The 'Big Bang' in Japanese Higher Education

JAPANESE SOCIETY SERIES

General Editor: Yoshio Sugimoto

Lives of Young Koreans in Japan
Yasunori Fukuoka

Globalization and Social Change in Contemporary Japan
J.S. Eades Tom Gill Harumi Befu

Coming Out in Japan: The Story of Satoru and Ryuta
Satoru Ito and Ryuta Yanase

Japan and Its Others:
Globalization, Difference and the Critique of Modernity
John Clammer

Hegemony of Homogeneity:
An Anthropological Analysis of Nihonjinron
Harumi Befu

Foreign Migrants in Contemporary Japan
Hiroshi Komai

A Social History of Science and Technology in
Contempory Japan, Volume 1
Shigeru Nakayama

Farewell to Nippon: Japanese Lifestyle Migrants in Australia
Machiko Sato

The Peripheral Centre:
Essays on Japanese History and Civilization
Johann P. Arnason

A Genealogy of 'Japanese' Self-images
Eiji Oguma

Class Structure in Contemporary Japan
Kenji Hashimoto

An Ecological View of History
Tadao Umesao

Nationalism and Gender
Chizuko Ueno

Native Anthropology: The Japanese Challenge
to Western Academic Hegemony
Takami Kuwayama

Youth Deviance in Japan: Class Reproduction of Non-Conformity
Robert Stuart Yoder

Japanese Companies: Theories and Realities
Masami Nomura and Yoshihiko Kamii

From Salvation to Spirituality: Popular Religious Movements in Modern Japan
Susumu Shimazono

Japanese Politics
Takashi Inoguchi

A Social History of Science and Technology in
Contempory Japan, Volume 2
Shigeru Nakayama

The 'Big Bang' in Japanese Higher Education:
The 2004 Reforms and the Dynamics of Change
J.S. Eades Roger Goodman Yumiko Hada

The 'Big Bang' in Japanese Higher Education

The 2004 Reforms and the Dynamics of Change

Edited by

J.S. Eades

Roger Goodman

and

Yumiko Hada

Trans Pacific Press

Melbourne

This English edition first published in 2005 jointly by:

Trans Pacific Press
PO Box 120, Rosanna,
Victoria 3084, Australia
Telephone: +61 3 9459 3021
Fax: +61 3 9457 5923
Email: info@transpacificpress.com
Web: http://www.transpacificpress.com

Ritsumeikan Center for Asia Pacific Studies
Ritsumeikan Asia Pacific University
Beppu, Oita 874-8577
Japan
Web: http://www.apu.ac.jp

Designed and set by digital environs, Melbourne.

Printed by BPA Print Group, Burwood, Victoria, Australia

Distributors

USA and Canada
International Specialized Book Services (ISBS)
920 NE 58th Avenue, Suite 300
Portland, Oregon 97213-3786
USA
Telephone: (800) 944-6190
Fax: (503) 280-8832
Email: orders@isbs.com
Web: http://www.isbs.com

UK and Europe
Asian Studies Book Services
Franseweg 55B, 3921 DE Elst,
Utrecht, The Netherlands
Telephone: +31 318 470 030
Fax: +31 318 470 073
Email: info@asianstudiesbooks.com
Web: http://www.asianstudiesbooks.com

Japan
Kyoto University Press
Kyodai Kaikan
15-9 Yoshida Kawara-cho
Sakyo-ku, Kyoto 606-8305
Telephone: (075) 761-6182
Fax: (075) 761-6190
Email: sales@kyoto-up.gr.jp
Web: http://www.kyoto-up.gr.jp

Japan, Asia and the Pacific
Kinokuniya Company Ltd.
Head office:
38-1 Sakuragaoka 5-chome,
Setagaya-ku, Tokyo 156-8691, Japan
Phone: +81 (0)3 3439 0161
Fax: +81 (0)3 3439 0839
Email: bkimp@kinokuniya.co.jp
Web: www.kinokuniya.co.jp
Asia-Pacific office:
Kinokuniya Book Stores of Singapore Pte., Ltd.
391B Orchard Road #13-06/07/08
Ngee Ann City Tower B
Singapore 238874
Tel: +65 6276 5558
Fax: +65 6276 5570
Email: SSO@kinokuniya.co.jp

ISSN 1443–9670 (Japanese Society Series)
ISBN 1–8768–4323–3

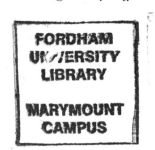

Contents

Tables

Figure

Contributors

Robert Aspinall is Professor of Social Systems, Faculty of Economics, Shiga University.

Jane M. Bachnik is Professor, National Institute of Multimedia Education, Tokyo.

J.S. Eades is Professor of Asia Pacific Studies, and Director of the Media Resource Center, Ritsumeikan Asia Pacific University.

Roger Goodman is Nissan Professor of Modern Japanese Studies, University of Oxford.

Yumiko Hada is Associate Professor in the Institute for Higher Education Research and Practice, Osaka University, Osaka.

Sachi Hatakenaka is Research Fellow, MIT Industrial Performance Center, Sloan School of Management, Massachusetts Institute of Technology.

Earl H. Kinmonth is Professor of Sociology, Taisho University, Tokyo.

Marina Lee-Cunin is Postdoctoral Research Fellow, Faculty of Economics, Shiga University, Hikone.

Brian J. McVeigh teaches the anthropology of Japan in the East Asian Studies Program, University of Arizona, Tucson.

John Mock is Professor of Anthropology, Global and Japanese Studies, Akita International University.

Akito Okada is Associate Professor in Comparative and International Education, Tokyo University of Foreign Studies.

Gregory S. Poole is a doctoral candidate, Institute of Cultural and Social Anthropology, Oxford University.

Patricia Walker teaches in the School of Education, Barking Campus, University of East London.

Shinichi Yamamoto is Professor and Director, Center for University Studies, Tsukuba University, Tsukuba, Japan.

Japanese Terms and Names

Japanese words have been transcribed in the conventional Hepburn system, with macrons used to denote long 'o' and 'u'. Loan words from English are given in the original English rather than a roman transcription of the Japanese Katakana forms.

In line with other TPP volumes, Japanese names in the main text are given in the usual Japanese order, with family names first, while the names of Japanese contributors to this volume are given in the Western order in the Table of Contents and the chapter headings, with personal names first.

The Japanese Ministry of Education has changed its official name both in Japanese and English over the last few years, as portfolios have been regrouped as part of the wider Japanese administrative reforms. Until 2001, the name most often used in both the English and Japanese literatures was 'Monbushō' (sometimes 'Mombushō'). From 2001, the brief of the the Ministry was widened, and it is now known as 'Monbukagakushō' (i.e. Ministry of Education and Science) in Japanese and 'Ministry of Education, Culture, Sports, Science and Technology' in English. In Japanese universities, the abbreviation 'Monkashō' is rapidly replacing 'Monbushō', while the Ministry itself is promoting the use of the acronym 'MEXT' in its English-language publications and web sites. Many of the papers in this volume cover the period when the name was changing, and so to avoid confusion and anachronism, we have used 'Ministry of Education' or simply 'the Ministry' as appropriate throughout the book.

Preface

This book has been a long time in the making, partly because of the complexity of the issues which it discusses, and partly because the higher education sector in Japan has itself experienced such rapid change over the last few years. Each time the editors drew breath and considered that the manuscript was complete, the goal posts seemed to move once again, with more major initiatives being announced by the Japanese government, or new studies being published which needed to be taken into account. Personal mobility was another factor, as our careers became part of our research material, with Jerry Eades moving to Ritsumeikan Asia Pacific University in 2000, Roger Goodman spending a sabbatical year in Osaka, and Yumiko Hada moving to Osaka University in 2004.

The idea for the book first arose from a research project led by Hada Yumiko in 1997, when we surveyed the university reforms which had already taken place in the United Kingdom and their possible implications for Japan. The Japanese Ministry of Education, it transpired, was also interested in the kinds of initiatives happening in Britain and elsewhere. From the late 1990s, the changes in Japan began to accelerate, with the announcement of such major initiatives as the 'Arima Plan' to turn national universities into autonomous corporations (announced in 1999), the 'Toyama Plan' to create Centers of Excellence (announced in 2001), the establishment of a new generation of international universities in Japan, (including Ritsumeikan Asia Pacific University in Beppu, established in 2000 and Akita International University established in 2004), and the hiving off by the Ministry of Education of autonomous agencies such as the Japan Society for the Promotion of Science to handle evaluation, peer review and the allocation of research funding (2003). Many of these issues were examined at a panel that we ran at Yale University under the auspices of the Japan Anthropology Workshop (JAWS) in May 2002, where much of the discussion was around how difficult it was to characterise such a rapidly changing situation. The end of 2004, however, seemed to provide a better point at which to draw breath than most. The previous year had seen the 'big bang' in Japanese higher education, the transformation of the national universities into independent trusts, together with the first batch of reviews of the Centers of Excellence (COEs) established by the JSPS in 2002. At the beginning of 2005, therefore, we feel ready to go to press.

Two academic meetings were particularly important in networking with contributors and generating the impetus for compiling a book. The first was a seminar organized by Yumiko Hada at Shiga University on education reform in the UK and Japan in 1998, in which participants included Professor Jyunichi Nishizawa, Chancellor of Tohoku University and Professor Akira Arimoto of Hiroshima University, in addition to Professors Okada, Yamamoto, Eades and Kinmonth. We would like to thank the Ministry of Education (the then Mombushō) for a Grant-in-Aid which financed the workshop and the research on which it was based. The second was the panel at the Japan Anthropology Workshop (JAWS) conference in 1992 mentioned above, which included contributions by Bachnik, Eades, Goodman, McVeigh and Poole, together with Bill Bradley of Ryūkoku University.

As the project has evolved, we have been very fortunate in assembling contributors, both Japanese and international, with extensive experience of teaching and research in Japan from a wide variety of perspectives. Okada has written extensively on the history of Japanese education, based on his doctoral work at Oxford University, while Hatakenaka is best known for her comparative work on university-industry partnerships in Japan, Britain and the U.S. McVeigh's widely-read work on the Japanese state and its relations with the university system is complemented by Yamamoto's experience as a bureaucrat-turned-academic. Kinmonth, Lee-Cunin, Walker and Aspinall have all carried out research relating to students, a surprisingly neglected topic in much of the work on Japanese universities. Their chapters describe the effects of the declining birthrate on admissions (Kinmonth), students attitudes to teachers and teaching (Lee-Cunin), the increasing numbers of students studying abroad (Walker), and the changing shape of the entrance examinations (Aspinall). Mock, Poole and Bachnik have also been able to draw on their own personal experiences, teaching English at a private university in Tokyo (Poole), establishing and running Japanese offshoots of American universities (Mock), and observing the implementation and impact of information technology policy

(Bachnik). We believe that the result is the most comprehensive and balanced survey of the field currently available in English, as well as the most up-to-date.

In preparation of the final version, our greatest debt is to Carolyn Dodd who shouldered the major burden of the copy-editing. The original Japanese versions of the papers by Yamamoto and Hada were translated and edited by Eades, who also did the final typesetting and preparation of the Index. He would like to thank Carla Eades for her usual forbearance in the face of terminal book production. Hada would like to thank her mother, Toshiko, and Kazue Morsbach for their moral support during the long course of the project.

Thanks are also due to Neil MacNeil of the Ritusmeikan APU Media Center, for technical help with the logo, the cover photograph, and uploading files to the printers. We are very grateful to Yoshio Sugimoto, for his ability to publish quality books on Japan in English with Japanese efficiency; this is particularly important in a field like Japanese university education where the reality is changing by the day.

Our final thanks go to Malcolm Cooper, Director of the Ritsumeikan Center for Asia Pacific Studies at APU, for a subvention to speed publication. This support is gratefully acknowledged, and it is hoped that this will be the first in a series of monographs in English bearing the RCAPS logo to complement the Japanese series already established.

Jerry Eades, Roger Goodman, Yumiko Hada
February 2005

1 W(h)ither the Japanese University? An Introduction to the 2004 Higher Education Reforms in Japan

Roger Goodman

On 1 April 2004, Japanese higher education underwent the kind of 'big bang' reform experienced by many other sectors of Japanese society during the previous decade. The reforms – which the US *Chronicle of Higher Education* (12 March 2004) described as 'the biggest higher-education reforms in more than 100 years' – aimed to set Japanese tertiary education on a completely new track for the twenty-first century. The chapters in this book set out to explain the background to many of the individual elements of the reform and show how the higher education system in Japan found itself in a situation where it needed them. As a means of introduction, this chapter will discuss the nature of the reforms themselves, why they have been considered necessary and how they will (or will not) affect the way that people think about *daigaku* (universities) in Japan.

The 2004 reforms

Most of the public attention on the reforms in Japanese higher education has been focussed on the fact that from 1 April 2004 Japan's national universities (which account for less than 20 percent of the students in higher education but 80 percent of the national budget)[1] were turned into independent agencies (*dokuritsu gyōsei hōjin*) and that their staff were no longer national civil servants (*kokka kōmuin*) guaranteed jobs for life. At the same time, as Hatakenaka Sachi explains in her chapter in this volume, the power of the heads of these national universities was greatly strengthened. No longer do they need to get permission from the Ministry of Education for every little decision, but they will have the power to hire and fire, set their own budgets, review their academic programmes and even adjust the pay of individual staff.

Management boards of these new corporations now include external members, thereby reducing the power of the professors' meetings (*kyōjukai*) to appoint their own choice as presidents.[2] In English, these new corporations are dubbed 'Independent Administrative Institutions' (IAIs) (see Yonezawa 1998: 21–2) and a clear recognition is made of the debt for this model to the reforms which took place in the UK higher education sector in the 1980s under Margaret Thatcher.[3]

What are the expected benefits, from the government's perspective, of such a reform process? Most immediately, according to a strong advocate of the plan, Atoda Naosumi, are the financial savings. Atoda (1997) estimates that this would be in the region of 1 trillion yen a year if public universities – which have twice as many staff (academic and support) per student – were brought into line with private university staffing levels and fees were increased (three times in liberal arts; five times in science subjects) to bring them also in line with those of private institutions. The reassignment of the 125,000 employees in national universities to the private sector would certainly also, as some critics of the plan point out, help the government in its drive to decrease the number of state employees by around 25 percent over a decade-long period starting from the mid-1990s (see Mulvey 2000).[4]

It would, however, be a mistake (a mistake indeed that many British universities made in the 1980s in the face of the reforms introduced by Margaret Thatcher) to dismiss the reforms being introduced into Japan in 2004 as merely about cuts in national budgets. The reforms are also ideologically based. As Royama (1999: 22) puts it, what is taking place is nothing less than a 'big bang', where market forces are expected to determine the future of both individual institutions and the sector as a whole. This ideological basis for the reforms can be seen more clearly when one looks at the other reforms which are being implemented alongside the 'incorporation' of the national universities, some of which are also discussed in her chapter by Hatakenaka.

From 1 April 2004, for example, the first two for-profit universities – Tokyo Legal Mind and Digital Hollywood – opened in Japan under a policy allowing for such institutions to be established in so-called 'Special Districts for Structural Reform'. Though small in nature (and with their academic programmes hotly criticised by more traditional universities), these institutions are perhaps the best exemplars of the new marketisation process that the government wants to see introduced into Japan's higher education system and which, as we shall see below, has already begun to appear in parts of its private sector as universities fight over a decreasing pool of students.

The Ministry of Education, Science, Sports and Culture (currently officially abbreviated in English as MEXT) is continuing to develop a policy of making its funding increasingly based on competition. As described by Jerry Eades in his chapter, in 2002 and 2003, the Ministry ran for the first time national competitions for universities to bid for funds as research-based Centres of Excellence (COE) and teaching-based Centres of Learning (COL). The funding, especially in the latter of these, was relatively large-scale and much was made of the institutions which did and did not succeed in the competitions, leading to serious discussion about 'winning' (*kachi-gumi*) and 'losing' (*make-gumi*) institutions and the possibility of the development of new hierarchies based on how universities fared in these competitions, just as the Research Assessment Exercise and Teaching Quality Assessments introduced in the UK in the 1980s led to new ways of ranking universities there (see, Nakai 2002; Yomiuri Shinbun Osaka Honsha, ed. 2003.)

The development of a rigorous assessment system is another of the major planks of the 2004 reforms. Until recently, it has been very hard not only to open new higher education institutions, but indeed even new faculties and departments as each have had to be rigorously vetted and controlled by the Ministry, a process which often delayed progress for many months or even years. Once set up, however, new institutions, faculties and departments were then subject to only the most cursory of subsequent evaluations, either internal or external. The new reforms are designed to reduce the difficulty in obtaining the external accreditation needed for the establishment of new departments and courses (and to some extent new institutions) and replace it with much tougher *ex-post-facto* assessments. All national universities, for example, have been required to produce six-year plans and targets against which their performance will be judged and on the basis of which their subsequent funding will be determined. Third-party evaluation agencies, accredited by the Ministry, have been set up in order to undertake evaluation of institutions' teaching and research, though the exact nature of these assessments is still to be determined. (Here, too, it is planned that market forces will be allowed to prevail, with provision for more evaluation agencies to bid to enter this market.) In short, this means that universities will have to take much greater responsibility for their own decisions and will be funded on the basis of their performance.[5]

The final plank in the recent reforms is the introduction of a greater emphasis on transparency and accountability in the higher education sector. Institutions will be required not only to submit to the Ministry a wealth of statistical data, but also to make this information public, so that individual consumers can make more informed choices about which institutions they (or their children) should enter. This is intended to move away from the current situation – where institutions are ranked almost solely on the basis of the average scores (*hensachi*) of their entrants – to being judged on a wider range of criteria, including drop-out rates, employment rates, research and teaching records, as well as the quality of the student body.

Almost as a footnote, though in any other year it would have been the main focus of attention, a new system of Law Schools started up in April 2004 as part of the biggest shake up of legal training in the past century, but also an indication of the development of universities as site of increasingly professional and practically-oriented graduate education (see Murakami 2003).[6]

While the above reforms are consciously based, in many cases, on reforms undertaken in the UK in the 1980s, they also fit into the overall reforms of the Koizumi government from the late 1990s of *kisei kanwa*, the relaxation of bureaucratic red tape, in the hope that a more entrepreneurial, deregulated system can help lift Japan out of its longest post-war economic recession. As we shall see in the next section, however, the need to reform higher education does not stem only from the same economic problems hitting other sectors of Japanese society, but has much longer – and in some ways more complex – roots.

Current trends in Japanese higher education

It is a strange coincidence (but nothing more than a coincidence) that the bursting of the Japanese economic bubble coincided almost exactly with the peak of the number of eighteen-year-olds (the group who have provided well over 90 percent of all university entrants) in the Japanese population. This generation, the second post-war baby boom, peaked at 2,050,000 in 1992 and then began a steady decline (31.2 percent) in numbers to around 1,410,000 in 2004. Due to the rapidly decreasing birth-rate in Japan since the late 1980s, there is no third baby boom on the horizon and the number of eighteen-year-olds will continue to decline to 1,183,000 in 2012 (an overall decrease of 42.3 percent over twenty years).

It might seem surprising, therefore, that during the period 1992–2004, the number of four-year universities actually increased by an even faster rate than the decrease in the eighteen-year-old population. In 1992 there were 98 national, 41 public and 384 private four-year universities in Japan; in April 2004, there were 88 national, 77 public and 545 private four-year institutions, an overall increase of 31.9 percent.

There are a number of explanations for this otherwise rather counter-intuitive situation. One is the fact that there has been a very rapid increase in the proportion of eighteen-year-olds going to four-year universities during the past decade. Between 1992 to 2002 – despite the drop in the *total* number of those leaving senior high school (and in Japan only about 4 percent of the age group do not complete senior high school, even though it is non-compulsory education) – the *actual* number going to university actually increased by 21.9 percent as the rate of advancement to universities of this group went up from around 37 percent in 1992 to just under 49 percent in 2002.

At the same time, many of Japan's two-year universities (*tanki daigaku*) converted into four-year institutions. In 1992, with 541 institutions (88 percent of them private), *tanki daigaku* constituted over 44 percent of all of Japan's university institutions and catered for nearly 23 percent of all university students (around 92 percent of their in-take being female); by 2004 they catered for only 9.6 percent of all university students, as more and more women entered higher status four-year institutions. In order to survive financially, close to fifty junior colleges converted to four-year universities (and many others were absorbed into their attached four-year institutions) during the decade after 1992.[7]

Despite the rapidly rising university enrolment rate in the 1990s, however, not only many of the two-year universities, but also many of the four-year universities increasingly found their financial situation becoming more difficult. As predicted in the late 1980s by the doyen of higher education studies in Japan, Amano Ikuo (1997: 138–39), the decade also saw an increasing diversification between universities – a process which the current reforms are designed to speed up. According to a detailed study carried out by the huge Mainichi newspaper group (and published in the weekly magazine Sunday Mainichi over a number of weeks at the end of 2003), one can begin to see a clear bifurcation of the situation of Japanese universities based around the *hensachi* mark (the average score of their entrants) from 1992. Those which at that time had an average *hensachi* of 55 or over have maintained, and in many cases increased, their competition-for-places rate and the average score of their entrants; those which had an average of under 55 in 1992 have seen both plummet. Many universities which enjoyed a huge number of applicants in the early 1990s have seen that number dwindle by as much as 90 percent so that now they no longer attract even enough to fill the places they have available, a situation widely known as *teiin ware*. As many as 30 percent of all universities now find themselves with some faculties in that situation and many of these (especially in private universities where fees account for over 80 percent of total income) are facing the possibility of financial collapse.[8] A whole spate of books have appeared in recent years which reflect this situation such as Furusawa's *Daigaku Survival* (University Survival); Satō's *Daigaku no Ikinokori Senryaku* (Universities' Strategies for Survival); and Yomiuri Newspaper Group's *Tsubureru Daigaku; Tsuburenai Daigaku* (Universities which will Collapse; Universities which will not Collapse).

The growing perception of the need for reform

The changing demography of Japan explains in large part the current reforms. Sometime between 2004 and 2009 according to differing estimates (Doyon 2001: 445; Royama 1999: 22), the places available in higher education institutions will be the same as the number of applicants, an era which is already dubbed in Japanese as *zennyū jidai*. One interesting indication of this is the rapid increase in the number of students who enter university directly from high school and the concomitant decline in the number who need to spend a year at cram schools as what are popularly known as *rōnin* (the term formally used for samurai retainers without masters), before they can enter their university of choice.[9] This does not mean, of course, as some have intimated (Obara 1998), that competition to get into university will disappear altogether; this will, as we have seen with the polarisation effect, probably become even more intense in the case of those still seeking entry to the top universities.

If the current demographic change explains the immediate pressure for reform, it is important to recognise that there has for a long time been the widespread perception (both inside and outside Japan) that the higher education system has not been serving either national or individual needs as it should. In international terms, it has been seen as uncompetitive. As Jane Bachnik writes in her chapter, according to the 2001 *World Competitiveness Yearbook* issued by the International Institute for Management Development and widely reported in the Japanese press, Japan ranked last among the 49 economies surveyed with regard to university education meeting the needs of the economy (*Japan Times* 26 December 2001). It has become a commonplace to describe universities as a kind of moratorium between the horrendous rigours of school 'examination hell preparation' which proceed it and the rigours of the company life which follow it (see, for example, Tsuda 1993). They have, as Brian McVeigh in his chapter suggests, long been 'difficult to enter but easy to graduate from' (*hairinikui, deyasui*). Some critics have even argued that Japan's economic growth was achieved *despite* its institutions of higher education. Edwin Reischauer (1983: 178), for example, a former Harvard professor and US ambassador to Japan often criticised for his overly positive view of all things Japanese, expressed such a view in the early 1980s: 'Higher education remains one of the major problem areas in contemporary Japanese society...That Japan continues to operate as well as it does despite the problems of higher education seems at first surprising'. This view was echoed by John Zeugner (1984), in an oft-cited article based on his four years as a visiting professor at four Japanese universities in the same period. After describing the general poor quality of the physical conditions of many Japanese national and public universities, Zeugner went on to criticise them more generally on a number of other points that can be summarized under three main headings:

1. lack of adherence to class attendance by both professors and teachers;[10]
2. lack of seriousness about teaching and grading compounded by day-time 'moonlighting' (*kakemochi*) activities of the academic staff;[11]
3. intense internal factionalism.[12]

Many other commentators over the past two decades have appeared to support Zeugner in his views (see for example Clark 2002; Fujii 1997; Kitamura 2002; Kusaka *et al.* 2003; McVeigh 2002; Shimbori 1981; Shimahara 1984; Schoolland 1990). Even though as Eades notes in the final chapter of this books, the top Japanese universities do not perform that badly in comparison with other non-Anglophone countries in international rankings based on research, these kinds of commentaries are still widespread.

While the apparent inefficiencies in the higher education system were tolerated during the decades of economic growth of the 1970s and 1980s, there is little doubt that the prolonged recession in Japan since the start of the 1990s has played a major role in the development of the belief that the system needs to be more productive in relation to the Japanese economy. As the economy has become increasingly deregulated in order to stimulate economic recovery, so the belief has hardened that the university sector also needs to be made accountable for its contribution to economic development, as happened in the US and the UK under Reagan and Thatcher in the 1980s (see Miyoshi 2000, for a bitter critique of this view of higher education in the US and Japan).[13]

In order to understand how higher education in Japan came to be seen as such an anachronism in a society whose education system has generally been perceived as both geared to meeting national needs and also highly efficient in training young people for the work place, it is necessary to have an understanding of some of the key underlying features of Japanese education, in general, and higher education, in particular. The sociologist of education, William Cummings, has set out some of the key comparative features of a number of education systems, which can provide a useful framework for such a discussion. In his comparative study of the 'educational models' of Prussia, France, the United Kingdom, the United States, Japan and Russia, Cummings (1999, 2003) identifies for each a period of genesis an ideal type of product of the system, a representative school, the scope of education, and a distinctive theory of learning and teaching as well as distinctive modes of administration, administrative style and sources of finance.

In Cummings' model, the period of genesis in the case of Japan is identified as the early Meiji period, when it was recognised that a modern education system was needed to drive the very rapid industrialisation that was Japan's only hope of avoiding colonisation. As is well documented (Dore 1984), Japan already had a relatively well-developed education system in the pre-Meiji period but this was rapidly expanded under Meiji state direction. The system was designed, as Cummings points out, to create citizens who were prepared to work for the good of the state as a whole and not in the narrow interests of region, class, gender or themselves. Particular emphasis was placed on primary school education and the training of the population in literacy and numeracy. Effort was – and, until the most recent reform debates, has remained – the key to success; hardship was seen as integral to the learning process. The teacher passed on information either to whole classes (or classes divided into groups) and this information was tested assiduously to ensure that it had been absorbed. The basis of the education system was made to look meritocratic to ensure that all those in it felt that they had an equal chance of success. As Dore (1982) memorably put it: 'One has to think of education in Japan as an enormously elaborated, very expensive testing system with some educational spin-offs, rather than as the other way around'. In order to make the system appear meritocratic, the curriculum has been the same in all schools (public and private); multiple-choice examinations have been favoured over essays; and even school buildings have tended to be built to the same (generally very functional) style.

As Okada Akito points out in his chapter, once it was decided that a modern education system was needed to serve the interests of the Meiji state, it was developed very quickly. The speed of development in the field of education as a whole in Japan is especially impressive in comparison with England (excluding Scotland which has been a separate case) and the United States. Japan started its modern education system in 1872 and had full enrolment at primary level by 1900, four years before the UK made a legal commitment to compulsory education (Cummings 1999: 433). At the tertiary level, in 1960, when around 7.5 percent of the eighteen-to-twenty age group were attending institutions of higher learning in England, the comparable figure in Japan was 9.5 percent and in the US it was already 37.2 percent (Azumi 1969: 24–5).[14] By 1980, 90 percent of all eighteen-year-olds were graduating from senior high school in Japan, compared with 74 percent in the US, while in England less than one-third of the population beyond the age of 16 was staying on in the non-compulsory education system (see James and Benjamin 1988: 55). At the higher educational levels, by 1980, 38 percent of all eighteen-year-olds in Japan were entering junior college or four year universities (Wray 1999: 2), while in the UK the comparable figure was around 13 percent (Smith 1998: fig. 4).[15] By the end of the 1990s, the proportion of students going on to tertiary education in the UK had grown to around 35 percent with a commitment to reach 50 percent by 2010. However, Japan was already considered to be close to what many educationalists believe constitutes full enrolment at this level of the education system, with 50 percent at university and a further 25 percent at tertiary-level vocational schools.

While, by OECD standards, the total state expenditure on social and welfare programmes has always been relatively modest in Japan, a much higher proportion of it has been spent on education. State investment in education in Western Europe, for example, in the post war period has generally been around 10 percent of total government expenditure while, in Japan, it has been closer to 33 percent. The fact, though, that total government expenditure in Western Europe has been around 45 percent of GNP compared with only 10 percent in Japan means that the absolute sums spent per child have not been radically different (Cummings 1997: 280–2). However, in Japan the focus of this spending has been on primary education. Beyond the primary level, the state concentrates its resources on national priorities (which it will heavily subsidise) but otherwise it will allow the private sector (which in Japan provides around 75 percent of both secondary and tertiary education) to fill the gap between demand and supply. As a result of this emphasis on primary education, the proportion of state educational spending on higher education in Japan is only about one-third of the OECD average (Postiglione 1997: xvii).[16]

The search for new markets

Many of the chapters in this volume focus on the search by universities for new markets to maintain their student numbers as they attempt to diversify away from what has been their traditional entrant: the eighteen- or nineteen-year-old Japanese student who has entered either directly from high school or, a year later, after a period at a full-time cram school or *yobikō*.[17]

Hada Yumiko, for example, examines in her chapter the development of graduate education. Only about 8 percent of Japanese students currently go on to graduate education, as opposed to 13 percent in the UK and 16 percent in the US (*Mainichi Shimbun* 1 June 2001). One report from the early 1990s put Japan as second among industrialised nations in the percentage of its college-age youth going to university and last in the proportion going on to graduate school (*Daily Yomiuri* 19 Feb. 1991). In part, this has been thought to be due to the reluctance of Japanese employers to hire those they feel already so qualified that they will be difficult to train in their own company way of doing things (Urata 1996: 189–90). Ogawa (1999) explains that graduate education in Japan has generally been seen only as a training ground for those who want to go on to be academics and that there has been little use of it for gaining professional and other non-academic skills. The Dearing Committee[18] (Dearing Report 1997: 55) was told that the Japanese Ministry of Education planned to increase the number of graduate students by 33 percent between 1995 and 2000, mainly in science and technology. In part this reflected the fact that, as Teichler (1997: 286–7; 293) points out, major Japanese production companies changed their recruitment policies in the early 1990s in favour of increasing science and engineering graduates from Master's programmes, which largely explains the doubling in the number of graduate students from the mid-1980s to the mid-1990s. While the number of undergraduate students in engineering and the natural sciences going on to graduate courses rose to almost one-quarter and one-third respectively by the mid-1990s, in the social sciences it remained around 3 percent, perhaps because graduate study was still not seen as having employment value other than for those who wanted to be academics

As Hada points out, however, there has been a substantial growth in the last few years in professional schools. As previously mentioned, almost 70 universities opened Law Schools on 1 April 2004, as part of the process of radically reforming the training and increasing the number of lawyers in Japan.[19] At the same time, there has been the development of MBA (Master of Business Administration) and MOT (Management of Technology) courses (see Yamada 2002). These schools are having the effect of bringing *shakaijin gakusei* (mature students)[20] into universities. Most of these students, however, are taking courses in the evening and at weekends so that they can combine them with their jobs; there is not much practice of students taking career development breaks and there is even less of housewives coming back to university once their children are old enough to go to school. Housewives were a huge new market for universities and community colleges in the US in the 1970s when they were facing the same drop in eighteen-year-olds as currently faced in Japan (Kelly

1999). Establishing graduate courses, moreover, costs money; there are strict minimum requirements for staff-student ratios which are much tougher than for undergraduate programmes, and strict requirements for the qualifications of the teaching staff, especially at the doctoral level. The number of graduates will need to increase much more, therefore, before they become a significant means for universities to increase their income.

Another source of possible students has been those from overseas (known as *ryūgakusei* in Japanese). As Patricia Walker discusses in her chapter, these again have constituted a huge source of university income in Anglophone countries such as the UK, US and Australia over the past decade. In 2003, Japan finally reached the target of 100,000 overseas students enrolled (26 percent at graduate schools; 53 percent on undergraduate programmes; 19 percent at vocational schools) that had been set by the then Prime Minister Nakasone back in 1984. Much of this rise came about in the previous five years when the numbers doubled from 51,000 to almost 110,000 and it was a result of the easing of immigration requirements for overseas students in 1997 and the rapidly growing demand for higher education in China and South Korea. Nearly 65 percent of all *ryūgakusei* come from China and a further 15 percent from South Korea. If one excludes the further 4 percent who come from Taiwan, the rest of the world sends a mere 18,500 foreign students to the second largest higher education system in the world. *Ryūgakusei* are highly concentrated in the metropolises with more than 30 percent in Tokyo. This means that provincial universities, which are most under financial threat, have found it difficult to recruit them as a mean of easing their financial situation.[21] Even in urban areas, though, it is generally agreed that *ryūgakusei* programmes are more closely related to the image and public relations of universities than their finances; many such programmes indeed are run at a loss.[22]

One of the reasons for introducing *ryūgakusei* into the Japanese higher education system was as part of Nakasone's drive to internationalise Japanese society – up to the year 2000, about 15 percent of all *ryūgakusei* were on Japanese government scholarships.[23] In the same vein, as Walker describes, there was a great increase in the 1980s in Japanese students going overseas in order to study in foreign universities. In part, this was a response to the growing strength of the yen and the attraction, particularly for young women, of an overseas experience. In part, it was due to the feeling that employers, who had hitherto been suspicious of overseas qualifications, would be more responsive to them when hiring. At the same time, there were students who applied to go overseas in order to escape the 'examination hell', as they saw it, of competitive entrance into Japanese universities.

John Mock describes the rise and fall of a parallel development in Japanese higher education which arose from the internationalisation (*kokusaika*) rhetoric of 1980s Japan. At their peak, there were over forty Japanese campuses of American universities catering for a perceived demand for an American-style university education based in Japan. Mock describes how and why they gradually disappeared due to limited funding, poor management, and an over-estimation of their marketability. Ironically, their insistence on sticking to American ways of doing things (such as refusing to either promote or to graduate students automatically or to allow alcohol on their campuses), which they had thought was their competitive advantage, was also possibly part of their undoing. Ultimately, though, they were fighting after 1992 for a diminishing pool of students and, as that pool contracted and other institutions began to offer their own international experience in terms of overseas exchange programmes, they simply could not compete

If neither mature nor *ryūgakusei* students offer an immediate means of bringing more income into most universities, then what other means are available? There are three revenue-generating offices which one finds on many US and most UK university campuses which are just beginning to appear in Japan: research offices, conference offices and continuing education offices. Encouraging universities to undertake joint research projects with industry (*sangaku kyōdō kenkyū*) has been one of the driving forces behind the current reform movement. As is well known, a far higher proportion of Japanese Research and Development has been done in companies than in university laboratories and Japanese companies have generally favoured overseas rather than Japanese universities to do research for them. Spin-off companies, however, have recently been set up in a number of universities. Crucially, however, this is expected, at least in short-term, only to be a source of significant income for a small number of the larger, mostly national, universities with strong medical, engineering and natural science departments. The fact that very few private universities invested in these areas – because they were so expensive – now means they are unable to reap the benefits of closer university-industry relations.[24]

Another possible source of income for universities is to make better use of their physical facilities. Many of the older universities have campuses in prime sites in the middle of urban areas and many of the newer ones have superbly developed, designed and equipped facilities. Most universities, however, are still only utilized during the day and in term time. Recently, however, university administrators have been waking up to the revenue-generating possibility of utilizing their campuses during the evenings, Sundays and vacations. Similarly – and sometimes in conjunction with the above – some institutions are beginning to develop programmes of lectures and classes for members of the public, though here they face strong competition from the courses which have been available for many areas at local cultural centres throughout Japan. If neither using their facilities nor their teaching personnel to generate money has yet to yield major returns, these new programmes are indicative of the trend in Japanese universities, both public and private, to begin to diversify their income streams which, until recently, have relied almost entirely on student fees (for entrance exams, entrance, tuition and other fees) and (central or local) government subsidies.

If new markets and new forms of income-generating projects have, as yet, impinged only slightly on the experience of most who work in tertiary education in Japan, there has been a much greater emphasis over the past decade on reforming what exactly universities offer to their students, in response to the sorts of student demands outlined by Marina Lee-Cunin in her chapter. Students are beginning to be seen, as in the US and in the UK, as consumers

As Gregory Poole discusses in his chapter, during the 1990s, virtually all universities undertook some form of curriculum reform. Previously, under the guise of academic freedom and a belief in the specialist nature of academic work, the teaching of academics had been left almost completely up to individuals. They designed their own syllabi, taught their own courses, set exams for their own students and marked their students' papers, all without external evaluation or reference to colleagues. The result was that, while some teaching was excellent, much of it was described as routine and unimaginative and, just as seriously, there was no coordination between courses within and across departments. A vicious circle developed as students became disillusioned and stopped attending classes; meanwhile, professors decried the lack of student commitment, yet still continued to graduate them on the basis that this was the university's duty after it had accepted them (see Usami 2001, for a good description of this process). As jobs became more difficult to obtain during the 1990s, students became more selective about what they studied, and not just where (Yano 1997), and more demanding about what they got for their fees. Moreover, as Kitamura (1997: 148) put it, Japanese tertiary education was seeing the development of a buyer's market where 'students will be "courted customers" rather than "supplicants" for admission' (see also Kinmonth's chapter in this volume). Institutions of higher education were under increasing pressure to respond to these new demands (Arimoto 1997: 205). Many students indeed dropped out of university altogether or attended vocational schools alongside or after university in order to make themselves more attractive to employers. In response to these trends, universities instituted FD (Faculty Development) programmes to try and get their academic staff to think about their teaching (see Inoshita 2002).

It is not easy to gauge the success of university FD programmes. According to Ehara (1998a), Japanese professors think of themselves as researchers in the German mould, rather than teachers in the Latin American mould, or as both researchers and teachers in the Anglo-American mould. While it has always been difficult to get a full-time post in a Japanese university, once obtained it has offered both a very high level of security and, by global standards for academics, a very good salary. There has been little incentive, therefore, to reform teaching practices, which have been unchanged for many decades. In order to bypass such resistance, some universities have introduced new courses, often taught by new teachers, though generally on the same campus, which have a more practical element to them than those taught by their established professors. For example, students studying English may be able to take courses designed for passing TOEFL taught by teachers from a local language school, while those majoring in economics can take courses to prepare them for accountancy exams taught by teachers from a local vocational school (*senmongakkō*). Such universities see the need to offer practical training which will improve their students' chances of employment, as employment rates (*shūshoku ritsu*) begin to replace entrance scores (*hensachi*) as the means of ranking universities (see Asahi Daigaku Ranking 2004; Yonezawa, Nakatsui and Kobayashi 2002).[25]

University management

Many universities, both public and private, have found the process of introducing discussion about reform – let along implementing reforms themselves – during the last decade extremely difficult. Put simply, there are two basic management styles in Japanese universities (see Nihon Shiritsu Daigaku Renmei, ed. 1986, 1999; Oe 2003). One, generally known as the *kyōjukai shihai* (control by the professors' council) model has pertained in all national, public and many private universities. The other, known as either the *gakuchō-shihai* (control by the president) or *rijikai-shihai* (control by a management committee or university council) model, have until recently been found only in private institutions (Ehara 1998b), though by the end of the 1990s, the Ministry was arguing for stronger top-down management in national universities as well. Both management styles, as Ushiogi (2002) points out, have problems for the reform of higher education institutions.

As Yamamoto Shinichi explains in his chapter, in the *kyōjukai shihai* model, while financial decisions are made by the school board, all academic decisions rest with the professors' councils of each faculty. As a result, the *kyōjukai* have tended to have huge powers of veto over decisions which have financial implications for the institution as a whole, without being responsible for the financial effects of those decisions. Indeed, since the *kyōjukai* has generally operated on the basis that it will only make a decision when a consensus has been reached (and for reasons that Hatakenaka Sachi explains, it has often been very difficult to form that consensus), it has frequently been a negative and reactive rather than a positive and proactive force in the institutional decision-making process.

The *gakuchō-shihai* or the *rijikai-shihai* models are most commonly found in the newer private universities, many of which are part of family-run educational conglomerations (*dōzoku-keiei gakkō hōjin*), which have been passed on from parent to child (or adopted child) over two or three generations. Here, power over both academic and financial matters rests in the hands of individuals or a board made up of their close associates. In some cases these individual are respected academics in their own right, fully involved in the day-to-day running of the university, and able to balance the academic and financial aspects of their decisions. In many cases, however, decisions are made by individuals and boards who are far removed from the issues about which they decide. As a result, staff often feel not only disempowered but also that decisions are arbitrary, something which those who work in such institutions say can lead to the development of a culture of fear and mistrust. There is no doubt, however, that, with this model, decisions can be implemented much more quickly, and hence the Ministry has recently advocated strengthening the power of the heads of national universities so as to help them speed up their reform processes.

From an Anglo-American perspective, as Hatakenaka Sachi in her chapter in this volume points out, what is conspicuous about the Japanese model is the almost complete lack of academics with management and financial experience. These 'hybrids', as she calls them, are responsible for most management decisions in UK and US research universities and have allowed the widespread development of decentralized management where individual departments (or even smaller units) have responsibility for both the academic and the financial management of their own affairs.

Where will the reforms lead?

As the state relinquishes some of its hold on universities and allows them to set their own agendas, it has not withdrawn from the higher education sector altogether. Instead, its role has changed from one of control to one of supervision. It is here that the universities in Japan are beginning to learn yet another new language, one which universities in the UK and US have been learning for the past 15 years and which Strathern (2000) calls that of the 'audit culture'. As Shore and Wright (1999) outline, audit practices in education are associated with a whole cluster of new terms including 'performance', 'quality assurance', 'accreditation', 'accountability', 'transparency', 'efficiency', 'value for money', 'benchmarks', 'good practice' and 'external verification'. This 'audit culture' is powerful, they believe, because it promotes itself as 'emancipatory' in giving autonomy to institutions to run themselves and because the actual audits (in teaching and research at least) are generally carried out by peers in other institutions so that the profession, in effect, polices itself on behalf of the state. Form, they suggest, is often more important than content and it is a system which punishes rather than encourages those who are seen to be failing. Academics find themselves between two cultures: 'Between two conflicting notions of the professional self: the old idea of the independent scholar and inspiring teacher and the new model of the auditable, competitive performer' (Shore and Wright 1999: 569). The new forms of assessment and evaluation being introduced into Japanese higher education will bring with them this new audit culture (see Kiyonari 2003: 77–83). It is not individuals within institutions that will no longer be able to act in isolation, as hitherto, but also institutions themselves. In some ways, as Ichikawa (2003) argues, the deregulation of universities is actually leading to universities being less autonomous and more subservient to state political and economic demands.

To understand their full significance, the reforms taking place in Japanese higher education sector need to be linked to those in other areas of the education system. For example, from April 2002, major new teaching guidelines were introduced into Japanese schools. These guidelines included the reduction of the school curriculum by around 30 percent and the implementation, for the first time, of a five-day school week. New, so-called 'integrated learning classes' without textbooks were introduced in the curriculum which was intended to encourage students to develop their own interests and think for themselves as part of what was termed '*yutori kyōiku*' (relaxed education). At the core of the reforms was an emphasis on developing children's interest in learning for its own sake.

These reforms in the school system have met with considerable resistance from teachers, parents, the mass media and politicians and led to a rash of books – described by Earl Kinmonth in his chapter – decrying and forecasting the lowering of educational standards. The reforms of tertiary education in Japan, on the other hand, have generally been met with favour by parents, students, journalists and the media. They have also, as Yamamoto Shinichi explains, met with surprisingly little opposition from those working in universities. This is because, as we have seen, government reforms to increase the efficiency of the university sector are going in the same direction as reforms which are already taking place for demographic and economic reasons.

Some commentators, however, are nervous that the *overall* outcome of the educational reform process in Japan will be an increasing differentiation of student outcomes by social class. Social class is an immensely complicated issue in Japan and sociological data on it is both somewhat limited and frequently contradictory. All researchers though seem to agree, however, that at private universities and the top national universities, there has always been a direct correlation between economic background and educational success. Amano (1998) is among those who think that the current reforms are likely to lead to less rather than more social mobility in Japan. If so, it will exacerbate what leading sociologists of Japanese education such as Kariya Takehiko (see Kariya and Ronsenblum 2003) and Tachibanaki Toshiaki (1998) have already identified as a growing division, not only in the educational experience, but also in the educational outcomes of different groups of children. As they point out, the development of such divisions becoming increasingly visibly related to the financial resources of individual families undermines what some see as the principle of meritocracy (i.e. that anyone can succeed if they try hard enough) – even though others see this principle as no more than a myth. This will, in turn, lead to disillusionment and lack of incentive among those stuck at the bottom of the system. Further, these problems are likely to be exacerbated in times of continuing recession. In 2002, official rates of youth unemployment stood at around ten per cent or twice the national average. Increasingly, labour economists such as Genda Yuji (2000) and others have been arguing that the new phenomenon of *furitaa* (young workers who quit their jobs regularly to spend what they have earned before returning to seek another short-term, often temporary and part-time job rather than a life-time employment opportunity) are not so much exemplars of a new generation of individualistic Japanese with a new work ethic (sometime dubbed '*parasite singles*' because they are happy to live rent-free off their parents) as victims of a labour market which cannot fully accommodate them.

Life-time and secure full-time jobs are increasingly becoming limited to those who graduate from certain institutions. Entry to those institutions will continue to be via the extremely competitive entrance examination system (described by Robert Aspinall in his chapter in this volume) and such entry is becoming more closely related to family income and investment. At the same time, entry to lower level universities is becoming increasingly easy, as such institutions scramble for any student willing to pay their fees. As Aspinall points out, already over 30 percent of entrants to such low-level universities are exempted from taking any exam at all and can enter through a recommendation system (*suisen nyūshi*) which was established originally, as Earl Kinmonth explains, to help students with a wider range of talents enter university without having to go through the normal rigours of the 'examination hell' system. Ironically, therefore, some of those reforms which were introduced in order to allow students more time to explore their own interests – in the belief that this might reduce some of the social problems, such as juvenile delinquency, which have been identified as being related to the excessive pressures of the curriculum in Japanese schools – might simply lead to an increase in students who can no longer see the point of working hard either in school (because educational success is so clearly linked to class background) or in university (see Saitō2000, for an example of this argument). There are some indications of these trends, as drop-out rates in university begin to soar (see Yoshimoto 2003) and student behaviour becomes increasingly disruptive (see Shimada 2002, as an example of a new series of books written for university teachers on how to deal with disruptive university students).

The chapters in this volume

The chapters that follow elaborate and expand upon many of the points which have been made above. Okada Akito sets the current reform debates in Japan in the context of the historical development of the whole education system in Japan since the Meiji period at the end of the nineteenth century, while Hatakenaka Sachi describes the historical context for the recent incorporation of national universities, highlighting the lack of a role for 'hybrid' academic administrators in defining this reform agenda.

Brian McVeigh sets the reforms in the context of the role in Japanese society of the Ministry of Education and its bureaucrats, who until very recently have kept tight control over all aspects of the system, in the belief that education was for the nation rather than for the individual. He and many others suspect that, despite protestations to the contrary, the Ministry will continue to maintain that control. Yamamoto Shinichi, himself a former Ministry official, offers a fascinating insight in to how Ministry of Education officials themselves see their role and the current educational reforms. Earl Kinmonth sets the reforms more clearly than I have been able to do above within the context of Japan's changing demography and the financial pressures that this has brought to bear on Japanese private universities. Marina Lee-Cunin shows how the emergence of the student as a consumer, rather than passive recipient of education, is becoming a major factor in the reform process

Patricia Walker looks in detail at the 'internationalisation' of Japanese higher education, both in terms of foreign students coming to Japan and Japanese students going overseas for their higher education. John Mock complements her chapter with an account of the rise and fall of the foreign university campuses which were established in Japan in considerable numbers in the 1980s to give Japanese students a foreign university experience without needing to leave the country.

Robert Aspinall examines the university entrance examination system, which commentators have long seen as the key to reforming the whole education system in Japan since it is around these exams that the system is so clearly focused (see, Zeng 1995). Hada Yumiko examines the expansion of graduate education in Japan which, as we have seen, has been the largest new source of students in the university system over the past decade. Gregory Poole gives a detailed case study of how one relatively low-level private university is introducing reforms in its teaching and management in order to maintain its financial viability. Jane Bachnik discusses how and why the information technology revolution, which has affected so many other sectors in Japan, could – but as yet, has not – make a major impact on the tertiary education sector. Her chapter begs the question of whether the factors that impeded the implementation of technology will also impede broader university reforms, especially the establishment of the 'independent administrative institutions'. Finally, Jerry Eades, one of the few foreigners to sit on one of Japan's recent "Centers of Excellence" selection and review committees, explains how the research environment in Japanese universities is being reformed by the Ministry to make it both more effective and internationally competitive.

Together, we believe that the chapters in this volume constitute the most detailed account in English of the current reforms of higher education in Japan. It is clear, however, that we are all describing a situation which is very much in flux. Much will depend, for example, on what happens when the national universities face their first external evaluation after six years of the new system in 2010 and how private universities deal with the continuing decline in the number of eighteen-year-olds in the population. Collectively, therefore, we wait to see what will happen as the reform process unfolds during the next few years.

Notes

1 In his well-known typology of higher education systems, Geiger (1986) places Japan in a category with 'mass private sectors' along with the Philippines and the United States. The comparison with the United States, however, is somewhat misleading, since while in Japan 80 percent of undergraduate students are enrolled in private universities, in the US, 80 percent are enrolled in public ones (Asonuma 2002: 110). Levy's (1986) less well-known analysis – which places the Japanese system in a category where private education has more than 50 percent but less than 100 percent of total enrolments, and where the private sector relies mainly on private finance and the public sector on public finance – is probably more useful in finding close comparisons with the system in Japan. Levy includes the Philippines along with India and Brazil in this list, but South Korea could also be added (see Weidman and Park 2000).

2 Since April 2004, public universities have also had the choice whether they become independent organisations (as the national universities) or remain under the control of local governments. While only one public institution – Akita International University, which has risen out of the ashes of the Minnesota State University-Akita, the rise and fall of which is graphically documented by John Mock in his chapter in this volume – opened on 1 April 2004 as an independent entity (*Asahi Shimbun* 25 Mar. 2004), local governments with several public universities, such as Kobe, Yokohama and Osaka, have begun to rationalise the administration and teaching of these institutions as a means of reducing their burden on local tax payers. Efforts by the Mayor of Tokyo to introduce similar reforms in Tokyo have met stiff opposition, particularly from professors at Tokyo Metropolitan University.

3 'The IAIs will incorporate plenty of unconventional systems that have not appeared in any existing public organizations. Sometimes they could be compared to "Agencies" in the United Kingdom. The Agencies were an insightful reference for the making of the IAIs, for example, in light of the separation of the planning and drafting function from the implementation function, the introduction of transparent, autonomous, and flexible operations and so forth.' (Central Government statement on Transparent Government, 30 June 2001). This statement and a collection of articles in English by Japanese academics putting the case against making national universities into independent corporations can be found at http://fcs.math.sci.hokudai.ac.jp/dgh/e-index.html (see also the articles in Zenkoku Daigaku Kōtō Kyōiku Shokuin Kumiai, ed. 2001.) While the national

universities represent less than 10 percent of all Japan's institutions of tertiary education, the fact that they have always been seen including most of its most elite institutions has markedly increased the depth of national debate about the *hōjinka* process.See, for example, an editorial in favour of the process in the influential Yomiuri newspaper (*Yomiuri Shimbun* 30 September 2001.)

4 This explains, for example, why in 1998 the senates of both Tokyo and Kyoto University initially rejected a plan for turning their national universities into quasi-autonomous administrative corporations after years of complaining about government interference in their affairs (see Hirowatari 2000).

5 The beginning of this deregulation process can be seen with the reform in 1991 of the Standards for the Establishment of Universities Act, which gave universities both more control over, and responsibility for, matters such as curriculum reform, self-evaluation and the introduction of non-tenure staff, currently accounting for around 2 percent of all academic staff, mainly in medical schools (Yamada 2001: 277).

6 The complex recruitment and transfer of staff between universities, which surrounded the establishment of the 68 Law Schools, was perhaps the first example of market forces entering both the public and private higher education system.

7 It is interesting to note, in this context, that junior colleges (*tanki daigaku*) were initially established only on a provisional basis in 1950 – because not all institutions which wanted to upgrade to universities in the post-war system were considered to be of a high enough standard – and they were only accepted as a permanent feature of the education system in 1965 (Teichler 1997: 278). Not long after, in 1969, as Cummings (1976: 69) recounts, several junior colleges went bankrupt as the level of debt in all private institutions increased severely, precipitating the student revolts which marked universities in Japan during the early 1970s. There is no doubt, therefore, that the junior college sector in Japan, which caters almost exclusively to female students, provided a useful 'buffer zone' during the development of higher education in the post-war period, but that role is fast disappearing as the supply of places across the sector as a whole begins to equal demand.

8 In 2000, 28 percent of Japan's 474 private four-year universities and 58 percent of its 453 private two-year colleges failed to reach their enrolment capacities (*Japan Times* 31 January 2001). This was the peak number of junior colleges unable to fill their enrolment capacities. By 2004, the percentage had dropped back to 41 percent as the total number of junior colleges fell to 400, many being absorbed into, or transformed into, four-year universities. The number of four-year universities unable to fill their enrolments however increased slightly to 29.1 percent as the total number of such institutions continued to grow to 533 (*Asahi Shimbun* 4 August 2004).This was clearly a major threat to their economic viability, particularly since, until recently, a department became ineligible for government subsidies if it fell to under 50 percent capacity. In 2000 this rule was relaxed as long as the institution *as a whole* in which the department was situated was more than

50 percent full (Asahi Shimbun 28 June 2000). For recent detailed analyses of the financial situation and viability of private universities in Japan, see Maruyama (2002), Nakamura (2002) and Shimano (2004).

9 This means of course that not only institutions of higher education, but also those cram schools (*yobikō*), which prepare students for taking entrance examinations, have been reporting financial problems. Some *yobikō* indeed are reported to be taking students who they believe will get into top universities without charge so that they can use their success in attracting other students to enrol. For a brief outline of the effects of the reform process, changing demography and economic conditions on the supplementary school system in Japan (known as *juku* and *yobikō*), see Russell (1997).

10 Zeugner's account is very much limited to the fields of social sciences and humanities where he taught. As Teichler (1997: 282–3) points out, 'The number of hours spent on study varies in Japan more strongly by field of study than it does, for example, in the U.S. or in Germany'. Even in the 1980s, there was little evidence to suggest, for example, that students in the medical, scientific and engineering fields worked any less hard than their counterparts in other industrial societies.

11 According to a large-scale survey by Morgan (1999: 17–8), 69 percent of full professors and 49 percent of associate professors teach on a regular basis at other institutions as well as their own.

12 Nakane (1973), for example, has argued that while all areas of Japanese society are characterised by factionalism, this is particularly the case in Japanese universities. Factionalism occurs both between and within universities. Between universities, the phenomenon of *gakubatsu* (school factions) has long been considered an issue affecting recruitment throughout the bureaucracy and in industry where many ministries and companies have tended to employ graduates only from certain designated universities (*shiteikō*) in the knowledge that these new entrants will be tied into obligation networks to their seniors (*senpai*) who graduated from the same alma mater. Certain *gakubatsu* channels are legendary: for example, Tokyo University has provided 10 post-war Japanese prime ministers, and 60–80 percent of Japan's current elite bureaucrats (*Asiaweek*, 15 May 1998: 38). Cutts (1997: 183), as part of his withering if journalistic attack on the over-dominance of Tokyo University in Japanese society, presents figures to show that around 30 percent of the 800 directors in the various Mitsubishi companies are graduates of the university. Universities are also particularly prone to appoint to faculty positions their own graduates: 95.8 percent, 93.5 percent and 87.1 percent of Tokyo University's Engineering, Law and Liberal Arts Schools respectively all graduated from those same departments and similar patterns can be found at other top national and private universities such as Kyoto, Osaka, Keio and Waseda (Urata 1996: 185–6). Within universities, factionalism has often been related to the *kōza* (or chair) system – whereby individual professors control all the funding for, and prospects of, those in their research group – and the need for individuals within those groups therefore sometimes to put loyalty to their group before wider issues of intellectual (and occasionally moral) 'right'

and 'wrong' (see Kelly and Adachi 1993 for a good description of how *gakubatsu* operates in a university context).

13 As Kim (2004) points out, the same trend can be seen developing in higher education sectors throughout East and South-East Asia following the East Asian economic crisis of 1997. Across the region, governments have abandoned the model of the state-centred higher education system in favour of the Anglo-American model of the 'entrepreneurial research university', a stronger emphasis on market mechanisms in university governance and the introduction of market-led competition.

14 According to Nagai (1971: 3), already by the late 1960s, only the US, USSR and India had more students than Japan (in absolute terms) going to universities.

15 Some of the figures here need to be used with caution in that different countries define higher education differently. For example, when the UK Dearing Committee (1997: Appendix 5; 49) reported on Japan, it gave two figures: 62 percent of the 18-year-old cohort going 'to some form of post-secondary education' and the official figure of 44 percent, since the Japanese government 'tends to refer to the universities and junior colleges as higher education provision'. The 18 percent difference was made up largely by those studying at full-time vocational schools (*senmongakkō*), which in some other systems would have been defined as universities.

16 The public spending on higher education as a proportion of GDP in 1998 was 0.4 percent in Japan, 1.3 percent in the United States, 1.1 percent in the UK and 1.1 percent in Germany (Akao 2002: 76).

17 For an example of some of the new marketing theory which is beginning to be discussed in Japanese higher education circles, see Imai (2001).

18 The Dearing Committee was a wide-ranging review of higher education in the UK, undertaken in the mid-1990s, including surveys of comparable systems in other countries. It published its lengthy report in 1997.

19 The future of these law schools, however, does not lie in their own hands, but will rely heavily on how many graduates go on to pass the notoriously difficult bar examinations to become fully-fledged lawyers. Many fear that with the Japanese Bar Association (Nichibenren) currently setting the figure at around 34 percent of graduates (as opposed to the 75 percent originally proposed by the Ministry of Education), many of these new schools will founder and, indeed, applications for entry in 2005 were around 30 percent lower than those of the year below. Others, however, predict that the Bar Association will be forced to increase its quota as demand for lawyers in Japan increases (see Arakaki 2004).

20 There does not seem to yet be an official definition of a mature student in Japan. Universities which operate special entrance categories for *shakaijin gakusei* seem to have developed their own definitions, most of which include the idea that the candidate either currently is, or in the past has been, in full-time paid employment while not receiving full-time education. The fact that definitions vary, however, is a good indication of how undeveloped this market remains. The market in part-time students has similarly remained almost untapped in Japan despite Ministry of Education guidelines in 1991 that allowed universities to accept such students. Some argue, semi-jokingly,

that because so many students already do so many hours of part-time paid work (*arubaito*, from the German word, *Arbeit*) while on course, they are already *de facto* part-time students!

21 One university in Tohoku set up classrooms in Tokyo and taught some of its *ryūgakusei* in them via video-links so that they could combine their studies with doing part-time jobs in the capital where such jobs are much easier to come by than in the countryside.

22 The vulnerability of this market, and in particular its over-reliance on students from China, was clearly demonstrated in March 2004 when the Japanese immigration authorities refused to give student visas to a substantial proportion of students from China who had been offered places for the academic year that was about to begin. This was in the wake of a series of highly publicised crimes committed by Chinese *ryūgakusei* during the previous year.

23 Government funding for overseas students in Japan is still categorised as part of its overseas development aid (Tsuruta 2003).

24 At the undergraduate level, students in the natural sciences, engineering and medical sciences make up 55 percent of all undergraduates at national universities, but only 23 percent in private ones. At the postgraduate level, the difference is even larger: postgraduates in these fields constitute 24.9 percent of all postgraduates at national universities, but only 2.8 percent at private universities. The total number of researchers in natural sciences and engineering at the ninety or so national universities is 50 percent more than in the over four hundred private universities combined, as is the expenditure on research (Asonuma 2002: 111). As Eades points out in the final chapter of this volume, this is reflected in their success in the recent Center of Excellence program.

25 The best example of this change in the perception of how higher education institutions should be ranked can be seen in the growing status of *senmongakkō*, which supply employment-oriented education, over the past decade (see, Ōtsubo, et al. 2004).

Bibliography

Akao, Katsumi, et al. (2002) *Kyōiku databook* (Data on Education), Tokyo: Jiji Tsūshinsha.

Amano, Ikuo (1997) 'Structural changes in Japan's higher education system: From a planning to a market model', *Higher Education* 34: 125–39.

Amano, Ikuo (1998) 'The socio-political background of educational crisis in Japan', in Rohlen, Thomas and Christopher Bjork, eds. *Education and Training in Japan*, London: Routledge, pp. 168–85.

Arakaki, Daryl Masao (2004) '"Please teach the 3 H's", a personal request to Japan's new American-style law schools', *Hōgaku Kenkyū* (Osaka Gakuin Daigaku), 30 (1/2): 107–46.

Arimoto, Akira (1997) 'Market and higher education in Japan', *Higher Education Policy* 10 (3/4): 199–210.

Asahi Daigaku Ranking (2004) *Nihon no daigaku: 710 kō kanzen guide*

(Japan's universities: A complete guide to 710 Colleges). Tokyo: Asahi Shinbunsha.
Asonuma, Akihiro (2002) 'Finance reform in Japanese higher education', *Higher Education* 43 (1): 109–26.
Atoda, Naosumi (1997) 'A privatization plan for Japan's national universities', *Japan Echo* 24 (2): 34–9.
Azumi, Koya (1969) *Higher Education and Business Recruitment in Japan*, Teachers. New York. College; Columbia University, Institute of International Studies.
Clark, Gregory (2003) *Naze Nihon no kyōiku ha kawaranai no desu ka?* (Why can't Japanese education change?), Tokyo: Tōyō Keizai.
Cummings, William K. (1976) 'The problems and prospects for Japanese higher education,' in Austin, Lewis (ed.), *Japan: The Paradox of Progress*, New Haven and London: Yale University Press.
Cummings, William K. (1997) 'Human resource development: The J-model', in Cummings, William K. and Philip G. Altbach, *The Challenge of Eastern Asian Education: Implications for America*, New York: State University of New York Press, pp. 275–91.
Cummings, William K. (1999) 'The institutions of education: Compare, compare, compare!' *Comparative Education Review*, 43 (2): 413–37.
Cummings, William K. (2003) *The Institutions of Education: A Comparative Study of Educational Development in the Six Core Nations*, Oxford: Symposium Books.
Cutts, Robert L. (1997) *An Empire of Schools: Japan's Universities and the Molding of a National Power Elite*, New York: M.E. Sharpe.
Dearing Report (1997) *Higher Education in the Learning Society* (Appendix Five: Higher Education in Other Countries), London: National Committee of Inquiry into Higher Education.
Dore, Ronald (1982) *The Diploma Disease: Education, Qualification and Development*, London: George Allen and Unwin.
Dore, Ronald (1984) *Education in Tokugawa Japan*, London: Athlone Press.
Doyon, Paul (2001) 'A review of higher education reform in modern Japan,' *Higher Education*, 41: 443–70.
Ehara, Takekazu (1998a) 'Research and teaching – the dilemma: From an international comparative perspective', *Daigaku Ronshū*, 28: 133–55.
Ehara, Takekazu (1998b) 'Faculty perceptions of university governance in Japan and the United States', *Comparative Education Review*, 42 (1): 61–72.
Fujii, Kayo (1997) *Daigaku 'zōge no tō' no kyōzō to jitsuzō* (The truth and fallacies of the university's ivory tower), Tokyo: Maruzen.
Furusawa, Yukiko (2001) *Daigaku survival* (University survival), Tokyo: Shūeisha.
Geiger, R. L. (1986) *Public Sectors in Higher Education: Structure, Function and Change in Eight Countries*, Ann Arbor: University of Michigan Press.
Genda, Yūji (2000) 'Parasite singuru no iibun' (An objection to the concept of parasite singles), *Chūō Kōron* (April): 180–88.
Hirowatari, Seigo (2000) 'Japan's national universities and *dokuritsu gyōsei hōjin-ka'*, *Social Science Japan*, 19: 3–7.

Ichikawa, Shogo (2003) 'Kōtōkyōiku shisutemu no hensen' (Critical changes in the Japanese higher education system), *Kōtō Kyōiku Kenykyū*, 6: 7–26.
Imai, Susumu (2001) *Daigaku marketing no riron to senryaku* (The theory and strategies of marketing universities), Nagoya: Chūbu Nihon Kyōiku Bunkakai.
Inoshita, Osamu (2003) 'FD no jissen' (The practice of faculty development), *Aera Mook*, Special Number 93: 30–2.
James, Estelle and Gail Benjamin (1988) *Public Policy and Private Education in Japan*, Basingstoke: Macmillan.
Kariya, Takehiko and James E. Rosenbaum, (2003) 'Stratified incentives and life course Behaviors,' in Mortimor, Jeylan T. and Michael J. Shanahan (eds.), *Handbook of the Life Course*, New York: Kluwer Academic/ Plenum Publishers, pp. 51–78.
Kelly, Curtis (1999) 'The coming educational boom in Japan: Demographic and other indicators that suggest an increase in the number of adults seeking education', *Japanese Society*, 3: 38–57.
Kelly, Curtis and Nobuhiro Adachi (1993) 'The chrysanthemum maze: Your Japanese colleagues', in Wadden, Paul (ed.), *A Handbook for Teaching English at Japanese Colleges and Universities*, New York: Oxford University Press, pp. 156–71.
Kim, Terri (2004) 'Neo-Liberalism, WTO and new Approaches to university governance: From reform to transformation', in *Organizational Reforms and University Governance: Autonomy and Accountability*, Hiroshima: Hiroshima University: Research Institute for Higher Education.
Kitamura, Kazuyuki (1997) 'Policy issues in Japanese higher education', *Higher Education* 27: 141–50.
Kitamura, Kazuyuki (2002) *Daigaku umarekawareru ka?* (Can universities be reborn?), Tokyo: Chūō Shinsho.
Kiyonari, Tadao (2003) *Daitōto no daigaku jiritsu kasseika senryaku* (The strategy of activating university self-eeliance in the great weeding-out period), Tokyo: Tōyō Keizai Shinpōsha.
Kusaka Kimindo et al. (2003) *Ima no daigaku wo dō suru ka?* (What is to be done with our current universities?), Tokyo: Jiyū Kokuminsha.
Levy, D. C. (1986), *Private Education: Studies in Choice and Public Policy*, New York: Oxford University Press.
Maruyama, Fumihiro (2002) *Shiritsu daigaku no keiei to kyōiku* (The financial and academic management of private universities), Tokyo: Toshindo.
Miyoshi, Masao (2000) 'The university and the "global" economy: The cases of the United States and Japan', *The South Atlantic Quarterly* 99 (4): 669–96.
Morgan, Keith J. (1999) *Universities and the Community: Use of Time in Universities in Japan*, Hiroshima: Hiroshima University: Research Institute for Higher Education.
Mulvey, Bern (2000) 'The *dokuritsu gyōsei hōjinka* reforms: Ramifications and opportunities', *PALE: Journal of the Japan Association for Language Teaching* 6 (1): 4–14
Murakami, Masahiro (2003) *Hōka daigakuin* (Law schools), Tokyo: Chūō Shinsho.

Nagai, Michio (1971) *Higher Education in Japan: Its Take-Off and Crash* (translated by Jerry Dusenbury), Tokyo: University of Tokyo Press.

Nakai, Kōichi (2002) *'Kachigumi' daigaku ranking* (The ranking of those universities in the winning group), Tokyo: Chūō Shinsho.

Nakamura, Chuichi (2002) *Daigaku tōsan* (The bankruptcies of universities), Tokyo: Tōyō.

Nakane, Chie (1973) *Japanese Society*, Harmondsworth: Penguin Books.

Nihon Shiritsu Daigaku Renmeikai (ed.) (1986) *Shiritsu daigaku: Kinō, kyō, ashita* (Private universities: Yesterday, today, tomorrow), Tokyo: Fukutake Shoten. Keizai Shinpōsha.

Nihon Shiritsu Daigaku Renmeikai (ed.) (1999) *Shiritsu daigaku no keiei to zaisei* (The management and finances of Japan's private universities), Tokyo: Kaisei Shuppan.

Obara, Yoshiaki (1998) 'A presidential perspective from Japan', *International Higher Education* 10: 11–12.

Oe, Atsuyoshi (2003) 'Gakusei boshū to nyūgaku shiken to keiei' (Student recruitment, entrance examinations, and university management), *Kōtō Kyōiku Kenkyū*, 6: 131–48.

Ogawa, Yoshikazu (1999) 'Japanese higher education reform: The University Council Report', *International Higher Education*, 18: 22–23.

Ōtsubo, Wakako et al. (2004), 'Kyōi no senmongakkō: Daigaku yo sayonara' (The amazing phenonemon of vocational colleges: Good-bye to universities), *Shūkan Diamond* (16 October).

Postiglione, Gerard A. (1997) 'Introduction,' in Postiglione, Gerard A. and Grace C. L. Mak (eds.), *Asian Higher Education: An International Handbook and Reference Guide*, Westport, Connecticut and London: Greenwood Press, pp. xv–xxviii.

Reischauer, Edwin O. (1983) *The Japanese*. Tokyo: Tuttle.

Royama, Shōichi (1999) 'Let schools be their own masters: Higher education policy needs its own "big bang"', *Look Japan*, (22 September).

Russell, Nancy Ukai (1997) 'Lessons from Japanese cram schools', in Cummings, William K. and Philip G. Altbach (eds.), *The Challenge of East Asian Education: Implications for America*, New York: State University of New York Press.

Saitō, Takao (2000) *Kikai fubyōdō* (Inequality of opportunity). Tokyo: Bungei Shunjū.

Satō Susumu (2001) *Daigaku no ikinokori senryaku* (Universities' strategies for survival), Tokyo: Shakai Hyōronsha.

Schoolland, K (1990) *Shogun's Ghost: The Dark Side of Japanese Education*. New York: Bergin and Garvey.

Shimada, Hiroshi (2002) *Shigo e no kyōiku shidō* (Guidance on how to deal with private talk in class), Tokyo: Tamagawa Daigaku Shuppanbu.

Shimahara, Nobuo K. (1984) 'The puzzle of higher education in Japan: A response', in *The Changing Functions of Higher Education: Implications for Innovation,* Hiroshima: Hiroshima University, Research Institute for Higher Education, pp. 167–74.

Shimano Kiyoshi (2004) *Abunai daigaku, kieru daigaku '05* (Universities in danger; universities which will disappear, 2005), Tokyo: Yell Shuppansha.

Shimbori, Michiya (1981) 'Two features of Japan's higher education: Formal and informal', *Japan Quarterly*, 28: 234–44.

Shore, Cris and Wright, Susan (1999) 'Audit culture and Anthropology: Neo-liberalism in British higher education', *Journal of the Royal Anthropological Institute* (N.S.), 5: 557–75.

Smith, David (1998) 'The changing idea of a university', Unpublished Wolfson Lecture, Wolfson College, University of Oxford, Spring.

Strathern, Marilyn (ed.) (2000) *Audit Cultures: Anthropological Studies in Accountability, Ethics and the Academy*. London: Routledge.

Tachibanaki, Toshiaki (1998) *Nihon no keizai kakusa (Japan's economic disparities)*. Tokyo: Iwanami Shoten.

Teichler, Ulrich (1997) 'Higher education in Japan: A view from outside,' *Higher Education*, 34: 275–98.

Tsuda, Takeyuki (1993) 'The psychological functions of liminality: The Japanese university experience', *The Journal of Psychohistory*, 20 (3): 305–30.

Tsuruta, Yoko (2003) 'Globalisation and the recent reforms in Japanese higher education', in Roger Goodman and David Phillips (eds.), *Can the Japanese Change their Education System?* Oxford: Symposium Books, pp. 119–50.

Urata, Nobuchika (1996) 'Evaluation issues in contemporary Japanese universities', in Hayhoe, Ruth and Julia Pan (eds.), *East-West Dialogue in Knowledge and Higher Education*, New York and London: M.E. Sharpe, pp. 177–91.

Usami, Hiroshi (2000) *Daigaku no jugyō* (Teaching in universities), Tokyo: Toshindo.

Ushiogi, Morikazu (2002) 'Shijō kyōsōka no daigaku keiei' (University management under market competition), *Kōtō Kyōiku Kenkyū*, 5: 7–26.

Weideman, John C., and Park, Namgi (2000), *Higher Education in Korea: Tradition and Adaptation*, New York and London: Falmer.

Wray Harry (1999) *Japanese and American Education: Attitudes and Practices*, Westport, Connecticut and London: Bergin and Garvey.

Yamada, Reiko (2001) 'University reform in the post-massification era in Japan: Analysis of government education policy for the 21st Century', *Higher Education Policy*, 14: 277–91.

Yamada, Reiko (2002) *Shakaijin daigakuin de nani wo manabu ka?* (What does one learn at professional schools?), Tokyo: Iwanami Shoten.

Yano, Masakazu (1997) 'Higher education and employment', *Higher Education*, 34: 199–214

Yomiuri Shinbun Osaka Honsha (ed.) (2002) *Tsubureru daigaku, tsuburenai daigaku* (Universities which will collapse; universities which will not collapse), Tokyo: Chūō Shinsho.

Yomiuri Shinbun Osaka Honsha (ed.) (2003) *Daigaku dai kyōsō* (Universities in competition), Tokyo: Chūō Shinsho.

Yonezawa, Akiyoshi, 1998. 'Further privatization in Japanese higher education?', *International Higher Education*, 13: 20–22.

Yonezawa, Akiyoshi, Izumi, Nakatsui and Kobayashi Tetsuo (2002) 'University rankings in Japan', *Higher Education in Europe*, 27 (4): 373–82.

Yoshimoto, Yasunaga (2003) *Daigaku ni wa haitta keredo* (You have gone to university, but…?), Tokyo: Sangokan.

Zeng, Kangmin, 1995. 'Japan's dragon gate: The effects of university entrance examinations on the educational system and students', *Compare*, 25 (1): 59–83.

Zenkoku Daigaku Kōtō Kyōshokuin Kumiai (ed.) (2001) *Kokuritsu daigaku no kaikaku to tenbō* (Future perspectives and the reform of the national universities), Tokyo: Hyōronsha.

Zeugner, John, 1984. 'The puzzle of higher education in Japan: What can we learn from Japan', *Change Magazine*: 24–31.

2 A History of the Japanese University

Akito Okada

Japanese higher education pre-1945

The Meiji Restoration of 1868 is generally regarded as the moment at which Japan entered the modern age and state intervention in the development of modern universities dates from the first years of the Meiji period. However, almost thirty years before the Restoration, the Tokugawa Shōgunate had settled on the modern university system as a means to enable Japan to meet the new foreign challenge (see Dore 1965). In the 1870s, the Meiji reformers were deeply conscious of the importance of mass education and advanced knowledge in the quest for rapid modernisation and industrialisation. The Meiji government, therefore, promulgated the Gakusei (School Code) of 1872, which ordered the provision of compulsory elementary education for all (see Ministry of Education 1972; Kokuritsu kyōiku kenkyūsho 1974). Beyond this compulsory sector of elementary schools (where education was confined to 'the three R's'), the government also established an imperial university sector for the elite, which led to prestigious posts in the government ministries. In addition, the government itself established the framework required for the development of a diverse multi-tracked middle school or post-elementary educational system. The most prestigious (although some would remark the narrowest) track through middle school and higher school into an imperial university was, and still is, attained through passing a series of very difficult examinations. Other tracks led to various vocational schools (*senmon gakkō*), normal schools (*shihan gakkō*) and technical and semi-professional schools, all of which expanded steadily during the late Meiji and Taishō eras. Child labour, however, was still indispensable amongst the lower social strata and participation in the post-elementary education system tended to reflect class distinctions and parental status.

The Meiji government's Imperial University Ordinance of 1886 (*Teikoku daigaku rei*) led to the foundation of the pre-war university system along lines of strictly determined priorities because the resources were limited. The Ordinance describes the main priority of universities as 'the teaching of, and fundamental research into, arts and sciences necessary for the state'. The basic philosophy underlying policies for establishing universities, implemented by such ministers of education as Mori Arinori, was to meet the needs of the state and contribute to national strength (see Hall 1973). Thus, from early on in the modern period, as Nagai (1971) has pointed out, 'signs of the utilitarian character of modern higher education were already in evidence in the early imperial universities' (Nagai 1971: 21). Tokyo University, which had been formed in 1877 by the joining of three of the Tokugawa Shōgunate schools (Shōheikō, Igakusho, and Bansho-torishirabesho – later renamed Kaiseikō), was transformed under the 1886 Ordinance into Tokyo Imperial University. The other imperial universities established in the pre-war period were Kyoto (founded in 1897), Kyushu (1903), Hokkaido (1903), Tohoku (1909), Osaka (1931) and Nagoya (1941). Keijo (Seoul) (1924) and Taihoku (Taipei) (1928) were also founded in the overseas colonies of Korea and Taiwan respectively. Whether in the government or the business world, a young man's future was largely determined by his attendance at one of the imperial universities. At the pinnacle of the whole hierarchy was Tokyo Imperial University whose graduates occupied the elite levels of the national government.

The Meiji government did not choose the American style higher education system, but that prevailing in England, France and particularly in Germany at the time, which was highly selective. The Japanese Ministry of Education, or Monbushō, formed in 1871, did not intend to realise perfect equality of opportunity beyond post-elementary education for the Japanese people (see Okada 1998) but instead concentrated on another aspect of education, that of inculcating spiritual training based on the Confucian ethic. This ethic emphasised a subordinate's duties towards the emperor and a strong sense of patriarchal responsibility in the case of the national elite. The Imperial Rescript (Kyōiku-chokugo), promulgated in 1891, gave both legal and moral justification to an education system that spawned militarism and ultra-nationalism up to the end of the Second World War. In order for Japan to be a great power, successive Japanese governments in the pre-war period needed a docile population. Through the Rescript, therefore, the Ministry promulgated the notion that Japanese morality and values were equally as significant as western science and technology. Unlike German universities, where an inner strength and vitality arose from a measure of academic freedom, the Japanese imperial universities were severely lacking when it came to the vital principles of 'freedom to teach' and 'freedom to learn'. Thus, in spite of overwhelming westernisation in the material aspects of national life, the concept of education being for the benefit of the state rather than for the individual continued to permeate the pre-war Japanese education system.

Although the Imperial University Ordinance of 1886 had clearly projected a role for the state in providing national universities, it did not proscribe (nor did it promote) the development of private universities. Continuing a tradition from the late Edo period, Tokyo and other major cities had numerous excellent private academies, several of which were significantly older than the imperial universities themselves. Compared to the imperial universities, the main role of which, as we have seen, was to contribute to the fostering of national talents and to meet the nation's needs, the private schools enjoyed an atmosphere of academic freedom and critical rationalism. Among the best known of them were Keiō (founded by Fukuzawa Yukichi in 1858), Dōshisha (founded by Nijima Jo in 1875) and Waseda (founded by Okuma Shigenobu in 1882).

Such was the demand at the time for university places that, when the public sector did not offer adequate provision, the private universities rushed in to fill the vacuum. Even though the private institutions were not officially recognised by the government in their early years, they were well received by the public due to the high quality of education they provided. Until the early twentieth century, the private institutions were not allowed the legal status of university (*daigaku*), neither were they provided with any financial backing by the government. Furthermore, the well-educated but officially unrecognised graduates of these institutions faced systematic legal discrimination when applying for official posts. These government-imposed obstacles only served to strengthen the resolve of many universities in the private sector to continue to produce high-quality graduates for important positions in areas other than government.

There are several other types of institutions that were significant in Japan's pre-war system of higher education: the technical or vocational colleges and higher technical institutions (*senmon gakkō*), the girl's high schools (*kōtō jogakkō* or *jogakuin*) and women's colleges (*jogakkō*) and the normal colleges (*shihan gakkō*). These institutions sorted the nation's children at an early age and then educated each group according to their likely future career.

By the closing decade of the nineteenth century, technical and vocational institutions already existed at various levels (see Taniguchi 1988; Yoneda 1992). The Education Ministry called for the expansion of these institutions at the secondary level as well as in higher education. The *senmon gakkō* provided more advanced technical skills for those middle-school graduates who failed to enter the more academic schools. The 1879 Education Ordinance (Kyōiku rei) had disqualified the *senmon gakkō* from being called universities on the grounds that they specialised in only one discipline while a university was defined as an institution teaching numerous subjects. The main goal of the *senmon gakkō* was to produce middle-level technicians (in subjects such as commerce, engineering, agriculture and clerical skills) in order to advance the nation's economic development. While the public *senmon gakkō* did tend to be tightly focused on a single specialty, the private ones often taught a broader range of subjects, including the more loosely-defined humanities and social sciences.

The highest level of education readily available to girls was provided by the *kōtō jogakkō* or *jogakuin* and the *jogakkō*, both of which were of an equivalent standard to the boys' middle schools and were often missionary-founded (for example Ferris Seminary and Kobe Jogakuin). Girls, no matter how talented, were denied access to the imperial universities. The differences in the expected social functions of male and female adults in Japanese society provided the underlying justification for this system which provided different education to boys and girls (see Fujimura-Faneslow and Imamura 1991; Hara 1995). In the case of the *kōtō jogakkō* or *jogakuin*, the curriculum became increasingly 'domesticated' with home economics, music and literature being the required subjects for training 'good wives and wise mothers' (*ryōsai kenbo*). However, only a handful of women, predominantly the daughters of the ruling elite, actually attended these institutions. By the mid-twentieth century, little had changed. Thus, in order to acquire a higher education, girls in Japan had to await a more generous view of their social position, greater job mobility and the construction of a wider system of schools to which they could gain access.

In addition to the *senmon gakkō*, *jogakuin* and *kōtō jogakkō,* the Ministry also emphasised the role of normal schools or *shihan gakkō* (see Kawahara 1968). Students at these schools received scholarships from either the national or prefectural government. The basic characteristics of the pre-war *shihan gakkō* were a militaristic atmosphere and organisation: military drill had been established in 1886 by the Minister of Education and from then on strict regimentation was the rule. Given the nature of this system, it is not surprising to learn that the teachers in *shihan gakkō* readily toed the government line and engaged in 'missionary' work to inculcate their students with patriotic sentiments such as 'respect for the emperor and love of the country' (*chūkun-aikoku*). By the latter part of the Meiji period, the salaries and social prestige of teachers in *shihan gakkō* were relatively high and graduates were virtually assured of a teaching position.

The first quarter of the twentieth century saw the implementation of a remarkable number of policies, particularly those with a view to expanding higher education. Several important factors influenced those policies aimed at the reform of the university system: (1) the perceived need for a higher degree of order within the educational system and, in particular, a closer connection between elementary, secondary and tertiary levels; (2) the increasing industrial and commercial competition from western countries and the acknowledgement by the Japanese government of an urgent need for scientific and technical education to train skilled workers to increase industrial efficiency; (3) the belief in a rigidly meritocratic selection process for a national elite to provide the government with a workforce of highly-trained bureaucrats; and finally, (4) with the emergence of a number of liberals and intellectuals in the Taishō era (1913–1925), the introduction of a new dimension to the educational debates with demands to extend social opportunity (see Smith 1972). The motivations of the advocates for reform were various but, apart from the liberal exponents of increased social opportunity, all were in favour of the continued merit-based selection of a national elite.

The University Code of 1918 was promulgated and provided a legal framework for the establishment of new universities alongside the existing imperial universities. Through the Code, the way was opened for greater expansion of the higher education system along two routes: (1) the establishment of single-faculty state universities and (2) the recognition, as universities, of private institutions such as Keiō and Waseda. As a result, between 1918 and 1928, the number of state colleges and universities, and the number of students in them, more than doubled.

The expansion was even more impressive in the private sector. As Beauchamp and Rubinger (1989: 141) point out, in 1938, for example, there were 25 private universities with 44,000 students and 120 private colleges with 80,000 more students while twenty years prior there had been no private universities and only 65 private colleges with a mere 34,000 students. Even more significantly, by 1938, over 70 percent of the students were enrolled in private universities – a ratio that still exists today.

The development of the post-war education system: 1945–1970s

The post-war education system in Japan was introduced by the American Occupation forces and aimed at the 'democratisation', 'demilitarisation' and 'decentralisation' of Japanese society, all of which had been achieved through a series of debates in the process of framing the New Constitution and the Fundamental Law of Education (Kyōiku kihonhō) (see Horio and Yamazumi 1976; Okada 1999). These reforms were clearly opposed to the dominant characteristics of the pre-war education system, namely the training of imperial subjects; a narrow nationalistic perspective; and a complex and hierarchical post-elementary education system comprising middle schools and imperial universities for the elite alongside more vocation-oriented education for the majority. The new model followed the American pattern: the first nine years of education were compulsory and were composed of six years of elementary school and three years of lower secondary (middle) school *(chūgakkō)*, followed by three years of non-compulsory upper secondary (higher) school *(kōtōgakkō)*. Separate education for boys and girls at any level was abolished.

As far as higher education was concerned, the report of the United States Education Mission (USEM) to Japan of 1946 contained very significant ideas that foreshadowed the coming trend in higher education. The USEM Report proclaimed as follows:

> The inalienable and universal rights of people are safeguarded largely through the process of education. Schools are established to supplement

> and enrich the experience of people. The education is most desirable which results in the individual's attaining progressively throughout life his own best self. In a democracy, individual human beings are, we repeat, of surpassing worth. Their interests must not be subordinated to those of the state. Educational opportunity, commensurate with individual ability, should be equally available for all persons regardless of sex, race, creed or colour... Intelligent citizenship, based on freedom of thought, communication, and criticism, should be an important outcome of education (U.S. Department of State 1946: 6).

Emphasising a new principle of 'equality of opportunity', the report's suggestions for higher education included: (1) that access be based on merit; (2) that it be free from exorbitant government and ministry control; (3) that it be guaranteed financial and academic freedom; (4) that it provide teaching in liberal arts subjects in the first two years of university experience; and (5) that it improve the quality of library and research facilities (see Beauchamp and Rubinger 1989:143–4). The School Education Law of 1946 (Gakkō kyōiku hō) provided more concrete regulations for the higher education system.

In response to these recommendations, all the pre-war institutions of higher education were integrated into either four-year universities (six years for medical students) or new American-style two-year junior colleges. As a result of this reorganisation, by the beginning of the 1950s, 201 new universities and 149 new junior colleges existed in place of the previous 49 universities and other 391 varied higher education institutions such as *kōtō gakkō* (high schools), *senmon gakkō* and *shihan gakkō*. About 250,000 students were enrolled in the 350 institutions and they were established in virtually every town and city. Although the equality of opportunity for higher education was much improved, many of the new institutions could not be said to have met the standards expected of four-year universities but were established to meet local demand. As a result, these new Japanese universities were often pejoratively referred to as the *ekiben daigaku* or 'lunch-box universities', a name derived from the ready-made lunch-boxes filled with local specialties and sold from train station platforms (see Beauchamp and Rubinger 1989:144).

In relation to the Japanese higher education system, although the 1950s can be described as essentially a period of consolidation, it also saw the beginning of an important challenge to the new system. Once the American Occupation ended in 1952, the Japanese government began to undertake a revision of various legacies of the Occupation and to modify them according to the domestic conservative ideology of the day. This process became known as the 'reverse course' (see Schoppa 1991; Aspinall 2001; Okada 2002) and it was during this period that the Education Ministry, which had had little administrative power during the occupation, resumed authority over every aspect of education.

The government, along with the Education Ministry and the business world (*zaikai*),[1] attacked two aspects of the occupation reforms of the education system. Firstly, the conservatives criticised the post-war education system as too 'foreign' and 'democratic' to suit the traditional image of Japanese education. Secondly, they expressed strong discontent with the perceived inefficiency of the newly established 6-3-3-4 system. The *zaikai*, in particular, was not satisfied with this system. It advocated its diversification as essential for industrial and economic reconstruction and suggested the strengthening of vocational education at the lower and upper secondary education levels alongside the establishment of separate vocational colleges.

For instance, in 1952, the Federation of Employers' Associations (Nikkeiren) issued a 'Recommendation for Reconstruction of the New Education System' that bluntly expressed its complaints about the quality of the graduates entering the work force and suggested 'at upper secondary education level, vocational and commercial education should be given corresponding to children's intellectual ability' (Nikkeiren 1952: 1–2). At the same time, it also urged a fundamental review of post-war university education in order to improve the quality of study in fields that had direct relevance to industry. The same view was echoed in the Ministry's 1957 Five-Year Plan which recommended the establishment of 8,000 new university places annually for science and technology students.

The 1960s saw a phenomenal expansion of the Japanese economy. Japan became one of the leading industrial countries of the world and efficient adaptation to the international economy became more urgent. Not only in Japan, but also in other industrial countries, the early 1960s saw an unprecedented surge in enthusiasm for expansion in education. In Japan, a national emphasis on preventing a waste of talent accelerated the speed of educational expansion, which covered the whole system from pre-school to higher education. The new elements introduced by the 'manpower approach' and 'human capital approach' provided a theoretical basis for this expansion and a rationale to justify changes to the educational system.

The government reaction to the issue of manpower and educational reform in line with its attempt to promote rapid economic growth was immediately reflected in a series of reports from the Keizai shingikai (Economic Deliberation Council).[2] The Keizai shingikai stressed the link between economic growth and education through a new concept – *nōryokushugi* or the 'ability-first' principle. The Keizai shingikai's 1963 report entitled 'Issues and Measures for Development of Human Abilities in Pursuit of Economic Expansion', introduced the idea of *nōryokushugi* as follows:

> The principle of equal opportunity means that educational opportunity is given equally among people who have equal ability. If we follow this interpretation, the principle of *nōryokushugi* must be applied. Selection by ability is not discrimination... the principle of *nōryokushugi* is not to have identical conditions going on to a higher level of education in the educational courses but to have a flexible education system corresponding to people's ability. (Keizai shingikai 1963: 38)

Thus the meritocratic principle was recommended and justified in the name of equal opportunity. In order to resolve the problem of securing the talents and capacities required to successfully realise the aim of high economic growth, it was logical for the Keizai shingikai report to conclude by condemning the post-war education system on the grounds that 'it is established on the principle of standardised egalitarianism' (Keizai shingikai 1963:38). The report recommended a diversification of the 6-3-3-4 system by establishing a much greater number of vocational and technical schools with the aim of increasing national efficiency by developing industry and commerce. Thus, the Keizai shingikai, like other conservative groups, recommended that the structure and curricula of the higher education system should be diversified to meet the demands of society as well as of individuals, varying according to their abilities, future career and local conditions. The introduction of the five-year higher technical school (*kōtō senmon gakkō*) was a notable step in the creation of a new system parallel with the formal 6-3-3-4 system. At the apex of both systems, the universities provided a high number of courses in science and technological subjects at both undergraduate and graduate level.

Student radicals kept the issue of central government control of education alive throughout the 1950s, 1960s and 1970s. The initial main issue was the revision of the U.S.–Japan Security Treaty by Prime Minister Kishi in 1960. The student opposition movement continued up to the 1970s when a variety of factors, including external suppression (the American involvement in the Vietnam War), brought about an intellectual ferment on the campuses of Japan's universities (see Wheeler 1979; Ōsaki 1991).

Meanwhile, however, under the successive leaderships of conservative Prime Ministers Kishi, Ikeda and Sato, the government was more determined than ever to bring the universities under tighter central control. In August 1969, the Liberal Democratic Party (LDP) majority enacted legislation that empowered the Education Ministry to determine emergency measures to assist the independent efforts of the universities in restoring order following student riots. This University Administration Emergency Measures Law was widely interpreted to mean that the government would take over the administration of a university where necessary. Eventually, with a few exceptions, campus unrest declined and the student movement broke into increasingly hostile rival factions, each claiming to be more ideologically pure than the opposition (Beauchamp and Rubinger 1989: 146).

In the following decade, the education reform process was centred on the deliberations of the Chuō kyōiku shingikai (Central Council for Education).[3] Between 1969 and 1971 the Chuō kyōiku shingikai issued a series of reports covering everything from the expansion of kindergarten schooling to the administration of graduate school research. A final report in 1971, entitled 'Basic Guidelines for Reform of Education' cited a great number of areas for improvement including: (1) the quality of teaching and administration of institutions of higher education; (2) the problem of under-funded, especially private, facilities; (3) the university entrance examination system; (4) the diversification of the aims of higher education institutions; and (5) the incorporation of the business world and higher institutions (Chuō kyōiku shingikai 1971: 3–12).

The Chuō kyōiku shingikai considered proposals which aimed at ending the supposed insularity and immobilism of the universities. For example, following the Chuō kyōiku shingikai's proposals, the government abolished the Tokyo University of Education and replaced it with a radically new type of national university (Tsukuba University). In addition to the structural reform, the Chuō kyōiku shingikai also dealt with the issue of university administration (Kuroha 1993: 42–48) by proposing the establishment of a central administrative machinery for the whole university sector. Such centralised administrative power, the council was convinced, would be more likely to meet the various demands of society as well as those of students. Moreover, the Chuō kyōiku shingikai underlined the need for further expansion of higher education to meet the demands of the people. To meet these needs, the Chuō kyōiku shingikai assumed the national government was going to foot a large part of the bill and its proposal for increased aid to private universities was quickly implemented. These ideas were backed most notably by certain business interests and also by the more politically ideological Chuō kyōiku shingikai members.

However, the council's recommendations for higher education also encountered a storm of criticism. Criticism came not only from external groups, particularly from the Association of National Universities, but also from within the conservative groups, as they would have radically altered the nature of Japanese higher education (Schoppa 1991: 171–210). The major national universities were unwilling to yield internal policy-making to a government or other non-academic board dominated by outsiders. The new Tsukuba University, therefore, did not become a model for other public universities.

Education reform under the Ad-Hoc Council in the 1980s

The late 1970s and early 1980s saw a sustained, predominantly right-wing, critique of the education system. Conservatives in many advanced industrial nations began to assert that egalitarianism had brought about a lowering of standards and a loss of traditional values in education. Japan was not excluded from this trend. The powerful conservative Prime Minister Nakasone adopted a 'New Right' philosophy, which encompassed both the neo-liberals who called for decentralisation and the neo-conservatives who called for tough steps towards centralisation in order to bring about a recovery in the nation's economy. Both of these factions shared the view that government intervention and investment in education, as well as in other public services, should come to an end and they called for abolition of the welfare state and adoption of the market economy in all public services (see Goodman 1989; Schoppa 1991: 221–250; Hayao 1993; Hood 2001).

The Rinji kyōiku shingikai (Ad Hoc Council on Education), which was set up in August 1984 as a supra-cabinet advisory committee to Nakasone, embarked on discussion of educational reform from a long-term perspective with the support of all the relevant government authorities. The Rinji kyōiku shingikai engaged in three years of concentrated deliberations from a broad perspective during which four successive reports were submitted to Prime Minister Nakasone. These reports identified a number of subjects as needing to be dealt with promptly and these included issues directly affecting the current educational scene such as the escalation of entrance examination competition ('examination hell'), school refusal, the problem of drop-outs, physical and psychological bullying (*ijime*) in schools, as well as the great social changes resulting from an increase in the number of middle-class families, the internationalisation of Japan and the spread of information media.

One of the prime targets for the Rinji kyōiku shingikai's proposed educational reforms was higher education where the three key words were '*jiyūka*' (liberalisation), '*tayōka*' (diversification) and '*kokusaika*' (internationalisation). Furthermore, the council emphasised '*jūnanka*' ('flexibilisation') by which was meant more parental choice and the placing of more importance on a child's individuality. The recommendations in relation to *jiyūka* involved proposals for increasing competition in all sectors of the Japanese education system; by *tayōka* was meant the introduction of ability-streaming into the system; and by *kokusaika* was meant the provision of education with a global perspective including international exchange among students, teachers and researchers. Some of the main recommendations include the following:

Diversification

- improvement of admission procedures system to national universities and introduction of a new examination in which private universities would also join
- reform of the university curriculum and the notion of a generalist education

Flexibility

- requirement of 'individuality' as the fundamental principle of the reform
- correction of the adverse effects of undue emphasis on the educational background of individuals

- changing from school-centred education to 'Lifelong Learning'

Internationalisation
- response to internationalisation and globalisation
- increase the number of international students in Japan

Others
- review of the Ministry's role in policy-making and financial administration
- incorporation of the national universities
- conversion of life-time faculty positions to contracted posts
- encouragement of financial investment for private sectors
- establishment of a Daigaku shingikai (University Council) to inquire on specific aspects raised by the Prime Minister

An analysis of these recommendations reveals that the council's advocacy of higher education reform seems to have stemmed from three major concerns: (1) the necessity to make a reality of consumer 'choice' in education and to restore notions of merit; (2) to shift the burden of welfare responsibility from the state and more towards the individual; and (3) the desire to make a greater contribution to the global community. These reforms clearly mirrored the conservative 'New Right' philosophies of the 1980s.

Although the Rinji kyōiku shingikai gained some standing by creating new ideological packaging for the conservative reform agenda, it was not able to acquire a firm endorsement of its proposals in most of the areas listed above. They were frustrated by fierce resistance from the opponents of reform not only in the opposition parties but also on the conservative side (Schoppa 1991: 221–50). The critics of the Rinji kyōiku shingikai's educational reform were sceptical about the advantages of the proposals for higher education. In their view, the proposed plan was based on an intellectually narrow-minded attitude, namely that the education system's main priority is to produce a workforce suited to the changing industrial framework while ignoring any of the other benefits that schooling might offer.

The recent debate on the reform of higher education

In spite of the fact that Nakasone failed to get the Rinji kyōiku shingikai's proposals implemented during his term as Prime Minister, the debate about reform of the higher education system was far from over (see Hood 2001). The council's recommendations eventually resulted in major changes which were implemented by the mid-1990s. Higher education reforms continued and remained the subject of debate during the 1990s, mainly led by the University Council (see Daigaku shingikai 1998). There were various reasons why university reform remained on the agenda, including the radical changes in society's expectations of universities after Japan's 'bubble economy' burst; the drastic decrease in enrolments due to population changes; the increasing demands for progress in scientific research and human resource development; and the growing need for 'lifelong learning'.

University reform in the new millennium takes place against the background of a sequence of economic recessions since the early 1990s. Koizumi Junichiro, Prime Minister from 26 April 2001, positioned himself to embark on a series of structural reforms aimed at revitalising the stagnant Japanese economy. His pledge to restore fiscal discipline by cutting the number of public servants and reallocating limited budget resources formed the cornerstone of his 'reform with no sacred cow' agenda. His intention was to overhaul the bureaucracy and reform the legal system. It was in this political context that the concept of 'independent administrative corporations' (dokuritsu gyōsei hōjinka) was proposed to change how public servants are employed, to reform public corporations and to encourage municipalities to merge. Ongoing reforms aim to cut 25 percent of Japan's current 1.15 million public servants by fiscal year 2010.

As expected, higher education institutions, and particularly national universities, came into the spotlight of the administrative reforms. As a result, the national universities were required to improve their administrative efficiency, quality assurance systems and accountability in response to the demands of the different stakeholders such as government, bureaucracy, business and industry in addition to students and parents. Reacting to Koizumi's administrative reform agenda, the Education Ministry, headed by Toyama Atsuko, issued a series of reports and plans. On 11 June 2001, Toyama announced the 'Structural Reforms Policies for National Universities' (the 'Toyama Plan') and submitted it to the Council on Economic and Fiscal Policy (Keizai zaisei shimon kaigi) chaired by Prime Minister Koizumi. The Plan proposed, among other things, that, during the same fiscal year, a panel of experts would design a scheme to turn national universities into 'independent administrative corporations'. The core proposals of the Plan were as follows:

1 *Take bold steps to reorganise and combine national universities*
- Reorganise and combine national universities based on the conditions in each university and in each sector
- Reduce and reorganise the system for training educational personnel, and consider transferring authority to local government
- Merge single-curriculum universities, such as medical schools, with other universities, and consider transferring authority to local government
- Reorganise and merge universities and faculties into units covering more than one prefecture
- Aim to reduce sharply the number of national universities
- Revitalise universities using a 'scrap and build' policy

2 *Introduce management techniques based on private-sector concepts in national universities*
- Employ outside specialists as university administrators and in organizational management
- Operate universities effectively and strategically by defining the responsibilities of management
- Introduce a new personnel system based on rewarding ability and results
- Include primary and secondary schools attached to universities and business schools in these considerations
- Move quickly to establish national universities as corporations

3 *Introduce the principles of competition in universities by using third party evaluations*
- Introduce a third-party evaluation system in which specialists and other private sector personnel participate
- Coopt the National Institution for Academic Degrees and other organisations
- Fully disclose the results of the evaluations to the rest of society, including students, companies and funding organizations
- Give priority to the distribution of funds based on the results of evaluation

Parts of the Plan were quickly implemented. The Education Ministry along with members of the governing coalition – the LDP, New Kōmeitō and Hoshutō (New Conservative Party) – were keen on the Plan, reasoning that it would enhance the competitiveness and efficiency of the universities. The Ministry made a number of further recommendations with regard to the relaxation of government regulations in terms of budget, organisation and other related issues, allowing for greater autonomy in decision-making and the evaluation-based distribution of resources. Another recommendation was made to relax the regulations by which the state had controlled national universities, and to leave the everyday management to the discretion of the universities themselves. In other words, it separated planning and implementation – with the Ministry in charge of planning and evaluation and the universities as 'independent administrative corporations' in charge of implementation. The Ministry began to quicken the pace for incorporating the nationa universities, setting a target date of April 2004. A Ministry report on the subject in 2002 provided an important basis for future discussion and required each university to submit 'medium-term plans and goals' (chūki keikaku/mokuhyō) for approval. A National University Evaluation Committee (Kokuritsu daigaku hyōka iinkai) was established by the Ministry itself, with enormous authority over budget distribution and assessing the degree to which the universities meet their stated goals (see Kitamura 1996; Hosoi 1999; Satō 2003).

However, the thrust of these administrative reforms remained controversial especially in academic circles, particularly the Japan Association of National Universities (Nihon kokuritsu daigaku kyōkai, JANU). For instance, Hasumi Shigehiko, the head of JANU, criticised the moves, stating that 'unlike tax collection or immigration control, it is clearly not possible to make university education and research more efficient merely by meeting numerical goals' (*Japan Times* 16 March 2001). Critics of the reforms suggested that they would strengthen state control over national universities and deprive them of academic autonomy and freedom. National universities would be ranked, based on merit and performance, and the distribution of resources would be linked to evalution. The reforms would reinforce the view that the main job of the national universities was to produce the various kinds of human resources necessary to meet changes in the industrial structure. The reforms would threaten the alreay fragile financial status of the universities, especially in provincial areas, and promote 'scrap-and build'restructuring and mergers between different institutions and their staff and faculties. The government would relinquish its responsibility to fund citizens' education, instead allocating resources in line with arbitrarily established priorities, and increasing the cost of education to the citizens themselves. The reforms would impose on universities the management systems of private companies, so that they would increasingly pursue and protect their own vested interests (see Nihon kagakusha kaigi 1999; Iwasaki and Ozawa 1999). In the view of the critics, universities would be unable to foster new and creative research unless they were free of state control.

One of the most important topics in this discussion related to the requirement for universities to produce a statement of their medium-term goals. Even though the 2002 report highlighted the requirement for the Ministry to consider the drafts compiled by the universities, it also stated that the Education Minister would stipulate the goals against which the internal evaluation committee would assess progress and that this assessment would be reflected in the calculation of financial subsidies and other matters. The inclusion of the obligation to consider the drafts produced by the universities, which was not previously highlighted in the 'Toyama Plan', was certainly a major step forward, but the idea that the state had a responsibility to stipulate goals was more controversial.

After much deliberation, JANU approved the Ministry's plans to create 'independent administrative corporations' (*Asahi Shimbun* 20 April 2002). The implication was that universities would need to become more independent on an array of matters previously left to the state, including budget distribution and personnel affairs. University presidents would be given greater powers over matters of management as well as education. The universities would have to decide how much money they would devote basic research. With greater freedom, therefore, comes new responsibilities, and the universities unable to meet these challenges will find it hard to survive.

Notes

1 The *zaikai* is generally considered to include the Federation of Employers' Associations (Nikkeiren); the Japanese Committee for Economic Development (Keizai Dōyūkai); and the Japanese Chamber of Commerce

and Industry (Nissō). The groups of the *zaikai* were, and still are, involved in various spheres of policy-making and, on the education issue, their views are taken seriously by the conservative political parties and Ministry bureaucracy.

2 The Keizai shingikai was set up as the overall co-ordinating body for the Liberal Democratic Party government's economic planning at the time. It promoted a policy of high economic growth under the slogan of 'Doubling National Income' in 1960 and played a significant role in deliberating educational reform in line with this plan.

3 The Chūkyōshin (Central Council for Education), established in 1952, is an advisory body to Ministry. At the request of the Minister of Education, the Chūkyōshin deliberates fundamental government policies in education and submits recommendations on vital educational policies, including legislative measures and curriculum revision. Since its creation, the Chūkyōshin has so far presented 30 reports recommending basic strategies for educational reform.

References

Aspinall, Robert (2001) *Teachers' Unions and the Politics of Education in Japan*, Albany: State University of New York Press.

Beauchamp, Edward R. and Richard Rubinger (1989) *Education in Japan: A Source Book*, New York and London: Garland Publishing Inc.

Chūō kyōiku shingikai (Central Council for Education) (1971) *Kongo ni okeru gakkō kyōiku no sōgōtekina kakujū seibi no tame no kihonshisaku* (Basic Guidelines for Reform of Education), Tokyo: Ministry of Education (Monbushō).

Daigaku shingikai (University Council) (1998) *Nijū isseiki no daigaku zō* (A Vision for Universities in the 21st century), Tokyo: Ministry of Education (Monbushō).

Dore, Ronald (1965) *Education in Tokugawa Japan*, Berkeley: University of California Press.

Fujimura-Faneslow, Kumiko and Anne E. Imamura (1991) 'The education of women in Japan' in Beauchamp, Edward R. (ed.), *Windows on Japanese Education*, New York: Greenwood Press, pp. 229–258.

Goodman, Roger (1989) *Who's Looking at Whom? Japanese, South Korean and English Education Reform in A Comparative Perspective*, Oxford: Nissan Institute of Japanese Studies.

Hall, Ivan P. (1973) *Mori Arinori*, Cambridge: Harvard University Press.

Hara, Kimi (1995) 'Changes to education for girls and women in modern Japan: past and present', in Fujiwara-Faneslow, Kumiko and A. Kameda (eds.), *Japanese Women: New Feminist Perspectives on the Past, Present and Future*, New York: The Feminist Press, pp. 93–106.

Hayao, Kenji (1993) *The Japanese Prime Minister and Public Policy*, Pittsburgh, PA: University of Pittsburgh Press.

Hood, Christopher P. (2001) *Japanese Education Reform: Nakasone's Legacy*, London and New York: Routledge.

Horio, Teruhisa and M.Yamazumi (1976) *Kyōiku rinen* (Educational principles), Tokyo: Tokyo Daigaku Shuppankai.
Hosoi, Katsuhiko et al. (1999) *Daigaku hyōka to daigaku sōzō* (University evaluation and creation), Tokyo: Tōshindō.
Iwasaki, Minoru and H. Ozawa (1999) *Gekishin! Kokuritsu daigaku* (A severe shock! National universities), Tokyo: Miraisha.
Kawahara, Tomitarō (1968) *Kyōshi no rekishi* (History of teachers) 4th edn., Tokyo: Sōbunsha.
Keizai Shingikai (Economic Deliberation Council) (1963) *Keizai hatten ni okeru jinteki nōryoku kaihatsu no kadai to taisaku* (Issues and measures for development of human abilities in pursuit of economic expansion), 13 January. Tokyo: Keizai Shingikai.
Kitamura, Kazuhiko (1996) *Daigaku hyōka towa nanika?* (What is university evaluation?), Tokyo: Tōshindō.
Kokuritsu kyōiku kenkyūsho (1974) *Nihon kindai kyōku hyaku nenshi* (History of modern Japanese schools over the past one hundred years), Tokyo: Tōyōkan.
Kuroha, Rōichi (1993) *Sengo daigaku seisaku no tenkai* (Development of the Post-War educational policies for universities), Tokyo: Tamagawa Daigaku Shuppankai.
Marshall, Byron (1994) *Learning to Be Modern – Japanese Political Discourse on Education*, Boulder, Colorado: Westview Press.
Ministry of Education (1972) *Gakusei 100 nenshi* (The school system over the past one hundred years), Tokyo: Ministry of Education.
Ministry of Education (2001) *Daigaku (kokuritsu daigaku) no kōzō kaikaku no hōshin* (Structural reform policies for national universities – Toyama Plan), Tokyo: Ministry of Education (June).
Ministry of Education (2002) *Atarashii kokuritsu daigaku hōjin zō ini tsuite* (Concerning the image of new 'national university administrative Incorporation' – Final report), Tokyo: Ministry of Education (March).
Nagai, Michio (1971) *Higher Education in Japan: Its Take-off and Crash*, Tokyo: Tokyo University Press.
Nihon kagakusha kaigi (1999) *Kokuritsu daigaku ga nakunarutte honto?!,* (Is it true that national universities will disappear?!) Tokyo: Suiyōsha.
Nikkeiren (1952) *Shin kyōiku seido saikentō ni kansuru yōbō* (Recommendation for reconstruction of the new education system), October 16. Tokyo: Nikkeiren.
Okada, Akito (1998) *Equality of Opportunity in Post-war England and Japan: A Comparative Study of Educational Policy 1944–1970*, unpublished DPhil. thesis, University of Oxford.
Okada, Akito (1999) 'Secondary education reform and the concept of equal opportunity in Japan', *Compare* 29: 171–89.
Okada, Akito (2002) 'Education of whom, for whom and by whom? Revising the Fundamental Law of Education', *Japan Forum* 14 (3): 425–41.
Ōsaki, Hitoshi (1991) *Daigaku funsō o kataru* (Narrating university conflict), Tokyo: Yushindō.
Satō Seiji (2003) *Daigaku hyōka to accountability* (University evaluation and accountability) Tokyo: Moriyama Shoten.

Schoppa, Leonard (1991) *Education Reform in Japan – A Case of Immobilist Politics,* London: Routledge.
Smith, Henry D., II (1972) *Japan's Student Radicals*, Cambridge: Harvard University Press.
Taniguchi Takuo (1988) *Nihon chūtō kyōiku kaikakushi kenkyū* (The study of secondary education reform history in Japan), Tokyo: Daiichihōki.
U.S. Department of State (1946) *Report of the United Education Mission to Japan*, Tokyo: Supreme Command of the Allied Powers (SCAP).
Wheeler, Donald (1979) 'Japan's postmodern student movement', in Cummings, Willam K. et al. (eds.), *Changes in the Japanese University: A Comparative Perspective*, New York: Praeger, pp. 202–16.
Yoneda, Toshihiko (1992) *Kindai nihon chūgakkōseido no kakuritsu* (The establishment of the secondary education system in modern Japan), Tokyo: Tokyo Daigaku Shuppankai.

3 The Incorporation of National Universities: The Role of Missing Hybrids

Sachi Hatakenaka

Introduction

The Japanese higher education system is undergoing massive reforms today. The government first announced its intention to incorporate national universities in September 1999, and this became a reality in April 2004. In June 2001, the Education Ministry also announced aggressive pro-competitive policies (the so-called Toyama Plan), which laid out the government's commitmenting to support the development of the top thirty universities into world class institutions. These policies were complemented by another aggressive challenge set down in a statement by the Minister of Economy and Trade and Industry (METI), the so-called Hiranuma Doctrine, by which universities were expected to play a greater economic role through setting up at least one thousand entrepreneurial spin-off companies over a three-year period. But it is not only the political agenda that is pushing the universities to reform. A rapidly aging population with a declining number of young people is exerting competitive pressures on universities. 'Compete or perish' is the mood within the Japanese higher education sector today.

What is particularly significant is that the governance and incorporation agendas have been under discussion for many years. Governance reforms, to change the relationship between national universities and the Ministry, were first discussed after World War II during the occupation, even though 'incorporation' itself was not on the agenda at the time. 'Incorporation' as a concept was first articulated in the early 1960s, and it was given further attention by policymakers at several distinct junctures after that, but remained unimplemented. Even during the round of public sector reforms in the late 1990s, national universities were initially left out of an incorporation list, which included all other government research institutes and associated agencies. It was not until later that the incorporation of national universities re-surfaced as a policy. The questions of incorporation and reforming the governance of universities were therefore on the policy agenda for a very long time: why did they take so long to be implemented, and why is this happening now? Addressing this question is particularly important today, as the answers highlight underlying structures that could also powerfully influence Japanese higher education in future.

The simplest explanation is that dramatic changes in the political and economic contexts, particularly with the worsening economic conditions of Japan in the 1990s, helped push the reform agenda. While these contexts certainly played a key role in bringing about the current set of reforms, they are incomplete as explanations. In this chapter, I argue that the concept of 'hybrid expertise' can help illuminate both the nature of the past inertia as well as the events that triggered the current set of changes, and provide insights as to what may lie ahead.

This chapter is structured as follows. First, the three on-going reforms in Japan and their historical development are described in order to highlight the importance of incorporation and to show how long governance reforms and incorporation have been on the policy agenda. Second, the three structural characteristics of the Japanese university system, centralisation, decentralisation and internal division, are highlighted along with their historical roots. The chapter then discusses how these structural characteristics have limited the accumulation of hybrid expertise, contrasting Japan with the UK reform experience to illustrate the nature of the missing expertise. Finally, conclusions and implications are suggested.

What is going on today? Three major reforms

As of September 2004, three sets of reform agenda had been proposed by the national government in Japan: the incorporation of national universities, pro-competitive policies for creating world class universities and policies to encourage universities to develop into engines of economic growth.

Incorporation of national universities

In April 1999, when Prime Minister Hashimoto's cabinet delivered its decision to incorporate 89 national bodies, the national universities were given additional time until 2003 to develop a plan of action (Kako 2000). In September 1999, the Minister of Education, Arima Akito, addressed all national university presidents to explain his view that incorporation should be regarded as a positive step for the future of national universities and that it should not be seen simply as an extension of public sector reform in other areas (Ministry of Education 1999). In May 2000, Arima's successor met with the presidents of the national universities to re-emphasise the government's position on their incorporation (Ministry of Education 2000).

A special committee was established to draw up a vision for national universities and it submitted its final report in March 2002 (Ministry of Education 2002). The Education Ministry presented draft laws for national university corporations in February 2003 (Ministry of Education 2003). These were enacted in October 2003, and the national university corporations came into existence in April 2004. National universities submitted their medium-term targets and plans in November 2003, which were in turn evaluated by the the National University Corporation Evaluation Committee and formally accepted by the Ministry (Ministry of Education 2004).

Pro-competitive policies for developing world class universities

Minister Toyama shook up the entire sector by her announcement in June 2001 that her vision was to have a competitive system of universities striving for excellence, in which she expressed a desire to support the development of the top thirty universities into world class institutions. The Toyama Plan initially had three components: to consolidate and reduce the number of universities through mergers; to incorporate national universities in a way that would introduce private sector management practices; and to introduce greater competition within higher education through third-party evaluation.

By September 2004, the number of national universities had been reduced from 99 to 89 as a result of mergers planned before incorporation, with several other merger plans under discussion. National universities became independent corporations in April

2004, with new governance structures that included 'private sector-like features' such as boards of directors with executive directors working as top management teams, and administrative councils on which outsiders comprised a majority. Pro-competitive policies were implemented through competitive funding programs such as the 21st Century Center of Excellence (COE) programme for research and doctoral training, the Center of Learning (COL) programme to support innovative undergraduate education, and the programme to support the development of professional schools.

The policy environment for quality assurance changed dramatically in a move that was commonly described as one 'from input control to output control'. Earlier government initiatives to introduce third-party evaluation by the National Institute for Academic Degrees in 2000 for ongoing programmes were strengthened further, giving the issue a renewed emphasis. Review requirements for establishing new institutions and programs were drastically reduced in 2003. While the policy framework of competitive funding and quality evaluation have been established, the overall effectiveness of such competitive policies will clearly depend on the universities' capacity to plan and act and, therefore, on the direction taken by the incorporation and governance reforms.

Universities as engines of economic growth

The third strand of the reform policies was the government's expectation that universities should play a greater economic role as engines of growth. In 2001, Minister Hiranuma at the Ministry of Economics, Trade and Industry (METI) announced his goal of having at least a thousand university spinoff companies established over a period of three years. The involvement of METI in university affairs reflects an international trend among OECD countries towards innovative policies to develop the knowledge economy. METI's actions bear a striking resemblance to moves made by the Department of Trade and Industry (DTI) in the UK in this respect.

METI and the Education Ministry have been working, sometimes jointly and at other times separately, to push forward this new agenda relating to the economic role of universities. A number of incremental policies have already been introduced, from the establishment of technology licensing offices and administrative units to support joint research, to de-regulatory measures to facilitate university handling of external contracts, or new regulations to permit university professors to act as consultants and be involved in technology transfer (Hatakenaka 2004).

It is also clear, however, that these incremental changes did not add up to the kind of autonomy that universities needed in order to be able to work with outside bodies in a business-like manner. The fact that the national universities (the most significant universities in terms of science and engineering in Japan) did not have a separate legal status had been a critical constraint. National universities could not negotiate contracts with external bodies autonomously, nor could they own intellectual property rights. While professors at national universities had been able to work as consultants since the late 1990s, the terms and conditions for their work were still formally subject to the Minister of Education's approval and to civil service regulations. While the cultural change was certainly beginning to enable university professors to become more active in the economy, much still hung on the incorporation of national universities.

In other words, the incorporation of national universities is a fundamental change that has altered the whole basis of university operation and will have a powerful influence on other on-going reforms.

History of incorporation as an agenda item

How did incorporation come to be on the agenda for national universities? Much has to do with the manner in which national universities were created by the Meiji government and with subsequent historical events, most notably the government reforms during the American occupation.

The first of the national universities, Tokyo University, was created in 1877 by the Meiji government through the amalgamation of several existing schools. These schools were both symbols and instruments of the Meiji government's aspirations to modernise Japan quickly with a massive infusion of foreign expertise (Bartholomew 1989; Terasaki 2000). Tokyo University was established as an integral part of the Education Ministry, so that academic autonomy was not part of the design at the outset. Rather, the notion of academic autonomy diffused into the organisation through the presence of foreign academics (Terasaki 2000). Through the early 20th century, national universities established a delicate balance of power with the Ministry, particularly around controversial personnel decisions, without systemic change either in their governance or their legal status (Takagi 1998; Ōsaki 1999).

Governance reforms to change the relationship between universities and the Education Ministry were first discussed after World War II during the American occupation (Kaigo and Terasaki 1969; Takagi 1998; Ōsaki 1999; Terasaki 2000). The initial proposal by the American occupation administration in 1948 was to establish boards of governors for individual universities similar to those of state universities in America, along with a central university council within the Ministry. Even though 'incorporation' itself was not on the agenda, the proposal met with strong opposition from the universities as they were extremely nervous about changing their relationships with the Ministry and the outside world. The main issue was to do with the establishment of governing boards, which were seen as a way to increase external influence on universities. During the post-war period, the academic community was particularly sensitive to the issue of academic autonomy, given their wartime experience of being subjected to military control.

In 1949, the Education Ministry commissioned a special committee headed by Professor Wagatsuma Sakae to review possible options for university management (Korea 1993; Takagi 1998; Ōsaki 1999). The committee proposed revised governance structures with a central university council that would report to the Ministry, and advisory councils rather than governing boards at the university level. The plan again met massive opposition and was abandoned.

After that, the history of higher education was peppered with attempts to change the arrangements governing national universities. In 1960, the Ministry came up with another proposal which was again abandoned in the face of massive opposition (Takagi 1998; Hada 1999; Amano 2002). Subsequently, in the early 1960s, Professor Nagai Michio articulated the concept of 'universities as incorporated bodies' for the first time in a magazine article, leading to much public debate (Nagai 1962). In the late 1960s, student movements led to more political debate about university operation and management, and the Democratic Socialist Party went as far as proposing to incorporate universities with governing boards, but once again this never came to fruition (Takagi 1998).

In 1971, the Central Education Council's final deliberations included recommendations to consider making national universities into legally autonomous entities along with the establishment of governing boards (Schoppa 1991; Takagi 1998; Amano 2002). The Japan Association of National Universities argued against such ideas because they feared that the selection of governors and the subsequent flow of public funds might jeopardise the academic autonomy of universities.

In 1984, Prime Minister Nakasone established the Ad Hoc Council for Education to review policy issues. Nakasone envisaged the need for radical reform in education and wanted to set up an ad hoc council at the cabinet level to avoid the conservatism of the Ministry (Schoppa 1991). Several members of the Council were strong proponents of the incorporation of national universities, which would enable these universities to seek funding from private sources. The Ministry put up strong opposition to this idea, with the result that the Committee's final report in 1987 merely noted that incorporation was a complicated issue and recommended that the government and universities should continue to explore various options.

The public sector reform committee under Prime Minister Hashimoto during the 1990s looked as though it was following a similar course of action. Their final report, submitted in December 1997, excluded the national universities from the list of agencies to be included in an incorporation plan (Kako 2000; Sawa 2001). Their recommendations were inherited by the Obuchi government and consolidated into a plan to restructure and streamline government ministries in which all non-policy executing agencies, including affiliated research institutes but excluding the national universities, were to become separate legal entities by January 2001. It was not until 1999 that national universities again re-surfaced as targets for public sector reform.

Possible explanations

If governance reform and ideas to incorporate national universities have been on the policy agenda for so long, then why have they taken so long to happen? The simplest explanation is that the political mandate for public sector reforms strengthened over time, both as leftist opposition weakened within universities and as economic circumstances deteriorated in Japan, legitimating the political call for change.

The political mandate for public sector reforms certainly appeared to strengthen over time (Kaneko 1998; Yonezawa 1998;

Yonezawa 2000). Whereas Nakasone was powerful both as prime minister and as a proponent of public sector reforms, his specific attempt to reform education through the Ad Hoc Committee fell short due to factional divisions reinforcing the tendency to conservatism (Schoppa 1991). Hashimoto was also known as a proponent of public sector reform and yet, again, his reform committee failed to touch the issue of incorporatiing the national universities. It took the Obuchi government, with its more ambitious goal of cutting the civil service by 25 percent rather than 10 percent, to include national universities in the plan. Finally, when confronted by Prime Minister Koizumi's strong push for public sector reforms, Education Ministry Minister Toyama Atsuko had no option but to come up with radical proposals. At the same time, the leftist opposition to reform within universities weakened significantly, partly because the younger generations remembered little of the struggles of the 1960s, and partly because the leftist agenda had weakened globally.

Changing economic circumstances in Japan also dictated the course of events. Until the 1980s, there were few economic arguments for universities to change. In the 1980s, Japanese export-oriented industries had caught up with other countries, and began to think explicitly about strategies for scientific innovation. This led to the pressure to liberalise and reform national universities that grew slowly but steadily through the 1980s and 1990s (Schoppa 1991; Hatakenaka 2004). It was the economic stagnation in the 1990s that added a new sense of urgency to national demands for change. Universities became the last resort in the search for economic revival and public demands for them to play a more proactive role in the economy became explicit.

All these explanations are plausible and shed light on the historical developments. However, they leave certain gaps in our understanding about 'the how' of the reforms. They provide little insight into the mechanism of how the incorporation process was delayed and how it came to be legitimated. As such they cannot illuminate how the proposed changes were shaped, or what implications there may be for the future.

To address these questions, it is important to examine the underlying structures. For instance, some would argue that the structures of the Ministry and the national universities prevented the development of a constituency for reforms (Kaneko 1998). More specifically, particular historical contexts gave birth to a form of academic autonomy within Japan based on the power of the faculty meetings (*kyōjukai*) rather than institutional autonomy at the university level (Ōsaki 1999). Indeed, the reform agenda involved too many complicated issues to disentangle. One fear was that discussions about incorporation could lead to discussions about privatisation (Yonezawa 1998). Another related fear was that changes in the relationship with the Ministry would dramatically alter government commitment to fund ingnational universities. Another fear was that incorporation would imply governance reforms, which could drastically change internal power relationships. Persuasive arguments had to emerge in order for the reform to proceed.

An alternative explanation: missing hybrids

I will build on these structural explanations and propose that one underlying factor has been the lack of individuals with the hybrid expertise essential interpret the new agenda across institutional boundaries and direct change. Parochialism and the inability to cross these boundaries were critical in preventing the emergence of a vision that was acceptable to different stakeholders.

This section further argues that the lack of hybrid expertise was itself a result of three related structures: highly centralised governance structures, decentralized administration and decision-making within universities based on the *kōza* system(see below for an explanation of this), and internal divisions within institutions resulting from the way in which they had been set up. It was individuals with unusual hybrid expertise which crossed the the boundaries between academia, administration and politics who were able to trigger change by developing new discourses with which to explain the need for incorporation.

Highly centralised governance structures

The Education Ministry was directly responsible for negotiating national university budgets with the Ministry of Finance. As a result, the budgeting process for national universities was an internal issue within government, opaque even to individual national universities. This led to the development of administrative practices and expertise to deal with these matters centred within the Ministry itself rather than within individual universities.

More specifically, three types of administrative personnel had developed within the national university system. Most administrators working in universities were recruited directly into the universities themselves as civil servants. Members of this group then split into two streams as they advanced through through the ranks. One group was made up of those who were promoted to the managerial level and had the option of sitting for a national examination, which in turn enabled them to proceed as senior university administrators rotating between different national universities. The second group comprised both those who did not become managers and those who opted not to take the examination, all of whom stayed as local administrators within the same national university. This second type tended to fill the lower ranks of the university administration and provide the institutional memory as to how things were done. The third type of administrators were a handful of the elite civil servants recruited by the Ministry itself, who were assigned to higher level managerial positions such as finance directors within national universities as part of their career development.

Decentralised internal practices

The highly centralised governance structure at the national level contrasted with highly decentralised practices within universities, based on the *kōza* system, the Japanese system of professorial chairs. This is a system in which a professor, along with several junior assistant professors and assistants, are treated as a unit responsible for a particular field of study. Introduced in 1893, *kōza* came to be powerful units both in budgeting and hiring personnel (Terasaki 1992; Amano 1994). The Ministry's recurrent budget was determined largely by the number and types of *kōza* in each university.

People were recruited into the academic profession through apprenticeship within the *kōza* and assistant professors were expected to take over upon the retirement of full professors. The professor had supreme influence in personnel decision-making – it was assumed that he (rarely she) would know who would be the best replacement in his own field and could, therefore, select and groom his own successor. Departments or faculties were little more than collections of *kōza* organised by field whose main function was to protect and if possible increase the number teaching staff. Even with recent efforts to rationalise recruitment and amalgamate *kōza* into larger units, the institutional influence of *kōza*-oriented thinking remains powerful.

The consequence was that there was little room for the emergence of academics who had any real experience of administrative issues. Academics remained fiercely autonomous in their activities, ranging from personnel decisions to finance, but without assuming any formal administrative responsibilities. This pre-empted the need for a layer of academic administrators who might oversee budgetary or personnel decisions. Indeed, it was in the interest of academics collectively to avoid the creation of any such tier of academic administrators in order to protect their autonomy. Positions such as department heads, deans or directors of centers often became powerless posts with short-term incumbants precisely to avoid any individual becoming a heavy-handed administrator. Another problem was that financial and other administrative systems were designed by the Education Ministry for its own purposes, and were not adequate for decision-making at the level of universities.

Internal divisions

There were other internal divisions within national universities, in addition to those between *kōza*. During the post-World War II reforms, there was a massive move to merge specialist senior high schools or colleges into universities so that there would be a national university in each prefecture (Hada 1999; Amano 2002). The central government, under pressure from the occuption administration, mandated such mergers, and little was left to local discretion. As a result, most of the older national universities had historical and cultural boundaries within them that were hard to cross. Internal divisions were reinforced by the manner in which the Japanese academics interpreted academic autonomy, i.e. that all the key decisions should be left to academics in relevant disciplines at the faculty level (Ōsaki 1999), with little integration across faculties.

Consequences: missing hybrids

What were the consequences of these structures? The above discussion indicates that the system produced five types of career pattern, as follows:

- The education Ministry's elite career civil servants, a small number of whom had one or two year's of experience in university administrative management positions;
- University management level administrators who rotated between national universities, orchestrated by the Ministry, typically at intervals of two or three years;
- University administrators who remained attached to individual national universities, and who tended to remain in the lower tiers of the career structure;
- University academic administrators such as deans and heads of deparments, who tended to remain part-time researchers while holding these appointments, and who therefore did not develop significant managerial experience in dealing with budgetary or personnel decisions;
- University academics who remained autonomous in their activities in their respective faculties, some of whom might get involved in micro-level administrative issues, but without developing experience in understanding university-level issues.

These career patterns in turn reflected a highly segmented higher education sector in which hybrid expertise could not evolve easily. A striking omission was that of individuals with combineed academic and administrative expertise at the university level. Administrators either remained at the local level or they became senior administrators representing national universities collectively rather than a particular university. Academics engaged in administrative matters within their small academic groups lacked a perspective that went beyond their own disciplinary boundaries. At the university level, academics' understanding of financial matters was obscured by the complex and opaque national system of budgeting. The only individuals in the system who crossed boundaries were elite bureaucrats and high level university administrators who moved systematically between universities and the Ministry, thus blurring the distinctions between individual national universities.

Another missing link was that there were few people inside government who brought a university academic perspective to policy making. There were hardly any academics in positions that influenced higher education policies. The most university-centric policy makers were the elite civil servants, some of whom had held positions within the Ministry related to universities and possibly even direct experience as university administrators. Indeed, there is some evidence that this small core of elite civil servants with direct experience of education provided an undercurrent of reform within the Ministry, though their voices were often stifled by opposition from the rest of the Ministry, as well as from academics and university administrators. Amagi Isao is a well-known examples of a elite bureaucrat who supported reform efforts in the 1970s (Schoppa 1991).

Images of missing hybrids

The experience in the UK can be used to illustrate and understand what this missing expertise might look like. The higher education system in the UK has gone through massive and continuous reforms since the 1980s. Universities in the UK, once seen as immobile ivory towers isolated from the rest of the world, have changed to cope with larger student populations and have become entrepreneurial and managerial. Interestingly, this reform also took some time in coming to fruition. The earliest signal about the need for reform came in 1969, when Shirley Williams, the then Minister of Education under the Labour government, expressed her frustration in thirteen demands delivered to the Committee of Vice Chancellors and Principals (DES 1969). Williams was ignored at the time. However, once the Prime Minister stood firmly behind the reform agenda, as Margaret Thatcher did when she came into power in 1979, the consequences were swift and dramatic, starting with a 10 percent budget cut in 1981.

The subsequent higher education reform in the UK is variously described depending on the political perspective of the author. One thing everyone agrees is that universities went through a massive cultural change. Interestingly, while Thatcher's resolve to reform universities was reasonably well known, neither the specific changes sought nor the ways in which they would be made were clear at the outset. Rather, the directions and agenda for reforms were developed by multiple players operating at different levels of the system.

Many of these players were hybrids who combined academic, university administration and policy perspectives and who were able to facilitate change by articulating proposals that made sense to academics as well as to non-academics. In other words, the academic hybrids played a key role in designing the reform process as a set of actions that could be understood by at least part of academe.

Implementing policies

The 1981 budget cuts were implemented by the University Grants Committee (UGC), a body that had been responsible for channelling government funds into UK universities since 1919. The UGC had been established as a buffer to ensure that universities remained removed from politicians. The UGC's initial reaction was to allocate the cuts unevenly (Bird 1994; Williams 1997) with newer and more technically-oriented universities, such as Salford and Aston facing much greater cuts (around 30–40 percent) than the average of around 10 percent. What the UGC apparently did was to protect the more prestigious institutions at the cost of the less prestigious ones.

The UGC was soon under fire for allocating the budget cuts without a clear explanation. Moving towards a transparent formula was tricky since many research-oriented elite universities would have immediately lost out. It was made even harder because it would have made it more apparent how expensive the universities were compared with the polytechnics, which offered degrees but were primarily teaching rather than research institutions. It was clear to the UGC as early as 1984 that teaching costs in the universities would have be reduced to become comparable to those of the polytechnics (Swinnerton-Dyer 1984).

The UGC's move was to introduce, in 1986, formula-based funding for teaching. At the same time, research funding was to be determined by the Research Assessment Exercise (RAE), which was a bold move to evaluate academic departments in terms of their overall research performance and then reflect this evaluation in funding for research infrastructure. Most of the people within the UGC who translated the policy agenda into this set of specific actions were hybrids in the sense described above.

Let us take the example of the head of the UGC at the time, Sir Peter Swinnerton-Dyer, a well-respected mathematician from Cambridge. He had served as a College Master for a decade (1973–83), an interesting grooming ground for academic administrators as Oxbridge colleges are microcosms of university affairs, covering student recruitment, finance and academic issues. He was the Vice-Chancellor of Cambridge at the time of the budget cut announcement (1979–81) and so had first hand experience of dealing with the new policy environment from the university perspective. His swift action in Cambridge to propose early retirement to cope with possible further cuts is well documented in his annual addresses – and appear to have set Cambridge on a sound financial footing (Cambridge Reporter 1980–1990).

Swinnerton-Dyer thus came to the UGC with solid academic and administrative expertise and credibility. It was he who stood firm as the RAE was introduced, persuading both politicians and academics of its logic. While he did not convince all the academics, he managed to persuade a critical number of academic leaders, sufficient to be able to implement such a drastic change.

University response

Salford University was one of several newer universities which received a disproportionately high share of the 1981 cuts, of the order of 30–40 percent. John Ashworth had been appointed as Vice Chancellor of Salford just days before the budget announcement. When the news came through, he was still in his previous position as Chief Scientist at the Cabinet Office. He remembers being asked if he would back out of his new appointment – his answer was a resounding 'no'. He went straight to Salford, organised a senate meeting on a Saturday morning (possibly for the first time in the the history of Salford University), to discuss how to deal with the severe cutbacks. Salford organised an early retirement scheme, negotiated with the government to give them support in the process, and created a plan of action to respond.

Ashworth recalls how critical it was to work closely with his Registrar who was the chief administrator of the university and had intricate knowledge and understanding of the administrative and financial issues. As an administrator, the Registrar could not have instituted the change without the academic leadership that the Vice-Chancellor provided. John Ashworth, as an outsider and an academic, could not have instituted change without the detailed administrative knowledge of the Registrar. Together, they were able to formulate and implement the appropriate response for the university.

John Ashworth was himself a hybrid. He had first been an academic, moving to the Cabinet Office on secondment, where he stayed on to serve as Chief Scientist. He thus had a more solid understanding of the political climate facing universities than an ordinary academic. He lacked administrative knowledge of the university itself, but was able to team up with his Registrar who had exactly this expertise.

These tales demonstrate that there were structures in the UK system that allowed the development of certain types of hybrid expertise. First, academics learned to cope with administrative issues – not as a part-time short-term sacrifice, but over a sustained period. Universities had a tradition of long-standing department heads, who then became heads of faculties or schools, and then vice-chancellors. Second, there were career administrators in each university who understood the intricate details of administration, and who could academic administrators by providing university-specific knowledge and perspective. Third, academic administrators often took up positions in which they helped shape policies in a way that made sense to academics as well as politicians. These were the hybrids who straddled the worlds of academe, administration and policy-making.

Are these hybrids really missing in Japan?

So far, this chapter has argued that hybrid expertise did not readily develop in Japanese national universities given their structures. This does not mean that these hybrids never appeared. Indeed, it was precisely the emergence of anomalous hybrids, such as Professor Arima Akito, that appears to have led to the formulation of the incorporation plans of the late 1990s.

As noted above, in 1997, when the final report from the Public Sector Reform Committee under the Hashimoto government recommended ministerial restructuring and incorporation of public bodies, national universities were excluded from the list. In 1998, a new political agenda to cut the civil service numbers by 25 pecent arose and, as part of this scenario, national universities again became the target of public sector reform (Kako 2000).

At the time, Arima was the Minister of Education and Culture and was actively opposed to such an idea. In December 1998, Arima is said to have had three private meetings with a Liberal Democratic Party politician, as a result of which he himself became a proponent of incorporation. Arima explained that he changed his mind because he was convinced that it was possible to go ahead with incorporation while avoiding key measures which he saw as inappropriate, such as privatisation and the loss of civil service status for university staff. He saw that incorporation made sense for national universities in the light of international experience but argued that the specific laws under discussion for incorporating other public bodies were inappropriate for universities. As a result, he agreed to explore the options for incorporation of national universities before 2003.

Thus Arima changed his position, accepted the principle of incorporation and then negotiated the terms and conditions under which further discussions could take place. His actions did not stop there. Under his leadership, the Ministry persuaded the leadership of the Association of National Universities to explore options of incorporation in March 1999. President Hasumi of Tokyo University enlisted President Matsuo from Nagoya University to begin exploring the options for incorporation and, based on this preparatory work, officially launched a committee to explore incorporation as an option in June 1999. In September 1999, Minister Arima made a public speech, which shook the whole sector – at a gathering of national university presidents, he clearly stated the rationale for incorporation for the first time. While he was also clear in opposing the specific law proposed for incorporating other public bodies which he viewed as inadequate for universities, this was the key moment when the sector began to move in the direction of incorporation (Ministry of Education 1999).

Arima had been a respected physics professor from Tokyo University, where he served as President between 1989 and 1993. He then moved to head Riken, an incorporated public research unit, and later assumed the position of Minister of Education as a member of parliament elected through the system of proportional representation. His was a very unusual case of an academic with some administrative experience turned policy-maker. This hybrid expertise enabled Arima to analyse the situation and so change from opposing incorporation to one of supporting it. He was able to make a personal judgment as an academic and as a policy-maker as to whether the proposal made sense and the conditions that would need to be satisfied to make the proposal acceptable to national universities. It was also his respectability as an academic that made him persuasive in the academic community.

Arima was an anomaly as an academic becoming a minister and entering the world of policy-making. However, the academic-administrative aspect of his hybrid expertise has become more common. Various changes made in the 1990s strengthened the leadership of the national university presidents (Ōsaki 1999), for instance, by lengthening their term, emphasizing their role in resource allocation, and weakening the influence of the *kōza* (Ogawa 2002). Incremental changes during the course of the 1990s forced some heads of departments and deans to think proactively about their roles. More academics have begun to understand administrative issues at organizational levels. A small but growing number of academics have even become involved in policy discussions in the University Council which was established in 1987 to be the engine of incremental reforms.

There were others who came close to being hybrids who played critical roles in shaping the course of reforms. Satō Teiichi, an elite civil servant with an unusually detailed experience of university reform issues and a perspective that reflected the concerns of university administrators, served as the secretary general of the Education Ministry for over three critical years, twice the average for the decade. Toyama Atsuko, another anomalous case of a career civil servant from the Education Ministry turned politician, became the longest-serving Minister of Education in recent years, remaining in office for 29 months, compared with an average of 9 months during the previous decade. By crossing the boundary into the political world, she straddled the worlds of policy-making in the Ministry and the world of politics, and was able to initiate some aggressive reforms. It is interesting to note that both Satō and Toyama had held key higher education-related positions in the Ministry both during the period of Nakasone's Ad Hoc Council on Education in the mid-1980s and the subsequent incremental reforms of the early 1990s. They represented a new breed of elite civil servants who had experienced university reform issues at first hand, and who rose to power at a critical time.

It is striking that the most controversial moves towards incorporation were made during the tenures of these two Ministers. The three Ministers who served between Arima and Toyama, and the two who served after Toyama, were all politicians with little significant backgrounds in higher education, and they hardly made any moves on the issue at all. Indeed, there is some evidence that Koizumi selected Toyama as his Minister of Education precisely to deal with the issues in a way others could not, and pushed her to undertake serious reforms (Nikkei 2001).

Conclusions and implications

The central questions in this chapter have been why it took so long for incorporation and reform of the governance of national universities to happen when the issue had been on the agenda for such a long time, and why it happened when it did. The most common-sense explanation is that the political and economic contexts were not conducive to reforms. It was only when the economic situation of the nation as a whole had deteriorated sufficiently that the call by politicians to incorporate the national universities became legitimated. This chapter has argued that there was another structural factor at work, namely the lack of hybrid expertise, which was critical in delaying the incorporation agenda. These hybrids were needed to champion reforms by clarifying the options in ways that were acceptable to multiple stakeholders, most notably the academics. Parochialism and the lack of expertise that crossed boundaries were at the heart of the systemic inability of Japanese universities to change.

What were the structures that acted to prevent the development of such a hybrid expertise? First, there were few people in national universities who could comfortably cross the boundaries between the academic and administrative worlds. Second, there were few opportunities for individual academics and administrators to work closely together over a sustained period on university administration. Third, there were few policy-makers working on university issues who had an in-depth understanding of academic perspectives, particularly at the highest levels. What was missing were the structures that enabled people to cross boundaries between the three separate worlds of academics, administrators and policy-makers.

Indeed the system was not conducive to the development of administrative expertise at the university level in general. The fact that university academic actors were missing from administrative or policy decisions meant that there was nobody who was able to make sense of the reform agenda in a way appropriate to universities. There were very few hybrids who straddled the three worlds of academia, administration and policy-making. It took these anomalous hybrids such as Arima to change the course of events.

All that is in the past. Some may argue that since things are now changing so rapidly that none of their historical causes matter today. I would argue otherwise. If the absence of hybrids mattered in the past for the initiation of the reforms, it is at least as important today for the task of implementing them. The intervention of Arima or Toyama was short-lived and it is not clear that other academic hybrids have been centrally involved in the process as active designers rather than passive reviewers.

Today's process of incorporation, which will form the basis of Japanese higher education for the next few decades, risk being carried out without the benefit of synthesising multiple perspectives. What might be the consequences? If policies are implemented without taking into account all three perspectives perspectives (policy making, administrative and academic), they may turn out to create little more than structures which will continue to constrain university actions. There may be large numbers of changes in names and appearances but the fundamental relationships may not change much.

There are already signs that real changes stemming from incorporation may take a long time to fully materialise. In many cases, the preparatory activities for incorporating national universities appear to have focused on routine administrative issues rather than on strategic ones. This is not surprising given that the first step for each university is to develop an in-depth and shared understanding about how it currently operates, critically important knowledge at an organisational level that has not been fostered in the past.

More significant are the structures set up by the laws, such as the new governance arrangements, which look highly idiosyncratic and are at variance with those in the US, UK or continental Europe. For instance, there is no Board of Trustees or university governors to which the university president will report. The newly created Board of Directors (*yakuinkai*) includes members (*riji*) who are mostly Vice-Presidents appointed by the President, and is essentially an internal body designed to work as a top management team. This system is seen as the main way of importing private sector management practices, and indeed mimics the Japanese corporate governance structure which is itself unusual in having so few outsiders at the highest level. The Management Councils (*keiei kyōgikai*), with a majority of their membership coming from outside the university, look more like a board of trustees, but it only plays an advisory role to the President, together with the Education and Research Council (*kyōiku kenkyū hyōgikai*), comprising senior academics.

That the structure is idiosyncratic is not itself a concern. Japan clearly must develop systems that match its needs and culture. But the legal blueprint looks like a compromise between the politicians who wanted to have private sector management brought into universities (in the guise of the Board of Directors), reformers advocating external oversight of management (represented by the Management Council), and academics who wanted neither of the above (but who ended up with the Education and Research Council). What is lacking is coordination between the academic, administrative and policy perspectives.

The real question is whether the system is workable. For instance, though power is highly concentrated around the university presidency, which could work well with managerially-experienced Presidents who knew exactly what to do, what mechanisms are there to provide checks and balances when a President fails to deliver? One mechanism might be the two auditors nominated by the Ministry to sit on the Board of Directors, who are expected to report back to the Minister in the case of serious problems. The other mechanism is the evaluation system for medium-term goals and plans, as will be discussed below. Both of these are dependent on the Ministry to take action, a source of concern for many who are worried about Ministry intervention, but it is more likely that they will be concerned with serious cases of fraud or other illegal actions rather than with issues of mismanagement or misdirected strategies.

The system has virtually no drivers for change other than the Presidents themselves, and so when a President is not charismatic enough to push for change, the result may be stasis and stagnation. The Administrative Councils can offer their advice, but it is in the power of the President to accept it or not. In controversial issues over which there is substantive resistance inside the university, the president has to assume the sole responsibility for taking unpopular decisions, rather than sharing it with the Council, as would be the case had the Council more powers over decisions. The initial views of lay members of Administrative Councils are optimistic as 80 percent of them think their universities are taking their views seriously (Nikkei, 2004). The question remains as to whether they will continue to be satisfied by their 'advisory' role beyond the initial honeymoon period, and continue to use their professional experience to formulate realistic advice rather than simply present ideas.

It is interesting that a significant number of former Ministry bureaucrats have become external members of Administrative Councils, which is unusual in the international context. This may have arisen for several reasons (*Yomiuri Shimbun* 26 March, 2004). First, it is possible (as some critics suspect) that national universities believed in the continued influence of the Ministry, and so recruited these 'old boys' to safeguard for their future. This is normal practice in Japanese private companies, many of which have former civil servants on their corporate boards. Equally, it is possible that national universities saw them as individuals with useful expertise during this critical transition. In other words, their presence may be an indication that critical expertise is lacking, rather than of the power of the Ministry.

The use of medium-term goals and plans as an accountability mechanism was a result of the broader public sector reform that incorporated government agencies. The Ministry emphasizes the critical difference between the national universities, which were allowed to come up with their own goals and plans, and other national bodies which are evaluated in relation to goals mandated by the government. The first review of medium-term goals and plans was completed in the first half of 2004. The minutes of the discussions show that the agendas were largely set by the civil servants who served as a secretariat, with the committee caught between the desire to provide strong guidance to encourage good practice and the need to respect the independence and diversity of national universities. Although it is too early to tell how the full system will operate, a glimpse of this first review suggests that the committee will have difficulty in playing both an evaluative and a proactive role for the 89 national universities unless substantive structural change is made. This is partly because of the lack of resources, and partly because the committee is too close to the Miniswtry, and will therefore most likely avoid playing a strong independent role.

It is as if those who drafted the laws did so to satisfy all the stakeholders at a superficial level, but without focusing on what it really takes to manage and change academic systems. What is missing is the mechanism to combine academic and administrative concerns at the university level. As a result, the legal framework may provide an adequate institutional context for facilitating real change within universities. This problem is further compounded by the fact that academic administrative hybrids are still in short supply, while administrative systems, particularly at the university level, are inadquate to provide the driving force for change. Indeed, real change may only take place once more hybrid individuals have developed who can then produce realistic proposals that address academic, administrative and policy concerns. It may take another decade before a new generation of leaders emerges with sufficient organizational vision and an in-depth understanding of academic and administrative issues gained from management experience at the department and faculty levels. The question is, what will happen in the meantime?

References

Amano, I. (1994) *Daigaku: Henkaku no jidai* (Universities: The era of reforms), Tokyo: Tokyo University Press.

Amano, I. (2002) '*Sengo kokuritsu daigaku seisaku no tenkai*' (Developments in university policies in the post-war period), *Kokuritsu Gakkō Zaimu Centre Kenkyū Hōkokusho: Kokuritsu Daigaku no Kōzō Bunka to Chiiki Kōryū* 6.

Bartholomew, J. (1989) *The Formation of Science in Japan,* New Haven: Yale University Press.

Bird, R. (1994) 'Reflections on the British Government and higher education,' *Higher Education Quarterly* 48 (2).

Hada, T. (1999) *Sengo daigaku kaikaku* (Post-war university reforms), Tokyo: Tamagawa University Press.

Hatakenaka, S. (2004) *University-Industry Partnerships in MIT, Cambridge and Tokyo: Story-Telling across Boundaries*, New York: Routledge.

Kaigo, T. and M. Terasaki (1969) *Daigaku kyōiku* (University Education), Tokyo: Tokyo University Press.

Kako, Y. (2000) 'Kokuritsu daigaku ga kieru hi: semaru dokuritsu hōjinka' (The day national universities disappear: Imminent incorporation), Tokyo: Tokyo Shinbun.

Kaneko, M. (1998) 'Seifu to daigaku: Jiritsusei, shakaisei, kōkyōsei' (Government and universities: Autonomy, social and public characteristics) in *Henbō suru kōtō kyōiku* (Changing higher education), Tokyo: Iwanami Shoten.

Kuroha, R. (1993) *Sengo daigaku seisaku no tenkai* (Post-war developments in university policies), Tokyo: Tamagawa University Press.

Ministry of Education (1999) 'Kokuritsu daigakuchō daigaku kyōdō riyō kikanchō kaigi niokeru monbudaijin aisatsu' (A speech by the Minister of Education at a conference for national university presidents and heads of joint use organisations), Sept. 20 Tokyo.

Ministry of Education (2000) 'Kokuritsu daigakuchō daigaku kyōdō riyō kikanchō to kaigi ni okeru monbu daijin setsumei' (Explanatory documents by the Minister of Education at a conference with national university presidents and heads of joint use organisations), May 26.

Ministry of Education (2002) 'Kokuritsu daigakuchō daigaku kyōdō riyō kikanchō kaigi niokeru monbukagakudaijin no aisatsu' (A speech by the Minister of Education at a conference for national university presidents and heads of joint use organisations), April 3 Tokyo.

Ministry of Education (2003) 'Kokuritsu daigaku hōjin hōan' (Proposed national university corporation act).

Ministry of Education (2004) 'Kokuritsu daigaku hōjin hyōka iinkai gijiroku' (Minutes of meetings of the National University Corporation Evaluation Committee).

Nagai, M. (1962) Daigaku kōsha no teian (Proposing university corporations), Tokyo: Sekai.
Nikkei (2001) 'Futatabi kyoiku wo tou: Ichiritsu kara dokuritsue haikyugata gyoseiha genkai' (Questions about education revisited: moving from controlled equality to independence: the limit of supply driven policies) June 28.
Nikkei (2004) 'Gakugai iin, kokuritsudai teihyoka de touta 66% Nikkei chōsa' (66 percent of external committee members in national universities agree to closures in cases of low evaluation, Nikkei research finds) August 3.
Ogawa, Y. (2002) 'Challenging the traditional organisation of Japanese universities', *Higher Education* 43: 85–108.
Ōsaki, H. (1999) *Daigaku kaikaku 1945–1999* (University Reforms 1945–1999), Tokyo: Yūhikaku.
Sawa, A. (2001) 'Kenkyū soshiki no dokuritsu gyōsei hōjinka to daigaku kaikaku' (Incorporation of research organisations and university reform), in M. Aoki, A. Sawa and M. Daito (eds.) *Daigaku kaikaku: Kadai to ronten* (University reform: agenda and issues), Tokyo: Tōyō Keizai Shinpōsha.
Schoppa, L. (1991) *Education Reform in Japan: A Case of Immobilist Politics*, London: Routlege.
Swinnerton-Dyer, P. (1984) 'The Allocation Process', Internal handwritten memo.
Takagi, H. (1998) *Daigaku no hōteki chii to jichikikō ni kansuru kenkyū* (Research on universities' legal status and autonomy), Tokyo: Taga Shuppan.
Terasaki, M. (1992) *Promenade Tokyo daigakushi* (Tokyo University history promenade), Tokyo: Tokyo University Press.
Terasaki, M. (2000) *Nihon ni okeru daigaku jichi seido no seiritsu* (Establishment of institutions around autonomy in Japan), Tokyo: Hyōronsha.
Williams, G. (1997) 'The market route to mass higher education: British experience 1979–96', *Higher Education Policy.*
Yomiuri Shinbun (2004) '*Kokuritsudai keieikyōgika ni zaikaijinra shugo*', March 26.
Yonezawa, A. (1998) 'Further privatization in Japanese higher education', *International Higher Education* (Fall): 20–21.
Yonezawa, A. (2000) 'Changing higher education policies for Japanese national universities', *Higher Education Management* 12 (3): 31–39.

4 Higher Education and the Ministry: The Capitalist Developmental State, Strategic Schooling and National Renovationism

Brian J. McVeigh

Introduction: 'State guidance'

I begin this chapter with an anecdote: an American professor at a private university in Japan, while renewing his visa at an immigration office, was informed by an official that certain information was necessary because, although there are national (*kokuritsu*), public (*kōritsu*) and private (*shiritsu*) universities in Japan, the category of 'private' in fact has little significance. After all, he was told, *all* institutions of higher education receive 'guidance' (*shidō*) from the state.

There are different ways to interpret this incident but note the use of the word *shidō*, a favourite term of Japanese bureaucrats that, among other things, is used by officialdom to justify its demands from, pressures on, and sometimes interventions in, the non-official sphere of corporate culture, family life and personal affairs. Of course, all states exert some type of influence over their higher education systems but we should be careful to note the differing degrees of influence and the often subtle manner in which centralised state agencies influence education.

Whatever problems are evident in Japanese higher education, they become clearer once the impact of Japan's 'capitalist developmental state' is taken into account. Accordingly, in order to meet its goals of producing diligent workers and accumulating capital, the state has made great efforts to 'guide' society. One result of this officious guidance has been a weakening (though not a total colonisation) of non-state spheres, in other words a blurring of private (personal and kinship relations), social public (non-state associations and organisations) and official public (state and government) realms. Another more specific result of the capitalist developmental state concerns its vision of the primary mission of education: the cultivation of dedicated and obedient workers with basic knowledge useful for capitalist production. Consequently, the state has given more attention to preschool, elementary and secondary education and the main goal of schooling has been preparation for being selected and shunted through an 'educatio-examination system'. Acquiring knowledge for knowledge's sake has often taken a back seat. It is, of course, *de rigueur* to make such charges against any education system, but it is a matter of degree. In any case, as the last rung on the 'educatio-examination' ladder, Japan's higher education system suffers from a salient amount of institutionalised listlessness.

The consequences of a lack of a clear educational mission are these: in spite of a mass schooling system that more or less successfully inculcates knowledge forms (mathematics, literacy and science) and attitudes indispensable to a super-rationalised, post-industrialised, and technologically-advanced capitalist system, Japan's educational system founders at its apex. Universities and colleges (in the rest of this chapter discussed together as 'universities') are widely criticised by the Japanese (and much of the international community) as superfluous, pointless and devoid of academic content. Universities are institutionalised as employment agencies that provide 'human resources' for the economic system. Many schools are self-contained, inward-looking, isolated institutions that see little need to form academic linkages with other universities or develop community or adult education programmes. Indeed, until recently, few schools have utilised class or instructor evaluations. As poignant as the media images of hopeful test-takers braving bad weather to see if they passed an examination for one of the few prestigious universities are, we must remember that the vast majority of students attend universities whose quality would appal those unfamiliar with Japanese education. These are schools that regularly graduate students who never come to class; are run for profit; practice a form of institutional incest in which they only hire their own graduates as instructors, and lack a system of mutual evaluation. Many employers do not expect universities to teach students since they expect to train graduates in company-run programmes. Indeed, as I have argued elsewhere, Japan's higher education may be described as a system of 'institutionalised mendacity', which deploys 'simulated education' (McVeigh 2002).

Purpose

In this chapter, I argue that modern Japan's lathered drive to economic power has cost it a quality higher education system.[1] After introducing the meaning of the capitalist developmental state, I trace the institutional evolution of those internal units of the Ministry of Education, Culture, Sports, Science and Technology's (abbreviated in what follows to 'Ministry of Education' or 'the Ministry') which are devoted to monitoring and administrating higher educational sites.[2] Such an accounting, which illustrates how tightly tied the state has been to higher education since the Meiji era, is necessary in order to historically contextualise 'reform' attempts. Here it must be stressed that, all things considered, what has hindered the establishment of an effective tertiary-level education system has not been a direct and obvious attempt at 'ideological control' as conventionally understood, but rather various projects of 'strategic schooling' (McVeigh 1998) that have produced an administrative package of overbearing 'guidance, advice, and assistance'. These state operations have orientated the higher educational enterprise towards exam passing and conformity, not schooling and self-cultivation. As mentioned above, the lack of a clearly delineated social public sphere – legitimated by and grounded in civil society and a social public of autonomous individuals (i.e. not an official public of bureaucrats) – is not fertile ground for a flowering of educational innovation, institutional independence or liberal thought. Although I will not explore these issues here (see McVeigh 1998, 2002), I will note at the outset that the lack of a genuine, non-state public sphere – rather than merely, marginal, residual non-state spaces – precludes effective reform. Indeed, tacit in much of the discourse about reform is an understanding that any change should be authorised by the top, in other words by the Ministry. The implication is that education is an extension of the state and not an array of institutions rooted in civil society.

Reform and reactive nationalism, I contend, have motivated Japan's capitalist developmental state since the midle-to-late 19th century. The consequent ideological turmoil can be characterised as 'renovationist nationalism'. This tradition of national renewal – restoring the rightful political structure and purifying the land of foreign influences – can be traced back to the 'Meiji Renovation'[3] which triggered a never-ending project of national-state construction and improvement. More specifically, renovationism can be characterised as: (1) a keen sensitivity to the intensity of the speed of sociopolitical changes associated with modernity; (2) a fixated self-referencing tendency and great concern with cultural 'authenticity'; and (3) concentrated attention to emulating the great powers in order to increase prestige and power. Importing foreign models to bolster power is not unique to Japan; however, Japan has done so quite explicitly and systematically.[4] Renovationism was configured by international developments: Japan, being late to industrialisation, sought to 'catch up' with the west by bureaucratically 'guiding' society. Such national mobilisation accounts for an economic nationalism that in turn demands educational policies geared toward strategic schooling. Examinations of educational 'reform' should be understood as recurrent attempts to renovate schooling structures. For example, during the post-imperial period, repeated claims have been made that during the occupation, the Americans 'overly democratised' education and diluted the nation's Japaneseness; thus, Japanese conservatives assert, academic standards have dropped and students do not respect teachers.

The evolution of the bureaucratic guidance of higher education

Japan's system of bureaucratically-guided economics – legitimated by nationalism, fortified by war and implemented via neo-mercantilist policies – is best described as a capitalist developmental state (which to varying degrees appropriately describes certain other Asian states). 'A developmental state is like a revolutionary state, although at a less sweeping level' (Johnson 1993: 64).[5] In order to accomplish its economic nationalist projects, Japan has carefully cultivated its human resources – social cooperation, collaboration and coordination, at least ideally, have been the order of the day. Indeed, the educational counterpart of 'developmental orientation' – Johnson's term to highlight Japan's economic political philosophy as opposed to the Anglo-American model of 'regulatory orientation' – may be called an 'education of cultivation'. The Japanese state's attitude that it is responsible for directing and managing its citizenry is evident in economic practices. 'Industrial policy' and 'administrative guidance' are the practical outcomes of such an approach to economic matters (Johnson 1982: 18–19). As a package of specific policy measures and programmes that is nationalistic in perspective, emphasises production, employs market constraints and is suspicious of excessive profit, economic developmentalism, though rooted in the Meiji period, was forged during the depression and total war mobilisation of the 1930s and early 1940s. But what was originally intended for military purposes became the basis of Japan's post-imperial industrial policy (Gao 1997).

From the outset, the Meiji elite intended Japan's advanced education to further state purposes, and in this sense, higher education was for the most part politically pragmatic, economically practical and ideologically controlled. However, in the Meiji period there were some higher educational schools founded by enterprising individuals who had philosophies different from those of the authorities. As the decades passed into the twentieth century, however, the state gradually tightened its administrative grip over the various post-secondary institutions, including the specialist and vocational schools (agricultural, commercial, technical), beginning with the 1883 General Regulations for Agricultural Schools and the 1884 General Regulations for Commercial Schools.[6]

Key components of the system for the masses were *senmon* schools. The term '*senmon*' was initially used by the Meiji state 'to refer to a miscellaneous grouping of post-elementary level schools that did not fit into any of the other categories covered in the 1872 Gakusei Plan' (Amano 1979: 21). These schools quickly grew in number, reflecting the energies of the non-state sphere, so that by 1903, the educational authorities felt compelled to administratively standardise them by enacting the Senmon School Order, aimed at higher education institutions other than the imperial universities and preparatory higher schools. This order stipulated that *senmon* schools would only admit graduates of male middle schools or higher women's schools (*kōtō jogakkō*) and would be ranked just below universities. The graduates of private *senmon* schools were 'often suspect, yet they made an important contribution to Japan's modernisation, especially since they tended to enter fields that were disdained by the graduates of the prestigious state institutions' (Amano 1979: 19). Indeed, their role in Japan's modernisation cannot be overlooked since their number, both male and female, 'far exceeded the number who studied in universities' (Clarke 1980: 28). 'Without their efforts in opening up the frontier of industrialisation, it would not have been possible for Japan to attain substantial economic growth' (Amano 1979: 31–2). Before the 1918 University Order, only imperial universities were allowed the designation *daigaku* (university), but with this Order, *senmon* schools were able to upgrade and acquire university status.

In 1881, the Specialist Education Affairs Bureau was set up within the Ministry to monitor *senmon* schools. This Bureau would exist until 1885, and then re-emerge in 1887; be absorbed into the Higher Education Affairs Bureau (*Kōtō gakumu-kyoku*) in 1897 and be reassembled (with parts of the Commercial Education Affairs Bureau, or *Jitsugyō gakumu-kyoku*) in 1898. By mid-Meiji, *senmon* schools became an official category that 'included public institutions at the post-middle school level that were not officially designated either higher schools or universities. It also included private schools' (Marshall 1994: 68–9) and by 1905, 'a complex pyramid of vocational and technical training programmes that paralleled the academic track at the primary, secondary and advanced levels' (Marshall 1994: 72) had developed.

Mention should be made of the numerous medical schools, many established by prefectures. By 1884, there were thirty-two medical schools (two were private). Originally, the Department of Education oversaw medical knowledge and instituted the Medical Division *(Igaku-ka)* in 1871, which became a bureau in 1873 and, in 1875, was transferred to the Department of Home Affairs. In 1882, the Department of Education issued General Regulations for Medical Schools and, in July of that same year, issued General Regulations for Pharmaceutical Schools. Mention should also be made of private schools that offered programmes in legal and political studies, several of which would evolve into prestigious universities: Tōkyō Hōgakusha (forerunner of Hosei University, established in 1879); Senshū gakkō (forerunner of Senshu University, 1880); Meiji hōritsu gakkō (forerunner of Meiji University, 1881); Tōkyō senmon gakkō (forerunner of Waseda University, 1882); and Igirisu hōritsu gakkō (forerunner of Chūō University, 1885).

Within the Ministry, the Higher Education Affairs Bureau was established in 1897 from elements of the Specialist Education Affairs Bureau (absorbed into the Specialist Education Affairs Bureau in 1898) and monitored post-secondary education.

Reigning in a 'critical spirit': Elite education

The elite track culminated in Tokyo University (usually abbreviated to Tōdai) as it still does today.[7] This university was founded in 1877. Tokyo University has become the pinnacle of the entire educational system in terms of prestige, actual institutional clout and as the ideal model for other universities. It was, and is, a well established sorting and screening institution for future state officials, as well as other types of elites (Amano 1979: 19). Its predominance in the production of elites is 'difficult to exaggerate' (Marshall 1992: 191). In 1886, Tokyo University was designated Imperial Tokyo University. Later, other universities directly supervised by the state were established: Kyoto Imperial University (1897), Tohoku Imperial University (1907) and Kyushu Imperial University (1910).

As Japan sank deeper into militarism, the state focused its gaze on any activity that did not square with its objectives. The Home Affairs Ministry was particularly concerned with leftist student activities on university campuses. For its part, in the early 1930s, the Ministry of Education placed about 700 officials in higher education institutions to monitor students (Marshall 1994: 130). Meanwhile, the Student Affairs Department (*Gakusei-bu*) was upgraded to the Ideological Control Bureau in 1934.

Though many faculties at universities supported Japan's war efforts, not all did. Beginning in the late 1920s and lasting until the late 1930s, a series of purges decimated liberal and opposition views in Japan's universities, culminating in purges of leftists at Imperial Tokyo University from 1937–9 (Marshall 1994: 126). However, it would be a mistake to believe that these ideological cleansings were simple cases of 'state-against-society' manoeuvres. Often, faculty who supported (or feared repercussions for not supporting) Japan's militarism pressured those with opposing views to resign from their positions. But the best example of how state projects colonised the non-state sphere and individual subjectivities is illustrated by how

> Agitated students joined in harassing professors suspected of harboring Western liberal ideas or of lacking enthusiasm for Japan's mission in China. Right-wing students visited the classrooms of suspected liberals, and at other talks on campuses they frequently raised politically embarrassing questions. They visited professors in their offices to demand clarification of their interpretations of the national polity or an explanation of why a course syllabus was heavily weighted toward Western works on political science. (Marshall 1994: 127)

As the war continued, the authorities increasingly implemented policies that directed higher education efforts towards the goals of the military. In 1943, all students were mobilised, with only those in science and technology or in teacher training programmes exempt. Two years later, even the latter were ordered to rotate every year between academic work and four-month mobilisation duties. During this time there was a remarkable increase in women attending higher education, apparently due to wartime needs. In 1935, there were 15,500 women in various higher educational institutions; by 1945, there were over 58,500 with 10,000 of these in medical schools (Marshall 1994: 138). Meanwhile, within the Ministry, the Specialist Education Affairs Bureau changed its name to *Senmon kyōiku-kyoku* in 1942 and, three years later, this Bureau became part of the School and Educational Affairs Bureau.

After the war, there was much debate about how to reform higher education, particularly what measures should be taken to open its doors to more students, especially women who had traditionally been blocked from post-secondary schooling. Though I will not explore these issues here, it is worth noting that early post-imperial attempts at renovating the educational system reveal efforts by the Japanese authorities at maintaining central control.

By 1948, there were 580 old-system higher educational institutions (64 with university status, 352 *senmon* schools, 62 normal schools, and 39 higher schools); by 1955, there were 228 new universities (72 were state universities, 33 local state – i.e. 'public' universities – and 122 private). By 1955, 72 state universities had been established. But these were divided into two groups: the more prestigious group composed of the old-system universities and a less prestigious group composed of newly-established state universities (Amano 1979: 33–4). Two-year colleges (*tanki daigaku*), which were originally intended as provisional schools, opened their doors in 1950. Gradually, these schools underwent 'feminisation' (*joseika*) so that, by 1994, 91.8 percent of their students were female thereby constituting the gendered dualism of Japan's higher education that feeds into gendered employment practices.[8]

The development of post-imperial higher education

In order to organise my discussion about the evolution of Japan's post-imperial higher education, I borrow the four-phase system developed by Mosk and Nakata (1992: 64).

1 Democratisation period (1945–55)

In 1947, the All-Japan University Council was appointed and, in July of that same year, the state-affiliated Japanese University Accreditation Association (formally independent of the Ministry of Education) set standards for universities. In 1949, the Japanese University Accreditation Association established standards for graduate schools (the first four at private universities were established in 1950). In 1953, the Ministry issued the 'Academic Degree Regulations'. In1949, within the Ministry itself, the University and Science Bureau was formed from parts of the School Education and Science Education Bureaux. This new bureau was composed of General Affairs, University, Technical Education, Teacher Training, Student Life, Research Support and Science Divisions.

It was during the democratisation period that the relations between the state and the non-state educational institutions were formalised. In 1949, the Private School Law was promulgated and implemented approximately one year later. This legislation defined the extent to which the state could control private universities and other private schools. It was at this time that 'school juridical persons' (*gakkō hōjin*) were legislated into existence, thereby establishing the post-imperial legal framework for non-state educational institutions.

In order to assist private institutions destroyed or damaged during the war, the state stepped in, offering loans for reconstruction and, as evidence of how quickly the authorities could change their stripes, converted military bases into private educational facilities. The state moved to offer more permanent assistance. In 1952, the Japan Private School Promotion Association Law was promulgated and, on the same day, the Japan Private School Promotion Association was established. These manoeuvres to support higher education were responses to the explosion in tertiary-level education beginning in the 1950s. Between 1953 and 1971, the university population increased 3.3 times while the college population increased 4.3 times.

In order to meet the growing demands for 'industrial education', the need to train specialists who also had a solid academic background was often debated. In 1951, the Provisional Reform Discussion Committee suggested a return to the pre-war two-layered system: newly formed universities would focus on research, while two- or three-year specialised universities would provide practical training in engineering, commerce, agriculture and education. During the 1950s, the Japan Federation of Employers' Associations urged a return to the pre-war two-layer system in five different reports (Amano 1979: 36). In 1961, a revision of the School Education Law was made for 'colleges of technology' (*kōtō senmon gakkō*), operating since 1962, with their curricula specifically designed for 'industrial education'.

2 Expansion period (1956–74)

Education is tied to economic development everywhere, but in Japan – with the strong approval of the political elite motivated by economic nationalism – it has become not only institutionally interwoven with business demands but to a large degree determined by them, so that the development of human resources has come to shape an 'education investment theory' (*kyōiku tōshi-ron*). Discussions about education have revolved around an official idiom of 'manpower development', 'human resource utilisation' and 'demands of industry'. This is why the Economic Investigation Council reported that 'we must be concerned with ways to cultivate skilled workers and ways to use those workers effectively' (*Problems and Strategies in Manpower Development during Economic Growth: Report of the Economic Investigation Council*, 1994: 159 [1963]). In the words of Prime Minister Ikeda, 'if we are to build the nation of Japan, we must build human beings'; and 'the Japanese people themselves have an excellent constitution. Through education, the Japanese people can continue to cultivate this superb character and contribute not only to their own country but also show their fibre to the world through their efforts toward the peace of our nation and that of the world' ('Prime Minister Ikeda's campaign speech for the Upper House of the Diet', 1994: 155 [1962]).

Post-imperial state-driven economic projects have only strengthened the link between the 'formation of human beings' (*hito-zukuri*) and 'nation-building' (*kuni-zukuri*). Commenting on the Ministry's1962 white paper, *Japanese Growth and Education,* Horio notes that '"Growth" here did not mean the child's growth, but economic growth. This report was a landmark in the sense that it signalled the direct subordination of educational policy to economic policy' (Horio 1988: 216); it was peppered with terms such as 'stock of educational capital', 'expansion' or 'spread of education', 'educational goals (of the state)', 'educational planning (of the state)', 'development of education', 'returns from education' and numerous statistical figures, such as one detailing 'Trends of National Income, Labour Force, Physical Capital and Educational Capital'.

There were various reasons for the expansion of Japan's higher education. Economic growth, spurred on by Prime Minister Ikeda's 'Income Doubling Plan' of the early 1960s, made it possible for more parents to send their children on to university and this same growth created a demand for more qualified employees, especially in science and engineering. Various types of schools were upgraded to universities and procedures to establish them were greatly simplified. Meanwhile, the Standards for Universities were codified into the Standards for the Establishment of Universities and made part of official state policy by the Ministry in 1956. Demographics played their role in higher education expansion, with the post-imperial baby boom fuelling the increase in higher education students; the 18-year-old population increased from 2.0 million in 1955 to 2.5 million in 1961. The first wave entered elementary schools in the mid-1950s, middle school around 1960, high school in the early 1960s and universities in the mid-1960s. In 1965, there were 250,000 freshmen; by 1975, there were 420,000. As for the financing of higher education, in 1964 the Special Account for National Educational Institutions was established. This special account is separate from the General Account although it receives transfers from the latter.

The late 1960s witnessed widespread campus disturbances, turbulent protests, and student radicalism. There were many reasons for this agitation, including student dissatisfaction with university life. Alarmed at the upheaval, the state, corporate elite, and educational authorities supported legislation to contain the turmoil and passed the University Administration Emergency Measures Law in 1969. This legislation evidenced the state's attempt at re-centralising its control over higher education. Part of this re-centralisation included state-offered subsidies and loans, thereby making private schools more dependent on official largesse. In 1970, the Japan Private School Promotion Foundation Law was enacted and, in July of that same year, the Japan Private School Promotion Association was dissolved and replaced by the Japan Private School Promotion Foundation. The private schools were, not surprisingly, happy to accept state support. After all, throughout the 1960s, in spite of loans, direct subsidies and tax reductions and exemptions, many private schools were still in dire financial straits.

The Central Council for Education, concerned about the glaring problems in universities, submitted its suggestions for higher education reform in 1971 to the Education Minister. These suggestions set the stage for later debates about reform. Some of these suggestions have failed to gain support, others have been implemented, and others are still being deliberated.

By 1970, the University and Science Bureau was composed of the General Affairs, University, Technical Education, Teacher Training, University Hospital, Student Affairs, Foreign Student Affairs, Science, International Science, Research Support, Information and Library Divisions. In 1974, the University and Science Bureau was split into three: the University, Science and International Affairs Bureaux. The former Bureau became the Higher Education Bureau ten years later and, on the same date, the Private Education Institution Department was established and put under the Higher Education Bureau. The latter was formed with elements from the former Management Bureau.

3 Quality improvement period (1975–82)

Concerned about the disheartening deterioration in the standards of private universities during the period of rapid expansion, the Ministry attempted to improve their quality with the 1975 Private School Promotion Subsidy Law. This law, which reinforced earlier aid efforts, was intended to improve universities by subsidising their general expenses. It was also the culmination of an official policy which effected a change from 'no support, no control' to 'support and control' of universities (Kitamura 1979: 78).

4 The second expansion period (1983–present)

Although the eighteen-year-old population has been declining, the number of university applicants has been steadily rising. In 1986, there were 1,850,000 eighteen-year-olds and, of this number, about 640,000 entered university that same year. By 1996, there were about 1,730,000 eighteen-year-olds and, of this number, about 800,000 entered university in that year. In 1989, there were 1,083 universities but, by the year 2000, there were 1,221 (*Monbu tōkei yōran* 2001: 2, 180–1). Confronted with the prospect of more students of higher education and an increase in the number of universities, the Ministry has continued to look for ways to improve the quality of Japan's higher education. In 1987, the University Council was established as a body to advise the Ministry on reform and to give guidance as to in which direction the policies of universities should proceed. In the late 1980s, the Ministry further simplified chartering rules, granted more autonomy and suggested 'self-evaluation' for institutions of higher education as a way to improve their quality. In 1989, the Ministry issued Standards for the Establishment of Graduate Schools and Standards for the Establishment of Universities.

By 1999, the Higher Education Bureau had five divisions and oversaw the Private Education Institution Department. After a major reorganisation of Japan's bureaucracies in January 2001, the Higher Education Bureau contained six divisions: Higher Education Planning, University, Vocational Education, Medical Education, Student Affairs and Foreign Student Affairs. The Private Education Institution Department has two divisions: Private Education Administration and Private Education Aid.

Universities as 'superfluous institutions'

The state does not regard higher education as strategic to its projects in the same manner as elementary and secondary schools and, in this sense, has taken a *laissez-faire* attitude towards universities. Nevertheless, it must be stressed that within the context of post-imperial higher education, state interference has been for the most part restricted to bureaucratic monitoring and the sort of prying that not a few schools' administrators describe as meddlesome, officious and unnecessary.

The state's *laissez-faire* attitude is apparent in the fact that the bulk of tertiary-level educational institutions are private. However, despite their official designation as 'private', these institutions are to a limited but not negligible degree tied to the state bureaucratically and financially, thus constituting a system in which some schools are closer to the central state in terms of influence and status (though not necessarily quality) than others: 'This rank order is based not upon quality or university programs or faculty, but upon the reputation of the university' (Kerbo and McKinstry 1995: 139).

The state has so thoroughly colonised institutions of higher education, thereby over-administrating genuine education out of existence, that some administrators and professors have apparently forgotten the purpose of tertiary-level learning and have become over-dependent on the state. I have heard of how university administrators would phone the Ministry, asking for advice on how to design the curriculum and deal with the kind of administrative problems that one would imagine (at least at a private school), should have little to do with a central state organ. On the other hand, more than one university official complained that the Ministry treated them like 'children'. There are, of course, some good schools, serious professors and diligent students but, *as a system,* Japan's higher education is a failure, a victim of state interference and colonisation by corporate culture. Nevertheless, there are certain circles within the Ministry who are, in fact, embarrassed by the malfunction of institutions they are responsible for and by the stinging international criticism, and who are concerned with genuine higher education reform. Such sentiments are obvious in the discourse emanating from the Ministry in reports about the need to reform higher education.

Whatever the intentions and plans of the Ministry, two points should be kept in mind. First, there is considerable resistance at the higher education sites themselves to real reform. Schoppa reports that organisations such as the University Bureau of the Japan Teachers' Union, the Japan Scientist Association, the Japan Science Council and the Association of National University Presidents (*Kokudaikyō*) are wary of Ministry-initiated reforms and work hard to maintain the status quo of 'university autonomy' (1991: 164) – though this latter term is perhaps better described as 'university isolationism'. Note the opinion of one professor, who writes that when 'autonomy' was given to universities after World War II, it was pursued for its own sake: 'As a result, the university ironically turned into a "fortress of self righteousness" and a "heaven for the lazy" and finally a "fool's Elysium"' (*Japan Times* 14 March 1997). As Schoppa points out, many universities defend the status quo and do not want more autonomy. Indeed, they are prone to ask the Ministry what to do when given more freedom (1991: 165). For illustration: though the Ministry has strongly suggested that universities implement self-evaluation programmes, not many seem sincerely interested. The second point is even more problematic: the academic abilities and learning style of incoming students. The problems in Japan's higher education are very much rooted in the pre-tertiary level.

Conclusion

Since the Meiji period, Japan's elites have not stressed the need for the values that usually characterise higher education: learning for the sake of learning, the pursuit of knowledge for its own sake, and pure research. The dictates of the developmental capitalist state have deemed such practices a luxury. This is why many charge that Japan, though strong in applied research for its hungry capitalist developmental system, is weak in pure research. Thus, most research is not done at universities, but in private companies or their research centres. Some may say that it does not make any difference where research is carried out, as long as it is done. But such a view does not appreciate the critical role higher education has played (in spite of its reproduction of an elite class and hegemonic ideologies) as society's conscience and watchdog.

Since the war, Japan's universities have struggled to balance their public-minded character, academic independence and financial stability but, despite their rapid expansion and impressive statistics, they have been plagued by mismanagement, corruption and substandard education. Among many private institutions, profiteering, like an acid, has eaten away at teaching and learning. Most of these problems can be traced to how Japanese society has allowed the unchecked colonisation of universities by corporate interest, turning the institutions of higher education into degree-granting services rather than teaching and learning sites. As in other industrialised societies, employers have set the certification bar higher and higher as more students enter school and then seek employment, successively deflating the value of secondary and then tertiary-level educational degrees (see Kitamura's discussion of the 'iron law of educational growth', 1979: 68). But in Japan, this process, driven by the demands of economic growth at any cost, has reached excessive proportions. The result is that schooling, especially at the institutional apex of higher education, loses its character of learning and becomes 'only qualification, a mere process of certificating – or "credentialling"' (Dore 1976: 8). Moreover, the capitalist developmental state, with its projects of strategic schooling and guidance, has blurred the lines between state and non-state, discouraging the growth of the societal public sphere within Japan's political, economic and educational arrangements.

After Japan's defeat, the shift from politico-economic institutions defined by national polity (*kokutai*), militarism and statist nationalism to those grounded in citizenship (*kokumin*), democracy and economic nationalism did not terminate culturalist definitions of the Japanese people (*nihon minzoku*) and the state's (*kokka*) drive for capitalist expansion. Some observers, stuck on ideas of prewar ideological control of education by a highly militarised state, search for signs of such control, cannot detect any and thus conclude that there is very little direct state configuration of education in Japan's post-imperial democratic polity (however that is defined). Consequently, they have a tendency to 'see through' the more indirect, mundane and insidious forms of administrative intervention. Moreover, they fail to appreciate how the bureaucratic-corporate nexus – i.e. the capitalist developmental state – generates an educatio-socialising paradigm that discourages learning for learning's sake. Though the state has been heavily involved in higher education in some ways (funding, inspections, monitoring), in other ways it has displayed benign neglect with a vengeance. Indeed, it has not encouraged evaluative practices that, needless to say, are the very point of advanced education. The lack of evaluation at different levels – of students as students, of courses by students, of academics by academics, and among universities – is another serious problem. It is ironic to claim that evaluation is weak in an 'educatio-examination system', but often students are being assessed on the wrong things (such as how much they can cram – not learn – and 'moral character'). Some universities have only recently introduced course evaluations. As for the university accreditation process carried out by the Ministry, this clearly has not worked. Though in April 2000 the National Institution for Academic Degrees was renovated as a 'new' body with an additional mandate for evaluating universities, until now no third-party evaluating mechanism has existed. Having the state reorganise one of its own agencies, however, in order to implement a procedure that the former has, as of now, been unable to accomplish suggests an example of rhetorical, makeshift reform.

With all this said, will the quality of higher education improve? Perhaps, but it seems more likely that the institutions of the capitalist developmental state will manage, adjust and renovate where needed, making do with 'guidance' and the strategic schooling with which the Japanese are most familiar. Any adaptations will, in the end, be of and for the Japanese.

Notes

1 I will not comment on issues of reform, since others have done so in this volume. Also, I restrict most of my discussion to *daigaku* (universities and colleges) and leave aside treatment of other post-secondary schools (i.e. various types of vocational and technical schools).
2 The Education Ministry (Monbukagaku-shō) was known as Monbushō until January 2001. It is now popularly known as 'Monkashō', and the name is officially abbreviated in English as 'MEXT'. It was established in 1871 under the Grand Council, and was technically the 'Department of Education' until December 22 1885, when the Grand Council was replaced by the Cabinet.
3 Conventionally called the 'Meiji Restoration', but see Sims (2001) and McVeigh (2003).
4 For an elaboration of renovationism, see McVeigh (2003).
5 See Castells (1992), Ōnis (1991), and Bello (1996). Also see Dower's discussion of a 'strong capitalist state' (1990: 66).
6 For historical background see: *Gakusei hyaku nen shi* (1971); *Monbushō, Gyōsei kikō shiriizu* no. 105 (1980); *Kokushi daijiten* (1992) and *Kyōiku – bunka* I, II (1986).
7 Though a small number of other universities (for example, Kyoto University and private schools such as Waseda and Keio Universities) also furnish the elite strata with personnel, it has been Tokyo University (which regained its original appellation after the war) that has traditionally maintained the closest connections to officialdom.
8 See McVeigh (1997) for an ethnography of a Japanese women's college.

References

Amano, Ikuo (1979) 'Continuity and change in the structure of Japanese higher education' in Cummings, William K., Ikuo Amano and Kazuyuki Kitamura (eds.), *Changes in the Japanese University: A Comparative Perspective*, New York: Praeger, pp. 10–39.

Bello, Walden (1996) 'Neither market nor state: The development debate in South-East Asia', *The Ecologist* 26 (4): 167–75.

Castells, Manuel (1992) 'Four Asian tigers with a dragon head: A comparative analysis of the state, economy and society in the Asian Pacific Rim', in Appelbaum, Richard P. and Jeffery Henderson (eds.), *States and Development in the Asian Pacific Rim,* Newbury Park, California: Sage Publications, pp. 33–70.

Clarke, Elizabeth J. (1980) 'The origins of women's higher education in Japan', *Japan Christian Quarterly* 46: 26–33.

Dore, Ronald (1976) *The Diploma Disease: Education, Qualification and Development,* Berkeley: University of California Press.

Dower, John (1990) 'The useful war', *Daedalus* 119 (3): 49–70.

Gakusei hyaku nen shi – shiryō-hen (1971) Tokyo: Ministry of Education.

Gao, Bai (1977) *Economic Ideology and Japanese Industrial Policy: Developmentalism from 1931 to 1965,* Cambridge: Cambridge University Press.

Horio, Teruhisa (1988) *Educational Thought and Ideology in Modern Japan: State Authority and Intellectual Freedom* (ed. and trans. Steven Platzer), Tokyo: University of Tokyo Press.

Johnson, Chalmers (1982) *MITI and the Japanese Miracle*, Stanford: Stanford University Press.

Johnson, Chalmers (1993) 'Comparative capitalism: The Japanese difference', *California Management Review* 35 (4): 51–67.

Kerbo, Harold and John A. McKinstry (1995) *Who Rules Japan? The Inner Circles of Economic and Political Power,* Westport, Connecticut: Praeger.

Kitamura, Kazuyuki (1979) 'Mass higher education', in Cummings, William K., Ikuo Amano and Kazuyuki Kitamura (eds.), *Changes in the Japanese University: A Comparative Perspective*, New York: Praeger, pp. 64–82.

Kokushi daijiten henshū iinkai (1992) *Kokushi daijiten* (Dictionary of Japanese History), Tokyo: Yoshikawa Kōbun-kan.

Kyōiku gyōsei kenkyūkai (1986) *Kyōiku – bunka I, II: Gendai gyōsei zenshū 22* (Education – Culture I, II: Complete modern administration 22) Tokyo: Gyōsei.

Marshall, Byron K. (1994) *Learning to Be Modern: Japanese Political Discourse on Education,* Boulder, Colorado: Westview Press.

Marshall, Byron K. (1992) *Academic Freedom and the Japanese Imperial University, 1868–1939,* Berkeley: University of California Press.

McVeigh, Brian J. (1997) *Life in a Japanese Women's College: Learning to Be Ladylike.* London: Routledge.

McVeigh, Brian J. (1998) *The Nature of the Japanese State: Rationality and Rituality,* London: Routledge.

McVeigh, Brian J. (2002) *Japanese Higher Education as Myth,* Armonk, NY: M.E. Sharpe.

McVeigh, Brian J. (2003) *Nationalisms of Japan: Managing and Mystifying Identity*, Boulder: Rowman and Littlefield.

Ministry of Education (1980) *Gyōsei kikō series 105* (Administrative Structures Series 105), Tokyo: Kyōikusha.

Ministry of Education (2001) *Monbu tōkei yōran* (Statistical Abstract of Education, Science, Sports and Culture), Tokyo: Ministry of Education.

Mosk, Carl and Yoshifumi Nakata (1992) 'Education and occupation: An enquiry into the relationship between college specialization and the labour market in postwar Japan', *Pacific Affairs* 65 (1): 50–67.

Ōnis, Ziya (1991) 'The logic of the developmental state', *Comparative Politics* 24 (1): 109–26.

'Prime Minister Ikeda's campaign speech for the Upper House of the Diet' (1994) [May 25, 1962] in Beauchamp, Edward R. and James M. Vardaman, Jr. (eds.), *Japanese Education Since 1945: A Documentary Study,* Armonk, NY: M. E. Sharpe, pp. 154–6.

'Problems and strategies in manpower development during economic growth: Report of the Economic Investigation Council' (1994) [January 14, 1963] in Beauchamp, Edward R. and James M. Vardaman, Jr. (eds.) *Japanese Education Since 1945: A Documentary Study,* Armonk, NY: M.E. Sharpe, pp. 159–63.

Schoppa, Leonard J. (1991) *Education Reform in Japan: A Case of Immobilist Politics,* London: Routledge.

Sims, Richard (2001) *Japanese Political History since the Meiji Renovation, 1868–2000,* New York: Palgrave.

5 Government and the National Universities: Ministerial Bureaucrats and Dependent Universities

Shinichi Yamamoto

Introduction

In Japan, since the early 1990s, the pace of university reform has been accelerating. The old university system is facing a changing environment and there is a great need for this system to change. In fact, during the period of high-speed economic growth in Japan in the 1960s, the universities moved into what is generally called the 'mass' stage of development, but in recent years they have been allowed to carry on without fundamental change. However, one thing that should be said is that if the current outdated and dysfunctional system can be reformed, universities can help the society of today by providing knowledge to meet its requirements, the most urgent of which are in the fields of education, science and technology (Yamamoto, 1996).

On further consideration, however, while the mood of reform has spread quickly, relations between the government (represented by the Ministry of Education) and the universities have undergone a subtle but fundamental change. This concerns the future nature of the universities and there is anxiety that it will have an unexpectedly large impact. Even though the relations between them are not particularly strained, the changes will definitely be radical. In this paper I look at the direction in which the university system is moving as the reforms take place, both from the point of view of the government and of the universities themselves.

The characteristics of the recent university reforms

The Ministry of Education Advisory Panel on Universities was established in 1988 and has been extremely active, publishing 24 position papers and reports up to 1999. These publications include plans for changes that will fundamentally affect the future of the universities, such as the reform of university education; rethinking the postgraduate system; higher education planning; the staff tenure system and university evaluation systems. The necessary measures to make these changes possible are steadily being implemented. Many of the effects will become apparent only gradually, but we can already observe various interesting trends resulting from the university reform process.

First, the universities have become more docile. Formerly the universities and their staff were conscious of their previous imperial status when, as seats of learning, they had been contemptuous of the real world and had possessed the self-confidence that came from acting as arbiters and leaders of public opinion. In response to criticism of role of the university, there were often fierce arguments in those days, given university autonomy and freedom of speech, and society condoned the special status given to the universities. Nowadays, however, the universities are more in touch with 'the real world' and they have also become the targets of 'reform'. Perhaps surprisingly for anyone who knows about universities in Japan, there has been no particular campaign of opposition to the reforms from either the universities or staff associations. It is rather as if they are expecting the reforms to improve their own teaching and research environments. The reality of university reform is that the balance of interests between university and society, which until now has favoured the universities and their staff, should shift in the direction of society. For many universities and their staff, reform means losing some of the benefits that they have enjoyed up to now. Having been a Ministry of Education official myself, however, I personally believe that the importance of reform is painfully obvious.

Second, rather than attempting to resist the reforms proposed by the government in order to protect their autonomy, the national universities are treating this as a good opportunity to increase their incomes and they are becoming enthusiastic participants in the competition for budgetary resources. This does not mean, however, that the national universities will be financially independent. Under the system of budgetary requisition, which is peculiar to the national universities, the Ministry of Education submits requests for funds to the Finance Ministry. National universities have to submit provisional requests for funds to the Ministry of Education and are subject to the its assessment. It requires effort for a university to get an advantageous assessment where the budget is limited and it is clear that one strategy is to monitor carefully trends in Ministry policy. Nowadays, phrases such as 'the Ministry says so' are often heard in university meetings. Formerly, university administrations were diametrically opposed to the 'Ministry line', at least on the face of it, but now toeing the line is becoming something of a requirement.

Against this background – and given that there is a strong tendency in Japan to fall into line – if one university is successful in its bid for funds, this directly affects the ways in which other universities bid for funds the following year. The increased emphasis on postgraduate training began at the University of Tokyo in 1991 but it had an effect on the whole of the former imperial university sector; and this stress on graduate education has had a considerable effect on the administration of other national universities as well. Recently, various research groups on higher education took on board the issues of 'reform fatigue' and what to do next. This was, perhaps, because many people in the universities were wondering privately whether they were able to keep up with the pace of the various reform campaigns.

Thirdly, university staff are clearly becoming overloaded. Formerly, university teachers in the humanities were not pressurised for time; to some extent the same was true in the physical sciences. However, for university teachers now, whether in the humanities or social sciences, the pressures of work are considerable. According to research carried out in 1995 (Takuma 1996), about 20 percent of the standard weekly schedule of many university teachers was used for purposes other than teaching and research and, significantly, this percentage was rising. (It may be noted that, when lecturing, staff spent about 40 percent of the week on teaching compared with 20 percent when there were no lectures, while the rest of the time was available for research.) The sense of overwork was reflected in the feeling that there was not enough time for research. Reasons given by respondents for the lack of research time included teaching and preparation (46 percent), meetings (49 percent), preparation of documents (43 percent) and the pressure of other responsibilities (47 percent). The largest group of respondents (63 percent) who said that their responsibilities had increased in the previous five years named 'internal university meetings' as the reason. In responses to other questions, 41 percent answered that research time had been reduced as a direct result of university reforms.

Stricter regulation in the universities

There are a number of possible explanations for the observations in the previous section. Firstly, society and the government are looking at the universities increasingly strictly. Formerly, the university was sacrosanct as a place for research based on the logic of the academy and for the education of the future elite. Now, however, intellectual activity within universities is no longer governed by academics in isolation from society but by the logic of social needs and accountability. The university is no longer an ivory tower, but is a public resource that must survive by being recognised as such by the people who make up the social system.

One thing evident in all this is the change in student requirements that has accompanied the wider provision of university education. In 1992, the population of eighteen-year olds reached a peak of 2.05 million. It is expected that this will fall to 1.2 million by 2009, though in the 1990s the proportion of eighteen-year olds going on to higher education increased rapidly, from 39 percent in 1992 to 49 percent in 1999. There was also a rise in the rate of applications to higher education institutions and this accelerated rapidly. However, universities now are in competition with each other for a share of this decreasing population of eighteen-year olds. Formerly, universities used to select students on the basis of the entrance exam, but from now on the students will be able to pick and choose between universities, and the question they will ask is how the university suits them. First, the content of university education is changing in response to the diversification of student needs and more consideration is being given to making it more attractive. According to research carried out by the Ministry in 1995, in relation to students in faculties throughout the country, more than half the students responded that they wanted materials that would be useful to them taught in a way that was easy to understand (Ministry of Education 1995). In other words, this suggests that students prefer practical education geared to work rather than abstract academic education. In fact, universities were given more discretion, following the changes in the general standards for establishing universities in 1991 and, as a result, in many universities, the curriculum is being revised in various ways to give it more individuality and character. There has also been a sudden move towards faculty development programmes to improve the content and presentation of lectures (Monbushō Kōtōkyōikukyoku, 1998). In addition, in response to the increasing importance of environmental education, together with internationalisation and globalisation, mature students and overseas students are being actively encouraged to enter Japanese universities. These students are sensitive to the benefits that their degrees will provide in terms of content and results and their increasing numbers therefore means that the voice of the 'consumer' is becoming more important. As a result, a more precise response is becoming necessary on the part of universities and university teachers, in contrast to the previous situation. It is inevitable that institutions will be judged strictly according to the laws of the market.

The second factor is a growing recognition of the importance of technological development and related research and that this necessitates a closer relationship between society and the university. In recent years, developed countries have become aware of the importance of basic research centred on the universities, and that this is a means of strengthening international competitiveness where it exists. It is also beginning to be seen as a basic social resource without which economic development is impossible. In Japan, a subtle change is also becoming apparent in relation to academic research by universities and the demands of society.

In 1973, a report of the Advisory Committee on Higher Education for the first time discussed the basic measures for the promotion of learning and, in particular, for basic research – 'the search for the unknown' which is 'the source of human intellectual activity' (Gakujutsu Shingikai, 1973). Moreover, in relation to the needs of society, it concluded that 'as well as representing an accumulation of resources for all mankind, the application and advancement of knowledge is of great benefit to our lives, as the basis of the prosperity of modern society'. It describes the way in which its usefulness of basic academic research to society has been clearly realised, along with the processes of its application and development. In short, it recognises that an improvement in academic research should come about using the logic of academic research itself.

In relation to this, a 1992 report from the same advisory committee (Gakujutsu Shingikai, 1992) discussed ways of stimulating academic research. One section dealt with the importance of the independence of the researcher and the expectation of social benefits. Outstanding results can only be achieved in academic research if the researchers think for themselves and are highly motivated. In contrast to previous reports, the 1992 report came to the clear conclusion that the significance of academic research lay in its social benefits. 'Researchers should respond positively to the demands of society for research which addresses issues such as the global environment, and they should attempt to select these kinds of substantive research problems. In this way, they can be expected to make a positive and active contribution to society' (Gakujutsu Shingikai, 1992).

Partnerships between industry and universities are also encouraged and this implies a move to make the universities part of the whole science and technology system. This means that not only is it expected that universities will operate in fruitful partnership with the government and the world of business, but more generally that they cannot survive in isolation from the operation of the rest of society. If we look at the Science and Technology Basic Plan for 1996, the Report of the Academic Advisory Committee for 1999, and the Plan for the General Science and Technology Council which began work in 2001, this trend is all the more apparent.

The increasing necessity of funding individuals in university research

Resources, especially research funding and the way in which it is distributed to staff, have a considerable influence on universities and the activities of teachers. Unlike the United States, Japanese universities do not have a system of accumulating research money and manpower based on the sum total of individual research projects. Instead, most of the resources are distributed according to a budgetary formula based on factors such as whether there is a graduate school or not, or on the number of staff. In addition, the management style was one in which, in times of high-speed growth, people were concerned with the distribution of an increased budget.

The general principle according to which resources are distributed in Japanese universities is this: even though there might be considerable differences between universities, or an unfavourable distribution of resources between teachers in the same university, generally the professors were able to work within the limits of unit costs based on teaching staff numbers as long as they were not involved in much large-scale research,. More importantly, the length of research time available, together with academic freedom, was an important privilege for university researchers. Generally, it was only in areas where the distribution of time or the equitable distribution of resources was difficult that it was necessary to draw on the strength of the government or of companies. This was true in the case of some liberal arts faculties when they became involved in setting up courses in the physical sciences or in large-scale research. In the case of medicine or engineering where there was a possibility of getting funds from sources other than the Ministry, or in the case of humanities where research did not require much by way of resources, there were only a few cases where additional help was required. These were most clearly concentrated in fields where research institutes were set up as national resource centres with the same status as national universities. However, in recent years, the competition for resources has become more severe in most fields and getting funds has become increasingly difficult, even where it was once possible to access resources from the Ministry.

As shown in Table 5-1, the relative stagnation in the distribution of research funding on an equal basis, coupled with the expansion of funding for individual research through Ministry of Eudcation research grants (*kakenhi*), means that an extremely competitive environment has developed for individual academics. In this context, in order to achieve success where resources are limited, researchers have had to become supplicants to the Ministry, symbolised by the idea of toeing the 'Ministry line' as discussed above. Reliance on funds which are divided up semi-automatically, if they are released at all, is not a good system. Clearly the strong relationship between the national universities and the Ministry is undergoing a change.

Personnel changes in the universities and the Ministry

According to Burton Clark's (1983) analysis, the dynamics of decision-making in universities involves a balance of power between three groups – the government, the university administration and the faculty meeting (*kyōjukai*). In other words, many sections can make their own decisions, and in Japanese universities the government and faculty meeting are both powerful. In this system, the university administration finds itself caught between government regulations and the reactions of the faculty: it has to make decisions, but it is not easy for it to do so. This has been the basic framework of university autonomy in Japan since the Second World War (Shimizu, 1989).

Table 5-1: Recent changes in sources of research budgets (Unit: hundred thousand yen)

	1992	1999	% Increase 1992–1999
Research money per laboratory/department	7,635	7,975	4
Total Ministry research grants	64,600	131,400	103
Total scholarships	48,184	52,783	10
Total budget of national universities	2,217,269	2,276,072	23

Source: Ministry of Education Annual Statistics.

However, this pattern is changing fundamentally as university education provision widens and the standard of academic research rises. As mentioned previously, a significant factor in this, along with the obligation to meet the needs of society in regard to students, is the changing relationship between the government and universities in relation to resources such as research money.

One more background factor should be noted in relation to this change, and that is the change in the personnel who make up the university management and administration. First of all on this issue, there has been a change in the constitution of the faculty meeting. There are now no teachers left with direct experience of the difficulties of the pre-war and wartime period. The so-called 'argumentative generation' who made university autonomy a serious issue are now in the process of retiring. Those who will be left belong to a generation with no experience of university conflict. In fact, there have been hardly any nation-wide university conflicts or student movements in Japan since the 1970s, an interesting contrast with the preceding decades. During this period, individual academics have been competing desperately to be recognised within their own research fields. According to comparative international research by the Carnegie Foundation (Boyer 1994), it appears that university teachers in Japan are relatively more interested in research as opposed to teaching than is the case in other countries. If we put this alongside the problems of Japanese university teachers feeling overworked, which I mentioned above, we might deduce that they are becoming less interested in university management or in the idea of university autonomy.

Like the university administrators, the staff of the Ministry is also changing. Among the career officers, i.e. those that have passed the exams for higher-grade civil servants, the proportion of new entrants who have graduated from Tokyo University Law Faculty has been increasing in recent years. This ratio, which had previously fallen, began to increase once more from around 1970. The average for the period 1957–70 was 17 percent but this more than doubled to 35 percent in the period after 1971. In particular, those who entered the Ministry during the 1970s now form the core of the educational administration as council members and heads of sections. The proportion of Tokyo University law graduates on the staff does not directly determine the quality of government officials, but it can probably be said that their thinking has a subtle influence on policy. Since the proportion of Tokyo University law graduates is high in other parts of the central administration, it raises the question as to whether this will mean more consensus or more confrontation. In line with the reform of the government bureaucracy in recent years, Ministry of Education officials and those in other ministries are now more closely integrated.

To summarise, in its relations with the universities, the Ministry has moved away from its traditional secretarial role to become more of an administrative authority, the kind of ministerial role traditionally carried out at Kasumigaseki, the district in Tokyo where the central administration is located. This will probably have an influence on the relationship with universities as they come under increasing administrative control.

The next thing that is apparent is that, in the Ministry, the officials in charge of universities have less experience of university administration. Research has been carried out on senior officials working in the higher education office of the Ministry (excluding the division in charge of private universities) and its predecessors, including heads of departments, council members, section heads, heads of offices and project officers. (Heads of subsections, supervisors and specialist personnel were not included.) The research involved officials who were in post at the beginning of 1977, 1982, 1987 and 1992 and looked at the ratio between the length of their experience of university administration and the total length of their work in the Ministry. (Only the national universities were included in this research).

As is shown in Table 5-2, the findings were that the number of officials with lengthy experience outside university administration is increasing. For instance, many of them have long experience in primary and secondary education administration. I personally think

Table 5-2: Experience in university education among senior Ministry officials: Number of officials already in post by year

Percentage of experience in universities	Year 1977	1982	1987	1992
Under 25%	2	4	6	6
25–50%	6	5	4	4
50–75%	1	1	1	0
Above 75%	0	0	0	1
Total	9	10	11	11
Average percentage	35	30	23	*28(22)

Source: Bunkyō News-sha 1996.

Note: In the 1992 data, there was one official who had spent 90 percent of his areer in university administration, where he had worked continuously before entering the senior grades. If this atypical case is excluded to make the calculation more representative, the average becomes 22 percent.

that acquiring a balanced experience of educational administration is a good thing, but the basic assumptions of the university administrators of the past, who assumed that universities should be taken seriously as an academic interest group and that university staff should be autonomous, probably had a subtle influence on the way that universities were dealt with. As educational provision has become more widespread, it seems that universities are increasingly being treated not so much as seats of advanced learning, but more like high schools.

These two processes I have suggested, in which bureaucrats are behaving more like ministers, and universities are behaving more like high schools, are only hypotheses based on my own research up to now. More detailed testing will have to await further research, but at least it can be said that the human environment in which universities operate is clearly changing.

Developing universities for the knowledge society of the 21st century

It is said that the 21st century is the century of the knowledge society, and this means that the university will act not as a mechanism for selecting young people according to their latent ability, but as a place where knowledge and skills useful to the whole of society can be created and disseminated. In order to realise this, it is necessary to think about ways in which the facilities of the universities and the abilities of the people who work there can be utilised as fully as possible. We have to discuss immediately the steps necessary to achieve this, such as deregulation, the development of a fair evaluation system and the injection of the necessary resources. However, in the present climate of university reform, it is not clear whether the officials concerned are really aware of the future role of the universities, whether they are just embarking on reform for reform's sake, or whether they have already missed the boat. So far it is too early to judge. Even though there are numerous conflicting opinions, however, I personally think that it is necessary to move in this direction, in order to develop universities for this borderless age. If we look back at Japan's unhappy history, we see that the existence of a healthy and strong opposition is a crucial factor in developing sound and effective policies. Those concerned with universities should take this to heart, and in future, while protecting the autonomy of the universities, they should think about the best way to turn them into arenas for the real production and dissemination of knowledge.

References

Boyer, Ernest L. (1994) *The Academic Profession: An International Perspective*, New York: Carnegie Foundation.

Bunkyō News-sha (1996) *Monbushō kanbu shokuin meibō, Heisei 8 nendo* (Directory of Senior Ministry of Education Officials 1996).

Clark, Burton R. (1983) *The Higher Education System*, Berkeley: University of California Press.

Gakujutsu Shingikai (1973) 'Gakujutsu shinkō ni kansuru no toumen no kihontekina seisaku ni tsuite – tōshin' (On the basic urgent policy regarding the promotion of science – Draft report), Tokyo: Gakujutsu Shingikai.

Gakujutsu Shingikai (1992) '21seiki wo tenbō shita gakujutsu kenkyū no sōgōteki isshin hōsaku ni tsuite – tōshin' (On general support policies for scientific research in the 21st century – Draft report), Tokyo: Gakujutsu Shingikai.

Ministry of Education (1995) *Ware ga kuni no bunko shisaku Heisei 7 nendo: Atarashii daigakuzō wo motomete* (Japanese education policy 1995: In search of a new image for universities), Tokyo: Ōkgurashō Insatsukyoku (Ministry of Finance Printing Office).

Monbushō Kōtōkyōikukyoku (Ministry of Education, higher education division) (1998) *Daigaku ringikai nyūsu* (University Advisory Council News),16.

Shimizu Izō (1989) 'Shigaku keieisha kara mita kokuritsu daigaku' (How managers of private universities see national universities), *IDE Gendai no kōtō kyōiku* (Current Higher Education) 307: 24–29.

Takuma, Hiroshi (1996) 'Daigaku nado ni okeru kenkyūsha no seikatsu jikan ni kansuru chōsa kenkyū' (Research into the lifestyle time available to university researchers), Ministry of Education Research Subsidy Report.

Yamamoto, Shinichi (1996) 'Mass kōtō kyōiku system to kenkyū daigaku' (The mass higher education system and the research university), *Hōsō kyōiku kaihatsu sentaa kenkyū hōkoku* (Distance Education Development Center Research Report) 91: 271–84.

6 From Selection to Seduction: The Impact of Demographic Change on Private Higher Education in Japan

Earl H. Kinmonth

That the Japanese population is aging and that in the future Japan will have an exceedingly high ratio of benefit-receiving elderly to productive-age workers, is well known. Less well known, but of considerably more immediate importance in terms of higher education, is the rapidly declining number of college-age students. In 1992, there were 2.04 million eighteen-year olds; ten years later in 2002, there were 1.49 million; and it is projected that there will be only 1.21 million in 2010 (*Daigaku mirai mondai kenkyūkai* 2001: 15). According to projections made by the Ministry of Education, by 2009 the number of undergraduate places in colleges and universities will equal the number of would-be students. Anyone wanting to go to college will be assured of a place (*Nihon Keizai Shimbun* 4 July 1999; Kuroki 1999: 17). Other calculations put the date at 2007 or even earlier (Kuroki 1999: 28–29).

A few commentators have gone so far as to proclaim that this demographic shift will mean the end of Japan's so-called 'examination hell' or *shiken jigoku*. Others have suggested that the 'examination hell' will continue in altered form and will be coupled to a 'recruitment hell' or *boshū jigoku* (Nakamura 2000: 33–34). In this scenario, a relatively small fraction of all would-be college students will continue seriously studying for entrance to a small group of prestigious colleges and universities. A much larger body of students will study the relative attractiveness of competing admission offers from a large number of colleges and universities desperate to fill places and generate enough tuition revenue to avoid bankruptcy. Developments to date suggest the second reading is more accurate than the first.

Although demographic change is also having an impact on public institutions, this chapter concentrates on the private sector, which is much larger than the public sector in terms of numbers of students, faculty, and institutions. Due to the fact that Japanese private institutions are highly dependent on tuition fees paid by students, they must respond more rapidly to change than institutions reliant on public money. To the extent that pre-college education in Japan is influenced by college entrance requirements, or the lack thereof, changes made by private colleges to recruit students in a buyers market will almost certainly have an impact on the Japanese education system as a whole.

Japan is one of a small number of countries with a large, private higher education sector. In 1999, 73 percent of four-year college students and 92 percent of two-year college students were enrolled in schools operated by 'educational juridical persons' or *gakkō hōjin* (Amano 1999: 21). In Japanese the four-year institutions are usually referred to as *daigaku* and the two-year institutions as *tanki daigaku.* Typically, *daigaku* is translated as 'university' and *tanki daigaku* as 'junior college' although these translations are inappropriate in terms of both British and American usage. The term 'university' carries connotations of a breadth and level of research and education that are inapplicable in the Japanese context. Many four-year institutions are quite small with only a few thousand, or occasionally as little as a few hundred, students and many offer only a single course such as business, literature or information studies. A much smaller number of institutions cover virtually all fields, including medicine, and have tens of thousands of students. The term 'university' is not, however, really applicable here either because such institutions are collections of single subject units often at widely separate locations and would-be students gain admission to these units not the 'university' as such. Transfers from one department (college) to another within the same 'university' are unusual.

Although two-year institutions are somewhat distinctive in having a student body that is 90 percent female, and in concentrating on liberal arts or home economics, they are best seen as providing a truncated version of what many of the four-year institutions offer.[1] There is considerable interchange in faculty between two and four-year colleges. Young academics move 'up' from two- to four-year colleges; retirees from four-year colleges spend a 'twilight' period at two-year colleges. Throughout this paper the term 'college' will be used to translate *daigaku* with two-year or four-year added where necessary.

Many of the older and more well known private colleges were originally 'mission schools' started by foreign Christian missionaries or Japanese believers. 'Law schools', set up in the 1880s and 1890s to compete with Tokyo Imperial University, were the basis for a number of the larger second-tier universities in Tokyo. In the early twentieth century, numerous schools with a business or engineering orientation were founded by businessmen either as a philanthropic gesture or to provide trained manpower for their own expanding corporate empires. Generally, these institutions have evolved into something that would fit an American notion of what private higher educational institutions, sectarian or non-sectarian should look like. There are, however, patterns to be seen in Japan that are highly unusual in the United States and unknown in the United Kingdom.

Many institutions in all size categories in Japan are in effect educational conglomerates operating several two-year and four-year colleges, high schools, middle schools, grade schools and even kindergartens. A few are 'international' in that they operate schools for expatriate Japanese in one or more foreign countries. Despite their nominal non-profit status, many institutions both large and small are actually family run businesses.[2] People bearing the same surname, or who are related to each other by marriage, hold most of the managerial positions.[3] Founders of some schools in this category are occasionally written up in the weekly magazines that specialise in scandals involving the lifestyle of the rich and famous.[4] Several institutions have even been rumoured to have links to organised crime.[5]

Compared to American private colleges and universities, the most striking difference in Japanese institutions is that they essentially live a hand-to-mouth existence covering current operating expenses and capital expenditures primarily from student fees. By American standards endowment income is almost non-existent. Compared to the United States, voluntary contributions from graduates, the general public or corporations, have little role in the financing of private institutions in Japan.[6] Only a few institutions with religious affiliations (both Buddhist and Christian) can expect more than token voluntary contributions. Since most private colleges in Japan concentrate on business, economics, liberal arts or social science subjects, they generate little research income. A few private institutions with medical schools have earnings from their teaching hospitals but such institutions are the exception rather than the norm (Nakamura 1999: 59–65; Nakamura 2000: 20).

In 1975, the government introduced a system of subsidising private colleges. At this time it was envisioned that eventually half of the operating costs of private schools would come from the national government. In fact, the subsidy rate peaked at 29.5 percent in 1980, declining to 13.3 percent in 1991 and 12.6 percent in 2001.[7] Given that governments at all levels in Japan are running substantial deficits, it is unlikely that the downward trend in the subsidy rate will be reversed. In the future, Japanese private colleges are almost certain to become more dependent on student fees, particularly tuition charges, rather than less.

While tuition charges as such require no special explanation, Japanese private colleges have two distinct and important revenue sources that are not found in the US. Entrance examinations were, and are, a major source of revenue, at least for those institutions that are relatively popular. In the so-called 'Golden Years' of the late 1980s and early1990s, when the number of would-be students was rapidly increasing, it was not unusual for even a third-tier private college with an intake quota of 3000 to have 20,000 would-be students sit its examinations at 30,000 yen ($300) or more per head.[8] Since the examinations were written in house by the faculty, the only cost to the college was that of printing the papers and renting a venue if the applicants could not be accommodated on campus. Essentially, entrance examinations were pure gravy for private institutions.

Following notice of admission would-be students have been required to make an immediate one-off payment, generally 200–400,000 yen ($2,000–$4,000), called 'admission money' (*nyūgaku-kin*). If the student fails to enroll, this payment is not refunded. Since Japanese private colleges give admission notice before public (national) institutions and lower prestige institutions give notice earlier than higher prestige institutions, some could always expect a certain amount of income from students who forfeited their 'admission money' when they received later notice from a more prestigious or attractive institution. For some institutions, revenue from this source is comparable in size to the government subsidies they receive. Recently, lawyers and parents have sued a number of colleges using a consumer protection law that came in to effect in 2001. They argue that the consumer protection law requires that cancellation fees be reasonably related to the expenses incurred by the service provider. Although as of April 2003, the issue was still in litigation, the Ministry of Education has issued guidelines 'encouraging' refunds and some colleges have started issuing refunds of advance tuition payments if not of the 'admission money' itself (*Nihon Keizai Shimbun* 5 March 2003).

While the overall fiscal impact of demographic change can be documented, the actual financial situation of individual private colleges is extremely difficult to determine. Despite receiving public money and being tax-exempt, private educational institutions are not required to publish detailed accounts or submit to public audit (Nakamura 2000: 23; *Nihon Keizai Shimbun* 28 March 2001). Only a few institutions publish detailed accounts and still fewer have had their credit worthiness assessed by rating agencies.[9] Assessment is made still more difficult because private colleges are legally required to use an accounting system that is quite different from that used in the private sector and published texts and manuals on the subject have appeared only recently.[10]

The Ministry of Education receives more information than most colleges publish but its reports on the state of private school finances give only aggregate figures for broad categories of institution. For example, a 1996 Ministry report indicated that there were 60 schools with 10–20 billion yen (100–200 million dollars) of debt and 35 schools with more than 20 billion yen (200 million dollars) of debt, but specific institutions were not identified.[11] Some commentators have used this and other aggregate data to assert that, overall, private colleges are already operating in the red, surviving only by selling off financial assets and drawing on reserves built up during the 'Golden Years' (Nakamura 1999: 65–68). The Ministry and the *Nihon shiritsu daigaku shinkō kyōsai jigyōdan* (The Promotion and Mutual Aid Corporation for Private Schools in Japan) have been reported as having prepared contingency plans to provide for students left stranded if their college goes bankrupt suddenly and ceases operations (*Nihon Keizai Shimbun* 23 Sept. 2001). Other colleges have decided that they should wind down before falling down. In the past four years (2000–2003), seventeen two- and four-year colleges have stopped recruiting in anticipation of ceasing operation.[12] In one widely reported case a provincial four-year college suspended operations without producing a single graduating class (*Nihon Keizai Shimbun* 24 Feb. 2003).

Barring large casualties from natural disasters, epidemics, war or other cataclysmic events, or a sea change in Japanese immigration policy, the number of potential college students for the next twenty years or so is already known. Two important variables are, however, unknown. One is the proportion of the population that will actually attend college. The other is the number of places there will be for them. When, in 1996, the Ministry published the often-cited applicant to place ratio of 1:1 by 2009, it assumed that 50 percent of the college-age cohort would in fact choose to attend college. Most observers regard this expectation as overly optimistic.

The Ministry projection was further based on two assumptions about the number of places, neither of which is being evidenced: first, that the increase in enrolment quotas allowed since 1986 to deal with the second baby boom would be eliminated by 2000; second, that the number of new places would be restrained. In other words, there would be a substantial net decrease in the number of places on offer. Although there has been some reduction in the enrolment quotas, colleges became dependent on receiving the tuition fees from 120 (or more students) while providing the mandated facilities for 100 and the Ministry has not forced a full roll-back (Nakamura 1999: 43; Nakamura 2000: 15–16; *Nihon Keizai Shimbun* 28 Sept. 2002). Moreover, rather than using its considerable regulatory power to lessen the impact of the declining number of eighteen-year olds, the Ministry has actually followed policies that have made, and will continue to make the situation worse.[13] Nominally, the Ministry has proclaimed a moratorium on the founding of new colleges. The declaration has, however, three exemptions to the general prohibition and these have, in fact, allowed a steady increase in new institutions and expansion in older institutions. Existing two-year institutions are allowed to retool as four-year colleges; new colleges can be founded and new programmes can be added if they are in areas deemed to fill a social or economic need (social work, nursing, information technology, international studies); new colleges can be founded that do not fall into the previous two categories if there is strong local support for the proposed institution.

As of 1999, more than 60 percent of short-course colleges were under quota, partly due to demographics and partly due to the advancement of women into four-year colleges.[14] Without conversion, many of the two-year colleges are almost certain to fail. Less certain is whether they will survive after conversion. As new four-year colleges with no reputation in terms of student placement, they will face stiff competition for new students from older institutions higher up in the pecking order. Students at an existing two-year college, who might otherwise consider carrying on in a four-year version of the same college, will be aggressively courted by existing four-year colleges that see transfer students as a means of making up their own enrolment shortfalls.

'Information society' (*jōhōka shakai*) and 'internationalisation' (*kokusaika)* have been buzzwords in Japan for nearly two decades. Neither seems to show any signs of declining in popularity. Both have been exceptionally popular components in the names of recently founded colleges and newly-created departments (Kuroki 1999: 23–24, 51–53). Frequently they are used in combination with each other and with other contemporary buzzwords such as environment (*kankyō*), welfare (*fukushi*), studies of the human condition (*ningen kagaku*) and so on. Indeed, college administrators speak in awe of one new college that received approval for a department incorporating eight popular buzzwords in the name. Both *jōhōka shakai* and *kokusaika* have been used to justify the creation of a large number of small-scale institutions, most of which prove exceedingly unpopular with would-be students and which almost immediately end up on lists of 'colleges that could fail at any moment'.

In 1984, the Ministry of Education first indicated that it would approve a new type of college that was based on public-private cooperation (*kōshi kyōryoku*). Initially few such institutions were created but, in the first half of the 1990s, 24 new colleges now described as 'publicly established, privately managed' (*kōsetsu minei*) were founded (Amano 1999: 102–03). Local government units, typically prefectures, have supplied the money but an 'educational juridical person' (*gakkō hōjin*) carries out the actual management. Such institutions have been created primarily as part of regional development programmes either with the intent of reducing the outflow of young people from an area or to bring modern, academic training to the preservation of traditional industries. By entrusting the management to a *gakkō hōjin*, the schools have management flexibility and possibly lower personnel costs than would be the case if the institution were part of a local government bureaucracy. Due to the fact that construction and other capital costs have been borne by government bodies, such schools start out with less debt and lower overheads than would be the case for a conventional, totally private venture. As they are legally private institutions, they can, and do, charge the higher tuitions fees associated with the private sector rather than the lower fees associated with the public sector (Nakamura 1999: 159–61). Such hybrid institutions are nonetheless only marginally better equipped to deal with enrolment shortfalls than are more conventional private institutions (*Mainichi Shimbun* 31 Jan. 2000). Further, because such institutions promise an ongoing payroll and tend to involve lucrative construction contracts that are handed out to local contractors on the basis of political connections, their establishment has typically more to do with politics than education. Indeed, just such a 'college for craftsmen' (*monozukuri daigaku*) has been at the centre of a scandal involving a level of bribery considered ostentatious even by Japanese standards.

In the context of a dwindling number of potential students and an increase in the number of institutions competing for those students, private colleges are currently pursuing three major strategies: (1) lowering costs; (2) cultivating new markets (non-traditional students); (3) trying new recruitment strategies.

On average, personnel costs consume 60 percent of the income of private colleges. Many private institutions have highly-skewed faculty age distributions, top heavy in the 50s and above. Unlike corporate employment were the pay curve has peaked in the mid or late 50s, academic pay has had an increasing length of service component up to age 70 or even beyond. By forcing retirement earlier in the length of service curve and then re-employing selected faculty on fixed-term contracts and lower salaries (typically two-thirds or less), institutions save in three ways: first, there is a *de facto* pay cut for those forced into earlier retirement; second, their benefits are cut because the very substantial termination allowances (*taishokukin*) paid in Japan are a function of final salary and years of service not counting any period on fixed-term employment; third, the institution can be selective in deciding who is given additional years on fixed-term contracts. The savings that can be generated this way can be quite substantial although making such changes in employment conditions requires a management structure that is not dominated by those in the age cohort that stands to lose the most (*Nihon Keizai Shimbun* 6 Dec. 1999).

Already highly dependent on poorly paid part-time instructors (*hijōkin kōshi*), private colleges are increasingly overloading their regular faculty. Instead of teaching the nominal five or six courses per term that has been the norm in Japanese private colleges, existing faculty teach eight, nine, ten or even more courses per term. Although there is usually some compensation for each course above the notional limit of five or six, this rate is, per course, half or less that which even the notoriously underpaid part-timers receive. Such overloads cannot but adversely affect the standard of teaching, which almost all Japanese commentators regard as low even at the outset.

Some private institutions have attracted popular press attention for cost cutting in the paper and pencils area. The fact that competitive bidding for construction projects, or that two or more quotations are required before any purchases are made above a certain monetary limit, could be regarded as managerial innovations worthy of press coverage indicates the degree to which Japanese private institutions have been living in a sheltered world divorced from even the most basic elements of managerial common sense. Nevertheless, no matter how carefully institutions manage expenditure on paperclips and toilet paper, this will not ensure their survival since such items are a small fraction of their overall operating costs.

On the revenue side, Japanese private colleges have very few options. For all practical purposes most have no endowments to manage. Even if they did, the so-called zero interest rate policy (ZIRP) adopted by the Japanese government, has meant very low rates of return on the sort of financial instruments generally considered appropriate for institutional trust funds. A few institutions have received press attention for constructing high-rise buildings, part of which they rent out to generate income, or by leasing their land for ventures such as hotels. (Waseda University is a prime example, see *Nihon Keizai Shimbun* 17 Aug. 2000). Such ventures are dependent on historical chance, i.e. the institution owning prime, urban real estate whereas most of the really weak institutions have unattractive provincial locations. Similarly, the growing emphasis on 'college-industry cooperation' (*sangaku kyōdo* or *sangaku rentai*) provides no guidance for the majority of private institutions that lack engineering, science or medical faculties.

For all but a few private colleges and institutions, survival essentially means finding students to fill places. This can be done either by competitive recruiting of traditional students at the expense of the other private institutions scrambling for this same dwindling pool, or by recruiting students from groups that did not previously attend college in Japan.

Foreign students have been seen as one alternative to the declining number of eighteen-year old Japanese and, after a long period during which it seemed that Japan would not reach its official goal of 100,000 foreign students (at all levels), that target seems to have been realised, albeit several years later than the original goal of 2000 (*Nihon Keizai Shimbun* 15 Nov. 2002). The collapse of various Asian currencies in the late 1990s sharply cut the number of students capable of studying in Japan even with generous visa provisions for side jobs. Stories of discrimination have not helped. Asian students who are serious about their studies do not necessarily find the standards of instruction prevailing in private colleges sufficient to justify the cost of study in Japan. Many lack sufficient preparation in Japanese for serious study or would prefer to pursue higher-level studies in English (Greenlees 1998; Kuroki 1999: 166–68). Japanese immigration regulations make it difficult for foreign graduates to secure employment in Japan even if they have skills that are in short supply (*Nihon Keizai Shimbun* 27 April 2002). Nonetheless, desperate private colleges cannot ignore any potential source of students and recent newspaper articles report college recruiters making the rounds of Japanese language schools offering admission on the basis of interviews and perfunctory 'examinations' (*Nihon Keizai Shimbun* 23 Nov. 2002).

English instruction can, of course, be offered in Japan. Ritsumeikan University, a well-known private university in Kyoto has set up a large-scale branch, Ritsumeikan Asia Pacific University (APU) in Beppu, Oita prefecture, with the express purpose of teaching a largely foreign student body in English. Even if APU succeeds in a nominal sense, it will not necessarily be indicative of a path to be followed by other private schools. Ritsumeikan, a large and generally well-managed institution, was aggressively courted by both the prefecture and the city involved and it received a very high level of direct and indirect subsidy including free land for its campus (Nakamura 2000: 130–133).

Smaller institutions already in trouble do not have the financial wherewithal to open new campuses or to hire faculty who are capable of giving serious instruction in English. Further, most such institutions have provincial or rural locations and are unattractive to foreign students who need to work to pay their expenses and for whom opportunities for relatively high-paid casual labour are greater in urban centres.[15] If deceptive claims are made, students may simply disappear as happened with a provincial two-year college whose largely Chinese student body moved en masse to Tokyo leading to the closure of the school.[16] Further, 'internalisation' may also work to the disadvantage of Japanese private colleges. Rather than paying a substantial price to attend a mediocre or worse Japanese institution, Japanese students may elect to study abroad. The large private supplementary schools (*juku*) that survive by attending to the needs of students have identified preparing Japanese students for study abroad as a growing market (*Nihon Keizai Shimbun* 7 Jan. 2000). Recent Ministry moves to recognise degrees from foreign institutions acquired through Internet-based distance learning, and rule changes that may make it easier for foreign institutions to be legally recognised as *daigaku* have caused some to speak of 'the coming of the black ships' and to fret that a proportion of the dwindling supply of eighteen-year olds will be poached by the foreign invaders.[17]

Minorities, and those previously excluded from conventional higher education by reason of physical disabilities, constitute a potential source of students for private colleges and at least one institution in Shikoku has aggressively courted such students including *burakumin*, resident Koreans, and the visually impaired (*Mainichi Shimbun* [regional edition] 7 Feb. 2000). For its part, the Ministry has revised its regulations to allow students from the tolerated but not legally recognised, (North) Korean high schools in Japan to sit regular entrance examinations.[18] Even with an aggressive (and unlikely) affirmative action plan in Japan, such students cannot be expected to be the salvation of struggling provincial private colleges. Able minority students will go to the best urban colleges they can. Others will not necessarily want to be publicly identified as members of minorities. Students with physical handicaps require additional expenditures that financially strapped institutions can ill afford.

For some private colleges, a partial answer to the shortfall in eighteen-year olds may lie in courting adult learners and post-graduate students of which neither group has been significant in Japanese college enrolments until now. Adult learners have largely been confined to night school programmes offered primarily by second-tier private colleges. With the exception of MS programmes for engineers that began to boom in the 1980s, graduate programmes in Japan, as in Britain, have been primarily for the training of academics. Again, as in the case of Britain, there are virtually no professional degree programmes. Law, medicine and business administration, which in the United States are largely entered after taking an undergraduate degree, in Japan are entered at the undergraduate level although some courses (medicine) may be more than four years in length, or others (law) may involve special training in government institutes.

Recent government moves to encourage American-style 'professional schools' in Japan, most notably for the teaching of law, will create a new market for some private institutions but those that can, and will, respond to this initiative are without exception large, strong institutions. Many of these latter institutions have also benefited from an upsurge of interest in domestic MBA (Management in Business Administration) degrees. It is these well-known and well-regarded colleges located in urban centres that can expect to recruit adult-learner students. Moreover, to cater to salarymen, these institutions must have, or rent, space near major rail stations and, even in the post-bubble era, high-quality facilities within a few minutes walk of a busy commuter station are very expensive.[19]

Given that there is no tradition in Japan, other than perhaps in engineering, for employers to recognise graduate qualifications (*Nihon Keizai Shimbun* 9 Aug. 1999), it would seem that the majority of private colleges would find few students through the creation of graduate programmes. Nonetheless, the creation of such new courses, especially in the social sciences, has boomed in recent years. How successful these will be remains to be seen. A portion of the graduate enrolment increase seems to be coming from students just out of college who see graduate school as a way to pass time until the corporate job market picks up or 'they find themselves'. They are referred to in Japanese as 'moratorium' types. The Ministry has also artificially stimulated the demand for social science graduate credentials. Before now nurses, and several other groups, have been trained in post-secondary schools that were not legally colleges and thus did not grant academic degrees. Instructors in these schools are usually graduates of the same school or a similar institution and lack academic degrees of any kind. Recently, these instructors have come under pressure to acquire academic degrees. They represent an attractive but inherently finite source of new students.

Adult learners seeking undergraduate degrees or cultural enrichment represent another potential source of students for private colleges. Private colleges have worked to erase, or at least paper over, the distinction between degrees earned in full-time day programmes and those earned part time or at night (Kuroki 1999: 179–84). Here again, location is all-important, as small provincial private colleges (or those in urban areas but distant from a major rail station) cannot expect to attract many students.[20] In the area of cultural enrichment, private colleges face stiff competition from a variety of other course providers, including local government agencies and the major quality newspapers through their 'culture centres'. Further, few of the faculty at private colleges have had any experience preparing interesting courses for adult-learners (who are selective consumers, not time-serving quasi-captives). The attitude of many undergraduates at low-ranked institutions may also well put off mature students.[21]

Until recently, a student of a two-year college in Japan who wished to transfer to a four-year college usually had to study for, and pass, the entrance examination of the four-year college and then spend four years in residence. Now, many four-year private colleges offer transfer admission to students from two-year colleges. Because two-year colleges ran into recruitment problems some years ago when their primarily female recruitment base began to prefer four-year colleges, admissions at all but a few institutions have been essentially open door. In effect, therefore, the open door of the two-year institution becomes an open door to the four-year institution (*Yomiuri Shimbun* 15 Jan. 2000). While there may be a few 'diamonds in the rough' to be found in those transferring from such colleges, it is far more likely that most students will be poorly qualified and marginally motivated. Further, as the two-year colleges continue to contract, the number of potential transfer students will also contract.[22]

Even if all of the sources for students noted above are fully exploited, ultimately the bulk of enrolments for most institutions will still come from recent high school graduates. It is in the recruitment of these students where the greatest changes have taken place and will take place in the future. Indeed, the situation has already changed from one in which all colleges had at least some degree of selectivity to one in which many institutions are willing to take almost anyone they can get. Since the 1980s, the most noted method of ranking colleges in terms of the difficulty of entering them has been *hensachi*. This is a rating based on the results of mock entrance examinations conducted on a nation-wide basis by the large chain *juku* such as Kawaijuku and Yoyogi Seminar. Performance in the mock examinations is correlated with admission results in the following year. Applicants to each faculty (college) are divided into standard deviation groups and the success rate for each group is calculated. The standard deviation group that has a 50 percent chance of admission to the given faculty is used as an index of the difficulty of entrance at that faculty. Colleges with broadly similar entrance requirements are grouped into bands and given alphabetic designations: SA, A, B, C, D, E. Institutions in the SA category are most difficult to enter while those in the E category are the least difficult.

In 1998, the rating system broke down due to the emergence of institutions that are mathematically off the scale. In essence, in these institutions, anyone who takes the entrance examination is admitted and, as a result, a new category of F-rated institutions has appeared. (Correspondence with the English 'F' for 'failing' is only coincidental). To be placed in this category by Kawaijuku, for example, the college must have an applicant to place ratio of 1:2 or less; a take-up rate of 65 percent or greater, and an applicant pool that comes from the 35 point deviation group or lower (*Nihon Keizai Shimbun* 8 July 2000). Given that, as we have seen, applicants often apply to multiple institutions and then enroll at the highest tier at which they are successful; and given the institutional response of admitting more applicants than are expected to come, the result is the emergence of a category of institutions characterised by the title of an article in a popular weekly magazine – 'Take the examination and they take you' (*Shūkan Asahi*, 23 June 2000: 145–46). Presumably such institutions have entrance examinations only for cosmetic reasons and, perhaps, in the hope of collecting fees.

Of the 194 colleges first placed in this 'F' ranking, most could be described by one or more of three characteristics: provincial, single-subject or for women, but a surprising minority were nominally science or engineering colleges, or had 'international' (*kokusai*) or 'information technology' (*jōhō kagaku*) in either the institutional name or that of the 'F' ranked department. That 'trendy' subjects should be associated with enrolment shortfalls is largely to be explained by the lack of content behind these names. Looking at the prospectus of a private college that touts itself as 'international' typically reveals nothing more than the teaching of 'business English' and possibly the presence of several peripatetic foreign teachers of English conversation. In the case of 'information studies', one typically finds pictures of brightly lit rooms filled with personal computers, but checking course listings shows no indication of anything approaching American computer science or software engineering programmes. The feeling is more of a secretarial programme in which spreadsheets and word processing programmes have replaced ledger books and typewriters.

Even in the case of colleges that can afford some level of selectivity, many students now enter without taking the traditional multi-day tests associated with Japan's notorious 'examination hell'. Some of the non-examination routes are not new and are unrelated to demographic change. Even the most prestigious institutions have long had special, albeit small, quotas for those with more athletic than intellectual ability. Buddhist institutions have offered automatic admission to any male who will inherit a temple of one of the sects supporting the college. Many private colleges have offered nearly automatic admission to graduates of high schools that are part of the same or closely affiliated to the institutional group. What has changed is that in recent years, the number of entry routes, with and without examination, has proliferated to the point that some colleges have eight or more admission procedures ranging from the traditional paper examination to self-recommendation. Pick one or more entry category or procedure that suits your tastes and qualifications – traditional examination, high school recommendation, self-recommendation and so on. Even within the traditional examination scheme some schools offer a choice, such as take three examinations but have only the best two (or even best one) count (Kuroki 1999: 12–14). Japanese commentators have somewhat cynically styled this pattern as *à la carte* admissions.

The first large, generally available, admission quota outside of the conventional entrance examination route was 'admission by recommendation'. Originally limited to 30 percent of all admissions for four-year colleges and 50 percent for two year-colleges, in 2000 the Ministry raised the permissible limits to 50 and one 100 percent respectively (Nakamura 2000: 39; *Nihon Keizai Shimbun* 2 Dec. 1999). Such admissions currently account for about 60 percent of all two-year college admissions and about 30 percent of all four-year college admissions. In theory, Ministry directives call for colleges to indicate what they expect in terms of academic performance and to publicise these criteria to high school principals who will then recommend students meeting these standards. The college will then make a decision based on an interview and/or an essay. The Ministgry has not, apparently, checked to see what institutions have actually been doing. In general, it would appear that strong institutions have used additional exams (discouraged by the Ministry) to maintain quality. At the opposite end of the spectrum is a desperate two-year college on the island of Shikoku that has gone so far as to make 'recommendation' by a current student sufficient for admission. Institutions that take 'admission by recommendation' find that students thus admitted are less well prepared than students who sit conventional examinations. While 'admission by recommendation' was intended to free final-year high school students from the peculiar rigours of preparing for entrance examinations, many students appear to take admission as a licence exempting them from further study of any type.

Of the items currently on the admissions menu in Japan, perhaps the most interesting is known as the 'admission office entrance examination' or *AO nyūshi* – a blend of American and Japanese terminology that is something of an oxymoron in that typically no 'entrance examination'(*nyūshi*) as such is required. The first Japanese 'admissions office' was part of the glitzy Shonan Fujisawa Campus of Keio Gijuku University (Kuroki 1999: 79), one of the most prestigious private institutions in Japan. The pattern spread rapidly from the top of the hierarchy downward and as it did so it changed from something that was originally intended to allow admission to bright, creative students who might be rejected by the conventional examination system, to a device by which colleges desperate for students could maintain the pretence of selection while in fact accepting almost any applicant (*Nihon Keizai Shimbun* 23 May 1999). Others see the system as a rationalisation for poaching (*aotakai*) students early in the application cycle (*Nihon Keizai Shimbun* 18 July 1999). As of the 2003 fiscal year, 286 primarily private colleges were using something they called *AO nyūshi* (*Nihon Keizai Shimbun* 2 March 2003).

Individual schools have different procedures but, in general, the Japanese system is based on prospective students being interviewed by faculty once they have passed only a minimal screening conducted by college clerical staff who basically check paperwork not credentials. If the college and department with an AO quota is relatively popular and in a position to turn away unimpressive students, the system has the possibility of identifying motivated students who might not make it through more conventional channels. Since AO decisions are made before exam-based decisions, the system also frees motivated students to study what interests them rather than, the sometimes rather arcane, material they need to pass the examinations. In the case of 'admission by recommendation', however, many students regard acceptance as a licence to go limp (*Nihon Keizai Shimbun* 5 Dec. 1999).

For colleges and departments that are not popular, particularly for colleges that may already be under-quota, admission office entrance might better be styled 'recruitment office admission'.[23] Indeed, an executive with Sundai *yobiko*, one of the large exam preparation chains, has suggested that the 'A' of 'AO' really stands for 'around' as in going around searching for students (*Nihon Keizai Shimbun* 23 May 1999). Many private institutions now have 'open campus' days or weeks in which the general public, particularly parents with children nearing college age, are invited to view the campus, listen to lectures, and in some cases attend parties. Some have gone so far as to offer entertaining lectures to high school, middle and, even elementary school students. Although this latter was originally part of a Ministry scheme for rekindling interest in science and engineering, colleges have seized upon these lectures as a way of reminding possible future customers of their existence (*Nihon Keizai Shimbun* 28 June 2003).

As more and more colleges become ever more desperate to recruit students, it is probable that some will take steps that amount to bribery. A few very weak institutions have offered what amount to enlistment bonuses. One college that has tried, and failed, to cash in on *kokusaika* has been reported as offering a free one week 'study tour' to the United States to anyone who would sign up for four years (*Mainichi Shimbun* 15 May 2000). Another weak school in the Tohoku area was reported as offering trips to Tokyo Disneyland to any high school student that would come to the college and listen to a pitch for the institution (*Yomiuri Shimbun,* Evening Edition, 21 Aug. 1999). Other private colleges have been reported as offering parties and premiums to high school counsellors willing to attend 'briefing sessions' about the college. One small private college for women was reported as 'pouring on the booze and food' for 220 counsellors. Since those participating were all public employees the 'briefing' became something of a minor scandal. For its part, the college admitted that handing out gift certificates might not have been the thing to do but 'holding briefing sessions with food, drink, and presents, is something that colleges all over are doing in order secure students' (*Asahi Shimbun* 23 June 2000). As private colleges become ever more desperate for bodies, it is quite likely that there will be an escalation in these 'briefings' and the extras that come with them. Indeed, it is not hard to imagine private colleges giving bounties to those who steer students to them.

Even for those colleges still popular enough to be able to use entrance examinations for actually selecting more able students, the change from a seller's market to a buyer's market has had a substantial impact. When the market favoured the colleges, entrance examinations were tightly clustered: one day, or set of days, for public institutions; one day, or set of days, for private institutions. Exams were college-specific. It was difficult to sit more than one public college entrance examination and one private college entrance examination in a given year. Typically, each examination was offered in one and only one venue. During examination season, hotels and inns, in cities with large numbers of colleges, offered package deals for provincial students and a parent, typically the mother, who came along as a combination coach and chaperone. Now, private colleges take their examinations and other admissions procedures to potential students. Some of the larger private institutions go so far as to offer examinations in every one of Japan's prefectures, plus Hokkaido. Smaller schools limit themselves to three or four venues or perhaps to only Tokyo and either Kyoto or Osaka. This approach is a complete reversal of past policy. Previously applicants bore the cost of travel to a location convenient to the college. Now colleges bear the not inconsiderable cost of renting venues and sending staff to locations convenient to applicants.

Each year an increasing number of private colleges allow applicants to use the results of the so-called 'Centre Examination' in place of their own institution-specific examinations. Originally called the 'Common First Tier Test of Academic Knowledge', the Centre Examination was first used in 1979 as a preliminary screening examination for applicants to national colleges who would then usually take an institution-specific examination, at least in the case of the more attractive national institutions. In 1990, the examination gained its present name, and private colleges were given the option of using it although initially few did (Amano 1999: 7). When there was a surplus of applicants, it was far more profitable for private colleges to force students to take highly expensive institution-specific examinations.

When using the Centre Examination, colleges are taking a risk. A student who uses the Centre Examination for multiple applications to one or more private institutions and one or more national institutions will, almost certainly, score permitting, select a more prestigious private institution over a less prestigious one, and a lower cost public institution over a private institution unless the latter is near the top of the pecking order. The Centre Examination appears to produce a larger number of applicants in the first year or two of use by a private institution but the effect is temporary (*Shūkan Asahi*, 18 Feb. 2000; *Nihon Keizai Shimbun* 20 Jan. 2001 and 8 March 2003). Nonetheless, having a higher competition rate makes an institution look better and as long as the 'admission money' system holds, students who hedge their bets are a significant source of income.

In parallel with the spread of multiple venues for sitting exams, private colleges are in the vanguard of a move to offer September admission in addition to the traditional April admission. This is most frequently explained in terms of the popular buzzword *kokusaika*. September admission makes it easier for Japanese students to take a term or year out in a foreign institution.[24] But, when even the weakest schools had two or three or more applicants for each place, institutions at all levels were quite content to work within the once-a-year tournament system. Having a second round may bring in a few students who have decided that another full year as a 'masterless samurai' (*rōnin*) is not worth the effort and expense.

To make applications less costly, some private colleges with so-called *à la carte* admissions schemes offer 'two for one' or 'three for one' deals in which the student applies under two different quotas but pays only one fee rather than paying each time. This is, in effect, a form of discounting and, while overt competition in terms of yearly tuition has not yet appeared, weaker schools have started waiving the 'admission money' or reducing non-tuition charges. Another approach is to offer a tuition fee discount to students scoring in the top n percent in the entrance examination on the assumption that these students have also received a high score and admission elsewhere (*Asahi Shimbun* 20 Nov. 1999).

Because the demographic crunch has just begun, private college administrators, at this point, are concerned first and foremost with simply recruiting students. Historically, retaining students has not been an issue. Academic failures, while not unknown, have been covered by ad hoc measures or an extra year. Even graduates from prestigious universities have been described by the term *tokorotenshiki* (a reference to a kind of Japanese jelly that squirts out of its container with little applied effort). As participation rates have increased, motivation has decreased. An increasing number of students are reported as being in college to please parents, to keep contact with friends or for want of anything more compelling to do. Such students are almost certain to increase in number and private colleges, usually weaker ones, have been trying to make changes that are thought to be useful in retaining existing students and preventing dropouts. These include allowing credit transfers; 'faculty development programmes' designed to help faculty produce more appealing courses; student evaluation of courses and so on (Kuroki 1999: 84–98).

Whether these programmes will have any serious impact remains to be seen. Articles about 'reforms' typically deal with their introduction. Follow-up evaluations are rare and tend to suggest that students are not particularly interested in reform as conceived by academics and administrators (*Nihon Keizai Shimbun* 21 July 2002). Introducing new patterns seems to be based primarily on their use in the United States rather than on any serious investigation of what Japanese students want that they are not already getting. Even in the United States, where these systems have been widely used for years, it is far from clear that they achieve the goals by which their use is justified. It is still less clear that these systems have any notable impact on how high school students select colleges.

Whereas in the past it could be said that colleges existed to measure and validate the ability, or at least the concentration skills, of their students through their entrance examinations, with more and more students entering without taking an examination or passing with lower scores, this is no longer the case. At least some students or their parents seem to think that the four or five years of college life should be more than a moratorium, that students should actually learn something useful in career terms. One pattern that has emerged in response to this is 'double school' in which Japanese college students in non-vocational courses (arts, humanities, social sciences and so on) enroll in highly vocational, often credential-oriented, training courses provided by a category of post-secondary institutions called 'specialised schools' (*senmon gakkō*). This pattern became notable in the late 1990s when many firms started restructuring or downsizing. Press stories reporting the difficulty that generic salarymen, with only company-specific knowledge, had in finding work once laid off stimulated an interest in portable and widely recognised credentials. A 1999 survey of 10,000 students at some 119 colleges nation-wide showed that 26 percent were engaged in 'double schooling' (*Nihon Keizai Shimbun* 7 Dec. 1999; Kuroki 1999: 48).

While 'double schooling' is not directly related to the fall in the number of eighteen-year olds, private colleges have sought to use the phenomenon to their own advantage. Some have moved to offer more vocational and credential-oriented training within their existing structure. For example, Ritsumeikan University in Kyoto offers courses geared to civil service examinations, licensing as a chartered accountant (*kōnin kaikeishi*), licensing as an estate agent (*fudōsan kanteishi*) and so on. Nearly a third of the student body at Ritsumeikan is enrolled in one or more courses.[25] Other colleges have tried to increase their attractiveness to students by facilitating the 'double schooling' on campus either by hiring in lecturers from specialised schools or by contracting with specialised schools to offer 'on campus' programmes (*Nihon Keizai Shimbun* 21 Nov. 2002). Others are turning to practitioners to teach courses previously taught by academics (*Nihon Keizai Shimbun* 28 Dec. 2002; *Daiyosoku* 72–5). Due to the fact that students with credentials even from less prestigious colleges are more successful in, the currently very tight, job market than those without and because the placement rate of its students is one public indicator of the attractiveness of a college, there is a further incentive for private colleges to facilitate 'double schooling'.

The changes in admissions criteria and procedures documented here are significant not only in terms of private college management, but in terms of Japanese education at large. While the importance of entrance examinations and the magnitude of the 'examination hell' has often been exaggerated, the need to pass relatively to extremely rigorous examinations for college admission has had an impact that has extended beyond just the minority of the age-cohort that sought to advance to a prestigious college. Secondary education institutions (middle schools and high schools) in Japan have almost universally practiced 'social promotion'. Serve your time and you graduate whether you have learned anything or not. College entrance examinations indirectly measured the mastery of secondary level material and the quality of education offered by the high schools from which successful applicants had graduated. Similarly, middle school standing, and mastery of the material taught at this level, has been measured by graduate success in entering 'good' high schools (*Nihon Keizai Shimbun* 3 Feb. 2001). Only elementary schools were largely exempt from this pressure. But, as college admission has become easier, students at lower levels, it is argued, have seen that they do not need to work as hard as in the past.[26] This phenomenon, coupled to policy changes made by the Ministry, has produced widespread debate over 'declining academic standards' (*gakuryoku teika*) in Japan.

Beginning in 1998, the mass media began to report a drop in academic ability among students entering college in that year.[27] Particularly striking was the inability of first year students in engineering to perform the kind of simple arithmetic calculations, such as 3/5 divided by 5/9, that they should have learned in elementary school. For several months, magazines, newspapers and the television networks competed with each other by sending out reporters who stood at the entrances of various colleges conducting highly unscientific surveys as to what college students did or did not know. Generally, the reporters were not disappointed. The proportion of students unable to recall things they should have learned in elementary or middle school, particularly basic arithmetic operations, was distressingly high,.

The Ministry initially took the line that there could be no problem because the performance of the Japanese in the Third International Mathematics and Science Study (TIMSS) had not declined compared to previous international comparisons.[28] In contrast, surveys of those actually working in higher education revealed a general sense of declining standards (*Nihon Keizai Shimbun* 20 Dec. 2000). This was soon backed up by hard data showing a real decline, not just at second- and third-tier private colleges, but even at the most prestigious of the national institutions. Remedial education was introduced on a wide scale and rapidly became a new major market for the *juku*. Such courses help to make up for the declining numbers of students enrolling in the conventional college prep courses offered by these schools.[29]

Numerous critics blame poor preparation on Ministry guidelines that, since the 1980s, have reduced the amount being taught in schools under the rubric of 'relaxed education' (*yutori kyōiku*) and encouraged the use of 'student centred learning' (*shirabe gakushu*). Both policies were intended to reduce 'cramming' and 'rote learning'. Critics argue that these changes reduced the total learning period. While there is still some controversy in this area, careful large-scale studies appear to confirm a long-run secular decline.[30] Assuming this is the case, the significance extends beyond Japan. A 1998 college student, who could not 'do fractions', would have entered compulsory education in 1986 and would have received his/her education in those years when Japan was being intensively studied by foreign observers who lavished praise on Japanese instruction in mathematics and science and who saw Japanese practices as the base for reforming instruction in their own countries. Space limitations prevent a full critique of the many problems with this foreign research but, at the very least, it would appear foreign observers failed completely to note the changes that were taking place.[31]

Other critics have seen the apparent 'dumbing down' as the result of changes introduced in college entrance procedures in both the private and public sectors. As of the 2002 academic year, approximately 40 percent of all college students were gaining entrance without taking any formal written test of academic ability (*Nihon Keizai Shimbun* 2 March 2003). Those who do take such tests face a regime quite different from that which faced students a decade ago. 'Choice' has been introduced with predictable results. Allowing would-be students to select 'a science' rather than, for example, requiring them to study physics, led to students concentrating on the science subject that was easiest for them. This has resulted in engineering students who have not studied physics, and medical students who have not studied biology.[32] Related changes have resulted in science and engineering college students who have neither studied nor used any substantial mathematics in the years preceding college entrance. Unlike the rather diffuse relation between content and pedagogy in the colleges and the skills of college students, there is no question that what would-be college students do, or do not study, is explicitly determined by what is required for the entrance examinations. Why these changes to the entrance examination system actually took place, however, is not well understood.

It is something of an urban myth in Japan that more latitude in entrance examinations was introduced in response to the declining number of eighteen-year olds. The change actually took place during the 'Golden Years' when the number of would-be applicants was surging and they came about, particularly in the private sector, in relation not to demographics, but to two other factors: first, the prestige that accrued from having a higher *hensachi* rating and second, the earnings to be made from examination fees. Lower-ranked colleges realized that by allowing students to pick and choose their examination subjects (and avoid unpopular fields such as mathematics and physics), they were able to increase the number of students sitting their exams. This, in turn, led to a higher failure rate at exam, a raised *hensachi* rating and greater prestige. Further, with more students taking the examinations, the schools raked in more in examination fees (Nakamura 2000: 36).

In the same period national institutions also relaxed their entrance requirements although not to the same degree as private schools (*Nihon Keizai Shimbun* 20 Dec. 2000). In the public sector, the prime motivation for such change was probably to meet criticism directly associated with the 'examination hell' although lower prestige national institutions did also gain status from higher competition rates.[33]

In the 1970s and 1980s, when Japan seemed to be No. 1 or at least on its way, numerous widely read works celebrated the astute leadership of the Japanese bureaucracy and the efficacy of Japanese industry and education. Japan seemed an unstoppable juggernaut that would soon dislodge the United States from its manifest destiny as the world's leader in every sphere. In 1989, a call by a prominent American journalist for 'containing Japan' because it threatened American hegemony, reflected the fear inspired by apparent Japanese success in just about everything, including education, at which Americans had thought they excelled.[34] At the beginning of the twenty-first century, however, Japan looks rather different than it did in the 1980s.

In education as in the Japanese economy at large, government seems confused and its policies contradictory. The Ministry has more or less formally recognised that Japanese higher education, even as represented by the most prestigious domestic institutions, is not 'world class'. Nevertheless, as Japanese commentators have observed, Ministry policy of late has led to a proliferation of small, weak private institutions that accept anyone they can get and whose existence only serves to further devalue the significance of attending college. The answer that the Ministry makes to the criticism that its policies are irresponsible is that it cannot go against the prevailing trend of decreasing government regulation (*Yomiuri Shimbun* 10 Jan. 2000). This argument rings hollow given that the Ministry has been increasing the regulatory burden on colleges in other areas, most notably in pushing highly bureaucratic British-style evaluation and review schemes.[35] While in part justifying this increased burden in terms of raising standards to give Japan 'world class universities', Ministry bureaucrats seem to have missed the essential point that the 'world class universities' in the United States and Britain developed with little or no government regulation or guidance of any kind.

In the primary and secondary education sector, the Ministry has prevaricated and waffled. Within months of their introduction, the guidelines introduced as part of a general move to put a cap on what children were expected to learn, were restyled as 'minimum standards'. The *juku* are advertising that 'the public schools are in danger' and attracting new custom from parents who fear that there children will not receive a proper basic education let alone gain entry to a college of any prestige. Major scholars have expressed a fear that Japanese education will have an increasingly strong class character.[36] Parents with the economic wherewithal will send their children to *juku*, heretofore unusual in the early elementary school years, or remove them from the public school system entirely leaving the public sector with an increasing proportion of less affluent and less motivated students.

Seen in this context, the demographic problem faced by private colleges is only one part of a general malaise that hangs over Japanese education. It is nonetheless an important issue because of the validating role and incentive for study that college entrance examinations have provided up to now. Without either a complete structural reform that would introduce new incentives and new validation mechanisms, or an equally radical reform that would give private colleges the financial security and incentives to be truly selective and rigorous providers of higher education, it is probable that further deterioration and bifurcation will follow.[37] A small number of young people from relatively affluent backgrounds will work hard during primary and secondary education to gain admission to the small number of private colleges that can maintain selectivity, while a vastly larger number will coast through primary and secondary education before spending four years at institutions that represent 'higher education' in name only.

Notes

1 For a concise description of the origin of the two-year colleges, see Satō (2001: 24–26). For a description of the 'finishing school' type of two-year college, see McVeigh (1997).
2 Amano (1999: 21) notes the entrepreneurial and expansive character of private institutions in Japan.
3 For a striking example of this, see the colophon for Tanioka et al. (1997).
4 Teikyō University is an extreme example of this. The various Okinaga family members who occupy top positions in this university regularly attract the attention of gossip and scandal sheets. As an institution, Teikyō has attracted the attention of the broadsheet newspapers as well as the tax authorities for the handling of 'donations' to its medical school, a large fraction of which

are alleged to have gone to one or more members of the Okinaga family (Nihon Keizai Shimbun 11 March 2003; Shūkan Shinshō, 31 Jan. 2002). Teikyō is part of a 'group' (Japanese jargon for conglomerate) that controls three colleges in the United States; six four-year colleges and five two-year colleges in Japan; ten high schools and a variety of related institutions (data from Daigaku Ranking 2001: 462–63).

5 As an example, underworld involvement is alleged in the takeover of Morioka College, a medium scale private conglomerate that was originally of the founder-owner-operator type (Kuji 1997). An Internet search on shiritsu daigaku (private universities) and bōryokudan (criminal gangs) will turn up numerous instances of local citizens asserting underworld involvement in private colleges.

6 As noted below, private institutions in Japan collect 'contributions' from enrolled students, but these 'contributions' are not voluntary and have to be considered a surcharge on tuition.

7 Amano (1999: 31); Nihon Keizai Shimbun , 5 April 2003. The most recent figure may be slightly overstated since it is based on data for the 133 colleges that are members of the Japan Federation of Private Colleges (Nihon shiritsu daigaku renmei).

8 Throughout this paper, an arbitrary exchange rate of 100 yen to the dollar has been used.

9 Hōsei University attracted considerable press coverage when it submitted to examination and received a rating of AA – putting it in a league with firms such as Mitsubishi Heavy Industries and Tokyo-Mitsubishi Bank (Nihon Keizai Shimbun , 8 March 2003).

10 Concerning the general lack of published financial data, see Iwauchi (2000: Ch. 6). For an accountancy manual specific to the legally mandated accounting procedures, see Nonaka et al. (2001).

11 See Kuroki (1999: 30–31). Reports on private institution finances issued by the Ministry tend to be three or four years out of date. It is not clear whether this is due to gross bureaucratic inefficiency or a desire not to create alarm by publishing dire information in a timely fashion.

12 '*Shōshika susumi 17 no daigaku, tandai ga boshū teishi*' (As the birthrate declines 17 universities and colleges stop recruiting) at asahi.com, http://www.asahi.com/edu/nyushi/OSK200303130010. html.

13 Ministry policy on the establishment of new colleges and faculties has varied considerably in the post-war years, see Amano (1999: 20–35).

14 Although many two-year colleges are explicitly for women, the category as a whole became overwhelmingly female through preference not regulation. Recently, the popularity of four-year colleges for women, has also been on the decline, see *Aera* 2 July.

15 For an example of a provincial institution under-quota despite aggressive recruiting of foreign students, see *Mainichi Shimbun* (Yamaguchi edition), 14 April 2000 and 27 April 2000.

16 See *Nihon Keizai Shimbun* 30 March 2002. According to an article in a popular weekly magazine, the management of this two-year college was also involved in golf course development and refuse removal (*Shūkan Shinshō*, 27 Dec. 2001: 30).

17 See *Nihon Keizai Shimbun* 20 Nov. 2002; Yomiuri Weekly, 17 March 2002. 'Black ships' (*kurobune*) is a reference to Commodore Perry and his gunboat diplomacy that broke Japanese seclusion. It is a standard expression used whenever Japanese think they are being forced to accept foreign competition.

18 For a readable and informed study of the portion of the Korean minority in Japan that has been oriented to the North, see Ryang (1997).

19 See Nakamura 2000: 126–30; *Nihon Keizai Shimbun* 13 Nov. 1999, 2 Feb. 2001 and 21 June 2002. Until March of 1999, private colleges were essentially prohibited from expanding their existing facilities in Tokyo as part of measures intended to relieve urban crowding. Those institutions that made the mistake of moving entirely to the Tama region find themselves at a severe disadvantage because of a poor transportation infrastructure and few opportunities for students to take side jobs.

20 One possible exception to this rule may be in suburban areas where women can drive during non-peak hours to a two-year college (*Nihon Keizai Shimbun* 4 Dec. 2002).

21 For a highly one-sided description of undergraduate behaviour at low-ranked institutions, see McVeigh (2002). In Japanese, see *Daigaku mirai mondai kenkyūkai* (2001: 110–15); *Nihon Keizai Shimbun* 5 Feb. 2001 and 16 Nov. 2002.

22 For a detailed description of the specific problems faced by two-year colleges, see Satō (2001: 39–59).

23 This description is based largely on the explanation of 'AO admissions' given in the on-line materials of Kawaijuku and the comments of Keio professor, Ono Hiroshi, contained therein. A more complete treatment can be found in Ono (2000).

24 See Kuroki (1999: 63–68). The Ministry has also made provision for the *Daigaku nyūgaku shikaku kentei* (College Entrance Qualification Examination) to be taken twice yearly. High school dropouts and graduates of 'ethnic schools' in Japan, which are not accredited or legally recognised, take this examination (*Nihon Keizai Shimbun* 9 Aug. 2000).

25 See Kuroki (1999: 49). Vocational programmes are not necessarily white-collar or clerical. One private college in Kyoto achieved some notoriety by offering the first course in 'cartooning' (*manga*) in Japan (*Nihon Keizai Shimbun* 24 Nov. 2002).

26 Preparation schools (*yobiko*) find students starting their examination-directed study later in the year than previously and surveys report as many as half of the students at mid-rank schools saying that they did little or nothing in the way of special study for their entrance examinations (*Nihon Keizai Shimbun* 8 July 2000).

27 A convenient collection of the more serious journalistic treatments of the subject is Nakai (2001); see also *Nihon Keizai Shimbun* 26 Sept. 1999. Publishing on this subject subsequently turned into a minor 'growth industry' to the point that even a partial listing of the available titles would take more space than is available here.

28 Both the Ministry and foreign observers, who have lavished praise on the Japanese education system on the basis of TIMSS, have overlooked, or deliberately ignored, the fact that TIMSS measures the knowledge of

elementary and middle school students, not college-age students, and most certainly not the general work force.

29 The heretofore distant, and sometimes overtly hostile, relationships between colleges and prep schools seems to be changing. In addition to 'out-sourcing' their remedial programmes to prep schools, some colleges also have these schools write their entrance examinations. A still more recent pattern is to get 'marketing' advice from the prep schools (*Nihon Keizai Shimbun* 4 March 2003).

30 The results of a large-scale study led by Kariya Takehiko (2002) received wide press attention. Others have subsequently confirmed the patterns he found.

31 Foreign scholars who studied Japanese elementary and secondary education from the mid-1980s were, to varying degrees, trying to explain Japanese economic and technological performance and to provide reform models for the US or the UK. That a prime worker in 1985 (aged 35) would have begun their education in the mid-1950s, or that a manager or executive (aged 55) would have started their education in the mid-1930s, does not seem to have been recognised by any of those scholars who examined Japanese education in the 1980s and later, in terms of the economic performance of the 1980s and later. Examples of scholarly works praising Japanese instruction include Stevenson and Stigler (1992), Stigler (1999) and Whitburn (2000). For a largely uncritical discussion of the context in which US research in this area was carried out, see LeTendre (1999).

32 See *Nihon Keizai Shimbun* 20 July 2002; in English, see DeCoker (2002).

33 After the debate on declining standards erupted, the Ministry in effect ordered national universities to return to the earlier pattern of seven tests in five subject areas. Critics immediately noted that while telling universities to tighten up, it was also telling high schools to 'dumb down' (*Nihon Keizai Shimbun* 16 Nov. 2000 and 23 Aug. 2000).

34 See Fallows (1989); and for a recent critique of this and other 'revisionist' writings, see Lindsey and Lukas (1998).

35 Unlike Britain where the Research Assessment Exercise (RAE) and the Teaching Quality Assessment schemes have been essentially ignored by the popular press, the administrative burden and financial costs of the mandated Japanese system have received attention even in popular weekly magazines (e.g. *Yomiuri Weekly* 2 Feb. 2003).

36 Kariya Takehiko (2002) is perhaps the most prominent but by no means the only scholar expressing this concern.

37 Serious reform proposals that go beyond tinkering with the traditional entrance examination system are few and far between. For a thoughtful counter-proposal that essentially disappeared without a trace, see *Nihon Keizai Shimbun* 22 Jan. 2001.

References

Aera (2001) 'Shiritsu kyōgakka no honryū' (Torrent of mergers in private universities), *Aera* 2 July, pp. 12–15

Amano, Ikuo (1999) *Daigaku: Chōsen no jidai* (Universities: Challenging times), Tokyo: Tokyo Daigaku Shuppankai.

Daigaku mirai mondai kenkyūkai (2001) *Daiyosō: 10 nen go no daigaku* (10 year forecasts for universities), Tokyo: Tōyō Keizai Shinbunsha.

Daigaku Ranking (2001) *Daigaku ranking: 2001 nenpan* (University rankings: 2001 edition), Tokyo: Asahi Shinbunsha.

DeCoker, Gary (2002) 'Deregulating Japan's high school curriculum: The unintended consequences of education reform' in DeCoker, Gary (ed.) *National Standards and School Reform in Japan and the United States,* New York: Teachers College Press, pp. 141–57.

Fallows, James (1989) 'Containing Japan', *Atlantic Monthly* (May): 40–54, available at http://www.theatlantic.com/issues/89may/fallows.htm.

Greenlees, John (1998) 'Japan shy of target', *Times Higher Education Supplement*, (March 20).

Iwauchi, Ryōichi (2000) *Shidai kakumei no jōken o tō* (An enquiry into the revolution in private universities), Tokyo: Gakubunsha.

Kariya, Takehiko. 2002. *'Gakuryoku teika' no jittai* (Is there a decline in academic standards?). Tokyo: Iwanami Shoten.

Kuji, Tsutomu (1997) *Morioka daigaku giwaku o tsuikyu suru* (Investigation of suspicions at Morioka University), Tokyo: Shinsensha.

Kuroki, Hiroshi (1999) *Meisō suru daigaku* (Universities losing direction), Tokyo: Ronsōsha.

LeTendre, Gerald (ed.) (1999) *Competitor or Ally? Japan's Role in American Educational Debates*, New York: Falmer.

Lindsey, Brink and Aaron Lukas (1998) 'Revisiting the "revisionists": The rise and fall of the Japanese economic model', *Trade Policy Analysis* No. 3 (July 31), available at http://www.freetrade.org/ pubs/pas/tpa-003.html.

McVeigh, Brian (1997) *Life in a Japanese Women's College: Learning to be Ladylike*, London: Routledge.

McVeigh, Brian (2002) *Japanese Higher Education as Myth*, Armonk, New York: M. E. Sharpe.

Nakai, Kōichi (ed.) (2001) *Ronsō: Daigaku hōkai* (Controversy: University collapse), Tokyo: Chūō Kōronsha.

Nakamura, Chūichi (1999) *Abunai daigaku: 2000 nenpan* (Dangerous universities: 2000 edition), Tokyo: Sangokan.

Nakamura, Chūichi (2000) *Daigaku tōsan* (University bankruptcy), Tokyo: Tōyō Keizai Shinpōsha.

Nonaka, Ikue, FujioYamaguchi and Morihiko Umeda (2001) *Shiritsu daigaku zaisei bunseki ga dekiru hon* (Analysis of private university finances), Tokyo: Ŏtsuki Shoten.

Ōno, Hiroshi (2000) *Daigaku AO nyūshiki to wa nanda?* (Introduction to the AO university entrance test), Tokyo: Mainichi Shinbunsha.

Ryang, Sonia (1997) *North Koreans in Japan: Language, Ideology, and Identity,* Boulder Colorado: Westview Press.

Satō, Susumu (2001) *Daigaku no ikinokori senryaku* (Strategy for university survival), Tokyo: Shakai Hyōronsha.

Stevenson, Harold W. and James W. Stigler (1992) *The Learning Gap: Why Our Schools Are Failing and What We Can Learn from Japanese and Chinese Education*, New York: Simon & Schuster.

Stigler, James W. (1999) *The Teaching Gap: Best Ideas from the World's Teachers for Improving Education in the Classroom*, New York: Free Press.

Tanioka, Taro et al. (1997) *Shiritsu daigaku no henkaku to kasseika no hōkō* (Directions for private university reform and revitalisation), Tokyo: Dōyūkan.

Whitburn, Julia (2000) *Strength in Numbers: Learning Maths in Japan and England*, London: National Institute of Economic and Social Research.

7 The Japanese Student Perspective on Universities

Marina Lee-Cunin

> University plays an important role when it's difficult for us to know what our own dreams are for the future but I think there are many students who are going to lose themselves by relying on university too much. I don't think we should graduate from university simply by obtaining the necessary credits for graduation. We must find out what we want to do in the future through the whole university process from the first year right up to graduating from university. (Student 163)

This was just one of the many comments made by first-year students when asked of their opinion of the university system in Japan. Their comments were part of the results of an exploratory survey into student perceptions of their university life. Within the context of the current Japanese higher education reform process, the student experience should be an important component. However, to date, much of the English-language literature has ignored the student voice (see Beauchamp 1991; Cummings 1980; Cutts 1997; Dore 1976; Dorfman 1987; Ellington 1991; Howarth 1991; Ishida 1993; Lynn 1988; Okano and Tsuchiya 1999; Rohlen and LeTendre 1996; Vogel 1979 and White 1987). Further, there seems to be an underlying assumption that Japanese students have not achieved a level of critical consciousness that would enable them to give an informed opinion on the education they are receiving. However, there are other societal changes and pressures affecting these young people today apart from their educational environment which could facilitate the development of a young critical self. It is important that students have the opportunity to reflect upon their status as students as well as comment on it, rather than allow a stereotype to effectively justify the exclusion of their viewpoint.

This paper presents the results of a survey that took place between December 1998 and January 1999 at the Faculty of Economics at

Shiga University. It examines students' comments regarding the educational environment which they were experiencing, explores some of the non-academic areas of student life and concludes that the student perspective is a necessary element of any viable reform and should be adequately represented and reflected as such.

Introduction: Images of Japanese students

Specific research on Japanese students is sparse but the literature that commented on students often made reference to two dominant images a) the quiet, uncritical student type; and b) the academically lazy student type who viewed university as a playground. With respect to the former image, Greenwood (1997) explained the Japanese student's silence in class was associated with elements in Asian culture. Silence was said to be a cultural sign of respect from the listener to the speaker. This was especially significant if the speaker was a person of high social status such as a teacher (Greenwood 1997: 82).

The concept of 'losing face' and issues of shame were also relevant in this context (Benedict 1946: 222). Taylor noted that Japanese students were afraid to ask questions because they were afraid someone might ridicule them for not knowing the answer (Taylor 1983: 98). The Japanese expression 'the nail that sticks up gets hammered down' (*deru kugi wa utareru*) was often cited as an explanation for students' possible reticent behaviour in class. Group dynamics and harmony in Japan were highly valued so that a person could be punished for standing out even for being too conspicuously intelligent or opinionated (Taylor 1983: 98). However, in the research on Asian students as English language learners, it was suggested that where there was student passivity or reticence, it was more likely that specific issues such as teaching methodologies and language proficiency level were to blame rather than cultural attributes (Cheng 2000: 436; Liu and Littlewood 1997: 372–3).

McVeigh (2001) suggested another perspective on Japanese students' shyness and reluctance to stand out. He stated that it could be 'a vague fear' resulting from a specific kind of schooling focused on taking examinations rather than spontaneous learning. He further argued that the students were more likely to question the value of schooling itself and overall, have lost confidence in education (McVeigh 2001).

Japanese students' lack of critical thinking or original thought was also said to be product of the education process (Ellington 1991: 127). A hierarchical, fact-based, exam-oriented education system was seen to produce un-inquisitive, uncritical and unreflective students (Davidson 1995). Davidson stated that Japanese students had trouble expressing ideas in English because, in general, 'they do not have any opinions; and if they have opinions, they often cannot explain or justify them'. However, he equally noted that many students were enthusiastic about being challenged intellectually (Davidson 1995).

The report of a survey of students commissioned by the Ministry in January 1995 was one of few sources that presented a specifically different image of students. 'The survey results indicate that students in this age of widespread higher education are strongly motivated to learn...Yet the results also show that many students are dissatisfied with university education." (Ministry of Education 1995)

The literature also noted that club activities and part-time jobs (*arubaito*) consumed much of Japanese students' time and energy. Students seemed to be at university to experience a full social life as opposed to an academic one. Club activities had particular importance, as they were often linked to future employment. Strong links were maintained between the club alumni and present club members and this relationship often assisted in introductions to prospective employers (Ellington 1991: 148). Part-time jobs also played a role as a semi-introduction to an independent adult life. Students tended to work in the service sector in establishments, such as the 24-hour convenience stores or fast food restaurants, or as private home tutors to high school students (Sugimoto 1997: 130).

Dropout rates for students in Japan were usually low. Kinmonth (2001) noted that in the past, there had been little to prevent students who registered for four years (or longer) from graduating. It was further noted that over 80 percent of students obtained their degree in the required four-year period (Dearing 1997). This high graduation rate was linked to the idea that graduates, particularly from the social science and humanities fields, tended to be recruited simply as 'raw material' for companies (Teichler 1997: 272).

Recently, however, as the percentage of high school students continuing to university has increased, there has also been an increase in the proportion of college students who drop out. Some reasons for leaving included students reporting a general lack of interest in higher education; a significant number of them stating that they attended university simply to please their parents; to remain in contact with their friends; or because there was not anything compelling for them to do at the time (Kinmonth 2001).

The results of the survey

Background information on the student-participants

The student survey was carried out between December 1998 and January 1999. Students were asked on a voluntary basis to complete a confidential questionnaire. During the academic year from April 1998 to March 1999, the total student population at the Faculty of Economics of Shiga University totalled 2,394. The total student number who participated in the survey was 272 (11.36 percent). However, it should be noted that the research primarily targeted first year students and in this case, 37.81 percent (197 students) of the total first-year student population (521 students) participated. Further, 75 second to fourth-year students also participated.

The division of the student-participants along gender lines showed that 73.5 percent were male, while 26.5 percent were female. Therefore, the proportion of women was slightly lower than the official Ministry statistics which stated that for the year 1998, students at four-year universities were 65.11 percent male (a total of 1,737, 215 individuals) and 34.88 percent female (a total of 930,871 individuals) (Japan Information Network 2000). The lower numbers for female students at Shiga University could perhaps be accounted for by the fact that Economics was still considered a 'male' subject area.

In terms of academic year of the student-participants; 72.4 percent were first year, 18 percent were second year and the remaining 9.6 percent were third to fifth-years. The students were largely in the traditional age range that would be expected with 18.4 percent being 18 years and younger, 64 percent being 19–20 years old and 17.7 percent were 21 years and over. Students would be generally expected to finish high school at 18 years old. However, some students may have taken a year out to specifically study for the university entrance examinations becoming what is known as *rōnin*. The results found that 23.9 percent of first-year student-participants had been *rōnin*.

The academic experience

1 The process of entrance to university

The transition from high school to university and the examinations that are taken within this process, all have some effect on a student's perception of the university which s/he attends and the major which s/he chooses. The majority of students surveyed followed the traditional path to university: 92.3 percent attended a general high school, then 94.8 percent took the national university examination together with a university specific one and 68.4 percent entered university directly or after one year (23.9 percent) having adopted the status of *rōnin*.

More than half of the students (51.2 percent) stated that the decision to go to university was one of their own but over a third (37.4 percent) confirmed that their parent/s encouraged them to attend university. Only 4.1 percent of students stated that friends and relatives had encouraged them but 7.2 percent checked 'Other' and stated that their high school or their high school teacher had encouraged them to further their education. This was important as showed that high school and high school teachers were another significant influence on a student's decision.

> I do not think everyone has to go to university. In fact there are many people without a BA who have succeeded in their fields, and there are many ways to go apart from going to university. However, I am not saying that going to university does not make sense. I think we can obtain a lot of things at university. (Student 8)

Students were also asked about their general views on the university entrance examination system. The strong belief that a person's career opportunities are dependent upon where s/he went to university is still prevalent in society. Therefore, the university entrance examinations can be said to play a most crucial role in the process from school to work. In the current recession, large companies in Japan are still more likely to ensure life-long employment with good benefits to graduates from prestigious universities rather than focus upon the competence of an individual graduate. Therefore, once a student has entered what can be considered a good university such as a prestigious private one or a national one, s/he may be fairly certain of a good chance of being recruited by an established company (Teichler 1997).

The results showed that 73.2 percent of the students stated that there should be an entrance examination system for universities in general. This could be due to the fact that most of the student-participants were in their first year and felt they had achieved a 'hard worked for' goal by passing the entrance examinations. Therefore, they were unlikely to criticise the system. Another reason could be that they did not know of any alternative to assessment for higher education apart from examinations.

When asked if the examination format should be changed from its current format, just over a half (54.8 percent) of students stated yes, while 21 percent said no, and 23.9 percent said they didn't know. Presently, entrance examinations take the form of multiple choice and short answer questions which require high school students to memorise the subject matter in detail. Takeuchi noted that the entrance examination had more to do with effort and accumulation of facts rather than intellect, cultural capital and native ability (Takeuchi 1997: 191). Therefore, students seemed to be aware of the failings of the examination process despite still being in favour of maintaining some kind of entrance examination system.

2 Choosing Shiga University, the Faculty of Economics, and a subject major

There were several reasons that students chose to attend Shiga University. The majority of students (36.2 percent) stated that they entered Shiga University either because they could not enter their first choice university or because they had failed the national university entrance examination but passed the entrance examination for Shiga University. This indicated that many student-participants had not specifically wanted to study at Shiga University and had hoped to attend university elsewhere.

A further 29.2 percent of students stated that they chose Shiga University because they felt that they needed higher education for a better job. This implied that any university would have filled this need. Yano suggested that by high school, most students had already considered that it made economic sense to continue on to higher education as the difference in lifetime earnings between a college graduate and a high school graduate was greater than the difference between a high school graduate and a junior high school graduate (Yano 1997: 208).

Twenty-one point eight percent of student-participants stated that they attended university because they did not wish to enter the labour market as yet. Traditionally, university has had, and still has to a greater extent, a reputation of being a leisure land for young people (Ellington 1991: 147). Therefore, while they delay working in the labour market, many students may simply view university as a) the place to improve their leisure and sports skills via the university clubs; b) to obtain a part-time job in order to have extra money for hobbies and personal use; and/or c) to live alone thereby experiencing a semi-independent life within a secure and 'socially approved of' environment.

Twenty-four point four percent of students stated that they chose Shiga University because it offered the course in which they wished to study. It should be noted that Shiga University is the largest economics faculty in the country and is ranked fairly high among universities. Fifteen point six percent stated that they chose Shiga University for reasons concerning intellectual enjoyment also implying that other universities could have also fulfilled the needs of these students by offering other types of academic programmes that interested them. However, only 4.5 percent of students specifically stated that they chose Shiga University because it was their first choice of university.

It should also be noted that 95.2 percent of students stated that Shiga University was the first university that they had attended. The remainder had come from a) a specialised high school; b) entered through the recommendation of their high school (*suisen nyūgaku*) or c) taken one of the following examinations to enter Shiga University: the examination for overseas students, for mature/working people, for students who have lived abroad for more than 3 years, or for students transferring to a four-year university. Therefore, for the majority of student-participants, Shiga University was their first experience of higher education.

Overall, these results indicated that the majority of students seemed to be at Shiga University by default rather than by specific choice and this would have a significant influence on their initial perceptions of Shiga University and university life in general. In reality, it would also mean that there were a large number of first-year students who were initially reluctant to be positive about attending Shiga University. This did not favour the university, but the results lead to a general understanding of some of the reasons for the general lack of enthusiasm among students with respect to their academic studies not only at Shiga University, but perhaps at other universities as well.

Students were also asked why they chose to study at a faculty of economics. Their responses were similar to those regarding their choice to enter Shiga University, although their reasons were prioritised differently. The results showed that the majority of students (37.5 percent) wanted to study for intellectual enjoyment, while the second reason given was the usefulness of an economics degree for a future job (26.5 percent). Although it has generally been confirmed in previous research that there is little relationship between what students study at university and the tasks which they carry out at their future jobs, on an individual level, some students may have still entertained the idea that the relationship between economies and the business world would make economics a good subject to study (OECD 1993: 25).

The other results indicated that students could not find any other interesting major in which they wished to study and therefore, opted to study within an economics faculty (17.3 percent). It should be noted that 13.6 percent of students stated that this faculty was automatically assigned to them on the basis of their application. These students also stated that the reasons they had been automatically assigned was because they had a) failed the national university entrance exams, b) scored low in the national exams but passed the Shiga University entrance exam solely or, c) did not get into their first choice university. Lastly, 13.2 percent of students stated that they had a mathematics problem and, therefore, chose economics as the next option area within which to study. The use of statistics and the field of econometrics made economics a likely second choice for these students.

It would appear then that although the results as to why students chose Shiga University were not favourable to the university, the results as to why students chose an economics faculty were a little more positive. Over 50 percent of students wanted to study economics either for intellectual enjoyment or for its perceived usefulness in future employment and a further 17.9 percent chose the Economics as a second choice toma mathematics-based major. This would then suggest that students' more positive attitudes towards studying at the Faculty of Economics could also have a significant impact on their general perceptions of Shiga University, thereby changing their initial negativity about the university into more positive perceptions regarding studying at the Faculty. It would appear that once students arrived at the university, well over half of them wished to study within the Faculty of Economics.

Students were also asked whether they had ever thought of changing their major. This was specifically aimed at examining the extent to which their particular major could be an influential factor in their initial perceptions of their academic experience. Within the Faculty of Economics, students could choose to major in one of six departments. It should be noted that over half of the student-participants (54.4 percent) majored in economics, followed by business administration (17.3 percent), accounting (11.4 percent), information processing and management (11 percent), finance (3.3 percent) and social systems (2.6 percent).

The results showed that 60.3 percent of students indicated that they would not change their major while 39.3 percent said they would. Out of the 39.9 percent, the largest number of students (37.6 percent) stated that they wished to change their major because they had found another one that they preferred.

> I wanted to change because Management is more interesting than Economics. (Student 192)

Although most courses in the first year were compulsory courses which had to be taken within each major, students were also able to choose some option courses from another department and, therefore, would have experienced a range of courses within and outside of their major in their first year.

A further 32.1 percent stated that they wanted to change their major because they could not initially choose the major that they wanted. This was because of the specific system of allocating majors at Shiga University. As there were only a specific number of places offered within each department, when a major became over-subscribed, students were simply allocated another major. This allocation was based on their scores at the Shiga University entrance examination and on what they had personally indicated as being their first, second or third choice major.

A further 22.9 percent of students stated that they wanted to change their major because they were disappointed in the major that they chose. In most instances, students had little or no prior knowledge of their chosen subject as they were unlikely to have studied it in high school. However, it could also indicate issues arising from the structure and nature of courses themselves, such as, how the courses were designed and taught, and the previous level of knowledge required in order to take them. Such issues were raised in the student interviews.

The other reasons (14.7 percent) for wishing to change majors were a) being influenced by family and friends, b) realising the major was not useful for future employment and/or c) that their major was too difficult to understand. It should be noted that half of all Economics majors wished to change this major (50.3 percent) whereas one third of students in the other five majors indicated that they wished to change.

However, the 60.3 percent of students who did not wish to change their current major seemed consistent with the results that indicated that a significant number of students were fairly satisfied with studying at the Faculty of Economics. Although, one third of students did wish to change their major, this was largely because (a) they had found another major that they liked; (b) experienced disappointment in the major that they had originally chosen; or (c) had been automatically allocated a major.

3 Do you like your university?

Given the fact that the majority of student-participants had stated directly, or indirectly, that Shiga University was not their first choice university, it is little wonder that when asked if they liked this university, the results showed that only 22.1 percent of students stated that they did whereas 51.8 percent said they were more or less neutral towards the university and 22.1 percent said they did not like it. These results were concerning as most of these students were in their first year. The implication was that a large proportion of these students will be attending Shiga University for another three years with either a neutral or negative attitude towards the university and this would certainly have some negative impact on their attitude towards their academic studies.

> I think that the majority of the students at the Faculty of Economics do not have a desire to come here to study, but just came somehow. (Student 207)

When students were asked whether they would still attend Shiga University if they had the opportunity to change to another university, 3.7 percent of students stated that they would definitely attend Shiga University if they had to start over; 19.5 percent stated they would probably attend this university; 40.1 percent stated they would probably not attend this university; and a further 36.4 percent said they would definitely not attend this university. Therefore, faculty members needed to be aware that a majority of their students did not have a real desire to attend the university and this should be considered in part, when developing teaching methods, classes and course structure.

4 Courses: structure, assessment, study skills, student comprehension

It is suggested that the students' ability to choose their own courses might also have some impact on their perceptions of the university as a whole. The results showed that the majority of first-year students at Shiga University took more than twelve courses in a semester (87.2 percent) while the remainder took between nine and twelve courses (11.7 percent). Each course was 1.5 hours per week therefore the total course-load in hours for most students was 18.0 hours per week.

> I think that there are some courses in which I can't learn anything useful for my future. Economics is different from what I expected and I often think that I should quit university. However, I don't have any job that I want to do. (Student 157)

The majority of courses for the first-year students were compulsory and there were a number of complaints about having to take such courses. However, there were also some courses that students could individually choose to take. The results showed that 94.1 percent of students stated that their first reason for choosing a course was because it was compulsory. (Students were permitted multi-answers in this question). Their second reason for choosing courses was split into two categories. The first category was choosing a course for intellectual enjoyment (54.6 percent) while the second category was choosing a course because it was 'easy-to-pass' (53.1 percent). Among the other reasons for choosing courses were a) because their friend had previously taken it (17.3 percent), b) because they liked the teacher – which could include liking a teacher whose class was considered 'easy-to-pass' (8.9 percent), c) because the course was connected to an outside interest or hobby (9.2 percent) and/or d) because the course was connected with future employment.

Regarding the forms of course assessment, most of the courses were the traditional, 'end-of-semester' 100 percent examination-based courses with the exception of some language courses, which included assignment work depending on the individual teacher. Over 95 percent of students confirmed that they sat written examinations at the end of the first semester and a further 93.4 percent stated that they would take between five and more than twelve exams at the end of the academic year.

Students were also asked about their general academic understanding of their courses. The course was defined as the course material and the lectures. The results showed that only 10 percent of students stated that they understood 75 percent of their entire courses. Only 36.9 percent understood about 50 percent of the courses, with 47.6 percent stating that they understood less than 50 percent or very little. In addition, there were 5.1 percent of students who said they did not understand the courses at all. Therefore, just over half of the students came away from courses understanding from less than 50 percent of it to nothing at all.

These results could indicate that students had insufficient time to 'digest' the amount and depth of information required for courses and subsequent examinations. However, students were also asked how much time they spent outside of the classroom studying for their various courses. The results showed that 32.5 percent studied less than one hour; 28.8 percent studied between one and three hours; 25.5 percent studied between three and six hours; and 13.3 percent studied from seven hours or more. These were significant results as they pointed to conflicting issues concerning the extent of student responsibility and genuine difficulties in the comprehension of courses which could result in students 'giving up' trying to understand them through personal study.

> University should give more education on general knowledge. Our general knowledge is limited and should be broadened because we study for twelve years only to prepare for the university entrance exam. (Student 38)

The reading skills of students were also questioned in connection with their study behaviour in order to determine the extent of extra information students were acquiring outside of the classroom. Approximately 75 percent of student-participants stated that they read between one to five of the assigned textbooks, while 12.5 percent read between five and ten and 10.3 percent stated that they had read no assigned textbooks. In terms of non-academic books,

39.9 percent stated that they had read one to five books; 18.8 percent read between five and ten; 15.5 percent read more than twenty; and 14.4 percent had read none.

The reading of articles in academic journals or news/current affairs magazines contrasted with the above in that over half of the students (53.9 percent) stated that they read no articles in the current academic year (1998–1999) while 36.2 percent said that they only read between one and five articles. Newspaper reading showed similar findings with 50.2 percent of students stating that they did not read the newspaper while the remainder (49.8 percent) stated that they did. Of these 49.8 percent of students, 86.2 percent read the television guide; 83.2 percent read the front page and/or headlines; and 66 percent read the sports section. On average, only one third of students read the world reports, the business section and the local news. Therefore, it would seem that unless students were assigned books to read, they did not read other material that contributed to their general knowledge of current and social issues, or directly to their major.

Further, over 80 percent of students stated that they either occasionally practice or never practiced the following: asked about extra reading on subjects; tried to apply acquired class knowledge to a practical situation; tried to see how facts and figures fit together; and used several sources and ideas for one assignment. TThis is very significant as it is these practices that need to be fostered in order to develop individual thought and critical consciousness; and it is these skills that are traditionally thought to be underdeveloped in Japanese students (Dorfman 1987; Beauchamp 1991). However, this was not necessarily the fault of lazy or apathetic students. First-year students are generally unaware of the specific study skills that are required for a university undergraduate course. They most likely use the same study patterns that they formed at high school and in most instances, these are irrelevant at university.

The results of the above sets of questions raised important issues of course structure, course content and student responsibility. Coming from a high school environment, which was full of rote learning and memorisation of numerous facts, many students wanted more general courses that would provide a framework for the numerous facts that they had memorised. They stated that the present course content was too specific and asked for more general knowledge courses and basic foundation classes in all of the majors offered by the faculty, thereby seeming to be quite aware of their own lack of academic ability.

> University should give us opportunities to study broader academic fields. (Student 87)

Some students held the professors personally responsible for the courses that did not take the students' previous educational background into account. It is suggested that a lack of understanding of courses is more likely to lead to students becoming disinterested and unenthusiastic about their academic studies.

> I have been doing my best to listen to the lecturer seriously and also to read the textbook but it does not make sense to make such an effort in his class. I want the lecturer not only to talk but also to consider how to teach, keeping in his mind what the students can understand. (Student 34)

It was expected that students would have less comprehension of classes if they only studied for an hour a week. Student responsibility was an important factor to consider when addressing students' perceptions of their academic experience as it could transform the dynamics of some of the issues that students raised in other areas. Some students had complained that they could not understand their courses but they spent few hours studying and did not read widely.

Further, many might have already prioritised their non-academic lives over their academic ones, such as being absent from classes due to club activities and/or working in a part-time job. The poor study skills of these students would certainly evidence why much of the higher education literature considered that the students' perception of university was one of a 'leisure land'. However, for students who studied for reasonable lengths of time, the return in comprehension levels did not seem to necessarily improve. This would then point to issues or problems arising within course structures rather than issues of student negligence. Students also noted that they chose their option courses based on the information written in the syllabus by the professor. However, when they attended the class, the material was often different from that which had been described and/or the course structure had been dramatically changed. This could lead to frustration among students as well as comprehension difficulties for those who were not prepared for the unexpected shift in content.

> There are also some teachers who lecture on their own research area, which is completely different from what they wrote in the syllabus. (Student 133)

With respect to course assessment, students stated that many courses were both examination and attendance-based ones. In practice, this meant that despite the regular examinations at the end of each semester, students were more likely to pass the entire course if s/he had attended the class on a regular basis. In fact, some students noted that even when they believed that they had failed the examination, they still ended up passing the course due to their attendance record. This type of class was said to be 'easy-to-pass'.

> Come to the class and you'll pass the course, the examination doesn't matter too much. (Student 116)

> I don't think it's good to take a course only to obtain the credit and also I think that the attitude of the teacher who gives easy credits is not good. (Student 119)

5 The faculty-student relationship

Contact and communication between students and faculty members is an important factor in the students' perception of their academic experience. Students were asked specific questions about the nature of their contact with faculty members. These questions had a 100 percent response rate, which was perhaps indicative of the importance of the topic to the students.

The results indicated that there was little contact between faculty members and students in general. Under half of the students (44 percent) stated that they occasionally to very often, talked with faculty members outside of the classroom. However, subsequent interviews with students indicated that they tended to have conversations with a particular minority of faculty members rather than the majority. A further 62.9 percent of students had asked a faculty member for information related to a course but over 82 percent of students stated that they had never made an appointment to see a faculty member in his/her office.

The fairly large number of students who asked a faculty member for course information could be explained by the fact that students tended to become very communicative with staff a) prior to the examination period, b) when important assignments were due or

c) because final grades/exam results were the focus of whether they moved to a higher year. First-year students tended to show more concern about getting information about courses from professors as they were new to the university system.

The majority of students who stated that they had never visited a faculty member in his/her office could suggest that the students' main queries were sorted out in or after the class itself or equally, that the students had labelled it an 'easy-to-pass' course based largely on attendance. However, it should be considered that some students might have felt uncomfortable making appointments to see faculty members out of some kind of trepidation or anxiety about talking to a staff member on a one-to-one basis. Coming from a high school setting, they may have preconceived ideas about university professors with their high social status, and might be uncomfortable about communicating with them.

> I haven't had so many opportunities to talk to teachers but honestly I don't know how to talk to them. (Student 130)

Students were aware that they had entered a new environment and seemed to be looking for a closer relationship with professors where the shared discussion of ideas could take place. However, it seemed that they were waiting for the professor to initiate such a relationship. The small seminar classes (*zemi*) did create such relationships and discussions and notably, these were the classes that students stated they enjoyed most and of which they wished to have more.

Overall, the present relationship that seems to exist between faculty members and students at Shiga University could be aptly described as one of a 'you leave me alone and I'll leave you alone' situation as suggested by Kuh et al. (1998) in commenting on the American faculty-undergraduate student relationship. They further suggested that faculty had disengaged themselves from an intense commitment to students which had resulted in less teaching, less emphasis on keeping office hours and more attention paid towards publications (Kuh et al. 1998: 7).

> There is no atmosphere at university for students and lecturers to talk to each other in a friendly way. (Student 79)

Students also pointed out in the interviews that peer group conversations greatly influenced them in terms of the faculty-student relationship. When one student had a negative experience with a professor, word would spread quickly across the student community, and the professor, his/her course and subject would all be held in the same poor light. However, a few students noted that when good experiences occurred with professors, they tended to have a positive effect in building good relationships between themselves and faculty members in general. They also stated that positive experiences with a faculty member encouraged them to take more of an interest in that course and other courses taught by that particular professor.

> When I questioned a teacher on a part that I couldn't understand in the class in the first year, I was treated unkindly by the teacher and I never asked the teacher again. However, there are also teachers who explain things very kindly even after the class...so much so that I got interested in that subject and class. (Student 197)

6 Future employment

The particular relationship between education and employment in Japan, one of lifetime employment, is crucial to understanding both the Japanese higher education and employment systems. Japanese students have been said to view employment as a lifetime matter and the companies, in turn, view graduates as a long-term investment issue (Yano 1997).

Recently, there have been claims of rising unemployment among university graduates given the current economic climate. Holden (1998) stated that unemployment among graduates and school-leavers has climbed to two or three times the national average. However, Yano (1997) has suggested that unemployment among university graduates is not quite the social problem it seems. Students who experienced difficulty in securing employment in the larger mainstream companies have instead turned to the new service industries or small businesses.

The students participating in this research were asked to name the ideal job they would like to obtain after graduating. The results showed that 12.5 percent stated working in the civil service; 8.8 percent stated they didn't know; 5.5 percent stated being a tax/chartered accountant or in a finance/accounting type job; 3.7 percent stated a job with a trading company, company/bank employee or self–employed; and 2.2 percent stated a variety of jobs from teacher and journalist to musician. The following question asked the students what job they thought they would get in reality. Approximately, 19 percent stated that they didn't know; 15.4 percent stated company employee; 7 percent stated a job in finance or a bank; 2.2 percent stated a job in local government, business, trade and planning departments; and 1.8 percent said they would be an 'office lady' ' – a gender-specific position of low status and with little promotion advantages.

Overall, it would appear that the majority of students either limited their choices in employment matters or were quite practical in their wishes for their ideal job as well as the job they thought they would gain in reality, citing jobs with stability and long term career prospects. For both their 'ideal' or 'realistic' job, the majority of students seemed to be studying within a field appropriate to their expected professions.

There were only a few students who displayed an imaginative or individual flair regarding their ideal job. An even smaller number stated that they were looking, for example, for a job which allowed creativity. It is interesting that those comments predominantly came from female students. Only 10 percent of students gave a reason when asked why they chose a particular job as being ideal. All of them stated that they wished to work for the civil service because it was a stable job. One student also wrote that there seemed to be less discrimination in the civil service. This was the only comment in the study which referred to issues of gender discrimination.

> It seems that there is no sex discrimination in the civil service. (Student 3)

In terms of what job the students thought they would obtain in reality, some students added comments such as:

> I am worried about the possibility of getting a job. (Student 23)

> I can't get a job in a recession. (Student 58)

This reflected the small number of students who were very aware of the current labour market situation for graduates. It was also noteworthy that this section saw comments, specifically from female students, stating that realistically they might end up as an 'office lady'.

> My ideal job is office work in accounting, as the job will improve my ability. I would become an office lady if I can't change myself. (Student 42)

> A job, which allows me to use a certificate, related to Economics because I want to be active in society as a woman. (Student 177)

It should also be noted that the students' demand for new courses all revolved around their future employment needs as 71.4 percent of students stated they would like to take university courses related to a future job; 64.3 percent said they would like to take courses related to general computer skills such as how to use a word processor, make a spreadsheet or browse the Internet; and 57.6 percent stated that they would like to take courses related to specific skills of speaking and listening in English and/or another language related to a future job.

Influences from the home, university and the socio-economic environment all contribute to a student's individual hopes for a particular occupation. Given that a large percentage of students stated that they had unclear goals and uncertainty about their future might be a significant factor in understanding why some students seem to be intellectually 'lost' at university.

7 Student views on the reform of the university system

> Since students are spending a lot of money as well as time, I think that teachers should try to improve their skills in teaching. I think there are many teachers who do not make an effort to improve the way they teach although they are spending time on their own research. It might be true that the quality of students has been reduced and their motivation has been decreasing. However, I do not think this means that teachers do not need to reflect [on how they teach] and this is even more so in national universities. (Student 53)

The students' opinions in the section on university reform were focussed on the three main areas of professors, lectures and teaching methods. The Ministry student survey in 1995 also found that students were most dissatisfied with teaching methods which included dictation and the use of the blackboard; with the lack of courses for gaining jobs or qualifications; with the information processing courses; and with class content and contact with teachers (Ministry of Education 1995).

> It is difficult to understand the teacher…all I get from the class is the points from attendance as well as knowing what the teacher will give in the exam. A 90-minute class has been absolutely wasted. (Student 18).

Students at Shiga University made similar comments regarding lectures and teaching methods. Although students were more critical than positive, their comments were noteworthy, as there appeared to be a consistency in their criticisms. A number of their comments were devoted to class content being uninteresting and their feeling that professors did not really care about the students. This particular comment was also an example of how students might have negotiated their role regarding the situation that faced them in the classroom. They seemed to be quite aware of what they needed to do to pass a course and often the literature on higher education emphasised what students did to gain their course credits and graduate. However, the literature gave little attention to what students said regarding how they would have liked to experience their courses.

> I promised my friends to attend all the classes at university during my rōnin period and am still keeping that promise but there are some classes at university in which I am only waiting for the bell to ring at the end of the period. In almost all of those classes, the lecturer checks attendance. Since there are many students attending the class because the lecturer checks the attendance, it seems that the lecturer lacks the incentive to increase the number of attendance by making the lecture interesting. (Student 105)

Kitamura stated that many professors had failed to attract students to their lectures and instead had turned to their research to find meaning in their lives. In general, few professors had changed or adapted their teaching practices to deal with the students of the nineties (Kitamura 1991: 314). The Ministry stated that with the diversification of the student body and the changing nature of university, teachers had to be aware of their changing responsibilities and continuously enhance their own abilities (Ministry of Education 1995). These comments were applicable to the Shiga University situation. Apart from a minority of faculty members, the majority of faculty seemed to be unconcerned with issues of training and updating their teaching skills or textbooks, or even that some students slept, talked or did homework for other courses in their classes.

> The classes are too noisy...although there are good students listening to the lecture, there are some students behind speaking loudly. The teachers should tell them off more and the faculty should let them not come to the class. (Student 226)

8 Small Classes

Students also requested smaller classes and frequently stated that they enjoyed their *zemi* classes because they were small and personal and they were able to participate in discussions. However, Gilbert argued that although there was a connection between small classes and improved learning, class size was much less important than the characteristics of the instructor, the way a course was organised, and how it was taught (Gilbert 1995).

> I hope that the university increases the number of tutorial classes where I can easily assert my opinion and also listen to others. Through the experiences of talking and giving my opinion, I can check how much I have really understood in terms of the materials, and then I can study further through the feedback. (Student 172)

9 Student Evaluation

Class evaluation by students is carried out in most courses in universities in the United States and the United Kingdom. However, the goal of evaluations was not simply to identify teaching problems but to correct them (Felder 1993:29). The Ministry was supportive of such evaluations taking place stating that it was important to have student evaluation and to apply the results to course developments (Ministry of Education 1995). However, many universities, including Shiga University, had yet to introduce any kind of university-wide evaluation process for faculty members or students.

> I also want the university to give students a questionnaire to ask us about the course at the end of each term and to fire lecturers who are not good at teaching. (Student 36)

Given the overall theme of this survey, it was unexpected that 78.3 percent of students chose to write additional comments at the end of the questionnaire and volunteered to participate in interviews. This suggested that many students, when given the opportunity, were genuinely interested in giving feedback regarding their experiences at university.

> I do not mind answering the questions in this questionnaire and I hope that this questionnaire can contribute to the reform of university. Study at the Economics Department could be more interesting and well-organised facilities are necessary to draw the interests of students. (Student 176)

10 Student as consumer

> Since national universities are supported by tax, teachers at national university should re-consider how they should improve themselves in order to properly educate all the students who have a positive motivation to study. Students are customers...they (teachers) should satisfy the students because we are paying money to the university. (Student 53)

A substantial number of students were also aware of the reform process that was being implemented by the Ministry. A small number of comments were particularly significant as they pointed to student awareness of the link between education, market principles, and their role as consumer. Perhaps these were the first seeds of real reform within universities where the students began to realise that they had some 'buying power' in the higher education market.

> I get angry with the lecturers who are saying that the students at Shiga University don't study. How can they say that when they don't know the students at Shiga University well? The fees of the national universities are not as high as those of private universities but it's still expensive. There are very few lectures which are worth this expense. (Student 133)

The non-academic experience

1 Club activities

> Now, I am not studying hard. But my life in this university is much better because I belong to a club. I can listen to the opinions of my friends or my seniors and I can think about many things. I don't think that university is only about study. I think that the life of university is to study,

> to think about relationships between people and to find new hobbies. (Student 62)

University clubs are extremely important in the lives of many Japanese university students. Club activities are vigorous and students work hard at them, showing a devotion and discipline equivalent to that of any professional sportsperson. This is a mindset that was rarely mirrored in their approach to their academic studies. General images of Japan as being a group-oriented, hierarchical society also found their expression in the behaviour of clubs and their members. Therefore, the club setting is an important area in student life where issues of cultural reproduction can be explored.

Out of all the student-participants, 66.9 percent stated that they were members of a club and 33.1 percent stated they were not. Out of the 74.6 percent of club members who responded, approximately 57 percent stated they attended their club events all the time and a further 32 percent stated that they often or occasionally attended. It should be noted that there was a wide variety of clubs at Shiga but the sports clubs were the most popular.

Club members were also asked if they thought that their club activities affected their schoolwork. Out of the 72.1 percent that responded, 57.1 percent stated that club activities never affected their schoolwork, while 36.2 percent stated that they sometimes affected their schoolwork. However, the interviews found a significant number of students being more honest about the affect of their club activities on classes.

> Once I entered university and joined a club, the club activities became more fun and we tended to be lazy in terms of our study. Fortunately, the club to which I belong definitely takes into account the lectures and it does not interfere with my study or the preparation for tests but I am honestly more interested in club activities than my studies. (Student 193)

Apart from the obvious personal enjoyment that club members experienced, they could also develop other personal skills that may be directly relevant to their future employment needs. Ellington (1992) described the hierarchical pattern of relationships among club members whereby first-year club members (*kōhai*) will use honorific language towards the senior club members (*sempai*). They may run errands for their *sempai* and perform menial tasks at the clubhouse. In return, the *sempai* assisted the *kōhai* in becoming more proficient in the club sport or activity and, more importantly, often assisted their former club members after university.

Therefore, club members continued to learn respect for authority, intensity of effort and loyalty, which were qualities that were often given a place of importance by prospective employers. This club-employment link might be an added incentive for new students to join a particular club and also may be part of the overall reason that clubs are so important to university life.

It seemed likely that *kōhai* would also listen and heed the advice of their *sempai* on academic course choices. Students were asked how often they discussed academic courses with other club members and 41.2 percent of students stated that they did this often or all the time; another 21.3 percent stated they had occasional discussion; and only 9.6 percent said they never had discussions about courses with other club members. This confirmed that students had access to information about academic courses from a variety of sources. Kuh makes an important point that it was the older students who taught the new students how much effort was needed to get by at university (Kuh 1998: 113). It would seem that, even on academic issues, syllabus and faculty advice could take a back seat to the advice of the club *sempai*.

2 The part-time job (arubaito)

> I do not think students at university can study, as we have to work hard. We do not have time. (Student 55)

An important part of student life is the part-time job or *arubaito*. Teichler (1997) stated that many surveys suggested that Japanese students spent almost 15 hours per week working part-time in comparison to the 25 hours they spent studying. He further commented that students in the Humanities or Social Sciences seemed to believe that their field of study, or the grades they obtained, would make little difference in terms of their career opportunities, thereby concluding that studying hard was almost pointless.

The results of the survey showed that 72.4 percent of students had a part-time job; 26.1 percent had no job; and 1.5 percent stated that they had a full-time job. The students were further asked why they had a part-time job. Approximately 35 percent of students stated that they worked for economic-based reasons.

> I can't put any burden on my parents. (Student 100)

> I work for living costs such as rent, food and transportation. (Student 169)

A further 28 percent of students declared they worked for pocket money; to support club activities or hobbies; or for 'extras' e.g. clothes, shopping, driving lessons and car maintenance. Finally, an interesting 16 percent of students said that they worked for work experience, social interaction and personal development: 'To meet people' (Student 35); 'To have experience in society' (Student 58); 'To know the difficulty of earning money' (Student 72).

It is noteworthy that one third of students declared that they worked for basic living costs as opposed to pocket money. Recent sources have indirectly pointed to the necessity of a part-time job for many students, as parents may no longer be able to completely support their children at university given the bleak economic conditions (Japan Information Network 1999). Therefore, like their counterparts in other industrialised countries, Japanese students may increasingly have to work in order to study which in turn may indirectly affect their academic capabilities and study habits.

In terms of the amount of time students spent working at a part-time job, out of the 72.8 percent that responded, 54.1 percent stated that they worked between one and ten hours a week, 33.3 percent worked between 11 and 20 hours a week and a minority of 9.1 percent worked 21 hours or more in a week. This would seem to be fairly average for a student working in a part-time job.

Finally, students were asked to evaluate how much they thought their part-time job affected their academic work. From the 74.6 percent who responded, 44.8 percent of students stated that their job did not affect their schoolwork; 49.3 percent said that their job sometimes interfered with their schoolwork; and only 5.9 percent said it always affected their schoolwork.

> On Sunday, from morning to afternoon, I have a part-time job. I get up at 5 am. I help prepare breakfast in a hotel. I carry the rice, vegetables and fish. It is hard work. I work eight hours with one break so I am very tired. (Student 27)

> Teaching is very difficult. My student understands nothing about English and Maths and he doesn't try to study. He doesn't have the

> passion for studying, so first of all I must give him the passion and will to study. Sometimes, I am not successful and, at times, it makes me confused...Teaching is not only for me but for him too. I want him to go to university. (Student 51)

Most students worked in either service sector jobs, such as in convenience stores or restaurants, or they worked as part-time tutors to high school students preparing to take the university entrance examinations. In the interviews, students generally expressed enthusiasm for their part-time jobs, as they felt that they were gaining 'real life' experience.

Further, the part-time job, similar to the club, played its role in reinforcing and exposing young people to the particular forms of socially acceptable behaviour in the workplace. An example was in the use of polite language (*keigo*) when addressing a senior or person of high status. The employment setting advanced the complex use of *keigo* from speaking to customers, to older employers and managers. In part-time jobs where students tutored junior and high school students, the first-year *kōhai* student became *sempai* to these younger students. Although this seemed to be an outward reversal of roles, the effect was a reinforcement of role behaviour that ensured that young people were consciously aware of and participating in, socially acceptable forms of adult behaviour.

In contrast, clubs and *arubaito* gave students an opportunity to learn or expand a particular sporting or leisure ability; develop social and personal skills; become economically semi-independent; and access larger networks of young people in which they made new friends from a variety of backgrounds and/or perspectives. Further, the club and part-time job were learning environments that continued the reinforcement of socially acceptable behaviour and the values that students had received in their homes and in school education, prior to entering university,.

Overall, the results of the survey demonstrated that the students' perspective on the important issues affecting higher education was in line with the Ministry's rationale for rethinking higher education, as well as with other leading ideas on reform. However, what is crucial is that only the students themselves can highlight the specific practical and realistic ways in which education ideology and policy directly affects them in the classroom. This is why it is essential to include the student viewpoint throughout the reform process.

The student-participants in this study have shown that they are much more conscious of their educational environment than previously thought and should not be underestimated in their understanding of the system of which they are part. Despite the drawbacks of the higher education system, young people are displaying levels of critical awareness in their judgments and insights on their education. These skills are perhaps being drawn from social experiences gained outside of the classroom.

Moreover, the student body is currently in a state of change and transformation. Due to the rapid advances in science and technology among other things, young people are being exposed to a huge variety of new social experiences, which are all having an impact on their ways of seeing the world. But with the introduction of the market principle, higher education will be entering an arena not quite so unfamiliar to this present generation of young consumers. It may be that once the connections are made regarding students as customers and universities as service providers that the student body may not remain so quiet and instead insist that its voice is heard.

References

Beauchamp, Edward R. (ed.) (1991) *Windows on Japanese Education*, New York: Greenwood Press.

Benedict, Ruth (1946) *The Chrysanthemum and the Sword: Patterns of Japanese Culture*, Boston: Houghton Mifflin.

Cheng, X. (2000) 'Asian student's reticence revisited', *System* 28: 435–46.

Cummings, William K. (1980) *Education and Equality in Japan*, Princeton, N.J.: Princeton University Press

Cutts, Robert L. (1997) *An Empire of Schools: Japan's Universities and the Molding of a National Power Elite*, Armonk, NY: M.S. Sharpe.

Davidson, Bruce W. (1995) 'Critical thinking education faces the challenge of Japan', http://chss.montclair.edu/inquiry/spr95/davidson.html (downloaded 05/05/2000).

Dearing Report (1997) *Higher Education in the Learning Society – Appendix 5: Higher Education in Other Countries*, London: National Committee of Inquiry into Higher Education, http://www.leeds.ac.uk/educol/ncihe/ (downloaded 21/09/1999).

Dore, Ronald (1976) *The Diploma Disease: Education, Qualification and Development*, Berkeley: University of California Press.

Dorfman, Cynthia (ed.) (1987) *Japanese Education Today: A report from the U.S study of education in Japan,* Washington, D.C.: U.S. Department of Education.

Ellington, Lucien (1991) *Education in the Japanese Life-Cycle: Implications for the United States*, Lampeter: Edwin Mellen Press.

Felder, Richard M. (1993) 'What do they know anyway? II. Making evaluations work', *Chemical Engineering Education*, 27(1): 28–29.

Gilbert, S (1995) 'Quality education: Does class size matter?', *Association of Universities and Colleges of Canada* 1 (1).

Greenwood, Catherine (1997) 'The quiet girls', *English Journal* (October).

Holden, Constance (1998) 'Crackdown by Japan's universities?', *Science* (Nov. 6).

Howarth, Mike (1991) *Britain's Educational Reform: A Comparison with Japan*, London and New York: Routledge.

Ishida, Hiroshi (1993) *Social Mobility in Contemporary Japan: Educational Credentials, Class and the Labor Market in a Cross-National Perspective*, Stanford: Stanford University Press.

Japan Information Network (2000) http://jin.jcic.or.jp/stat/stats/16EDU61.html, (downloaded 12/10/2000).

Japan Information Network (1999) http://jin.jcic.or.jp/insight/html/focus02/focus02.html (downloaded 06/06/2000).

Kinmonth, Earl H. (2001) 'From Selection to Seduction: The Impact of Demographic Change on Private Higher Education in Japan', paper given at the Asian Studies Conference Japan, Tokyo (June) www2.gol.com/users/ehk/shiritsu.htm (downloaded 18/02/2002).

Kitamura, Kasuyuki (1991) 'The future of Japanese education' in Beauchamp, E. R. (ed.) *Windows on Japanese Education*, New York: Greenwood Press.

Kuh, George D., Herman Blake, Mildred Garcia and Jillian Cans (1998) 'The final report: The undergraduate experience at the University of Nevada, Las Vegas' (May 1) http://www.unlv.edu/studentserv/interim_report/final/ (downloaded 11/10/1999).

Liu, Ngar-Fun and William Littlewood (1997) 'Why do many students appear reluctant to participate in classroom learning discourse?', *System* 25 (3): 371–84.

Lynn, Richard (1988) *Educational Achievement in Japan: Lessons for the West*, London: Macmillan Press.

McVeigh, Brian J. (2001) 'Higher education, apathy and post-meritocracy', *The Language Teacher Online,* 25 (10 October), The Japan Association for Language Teaching. http://langue.hyper.chubu.ac.jp/jalt/pub/tlt/01/oct/mcveigh.html (downloaded 29/01/2001).

Ministry of Education (1995) *Remaking Universities: Continuing Reform of Higher Education White Paper* http://wwwwp.monbu.go.jp/eky1995/ (downloaded 13/10/1998).

Organisation for Economic Co-operation and Development (OECD) (1993) *Higher Education and Employment: The Case of Humanities and Social Sciences,* Paris: OECD.

Okano, K. and M. Tsuchiya (1999) *Education in Contemporary Japan: Inequality and Diversity,* Cambridge: Cambridge University Press.

Rohlen, Thomas P. and Gerald Le Tendre (eds.) (1996) *Teaching and Learning in Japan*, Cambridge: Cambridge University Press.

Sugimoto, Yoshio (1997) *An Introduction to Japanese Society*, Cambridge: Cambridge University Press.

Takeuchi, Yo (1997) 'The self-activating entrance examination system: Its

hidden agenda and its correspondence with the Japanese "salary man"', *Higher Education* 27: 183–98.
Taylor, J. (1983) *Shadows of the rising sun*, Tokyo: Charles Tuttle.
Teichler, Ulrich (1997) 'Higher education in Japan: A view from outside', *Higher Education* 27: 275–98.
Vogel, Ezra F. (1979) *Japan as Number One: Lessons for America*, Cambridge, Mass.: Harvard University Press.
White, Merry (1987) *The Japanese Educational Challenge: A Commitment to Children*, New York: Free Press.
Yano, Masakazu (1997) 'Higher education and employment', *Higher Education* 27: 199–214.

8 Internationalising Japanese Higher Education: Reforming the System or Re-positioning the Product?

Patricia Walker

Setting internationalism against the background of reform

It is generally accepted that, as a nation, the Japanese are much given to self-criticism of their achievements not least the throughput and output of their education system. No country in the world discusses its system more, say the cynics, yet does so little about it.

My fieldwork in a number of higher education institutions in Japan provided important insights into the process of higher education as well as the end product. It is not so much a case of 'if it ain't broke don't fix it' (a maxim British universities might want to consider) and more one of 'let sleeping dogs lie' (as long as the loud snoring doesn't wake anyone up).

It is the case that, inside Japan, discussions of educational reforms are ubiquitous whereas the legislation to implement them is less so. Legislation that actually makes a difference on the ground is an even rarer phenomenon. Discussion of Japan's education system has generated miles of print over the years and developments, reforms, modifications and changes (whether proposed, alleged or putative, related to policy decisions or overhauls of the curriculum) are discussed just as feverishly in the generalist as in the specialist press. As the twenty-first century approached, changes were being proposed that would allegedly radically alter the quality of higher education but informed observers of Japan were not holding their breath.

The changes that took place until recently had two major characteristics. Firstly, not unlike those hailed as major reforms in 1987, which Schoppa (1991: 52) described as 'represent[ing] minor changes along the established lines of policy making', many of the actual changes were anodyne to the point of invisibility on the ground. Secondly, they were not educational objectives, producer-led, as the government hype proclaimed (Ministry of Education 1995), but were consumer-driven. One of these objectives is the aspiration to embrace internationalism.

Mass consumerism in Japanese higher education

With almost three million students enrolled in 559 junior colleges and 669 universities, Japan's higher education system is the largest in the developed world after the United States (Foreign Press Centre 2002). About half of Japan's youth passes through this system, which has enjoyed almost continuous growth since the first major reforms introduced by the American Education Mission to Japan in 1946. A staggering 96.9 percent of Japanese participate in post-compulsory education. Although the differences in currency values make international comparisons very difficult, the OECD has established purchasing power parities. Adjusting for real PPPs, it can be demonstrated (see Kitamura 1991: 30–8, among others) that the production costs of higher education in Japan have remained low, therefore giving producers a competitive advantage. Kitamura described Japanese education as a 'seller's market' with some of the highest participation rates in the world. With the sharp decline in the number of 18-year olds since 1992 (and it is worth remembering that, in Japan, 90 percent of college enrolments are in the 18–22 age bracket), the unabated prosperity of the higher education institutions has been severely tested.

As well as the demographic change in the Japanese population referred to above, there is another (not unrelated) major socio-economic factor that has a bearing on the demand for higher education reform in Japan and that is the fluctuating purchasing power of the yen. It is the latter that has an international dimension.

The first significant boom in higher education in Japan was during the 1960s – a decade characterised by a buoyant economy. Clearly, massive social changes fuelled the need for better educated Japanese to sustain economic growth and, in those optimistic years, people wanted better lives for their children and, as Yamamoto Shinichi (2000: 8) commented, 'a critical factor was that the education that people wanted became affordable'.

In the 1980s, the effects of the rising yen brought a number of problems for Japanese higher education. The notorious 'cocoon years' (see Tokyo denki kagaku kōgyō 1986) traditionally offer university students a welcome respite between high school 'hell' and company treadmill. However, as Ushiogi (1987) claimed, the strong yen was causing students financial hardship to the point where some of them were beginning to question whether they were getting value for money. Previously, in economic terms, education had always been seen as an essential good in Japan and, therefore, not price sensitive. Recently, however, young people began to demand more for their money from university experience and began eschewing campuses where education was absent. Put simply, a university education was becoming a luxury that many young people felt they could not justify.

The rising cost of education at home impacted on the demand for education consumed abroad. International education became a viable alternative since, for a time, it was actually cheaper for Japanese parents to send their sons and daughters to university in London than (especially when living costs are added) to Tokyo (British Council 1994)

The Japanese in general, in common with most East Asian peoples, are enthusiastic about education and they are prepared to pay for it. The high number of private educational institutions in Japan testifies to that and they are not cheap. About 73 percent of university students and 91 percent of junior college students are in private institutions. Paradoxically, the most prestigious universities in Japan are the cheapest. The national universities, which are the most difficult to get into, charge tuition fees of about ¥744,200 per annum; the local public or prefectural university about ¥844,943; and private institutions, even junior colleges, can charge more than a million yen for the cheapest humanities course. Japanese higher education also carries with it considerable extras which do not figure in other university systems. These include entrance exam fees (prohibitively expensive especially if the unlucky aspirant needs to re-take a number of times) and registration fee (Association of International Education Japan [AIEJ] 1999).

Where the price of the home-produced commodity rises to such an extent that it adversely affects customer satisfaction, it can price itself out of the market; customer choice is exercised and consumers elect to buy elsewhere. It is no coincidence, as Table 8-1 illustrated, that the explosion in numbers of students going abroad for university education, corresponded with the economic boom in Japan of the mid-1980s, and that the numbers of students entering

Table 8-1: Japanese students in the UK: total numbers for selected years (in relation to Sterling/Yen)

Year	Total numbers of Japanese students in the UK	Exchange rate (yen/sterling)
1982/83	369	370
1983/84	370	370
1987/88	829	230
1988/89	1 036	230
1989/90	1 445	220
1990/91	1 767	250
1991/92	2 316	225
1992/93	2 500	200
1993/94	2 726	160

Sources: Adapted from British Council; Department for Education, 1994; Bank of Japan.

British universities reflected the rise in the purchasing power of the yen against sterling.

During the economic crisis of the 1990s, foregoing the Japanese university in favour of an international education was not the bargain it had once been. Externally there was economic globalisation and internally the economic bubble had burst. At the International Centre for English Language Studies at Oxford Brookes University, in the academic year 1998–1999, a number of Japanese students cut short their studies and returned to Japan in mid-term recalled by anxious parents under severe economic pressure. British universities made financial support available place for Japanese and other Asian students who had started their studies before the crisis.

Japanese universities were swift to see their market advantage but, by this time, the demographic changes were kicking in as the shrinking pool of prospective clients was beginning to take serious effect. Once again the pendulum swung away from internationalism.

Internationalism – instrument of reform or sales gimmick?

Since the end of the 1980s, many academics and opinion-formers in Japan have been warning that Japanese higher education must internationalise in order to maintain Japan's global markets. Unlike universities in Europe and America, Japanese universities tend not to be comprehensive institutions and may have a curriculum limited in many cases to humanities and social sciences and they are, of course, predominantly undergraduate institutions.

Kida (1981) is amongst those commentators on Japan who put forward the view that opening up Japanese universities to international influences, across a spectrum of issues, was the way to bring about change. In particular, Kida suggested that internationalisation (*kokusaika*) could be a means of developing the higher education curriculum.

Best (1987) referred to the closed nature of Japanese universities. He saw an ever-present danger in Japanese society, of a decline into narrow nationalism, to which a more open internationalism within higher education acts as a bulwark. It is worth noting that as the world entered the 21st century, Japanese students abroad were being exhorted by their government to use foreign travel as a means by which to more fully appreciate the value of their own 'unique culture' (*Daily Yomiuri* 28 June 2000). Best (1987) warned that such is the severity of the major problems in Japanese universities, for instance the nature of the examination system and the faculty and academic structure, that it would be futile to expect leadership towards internationalisation to come from within. He saw the system as part of the problem rather than the solution. Only the commercial sector, Best believes, could exert influence on the universities to open up to international influences. Whilst this may be so the particular difference in Japan is that there is a very close, one might say symbiotic, relationship between higher education and the employment market.

This is a crucially important strand of investigation but it is not possible to do justice to it here. Briefly though, as Fulton (1984) explains, in times of economic constraints, expectations regarding higher education held by specific groups in society carry greater weight in policy-making as a proxy for analysis of national needs. In Japan, as in other post-industrial countries, employers are seen as major stakeholders. Unlike Britain and Sweden, for instance, with whom Fulton makes comparisons, companies in Japan do not expect the higher education institutions to do part of their work for them. On the contrary, there is a long tradition in Japan of firms providing their own recurrent education and training throughout an employee's career. Historically, companies have not been anxious for greater vocational preparation in universities and have preferred generalist to specialist knowledge in their graduate recruits, and positive character traits rather than achievements. The university in Japan faithfully reflects the pre-occupations of the Japanese economy and the employers are happy to maintain the status quo. El Agraa and Ichii (1985) list the following pre-occupations of high-growth industries; gender inequalities (the unemployment rate for women exceeds that for men – 2.7 percent of women progress to higher degrees compared to 6.9 percent of men) and clear sex variances in the wage structure – women are worse off than men across the whole spectrum. It has been put (Kempner and Misao 1993) that universities in Japan are devices for filtering students into powerful corporations and government positions. So, it seems business has been no more successful than academia in addressing the employment needs of Japan

In an effort to encourage a more global outlook, some Japanese academics have investigated the experiences of the leading receiving nations of international students (see Kawano 1989) who looked to the US, UK and France for examples of good practice.

In time, from these foreign models it was learned that an international dimension came to be seen as a 'value-added', bestowing a market advantage and opportunity for profit. Individual institutions keen to enhance their own position in a buyer's market, began to offer short-term international programmes (Junior Year Abroad or semester abroad) to lure prospective students away from enrolling in foreign universities. What is more, they further developed their commercial potential by operating as commercial agents. 'Study abroad' directors in the Japanese institutions bought places on British university courses and then sold them on with a marked up price to their own students. More and more stakeholders began profiting as the number of international programmes increased.

The international student plan

The Ministry's response to the call for internationalism in higher education was to come up with a one- pronged strategy, the '100,000 Foreign Students Plan', to which they attributed motives of noblesse and altruism:

> the existence and prosperity of Japan greatly depends on the maintenance of harmonious relationships with foreign countries. International exchange in education, especially the exchange of foreign students at the

> higher education level, plays an important role in raising education and research standards in Japan and other countries.
>
> Considering the important role foreign students, who are studying in Japan, will play after returning to their countries in the development and strengthening of friendly relationships with Japan, the Foreign Students Policy (sic) has to be regarded as one of Japan's most important national policies for the coming 21st century. (from Ministry of Education 1996)

There is no arguing with world peace as a long-term objective, but whether filling Japan's campuses with students from abroad would achieve this single-handedly is open to debate. Despite the Plan's critics, however, it seemed, as Yamamoto (1990) claimed, that within Japan there was a recognition that the country had reached a crossroads as it attempted to establish a system of foreign study that would meet its development goals.

The Ministry of Education hoped to achieve two objectives with their 'Foreign Students Plan'. It was pinning its hopes initially on the growing numbers of international students on Japan's campuses to bring influences to bear, as in the past, as a catalyst to university reform. The other was to rehabilitate Japan's tarnished academic reputation overseas – Japan has been pilloried as a beneficiary, rather than a benefactor, of the great intellectual currents of the world. Japan does not have an illustrious tradition as an exporter of education and culture (Goodman 1992) and throughout her history she has shown little inclination to make her very long-established and well-financed system of education available to other countries. This is seen by many as another example of Japan's balance of trade deficit.

The Ministry's goal of enrolling 100,000 international students assumed the acceptance of 30,000 graduate students funded by their own or the Japanese government. The policy can be seen, in part, as a response to the criticism that, as a nation, Japan continues to fail to make a contribution to world-wide educational needs that is commensurate with her financial position. The plan was due to mature in the year 2000. Now that the new millennium is upon us, we can see that the Plan had only moderate success, mainly because 91.5 per cent of the foreign students currently in Japan (predominantly China, South Korea and Taiwan) as Table 8-2 illustrates. This was not the client group Japan wished to attract.

In the *Times Higher Education Supplement* of 3 January 2003, Jannuzi claimed that Japan is back on track towards its target of

Table 8-2: Foreign students in Japan by year and country of origin

Country	Year 1988	1989	1990	1991	1992	1993	1994	1995	1996	1997	1998	2001	2003 (est)
China	7708	10850	18063	19625	20432	21801	23256	24026	23341	22323	22810	44014	58000
Taiwan	5693	6063	6484	6072	6138	6207	5648	5180	4745	4323	4033	4252	4000
Korea	5260	6575	8050	9843	11596	12947	12965	12644	12265	11785	11467	14725	16000
Malaysia	1201	1310	1544	1742	1934	2105	2276	2230	2189	2128	2040	803	
USA	964	961	1180	1257	1245	1192	1146	1087	1088	999	949	1141	1200
Thailand	753	831	856	898	894	992	1014	1010	1018	992	1059	1411	
Indonesia	671	824	948	1032	1154	1206	1178	1085	1052	1070	1140	1388	
H. Kong	428	618	422	455	496	520	479	392					
Philippines	339	413	479	477	503	528	487	433	448	447	434	490	
Brazil	268								390				
Bangladesh	200	394	423	479	581	637	710	791	732	750	805		
Others	2358	2606	2927	3242	3685	4326	4701	5050	5594	6248	6616	7845	

Source: Source: Ministry of Education, http:// jin.jcic.or.jp/stat/stats/16EDU61.html

100,000 international students with 95,550 students enrolled by May 1 2002 – an increase of 21.2 percent on the previous year. However, many of these students are not full-time but on short-term courses, which are more affordable to Asian students. So Japan *comme d'habitude*, follows the example of the western nations who, due to the same demographic changes, fill their classrooms with foreign students because they have not enough of their own. So as the pool of domestic Japanese students continues to shrink, institutions are filling up with students from China, Taiwan and other neighbouring Asian countries where demand for higher education exceeds supply. Fee-hungry Japanese universities and colleges are accepting students not normally seen on their campuses. Even a most inglorious junior college in Kansai was hosting block bookings of Chinese students for courses in management and computing and Japanese language in academic year 2001–02.

Re-thinking Japan's international responsibilities

The medieval universities of the west taught in Latin and accepted students from all over the world. Knowledge was thought to have no geographical or cultural boundaries. By contrast, the Japanese university is, and has always been, for the Japanese. Financial inducements have had some effect in that, as a result of receiving national funding, overseas student (*ryūgakusei*) centres had been set up in 31 national universities by May 1999 (Horie 2002). In 1991, Kitamura anticipated that 'if the (P)lan is realised, the existence of [100,000] foreign students may have an enormous impact on the education system of Japanese universities and colleges' (1991: 312). But we have seen that it did not and it is clear that, in terms of competing in the rising international market for students, Japan is not a real contender. Despite being ranked sixth in the world, her market share is insignificant compared to the world leaders and, despite economic swings, Japanese students continue to go abroad rather than study in marginal Japanese institutions as Table 8-3 indicates.

It is generally accepted that one of the reasons for the rigidity and over-centralisation of the Japanese higher education system (and its incipient nationalism) is due in part to the stranglehold of Tokyo University and the Ministry. An anarchic solution to reform was made during the last decade by *The Economist* (1990), which

Table 8-3: Japanese students abroad, 1999–2001, various years

Country	Number
US	46,497
China	13,806
UK	6,150
Canada	2,371
Korea	2,324
Germany	2,182
Australia	1,913
France	1,566
New Zealand	1,187
Austria	302

Source: Ministry of Education.

asserted that the only hope for change was if these two bastions were razed to the ground. A less dramatic solution they believed was the aspiration towards internationalism 'not from the suppliers of education but from its consumers' who would force Japan to internationalise: 'students are delivering a damning judgement on Japanese universities by choosing to study abroad instead' (*The Economist* 21 April 1990).

The consumer behaviour of the Japanese international student

Direct testimony received from Japanese students entering a British university (see Walker 1997) revealed that motivation for entering a foreign university has as much to do with the flaws in the Japanese system as it has in the perceived advantages of the host. Listed below are the push factors:

- There is irrefutable evidence of the dissatisfaction expressed by the Japanese young and their parents with the education system, including the higher education sector. In particular, they reject the 'examination hell' and the lottery of university entrance exams, which *The Economist* (1990) has described as 'a game of Trivial Pursuit writ large'.
- There is a demonstrable lack of opportunity, choice and level in Japanese universities. Marketing surveys by the British Council conducted at the Higher Education fairs in Japan indicate the desire of Japanese students to study those subjects not currently available to them in Japan.

- The motivation of growing numbers of women participating in study abroad can be explained as a rejection of traditional roles in favour of a more eclectic life style aimed at more fully developing their potential. The impact of the economic recession was felt more acutely by women (Inamura 1996)
- There is a certain amount of evidence that young Japanese are conscious of the need for Japan to become more pro-active on the international stage. Students expressed their aspiration to repair Japan's image as a xenophobic nation by taking on the role of ambassadors for Japan in the foreign environment.
- There is, in addition to this, a growing reaction in Japanese society against what has been described as the empty materialism of Japan, and a desire among the young and others to acquire alternative value systems.

There are also significant pull factors:

- The fear that foreign qualifications and experience are not acceptable in Japan (long a disincentive to prospective Japanese candidates for study abroad) is no longer an impediment and this has accelerated the demand for an international education. The acceptability of overseas-earned credentials in the Japanese employment market has been reinforced by the opening up of Japanese universities to the issue of credit transfer from abroad.
- The Japanese consumer buys designer labels. Any foreign mark will do but certain universities, such as London, Oxford and Cambridge (or even with the words London, Oxford or Cambridge in the title) have a cachet for which they are happy to pay.
- English is the badge of internationalism and Japanese students are drawn to programmes of study in English. Of the 76,000 Japanese studying overseas in 2001, 60,489 were in Anglophone countries.
- A preparatory curriculum is now in place in many British universities (Intensive English, English for Academic Purposes, Foundation courses, Post-graduate preparation courses). These have provided the 'safe house' students have long needed to acculturate and orient themselves to British higher education, which is a profoundly different system of education for which Japanese students require careful mentoring (British Council 1994).
- The sophistication of the Japanese education industry is such that where demand is expressed there is machinery to facilitate its

procurement. An infrastructure is in place in Japan that not merely facilitates, but also stimulates, undergraduate and graduate student mobility to overseas placements. The larger *juku* (private supplementary schools) have moved into the area of international placement and counselling because they see the potential for profit there (Walker 1999).

Japan is second only to China (with its vastly greater population) in the league tables of countries with numbers of students abroad. Every Japanese student, from the shrinking pool of consumers, who takes his or her custom elsewhere is adding to an increasingly critical situation for Japanese higher education. They are also delivering a damning indictment of the domestic product.

Consuming Japanese higher education

In Japan, a college education is almost a fashionable necessity. There is a general consensus throughout Japanese society that higher education is a matter of right and people have ceased to ask what it is good for. Refsing avers that extending education for young people in Japan has four functions: 'education, socialisation, selection and "safekeeping", i.e. school serves as a depository for the young until they are ready for the labour market, and especially until the labour market is ready for them' (1992: 119).

This latter is particularly pernicious in some junior colleges, which are little more than holding bays, keeping the young off the streets until the Japanese labour market is ready for them. In a buyer's market this situation is likely to exacerbate as institutions will take all comers rather than close down departments and fire professors (although in some colleges they are also doing this).

In the first spring of the new millennium, I observed students entering higher education institutions who were not only intellectually incapable of a higher education by anyone's standards but socially and psychologically unprepared for a higher education experience. Of one class of fourteen students at an institution in Shiga prefecture, one withdrew after the opening ceremony, a second did not formally withdraw but was not seen on campus again, a third attended for two weeks and was never seen again, yet another dropped out in the ninth week of term. Their parents were paying in excess of a million yen a year in tuition fees alone. The reason for non-attendance given by each of these students was 'psychological problems related to the relationships in the class' (direct testimony).

Those students who remained were able only to continue work of a similar nature and level to that which they had done (or couldn't do, as the case may be) in high school. Although they would have been inestimably better off getting a job, the marketing departments of the Japanese universities, desperate for income, had seduced them. Moreover, the crisis of discipline in Japan's schools is also spilling over into colleges, as students with a history of academic under-performance waste their own and other's time in the nation's lecture rooms. At one junior college with which I am familiar, local students who had enrolled because they could not afford to travel or live further afield in order to attend a more prestigious institution, discover that, far from being an engine for the production and dissemination of knowledge, the institution they are attending is providing little more than expensive day-care. They find themselves in company with students who are disaffected and, in many cases, dysfunctional. This is a dispiriting environment for students of average to good ability and the professors who teach them

The Ministry's reaction to criticism of the institutions at the lower academic levels and their 'playground' ambience is, typically, a financial one. As one daily paper reported, 'Top students may have loans forgiven...Given the marked decline in the levels of academic achievement of university students, (the Ministry) wants to motivate them to study and to revitalise campuses – which some say have degenerated into "playgrounds" for adult students' (*Yomiuri Shimbun* 14 March 2000).

To this end, the Ministry is considering a plan to exempt exemplary graduate and undergraduate students from repaying their student loans. How long then before application forms bear the legend 'Earn grade point average (GPA) of 4.5 and get your fees refunded – all we ask is that you appear on prime time TV to endorse Happy Days University'? These ultimate manifestations of commodification cannot be far away.

Higher education in crisis

The Japanese university was originally devised as an arm of the state for translating western technology for use in Japan and for protecting Japan from European cultural imperialism with its dangerous political ideas. As an institution it was always highly elitist. After the World War II, the American reformers insisted on widening opportunity and now only the United States itself has higher participation rates in higher education than Japan. Many Japanese, privately and publicly, have a tendency to believe the Americans are 'to blame' for much of what is wrong in Japan (including the problems with English language education but this is a topic in itself, see Walker 2000).

In the post-war era, schools have moved away from teaching the traditional Japanese values which emphasise responsibility to the community and the nation. Prime Minister Nakasone called for a return to these values, blaming the schools for a weakness in moral education; the teachers in their turn blame the 'where you went to school' system of achieving success in society *(gakureki shakai)* and the competitive exams (Beauchamp 1991: 60–61). However, school refusal, defined as 'skipping fifty or more days per year'...'has become a media headline topic in the last few years, replacing previous news leaders such as bullying and school regulations abuses' (White 1993: 85–86) and which was partly behind the last round of reforms, is not going away.

Children's complaints of physical ailments that keep them at home from school are neither truancy nor delinquency, but a silent protest at the pain of pressure. School violence continues to increase with female involvement in one case in five according to the National Police Agency. A common situation known as 'classroom breakdown' (*gakkyū hōkai*) involves violence against teachers and bullying. The English language newspapers in Japan in 2000–2001 were reporting fewer incidents than in the previous decade, however, those that were reported were spectacularly vicious, featuring extortion and beatings to the death. In recent cases, two middle school students extorted five million yen from a classmate spending it on long-distance taxi fares, for example, and other illogical extravagances; another case involved the unprovoked attack on a school boy who was beaten and left to die in a tunnel.

The Japanese dismiss such cases as examples of (*senshinkoku byō*) 'advanced nation disease' but such behaviour violates the fundamental code of Confucian-influenced, traditional educational values which require respect and obedience to teachers (Schoppa 1991: 54). This behaviour, which used to be confined to schools, is now spilling over into higher education, as the bad boys and girls of the high schools are being accepted into colleges and universities.

Although, 'in Japan there has generally been overproduction of formal education' (Evans 1991: 225) and, notwithstanding criticism of the Japanese university on all sides, there was previously a general consensus that they did impart skills for employment in that competent, malleable young salarymen and women were being produced for government service and industry. Now there are signs that they are not even doing that.

It was thought that changes in the employment market would force the universities to take on a value-added function, and not just act as a screening device, but the warning may have come too late. A recent white paper emphasised that many young people 'are not attracted by the prospect of working for a big company or gaining social status' (*Daily Yomiuri* 28 June 2000). The report went on to say that 'The ratio of graduates not seeking full-time work is increasing every year, with one in every three high school graduates and one in four university graduates without full-time jobs last year. Many part-time workers cited their reluctance to work full-time and the severity of working conditions as their motives for not trying to land full-time jobs. Young people want to be part-time workers, or so called freetimers, because they do not have specific goals for the future'.

The frontier within

The modern education system in Japan was set up in the Meiji period. The high costs (50 sen a month in 1883 when the average worker's income was 21 sen a year) meant, however, that the number of children enrolling increased only slowly until 1900 when tuition fees for elementary school were abolished (Evans 1991). One hundred years later the vice-minister for education, Sato Teiichi, reported that 'as incomes have risen to the first or second highest in the world, we've seen a very high rate of educational dissemination' (*Daily Yomiuri* 28 June 2000). But the Midas touch has a down side. Social extremes became more pronounced throughout the 1990s, as Emmott (1989: 70) predicted.

> There are suddenly a lot of rich Japanese…this arrival of a new class is important because it implies not only a change in consumption habits but also a widening of the gap between rich and poor…One reason [why Japan's egalitarian society is becoming less equal] is the high cost of education: the more you pay even for a kindergarten, the more likely

> your child is to get into the right schools and hence the best jobs. Those unlucky enough to be struggling to pay for housing will scarcely be able to pay for their children as well. (Emmott 1989)

What is more, young people growing up in affluence have a consumer orientation vastly different to that of their parents and their pursuit of pleasure is paramount. Yoshiki Fujii, a freelance writer, has researched lifestyles and values among the young and is convinced that a new group is emerging. He calls them 'event-oriented people' who seek constant stimulation and will sink to any means to obtain money to finance it even to the extent of selling their used underwear. '(T)hese high school girls live only for the pleasure of the moment without plans for the future' (*Japan Times Weekly*, 15/21 July 1996). Evidence abounds that they are squandering the resources carefully built up by their parents – 'the youngest generation of job holders, products of an affluent society, might even be innately lazy. They are products of parental indulgence' (Ohmae 1988: 18, in Stephens 1991) and, in the words of students themselves, 'Japanese higher education is hard on parents, easy on kids' (Walker 2000).

The need for reform in the national education system has been strongly expressed and the urge to internationalise equally so. Arguably the two are seen as mutually reinforcing, indeed, the former is thought to be predicated on the latter. A desire to learn from the foreigner, without betraying traditional Japanese values, has motivated Japanese rulers and educators since the first recorded 'overseas students' went to China bringing back a writing system, a medical system and an understanding of architecture and religion, in AD57. The Meiji emperor, in 1868, advocated overseas study with the express objective of achieving reform – ' (k)nowledge shall be sought throughout the world so as to strengthen the foundations of imperial rule' (in Hunter 1989: 192).

The withering birth rate in Japan is just one of many traits of a society in decline. Kitamura warned a decade ago that the foreign models to which Japan had traditionally looked for guidance are today wrestling with their own problems of post-industrial decline and the demands of a new millennium. He argued that Japan will have to look inwardly to find her own solutions and these may even serve to benefit the rest of the world (Kitamura 1991: 46–7). Clammer sees Japan as a unique post-modernist society facing specifically Asian issues (2000: 120–133). He reiterates that this time Japan is on her own to find a way out of the intellectual wasteland of much of her higher education enterprise. The Prime Minister's Commission seems willing to grasp this in the report of its deliberations, aptly named 'The Frontier Within' – 'The world no longer offers ready-made models…Japan's frontier lies within Japan' (Soeya 2000). Given the recently demonstrated fragility of the global economy and Japan's Pan Asia role, the rest of the world will be praying that she succeeds in finding a way forward.

References

Association of International Education Japan (1999) *Japanese Colleges and Universities,* Tokyo: AIEJ.

Beauchamp, E. R. (1991) 'The development of Japanese educational policy, 1945–1985' in Beauchamp, E. R. (ed.) *Windows on Japanese Education,* New York: Greenwood Press.

Best, Paul J. (1987) 'Japanese higher education and Japan's "internationalization" (*kokusaika*)', unpublished ms, Southern Connecticut State University, Requirement for Certificate of Advanced Study.

British Council (1994) *Access to UK Higher Education: A Guide for Overseas Students,* London: HMSO.

Clammer, J. and Michael Ashkenazi (2000) *Consumption and Material Culture in Contemporary Japan,* London: Kegan Paul International.

Department for Education (1994) *Students from Abroad in Great Britain 1982–1993,* London: Government Statistical Service (Statistical Bulletin Issue No. 15/94).

Ebuchi, Kazuhiro (ed.) (1989) *Foreign Students and the Internationalization of Higher Education*, Hiroshima: Research Institute for Higher Education.

The Economist (1990) 'Why can't little Taro think?' April 21, pp. 23–6.

El Agraa, A.M. and A. Ichii (1985) 'The Japanese education system with special emphasis on higher education', *Higher Education*, 14 (1).

Emmott, Bill (1989) *The Sun Also Sets: Why Japan Will Not Be Number One,* London: Simon & Schuster.

Evans, Robert Jr. (1991) 'The contribution of education to Japan's economic growth', in Beauchamp, E.R. (ed.) *Windows on Japanese Education,* New York: Greenwood Press.

Foreign Press Centre (2002) *Facts and Figures of Japan,* Tokyo: Foreign Press Centre Japan.

Fulton, O. (1984) 'Needs, Expectations and Responses: New Pressures on higher education', *Higher Education* 13 (2).

Goodman, R. (1992) 'Japan: Pupil turned teacher?' in Phillips, David (ed.) *Lessons of Cross-National Comparison in Education,* Oxford: Triangle Books (Oxford Studies in Comparative Education).

Horie, M. (2002) 'The internationalization of higher education in the 1990s: a reconsideration', *Higher Education* 43: 65–84.

Hunter, Janet E. (1989) *The Emergence of Modern Japan: An Introductory History since 1983*, London: Longman.

Inamura, Ann E. (ed.) (1996) *Re-Imaging Japanese Women*, Berkeley: University of California Press.

Kawano, Shigeto (1989) 'Policy trends and issues regarding foreign students in Japan', in Ebuchi, K. (ed.), *Foreign Students and the Internationalization of Higher Education,* Hiroshima: Research Institute for Higher Education.

Kempner, K. and Misao Makino (1993) 'Cultural influences on the construction of knowledge in Japanese higher education', *Comparative Education,* 29 (2).

Kida, Hiroshi (1981) *Japanese Universities and Their World – Their Features and Tasks,* Tokyo: National Institute for Educational Research.

Kitamura, Kazuyuki (1991) 'The future of Japanese higher education', in Beauchamp, E.R. (ed.) *Windows on Japanese Education,* New York: Greenwood Press.

Ministry of Education (1995) *Remaking Universities* (White paper), Tokyo: Ministry of Education.

Ministry of Education (1996) *Outline of the Student Exchange System in Japan*, Tokyo: Student Exchange Division, Science and International Affairs Bureau, Ministry of Education.

Ohmae, Kenichi (1988) *Beyond National Borders*, Tokyo: Kodansha.

Refsing, Kirsten (1992) 'Japanese educational expansion: Quality or equality?' in Goodman, R. and K. Refsing (eds.), *Ideology and Practice in Modern Japan,* London: Routledge.

Schoppa, Leonard (1991) 'Education reform in Japan: Goals and results of the recent reform campaign', in Beauchamp, E. R. (ed.) *Windows on Japanese Education,* New York: Greenwood Press.

Soeya, Yoshihide (2000) 'The frontier within', *Look Japan* (April). Tokyo: Ministry of Justice.

Tokyo Denki Kagaku Kōgyō (1986) *Video Letter from Japan Project*, in collaboration with School of Oriental and African Studies, London University.

Ushiogi, Morikazu (1987) 'Japanese higher education and its problems', unpublished paper, International Seminar, Current Issues in University Education in Korea and Japan, Seoul July 7–8

Walker, Patricia (1997) 'The Commodification of British Higher Education – International Student Curriculum Initiatives', PhD thesis, Oxford Brookes University, School of Education.

Walker, Patricia (1999) 'An outsider on the inside: viewing Japanese higher education', *The Japanese Learner* (Autumn), Oxford: Oxford University Press.

White, Merry (1993) *The Material Child*, Berkeley: University of California Press.

Yamamoto, Kiyoshi (1990) 'Foreign Students in Japan' (occasional paper), Tokyo: National Institute for Educational Research.

Yamamoto, Shinichi (2000) 'Making the grade: Japanese universities aim to outshine the competition', *Look Japan* (May), Tokyo: Ministry of Justice.

9 American Universities in Japan

John Mock

Broadly speaking, it seems safe to say that Japanese post-secondary education has very different functions and purposes than American post-secondary education. Phrasing it crudely, Japanese post-secondary education seems to have the basic premise that the entrance examination measures how 'good' students are and that further proficiency- based promotion is not terribly important. Conversely, American post-secondary education, although entrance requirements may or may not be stringent, seems to concentrate on a proficiency-based escalation of course work. Further, Japanese education remains rigid with 'majors' chosen at entry into the university. Transfer is precluded among educational institutions or even within the same educational institution while American education allows for enormous flexibility of courses of study as well as relatively easy transfer among educational institutions. Because of these differences, the recent experience of American higher education in Japan can be seen as being of considerable interest particularly in light of continuing cooperative and joint ventures.

Recent American university involvement in Japan can be crudely divided into the three phases: pre-bubble, bubble and post-bubble phases. All of these refer to the 'bubble' economic boom that Japan experienced, peaking in the late 1980s and then collapsing in the early 1990s. In the 'pre-bubble phase', ie. before 1985, there was a wide range of different relationships between those American institutions involved and the Japanese institutions. There were some consortial involvements, like the Inter-University Center in Tokyo (now in Yokohama), which were semi-free-standing and consortia, such as Michigan State, Illinois, Colorado and Hawaii linked to Konan University in Kobe. There were many straight sister-school 'exchange' relationships linking two specific universities, for example the University of Michigan and Kyoto University. Finally, there were independent 'university' involvements such as ones maintained by Temple University and Friends World College.

The 'bubble phase' showed a marked surge in American university involvement with literally dozens of American universities setting up either branch campuses, or the approximate equivalents, all over Japan. The huge expansion of the Japanese economy and the 'cash-rich' environment promoted a wide variety of arrangements, from single-university branch campuses (e.g., Southern Illinois University, Texas A & M-Koriyama) to system branches (Minnesota State University System branch in Akita) to consortial arrangements among groups of American universities (the Japan Center for Michigan Universities supported by the fifteen public universities of Michigan, Shiga Prefecture and, briefly, by the State of Michigan; and the Stanford Kyoto Center supported by Kyoto University and a group of American universities led by Stanford University.) Many of the new 'branch' campuses were created in the belief that they could be self-supporting or even make money for the 'home' institutions in the States. The idea was that English language education and its concomitant access to American higher education would be something so profitable in Japan, with its booming, cash-rich economy, that what might be considered one of the normal economic rules of higher education, that tertiary institutions are very poor money-makers, would be suspended.

The 'post-bubble phase' saw the almost immediate demise of many of these branch or semi-branch campuses as the ready flow of Japanese cash dried up. The institutions affiliated closely with Japanese universities were, to a certain extent, buffered from the full impact of the deterioration of the Japanese economy while the institutions that had gone 'independent', in whatever form, were hit extremely hard. By the beginning of 2003, out of more than forty institutions at the peak, only a few were left with Southern Illinois University's campus in Niigata clearly on its last legs. The recent termination of operations for Minnesota State University – Akita (MSU-A) is a clear case in point. In almost all cases, severe financial constraints had forced shifting configurations of the various institutions to forms that could be sustained with far less support. Basically, funding returned to pre-bubble levels but with some interestingly different purposes and structures. The expansion of purpose and structure that was created during the heyday of the bubble economy outlived the short-sighted expectation that money could be made in substantial quantities from teaching English and exporting American higher education.

Similarities

I am most familiar with the programmes run by Friends World College (FWC), now of Long Island University; Minnesota State University – Akita (MSU-A); the EAGLE [Engineering Alliance for GLobal Education] Japan Program; and the Japan Center for Michigan Universities (JCMU). Among these four institutions there are at least four common characteristics, which are shared by most if not all American institutions in Japan: limited resources, strong links with 'home' institutions, high quality 'residential' staff and extreme idealism of purpose – sometimes mixed with crass materialism, particularly during the 'bubble phase'.

Limited Resources

The limited resources were structural. None of these ventures were the 'main' part of the American institutions they represented. The funding was the least adequate at the East Asia Center of Friends World College, which was a very small and impoverished, Quaker-founded institution dedicated to international education and developed before the 'bubble economy' took off. The Japan Center for Michigan Universities (JCMU) and Minnesota State University – Akita (MSU-A) had the advantages and disadvantages of public state institutions and multiple participants. They also had functional partnerships, with Shiga Prefecture and Yuwa Town respectively, while Friends World College and the EAGLE Japan Program were completely independent.

The State Universities of Michigan and what is now the Minnesota State Colleges and Universities (MnSCU) have very substantial economic bases but also broad demands on those same resources. Small 'satellite' institutions located a great distance (half-way around the world) from the political 'centre' have virtually no chance of maintaining parity funding. As Japan studies became more 'fashionable' (due as much to the 'bubble economy' as to the tragedy at Tiananmen Square, which saw a substantial, if temporary, shift of students from Chinese to Japanese studies), the public institutions were able to maintain some support. But both the State of Michigan in the past, and MnSCU as of the summer of 2003, have substantially cut support for their higher education connection with Japan. MnSCU, in particular, supports a surprisingly small effort toward international studies of any kind.

In the case of Michigan, while the state terminated its funding, the fifteen public universities eventually put the Japan Center of Michigan Universities (JCMU) into their regular budgets. Conversely, Minnesota State Colleges and Universities (MnSCU) not only did not put Minnesota State University–Akita (MSU–A) into its regular budget but has also terminated all funding. Ironically, this decision was made a couple of years ago when the State of Minnesota was looking at surpluses in the hundreds of millions of dollars, perhaps as much as two billion dollars. As of March 2003, MnSCU terminated all operations at the MSU-A campus.

In addition, the JCMU and MSU-A have received very substantial support from their Japanese partners, Shiga Prefecture in the case of the JCMU and the town of Yuwa in the case of MSU-A. In the case of MSU-A, its demise was planned in an attempt to allow the transfer of 'sponsorship' from a small town (Yuwa) to the prefecture through the creation of a new prefectural institution primarily focusing on international studies. Akita International University (*Akita Kyōyo Daigaku*) opened in April of 2004.

The most highly funded of these programmes was the EAGLE (Engineering Alliance for GLobal Education) Japan Program, which was supported by a consortium of fifteen American institutions and funded by a very substantial AFOSR (Air Force Office of Scientific Research) grant. The aims of the EAGLE Japan Program were also far more limited. While the other institutions all sought general international education, focusing on Japanese-American relations, the EAGLE Program was specifically designed to provide somewhat intensive Japanese culture and language training for technically-trained American students and, where desired, to locate them in long term (one- to three-year) placements with Japanese companies. The funding for the eight-week summer programmes was excellent but it was only for two summers, very 'soft' and very short term. However, the EAGLE Japan Program, as with MIT's ongoing efforts, clearly demonstrated that it is both possible and profitable to expand the education of technically-trained students, by adding a substantial culture and language component sufficient to allow interested participants to actually work in the target culture and language for a minimum of a year.

In the case of MSU-A, however, as in the case of many of the other American involvements, the basic funding of the programmes was considerably underestimated and the capacity for the programmes to be 'self-supporting', in any significant manner, was overestimated. In these cases, the question of funding was not as extreme, at least in the beginning, as in other cases. With many of the branch campuses founded at the peak of the 'bubble phase', this underestimation/overestimation was even more extreme. As a result, their demise was far more rapid.

Texas A & M University – Koriyama (TAMU-K) presents an unusual case where the strong support provided by the City of Koriyama was withdrawn as a result of a change in the political leadership of the city. TAMU-K also shared with MSU-A a series of peculiar state accounting regulations that appeared to prevent a reasonable and balanced sharing of expenses as well as any surpluses. In both cases, there were state regulations restricting expenditure of state funds outside of the state which caused major headaches.

Links with home institutions

All of the institutions under consideration maintained as close a set of ties with the 'home' institutions as possible. The least directive were the ties maintained by the East Asia Center of Friends World College headquarters in Huntingdon, Long Island, in the early 1980s. Of all the year-round programmes, FWC maintained the least day-to-day control over its overseas centre in Japan due to the distance and the lack of 'hi-tech' facilities such as a fax machine.

The Japan Center for Michigan Universities, founded at the end of the 1980s when fax machines were commonplace, was kept in close communication with the International Studies Office at Michigan State University – the administrative base for the fifteen public universities of Michigan for this particular venture. However, there was substantial trust embodied in the person of the Director of the JCMU and day-to-day interactions in Japan were left pretty much up to the Director working with the resident faculty. As an exception, at one point there was a palpable attempt at direct 'management' of affairs of American students by at least one of the participating campuses. Fortunately, the overall management was left pretty much up to the local staff.

The EAGLE Japan Program (run by a fifteen university consortium) was a short (eight week) summer programme with virtually no 'management' by the 'home campus', in this case the Rose-Hulman Institute of Technology. There were frequent communications, however, particularly as the member institutions attempted to maintain and build-up more substantial networks in

Japan, both in the academic and business communities. There was also a relatively high 'visitation' rate with various deans, directors of programmes, and other interested parties either coming specifically to see the summer programmes or just 'dropping by' on the way to or from other projects in Asia. However, in spite of all of the contact and communication, the faculty running the two sites, under a resident 'director' who also served as a faculty member, were left with complete pedagogic and logistic autonomy.

At the other extreme is Minnesota State University – Akita, a branch originally of the eight campus Minnesota State University System (MSUS), then of the Minnesota State Colleges and Universities (MnSCU) System when the two-year community colleges and technical schools were combined with the state universities by an act of the state legislature. MSU-A has been kept very firmly under the direct control of the chancellor's office. The original structure had a 'provost' in Akita who reported to a 'director' in an office in St. Paul, Minnesota; the director then reported to the chancellor's office. This was later shifted to having the provost in Akita report directly to the chancellor's office with the director in St. Paul reporting to the provost. Finally, it appears that the St. Paul director reported to both the provost in Japan and the chancellor's office. Obviously, this sort of confused and confusing system was problematic.

Not only was the chancellor involved in decision-making vis-à-vis MSU-A but also the board of trustees became directly involved. In addition, toward the end there was also a 'work group' advising the chancellor about MSU-A. This work group had no faculty at all and of the ten Minnesota working members, none were directly involved with the Japan campus and none had any particular training or knowledge about Japan. Further complicating the mix, the three top administrators at MSU-A were listed as ex-officio members of the work group but it is not clear just how well they were able to communicate with a group meeting 8,000 miles away, or what was the level of their overall effectiveness.

There is also a significant difference in the training and experience, as well as the political roles, of the MSU-A administration compared with the other institutions discussed here. From an MSU-A faculty perspective, it seemed that the administration was ineffective in communicating effectively with the 'working group' and that this latter failed completely to understand the situation. This combination led to a number of misunderstandings and miscommunications that contributed significantly to the ultimate decision to close the Akita branch campus.

As the decision was made to 'phase out' MSU-A, more and more of the effective decision-making appeared to have been made in St. Paul and communicated to Japan. The administrators in Japan were repeatedly required to wait for specific instructions or information from St. Paul, which was often inappropriate, or simply never received.

Finally, there is a related observation concerning the training and background of the MSU-A administration. Most of the individuals fulfilling the 'provost' role in Akita and the 'director' role in St. Paul were minimally qualified in terms of administrative experience in general and experience of Japan, administrative or otherwise, specifically. At one point, during a search for a new provost, the faculty at Akita voted overwhelmingly to ask the search committee (in St. Paul) to re-open the search process since neither of the candidates who had just been interviewed in Akita had any significant Japanese experience or training. The response received was that the faculty should not expect to 'get a veto' in the search process. Of course, the faculty were not represented, at all, on the search committee. Nor were any of the administrators in St. Paul or in Akita ever subject to any significant review or evaluation process. In fact, at least one provost in Akita and all of the 'directors' in St. Paul were appointed without any consultation with the Akita faculty.

This pattern also appears to obtain for Texas A & M – Koriyama and the Southern Illinois University campus in Niigata. In these instances also the top administration seems to have been selected by the 'home' institutions without much if any faculty consultation and without sufficient consideration of background and ongoing interest in Japan. Thus, administrators who had little knowledge about Japan, including very limited language skills, seem to have been quite common at American institutions in Japan. Some of these administrators proved, of course, to be highly effective but they seem to have been the exceptions rather than the rule.

Residential faculty and staff

Because of the challenges involved in working with these institutions and the high level of interest in the positions, the 'residential' staff in all of these institutions was usually of a very high quality. This is in spite of usually low salaries in a land with a very high cost-of-living. Additionally, all of these institutions had heavy to very heavy faculty and staff work loads. Obviously, very small programmes, like EAGLE Japan Program and the East Asia Center of Friends World College, with literally handpicked staff, had a substantial advantage over larger institutions. However, even the somewhat larger Japan Center for Michigan Universities and the much larger Minnesota State University – Akita managed to maintain a very high quality of personnel, both faculty and staff.

In the case of the three smaller institutions, EAGLE, FWC and the JCMU, the total personnel were few enough not only to be very carefully selected, usually specifically by the director of the programmes, but also the director was able to pay close and effective attention to virtually all aspects of the activities of the staff. This meant, even without much in the way of authoritarian 'supervision', that communication, guidance and assistance could be provided relatively easily. The net result was that the institutions ran quite smoothly and functioned highly effectively.

MSU-A, on the other hand, was much larger and had several other marked advantages and disadvantages. Structurally, MSU-A was designed to have faculty from Minnesota 'rotate' into one of the academic departments. The home institution had a strong union developed from a history of very difficult labour relations between the union and management, and a number of employment rules and customs were adopted and maintained in MSU-A despite their obvious ineffectiveness. This proved detrimental to the ongoing operations of the institution. For example, faculty were simply appointed to Akita with no background in teaching non-native speakers of English and they received no training, even in minimal form such as a workshop, before being put into the classroom. Another example has to do with accountability where faculty could miss classes or cut classes short with apparent impunity.

Similarly, in all aspects of the operation of the institution, problems, such as poor, conflicting or non-existent supervision; unclear work assignments; short-term faculty appointments and administration, both in St. Paul and in Akita; and unfamiliarity with Japanese culture weakened what would otherwise have been a stronger faculty and staff. Neither faculty, administration or staff were involved in any significant evaluation process to enable them to avoid problems or to improve their work performance. Further, volunteer efforts by faculty and staff to expand areas of competence and improve the delivery of services to students were either simply ignored or actively suppressed.

On the other hand, a very high level of idealism, a generally shared interest in the mission of the school, and considerable care in selecting new employees, as well as a usually beneficial 'institutional culture' did, in fact, result in the relatively high quality of performance of most personnel.

Idealism

All four programmes were extremely idealistic. Notions of improving transnational, intercultural understanding, Japanese-American relations, and a whole range of other positive ideas, provided much of the motivation for creating and maintaining these institutions and others like them. There is also, of course, the realisation that economic relations between the US and Japan, the world's two largest economies, will depend, to a large extent, upon the mutual ability to communicate. To this end, therefore, the learning of both cultures and languages has a substantial economic motivation but this, to my mind, simply enhances the more idealistic notions.

There are, of course, counteracting forces. At MSU-A, for example, one school of thought was that the institution was created primarily for faculty from the state universities to be able to spend a year abroad, make some extra money for their retirement because of the cost of living adjustment, and be generally unaccountable. Avoiding selection of individuals who held this particular ideology involved quite a bit of time and effort. Another conflicting ideology sometimes encountered could be termed 'neocolonialism' where the idea (sometimes with religious overtones or even an overt theological rationale) was that spreading American cultural values was the imperative.

Differences

While there were at least four elements in common between the institutions under comparison, there were at least four structural elements that were somewhat different: public vs. private; size or scale; origin of initiative; purpose and the relationships with Japanese partners, if any. In addition, of course, there was a very complex mix of personalities, talents, skills and environments that made each institution unique.

Public versus private

In the United States, there is a considerable difference between private and public institutions although there are obviously all sorts of cases where this distinction is somewhat blurred. Here the critical differences would be flexibility, bureaucratic 'range', degree of acceptable innovation and, combined with size or scale, the number of 'constituencies' whose interests need to be addressed. Friends World College was a very small, private institution, which allowed local staff to do whatever they thought was appropriate to deal with local issues. The 'World Headquarters' staff, based on Long Island in New York, made no attempt to micro-manage. There was also very little need to conform to a variety of bureaucratic requirements.

At the other end of the spectrum, Minnesota State University – Akita was considered one of the universities of the MnSCU system and, as such, had to conform to all regulations laid down both by the State of Minnesota and by the MnSCU system offices such as accounting procedures, hiring practices and even policies dealing with the use of alcohol on campus. Specifically looking at alcohol, for example, MSU-A would certainly be one of the very few campuses in Japan, which is required to be absolutely 'dry' even for celebratory functions. MSU-A also had a unionised faculty and staff, thus forming yet other constituency that needed to be addressed.

The Japan Center for Michigan Universities, a product of a fifteen public university consortium, also had to conform to the lead administrative institution's policies on hiring and bookkeeping but was not as constrained by social policies as MSU-A. Further, because the director-in-residence in Shiga Prefecture was allowed substantial autonomy, at least in the early years, there was very little interest in micro-management of any kind.

The EAGLE Japan Program, born of a group of public and private institutions funded by an AFOSR grant, had to conform to the rules of the grant but was otherwise left almost completely autonomous. Also, because it was a short-term 'summer programme' lasting only eight weeks per year, there was probably very little impetus to try to direct the programme.

Scale

The size of the institutions is also a critical difference. FWC was a tiny institution with a couple of faculty members dealing with a maximum of 25–30 students. It was somewhat complicated because while the students were mainly in Japan, there were also some in other parts of East and Southeast Asia. The EAGLE Japan Program had two centres, each with 30–40 students, in the summer programmes. The Japan Center for Michigan Universities had several different programmes but a total of about 35 American students in residence.

In contrast, MSU-A had as many as 75 international students (mostly American) and more than 300 Japanese students, almost all in residence, with a resident faculty of up to 40 and a variety of administrators and other staff. The simple difference in scale meant that while small institutions could operate effectively in a 'personal' way, the larger MSU-A needed to develop institutional devices, both formal and informal, to deal with many of the same problems. Scale certainly contributed to each programme's 'institutional culture' or the pervading ethos of each of the different institutions. When one is talking about a very small face-to-face group, feedback among all involved – faculty, administration, students, staff – is very quick and immediate. In a larger community, feedback loops can become very extended or, as in the case of MSU-A, simply non-existent. Here also there seem to be parallels with the experience of Texas A & M – Koriyama and Southern Illinois University in Niigata. With administrators who were sometimes neither culturally skilled nor academically prepared, faculty and staff evaluations and personnel issues often were a source of conflict and considerable bad feelings.

Source of Initiative

FWC and the EAGLE Japan Program were both initiatives from the United States. The East Asia Center of FWC was only one of eight centres, worldwide. FWC had an extremely idealistic concept of the globalisation of education focusing on experiential approaches and students came from many countries. EAGLE was based on the idea of globalisation for technically-trained students, exclusively American. Given the source of funding, the Air Force

Office of Scientific Research, one cannot also help connecting this venture with previous military-assisted initiatives to promote critical languages and cross-cultural education such as the NDFL (National Defense Foreign Language) Act.

Both JCMU and MSU-A were Japanese initiatives. Shiga Prefecture had initially asked Michigan State University to construct a branch campus in the prefecture. Michigan State, for a variety of reasons, does not have branch campuses but the suggestion was made for a joint living/learning centre shared by all fifteen public universities of Michigan and this is what was eventually accepted. The small town of Yuwa, next to Akita City, had decided that having an American branch campus would be a good idea and had actually talked to a number of possible partners. The then Minnesota State University System (MSUS, later MnSCU) was eventually selected.

The reasons for both Shiga Prefecture and the town of Yuwa being interested in having an American branch campus are varied but include having access to high quality English language instruction for local residents, students and non-students; having access to American education in the United States; and wanting to 'internationalise' their communities, partly for economic reasons and partly for social reasons. In the case of both of these ventures, there does not seem to have been any intent to 'make money' out of education. However, in both cases, potential enrolment was overestimated and costs were underestimated which led to a variety of financial problems.

There is also one further school of thought concerning the purpose of the American institutions in Japan. Given the temporary increase in college-age Japanese during the late 1980s, the argument has been raised that the American institutions were invited specifically with the intention that they would 'bridge the gap' to cope with the temporary boom. Then, after the increase had passed, and college-age student numbers started to decline, this theory proposes that the Japanese establishment specifically intended the American institutions to fail leaving the Japanese tertiary education system untouched. According to this view, therefore, the leap to 40 or more American institutions in Japan, and the subsequent demise of almost all of these institutions, is seen as an intentional pattern and not just a massive miscalculation.

Aside from the rather negative perspective inherent in this argument, it also seems to come perilously close to a 'conspiracy theory'. One question that could be raised would be who planned this and who executed it? Since the Ministry of Education at the time steadfastly refused to recognise any of the American institutions (a policy which lasted until 2004), or really support them in any way, it is difficult to see a central planning agency at work. This is, however, a theory that has been raised repeatedly and often, but not always, by expatriate academics who see the lack of national support as of critical importance in the success or otherwise of these institutions.

Purposes

Friends World College was designed to promote international, experiential education for students from many countries including Japan. The focus of the programme was to go to other cultures to learn about them. The EAGLE Japan Program, on the other hand, was specifically for technically-trained American students, and provided an intensive Japanese language course with some cultural trimmings designed to allow students to be placed in longer term situations with Japanese companies. The JCMU and MSU-A both had dual roles. They were both windows to full second language competence and, if desired, American education for Japanese students and a fairly substantial 'study abroad' opportunity for American students.

MSU-A and the JCMU also had a very different view of education from that which is prevalent in Japan. Philosophically, both institutions were rooted in a system that saw 'general education' as the foundation of higher education with specialisation coming later in the undergraduate programme. One of the attractions of this system, for Japanese students, was the ability to use the ESL programmes and the first year or two of college life to sort out their career and educational goals rather than having to commit to a specific major at a specific institution while still in high school. Both MSU-A and the JCMU were associated with an extended system of institutions, in Minnesota and Michigan respectively, where students could proceed should they so choose.

More problematic, at least at MSU-A, was the American educational concept of 'allowing failure'. MSU-A, like almost all American institutions, allowed students to fail. In order to avoid failure, students were pushed to attend classes, study, do their homework and do other activities which are less common in

Japanese universities. This idea, where students had to take responsibility on a day-to-day basis, was one of the most difficult for Japanese students, their parents and the Japanese partners. However, as with the other American-based institutions, many of the students who chose the path of attending MSU-A were highly successful, suggesting that concepts such as grade point average, general education and transferability might be useful additions to Japanese higher education. As of the summer of 2003, there are several efforts (not all of them terribly serious) to incorporate these elements or components of them into Japanese higher education.

Relationships with Japanese partners

This is a very complicated question but one which appears to have been of major importance, particularly given experiences such as those of MSU-A and Texas A & M – Koriyama. Some of the American institutions in Japan, such as FWC and the EAGLE Japan Program, were independent. The oldest American institution in Japan, Temple University, has gone through several different types of partnerships.

Overall, there appear to be two major factors critical for Japanese-American partnerships – finances and social/academic expectations. It is critical for the American institution to have a clear institutional commitment. Similarly, it is key for the Japanese partner to also have a financial commitment and the financial base to back it up. When the State of Michigan, with a change in the governor's office, suddenly withdrew its financial support for the JCMU, the fifteen state universities were able, eventually, to cover but it did cause many problems, which threatened the continuation of the institution. Similarly, MnSCU withdrew its financial support and the Japanese partner did not have the financial base to absorb the increased deficit. However, in the case of MSU-A, there was also a very weak planning process with unrealistic projections both of income and of costs. It has been frequently repeated that Minnesota was promised that not one dollar of Minnesota money would be needed to run the MSU-A campus, a highly unrealistic view.

There were a number of other financial problems. There were 'sweetheart' deals made for housing and campus building that resulted in very high rents for faculty/staff housing and student housing costs that were extremely high. There also appear to have been charges made to students that were not justified but rather the funds were used to retire excessive debt. There does not appear to have been adequate auditing of either the construction costs or the student charges. These arrangements also resulted in extremely poor maintenance, shoddy construction and general user dissatisfaction. As the Japanese economy collapsed at the end of the 'bubble economy', the town was left with an extremely high debt that eventually may have led to the termination of the branch campus.

Socially and academically, it is also critical for any partnership to have shared understanding and goals. Again in the case of MSU-A, this was clearly not the case. Just what an American university is, and how it operates, were still not clear even after a decade or more of existence. The town employees running the physical plant administration and in charge of recruiting consistently wanted to recruit as many students as possible, regardless of qualifications or motivation. Further, the idea of failing students, for any purpose, was seen as being inappropriate. In the final analysis, one of the factors cited by the mayor for the demise of MSU-A was what he saw as a high attrition rate. Since the attrition rate was well below the average for the MnSCU system, clearly there was a difference in expectations. In addition, even in the face of inadequate admissions, the town did not consider effectively changing the administrative structure that dealt with admissions. The same person – a permanent employee of the town – who was consistently responsible for inadequate admissions not only remained in place but was actually promoted.

The idea of having bilingual staff to deal with a largely bilingual student body, faculty and staff was also only marginally accepted with two of the town employees being somewhat bilingual. Finally, the basic expectations of a university were not shared. Very few of the employees of the Japanese partner had ever had any university experience in any country. Thus, differences of perception, socially and academically, were almost inevitable in spite of whatever good will and idealism might have existed. In contrast, the Shiga Prefecture staff originally hired to manage the JCMU were all bilingual and most of them had university experience. Further, the working relationship between the prefectural 'support staff' and the academic staff, mostly American, was quite close and worked very well.

Lessons

Given the experience of American institutions in Japan, there are some clear lessons that should be kept in mind for further ventures.

The first lesson is that there needs to be a sufficient financial and educational base for any new institution. Tertiary educational institutions, historically, have not been noted as being money-makers and this rule seems to hold in this instance as well.

Second, having clarity of purpose, on both sides of joint ventures, is crucial. Some sort of firm agreement on the value of various outcomes needs to be reached right from the beginning. While finances are, of course, a critical foundation to any chance of success, social and academic expectations also need to be made clear.

A third element is that cross-cultural competence as well as the usual competencies is needed to run a tertiary institution. If the institution is going to be American and Japanese, then most if not all of the staff involved, and particularly the leadership, need to have these multiple competencies. Hiring an administrator who cannot function effectively in Japan, or an 'old Japan hand' who cannot administrate effectively, simply does not work well. Similarly, a fourth element is flexibility and allowing bi-cultural (or multi-cultural) institutions to develop paths somewhat different from the 'home' institutions. For example, locking a campus in Japan into a series of rules that culturally fit the United States does not necessarily make for the best system. Allowing competent faculty and staff to evolve what works best for that particular environment, and giving them as much flexibility as possible, seems to work best.

Given the history of the American institutions in Japan, looking into the future is not very easy. There are several ventures currently ongoing and being created such as Ritsumeikan's Asia-Pacific University (APU) which has a dual language degree programme; Temple University continues in Tokyo as does the California-Nevada Consortium and Lakeland College. Akita Prefecture has opened a new prefecture-based international university with an option for a double degree programme. Given the ongoing economic slump in Japan, the unrealistic economic projections of the 'bubble economy' seem unlikely but the opportunities for cross-cultural miscommunication appear to be as common as ever.

10 University Entrance in Japan

Robert Aspinall

Introduction

In November 1999, Japan was shocked by the savage murder of a two-year-old girl, Wakayama Haruna. When the mother of another two-year-old living in the same neighbourhood of Tokyo confessed to the murder the shock was compounded. The victim had just been selected for entrance to the top-level local kindergarten while the daughter of the murderess had failed to get in and this was immediately jumped on by the media as being a factor contributing to the jealous rage that caused the attack. The editors and journalists, behind the sensational media stories that followed this incident, knew that many people in Japan would have personal knowledge of children or adults who had snapped under the pressure of trying to get into the best schools. This linking of a terrible murder with Japan's national preoccupation with competition to get into good schools also caused the case of Wakayama Haruna to be taken up by the foreign media. Reporters from western nations were interested in something that seemed to them particularly 'Japanese'.[1] Both domestic and foreign observers, therefore, seemed to agree that, in Japan, rivalry over school entrance is so intense that it can literally lead to murder.[2]

Of all the rivalries related to getting into the 'right' school, the most intense is the competition that surrounds university entrance. Preoccupation with entering university is not confined to the two or three years that precede the actual act of university entrance but can be, as is shown in the tragic case above, a vital factor in the minds of the parents of children as young as two. This obsession is far from irrational given that success in university entrance exams will lead almost inevitably to a lifetime of social and economic inferiority. In a sense, the university entrance system is a victim of its own success. As Rohlen wrote in 1983, '[w]hat was an elite phenomenon three decades ago had now become a national preoccupation' (p.107). Although a good university education is regarded as a passport to future success in every modern nation, the Japanese university entrance system used to have an all-encompassing nature that set it apart from other systems. Many believed that future success could *only* be achieved through entrance to a good university. For others, entrance to a low-level higher education institution was better than none at all, regardless of what was (or was not) actually learned there.

This chapter examines the traditional state of affairs that existed up to the 1980s and which had become the subject of criticism for causing too much stress to Japanese children and their families. It will then examine the recent, and ongoing, reforms designed to reduce the intensity of the competition surrounding the education system. It will show how the chronic decline in the number of school-age children, combined with profound criticism of the existing system, has brought about a more complex and diverse university entrance system than that which previously existed. Although many aspects of the traditional system still persist, the process of university entrance in Japan is clearly going through a period of intense crisis and change in the first decade of the twenty-first century.

Getting into a Japanese university: How the traditional system works

The postwar Japanese education system combines a superficially egalitarian compulsory sector with a highly elitist and diversified post-compulsory sector. From the age of six to twelve, Japanese children attend elementary school and then from the age of twelve to fifteen, they attend junior high school and during this period of compulsory education the formal schooling of the vast majority is remarkably similar in content. After the age of fifteen, however, when they enter senior high school, children are divided into different tracks that will lead them to different careers or occupations. Entrance exams do not usually come into the picture until the end of compulsory education, therefore, when children undergo a selection process to determine entrance to senior high school.[3] In effect this is the first stage of the university entrance procedure because some high schools are designed to send their students on to good universities while others are vocation-oriented or have a poor academic track-record. Any account of the university entrance system in Japan would, therefore, be incomplete if it did not also include an account of the senior high school entrance system.

1 Entrance to senior high school

High-level academic-track senior high schools prepare their students for entrance into good universities and so the first hurdle for the ambitious child (and parent) is to gain entrance into one of these schools. Although the entrance exams for these schools take place in the final year of junior high school, preparation must begin much earlier if the child is to stand a realistic chance of success. This is why Rohlen has described getting into a good university as a 'marathon' that requires 'planning and stamina over a twelve- to fourteen-year period'(1983: 108).[4] Therefore, from an early age, Japanese children are encouraged to concentrate on schoolwork aimed solely at the passing of exams. Since exam questions are very factual and detailed, children have to start studying a large volume of factual information from an early age.[5] However, in spite of the hardships involved, and in spite of the wide usage of the term *jūken jigoku* (examination hell[6]) to describe the period of intense cramming that leads up to the exams, it is a widely held belief in Japan that the effort required to master this kind of task is a virtue in itself. In a recent wide-ranging study, Rohlen and LeTendre found that such stress on effort and persistence in learning was not confined to the experience of those of school-age:

> *Gambaru* (effort), *kurō* (suffering), and *gaman* (persistence) are words that are widely used in the spiritual or character-building contexts ubiquitous to Japanese learning. These terms are used in a specifically physical sense – we must note just how physical learning actually is – and often when endurance or exhausting repetition are involved...The new monk, the new potter, or the aspiring third-year [junior high school] student persist through painful repetitions because they fully believe that without experiencing these hardships or trials, nothing can be achieved. (Rohlen and Le Tendre 1996: 374–75)[7]

The suffering endured by children as they prepare for exams, therefore, is seen not just a necessary evil but, according to the point of view outlined above, it should be regarded as an end in itself – part of the whole character-building purpose of the learning process.[8] This helps to explain why criticisms of the exam system in Japan have often also tended to be tinged with a certain respect for the view that it helps to toughen up the younger generation. This tendency is described best by Dore in the following passage from his book, appropriately titled *The Diploma Disease*:

> One suspects that Japan's more conservative leaders, though they are prepared to shake their heads over the system with those who deplore it, are secretly well satisfied. The examination hell sorts the sheep from the goats; a man who can't take the psychological strain would be no use anyway...And as long as you keep adolescents, in those crucial years when they might otherwise be learning to enjoy themselves, glued to their textbooks from seven in the morning to eleven at night, the society should manage to stave off for quite a long while yet that hedonism which, as everybody knows, destroyed the Roman empire, knocked the stuffing out of Britain, and is currently spreading venereal disease through the body politic of the United States. (Dore 1976: 50).

Proponents of the reform of the entrance exam system – whether at senior high school or university level – have had to contend, therefore, with the view that if the tough, competitive side of the system is softened in any way it will no longer be able to produce the hard-working, self-sacrificing citizens who together brought about Japan's postwar economic miracle.

2 The 'unified university entrance exam system'

Once they have got themselves into a high-level, academic-track senior high school, the next task for students planning to get into a good university, is to prepare themselves for two separate rounds of entrance exams that take place between late January and early March in their third year.[9] The first round is called the *sentaa nyūshi,* or exams that are administered by the National Centre for University Entrance Examinations (NCUEE). This system was introduced in 1990 following recommendations made by Prime Minister Nakasone's Ad Hoc Council on Education or *Rinkyōshin* (an advisory body that met between 1984 and 1987). One of the key terms of the Nakasone-era debate on education reform was *jiyūka* (liberalization). The Prime Minister believed that it was important to 'introduce an element of competition into the whole school system' (see Schoppa 1991: 70) and, with this aim in mind, the monolithic university entrance exam system was an obvious target for reform. The declared purpose of the NCUEE exam system, therefore, is to add more choice and flexibility to the entrance process. It does this by allowing universities to freely choose the subjects they want candidates to study for the entrance examination. In the words of the Ministry, 'the NCUEE system gives universities greater latitude with regard to the selection and weighting of the subject areas used in the selection process while maintaining a high standard of examination questions. The result is an 'á la carte' system' (Ministry of Education 1996: 19).

The NCUEE system's predecessor, the *kyōtsū-ichiji shaken* (introduced in 1979), was a unified exam system which had been designed to set a national standard for students leaving secondary education to go on to university. This exam had required all applicants to take examinations in five subject areas – Japanese, mathematics, English, science and social studies. It was, therefore, criticised for being very inflexible. It was also criticised for including unnecessarily awkward and obscure questions and for contributing to the national obsession with ranking universities (i.e. rank was based on what score it was necessary to achieve in the entrance exam in order to enter a given university). The purpose of the system that replaced this was to maintain a centralised control over 'standards' while allowing students and universities more choice about what particular method they employed when deciding who would go where.

In its first year (1990), the NCUEE set exams in the five main subject areas subdivided into eighteen subcategories. Seven years later this was increased to six subject areas and thirty-four subcategories.[10] University faculties were allowed to decide for themselves the subjects they wanted candidates to take at entrance exam. Also, unlike the *kyōtsū-ichiji* system, the NCUEE system allowed private universities as well as public universities to make use of the exams.[11] This combination of universal standards with increased flexibility and choice has led some observers to compare the NCUEE exams with the GCE 'A' level of England and Wales or France's Baccalaureate (see Arai 1999: 18).

In addition to making use of the NCUEE exam, individual university faculties have their own procedures for selecting new entrants. Many continue to rely on the traditional timed exam requiring factual responses. However, in response to various pressures (not least of which is the demographic trend that will require, sometime before 2009, every single applicant to be given a place at university if student numbers are to be maintained at their 1999 levels[12]) many university faculties have increasingly adopted alternative methods of selection. Before moving on to an examination of the alternative methods, I will take a closer look at the traditional type of entrance exam.

3 Traditional university entrance exams set by individual universities

After taking the NCUEE exam in late January, the candidate then prepares him or herself for the next round of exams set by individual university faculties which are usually taken in February and March. A single candidate will usually sit for more than one set of exams in case he or she is unsuccessful in getting into their first choice of institution. Compared to previous generations, present day exam candidates have more choice about which exams to sit. Mathematics, for example, used to be a compulsory subject for all students sitting entrance exams for national universities but now it is no longer required if students are entering departments where the courses do not require high-level mathematical skills.

Although some choice and flexibility has been introduced into the system, the exams themselves remain similar in character to previously. The emphasis is still on detailed, factual answers. Timed, paper tests are a common method for selecting entrants for university the world over but exams in Japan have a reputation for an over-emphasis on detail and 'objective' trivia. The present day obsession with this type of exam can, in fact, be traced back to the nineteenth century. It is partly the result of the Meiji era reformers' success in abolishing privilege and patronage as routes to high public office. As Rohlen points out, 'Japan, as has been noted so often, is a group-oriented society – neither individualistic nor socialistic. Such a society can choke on its own narrow particularism if it does not have well-entrenched mechanisms that counterbalance its powerful tendencies to allocate rewards and favors on the basis of personal affiliation' (Rohlen 1983: 62). Impersonal, 'objective' exams were destined to become the 'mechanisms' that Japan needed in order to modernise. The passing of exams, therefore, rather than the use of wealth or family name, came to be the usual method for achieving high public office. As Japan industrialised, expanding private corporations followed the public lead and subscribed to the ideal of appointment based on merit and, in such an environment, exams had to be as objective and fair as possible. This led to the tendency for exams to concentrate on factual questions, the answers to which could not be open to differing interpretations, and to a culture of secrecy that surrounded the setting and the marking of exams.

At the same time as the establishment of objective exams as the main method by which people entered universities, companies or government offices; the Japanese lifetime employment system was also being established. Although 'lifetime employment' only ever actually applied to a minority of the Japanese workforce, it was still this kind of job that the majority of the population aspired to for their children. As the postwar economy expanded and affluence spread among increasing elements of the population, the desire to achieve secure, well-paid employment for the children of the family increased. At the same time, the number of attractive careers in private companies or government agencies also increased although the method of entry into this kind of career remained fixed in its prewar guise – i.e. entrance on the ground floor, after passing an exam and/or attending a well-known university which in turn had required the passing of an exam.

Japan's economy and bureaucratic machinery were modernising fast as Japan 'caught up' with the west in the 1960s and 1970s. Experts and non-experts alike, however, were all too aware that the methods by which personnel were chosen for the expanding range of careers offered by a modern late-twentieth century economy, had remained frozen in a form that was designed to meet the challenges of late nineteenth century modernisation. As Japan now moves into the twenty-first century, these problems are becoming even more apparent.

Problems with traditional university entrance exams

I have touched on some of the shortcomings of Japan's infamous university entrance exams and they have been well documented elsewhere. Briefly put, the most common criticisms are the following: children are required to spend much of their adolescence cramming mountains of facts into their tired heads (Woronoff 1997: 54–62); most students believe that most of what they are learning has little use beyond passing exams (Yoneyama 1999: 142–8); and an over-emphasis on mindless repetition and memorisation usually kills any possibility that a love of scholarship for its own sake will emerge.[13] Even though these criticisms have been voiced for many years there has been a general reluctance to face up to the task of completely overhauling the system. This may have been partly due to the previously mentioned Japanese respect for the virtues of perseverance and hard work, as well as the tendency for the powerful in Japan to believe that the system was producing the kind of workers that the Japanese economy needed. However, as Japan struggled with the lengthy economic recession of the 1990s this belief in the usefulness of the system was gradually eroded. It became more and more difficult to argue that the exam system was serving the national economic interest well.

Another popular belief that has come under threat recently is that of the fairness and impartiality of the system. It was always believed that merit alone – not family name, wealth or contacts – would secure advancement for those who deserved it. To this end an elaborate ritual of security and secrecy has developed that surrounds the setting and marking of exams.[14] The staff involved in these procedures are forbidden to take any exam-related documents out of the room where exam-setting or marking takes place. When exam papers do have to be moved from building to building they are carried in locked metal cases. On the day of the Tokyo University entrance exam, police with full riot gear available are stationed by the Komaba campus (the site of the exam) and admission is denied to all, including postgraduate students and research staff, who are not directly involved in taking or invigilating the exam. When the contents of exams are finally released to the public those set by the most prestigious universities are published in their entirety in the local and national newspapers.

The elaborate security that surrounds the exams, combined with the anonymous way in which they are marked (staff marking the papers cannot see the names of the candidates), is designed to prevent cheating or favouritism from tainting the system. Unfortunately, it also hides the arbitrary nature in which candidates can be passed or failed by a system that is not monitored by external agencies. In an unusual admission of fallibility, Aoyama Gakuin University in 1999 offered compensation to students who had been incorrectly marked on a question in the mathematics exam. A television documentary news programme made about the incident exposed the haphazard way in which the futures of young people were being decided by a testing system prone to inaccuracy and inconsistency.[15]

Many of the problems connected with the entrance exam system are derived from the fact that the people who set and mark the exams are not experts in testing and assessment. The Ministry is often critical of exams for containing difficult and obscure questions and yet this is almost an inevitable consequence of a system of tests that are set for high school students but are created by academics whose teaching experience is confined to higher education. The annual task of setting each entrance exam is usually allotted to a committee of academic staff from the relevant department. Since the personnel and chair of this committee usually change every year, their ideas about what to put in the exam are mainly guided by precedent. Another consideration is objectivity: as much as this is possible, questions are chosen that have a limited number of 'correct' answers. As well as setting the exam, the academic staff have to mark it and are, therefore, keen to avoid questions that will be time-consuming. This is an understandable consideration for large popular universities which have thousands of candidates sitting their entrance exams each year. The result, however, is that it is virtually impossible to set open-ended questions that may test the imagination, creativity or self-expression of the candidate. Furthermore, in spite of the fact that the questions are designed to have 'correct' answers only, and even in fields like mathematics where one would assume this to be a fair pedagogical approach, there is still the danger that the variations between one marker and another will be big enough to result in arbitrary and haphazard allocations of pass and fail grades.

Problems that have been found in the setting and marking of science and mathematics exams pale into insignificance next to the inherently problematic nature of 'objective' entrance exams in subjects like foreign languages and history. Foreign language entrance exams in Japan are overwhelmingly English and, in spite of the recent expansion of choice, the vast majority of Japanese school students continue to study English for all six years of junior and senior high school. The results of this intense effort on English are, to say the least, disappointing. When actual communicative ability is examined Japanese students compare very unfavourably with their contemporaries in other Asian nations.[16] It is not uncommon to meet a Japanese student who has studied English for ten years but who cannot take part in a simple conversation in the language. University entrance exams are often accused of being the main cause of this failure to teach practical, communicative skills in foreign languages for, with their emphasis on short, right-or-wrong written answers, they do not encourage the nurturing of communicative skills. The recent increase in the number of listening tests included in English entrance exams has helped to encourage the development of aural skills, but the testing of oral communication remains close to non-existent. Because of the crucial importance of entrance exams in the current system, students and their teachers cannot be blamed for focusing exclusively on those skills that will be tested and neglecting those that will not.[17]

History suffers in a similar way to English from the emphasis on short, 'objective' questions. History exams have been criticised for being little more than giant quizzes focusing only on historical 'facts'. The student who will perform best at this kind of test is one with very good memory skills. Other skills that are important in the academic study of history, for example analysis, empathy, interpretation, the ability to weigh up competing accounts of the same event and so on, are neglected. High school history teachers, like their colleagues in the English departments, have no choice but to focus on what is required for the entrance exam. It is no exaggeration to say that all teaching at an academic-track senior high school is focused on these exams. Due to the way that they are set and marked, these exams will continue to be seriously flawed and, because of the vitally important role they play in determining someone's future, they will continue to dominate what is taught at high school. Such a flawed system has frequently been criticised in Japan. Before going on to an examination of the reforms that are a response to this criticism, I will first take a look at another vital part of the entrance exam system – the private 'cram school' industry.

The (big) business of cramming

Getting into the right university is such an important undertaking that the majority of Japanese families do not leave entrance preparation solely to their children's formal schooling. Each year a vast amount of time, money and effort is invested in Japan's *juken* industry, i.e. the system of private cram schools and tutors that is designed primarily to help children prepare for university entrance exams. Tuvia Blumenthal comments that '[w]hile cram schools exist in other countries, they do not have the same magnitude and importance as they do in Japanese society' 1992: 448). There are three ways in which a Japanese family can pay for professional exam preparation help: they can send their children to classes at evening or weekend cram schools (*juku*); they can employ *katei kyōshi* (personal tutors who visit the home); or they can send their children to full-time cram schools (*yobikō*). The last-named category usually applies to students who have finished formal schooling, did not get into the university of their choice at the first attempt and are now spending an extra year in full-time entrance exam preparation. Students in this situation who are living in the grey area that falls between leaving school and university entrance are know as *rōnin,* the name historically given to samurai warriors who have no liege lord.

It is difficult to get an exact picture of the size of the *juken* industry since it encompasses so many small businesses and part-time workers. There is also, in Japan, a great deal of private tutoring in subjects completely unrelated to university entrance exams which is often carried out by the same private schools. Whatever the actual size of the industry, there is no question that it is huge – one estimate for 1989 put its annual total revenue at over one trillion yen (Blumenthal 1992: 453) and another for 1994 put it at 1.4 trillion yen (Ukai Russell 2002:158). The single-minded focusing of these private schools and tutors on university entrance has meant that school students can be tempted to pay more attention to these private classes than to their formal day-time classes. This phenomenon has made it very difficult for local boards of education to institute meaningful education reform at the high school level. If high school teaching starts to deviate from the path of university entrance preparation then students will simply neglect their high school studies and focus more on what they are taught at *juku.*[18] The Ministry's emphasis on alternative credentials for university entrance (outlined below) is clearly designed to break away from the grip that exam preparation has had on Japan's teenagers. It remains to be seen what effect this will have on the *juken* industry. Those in charge of the industry are likely to be more concerned about the demographic trends that are severely reducing the number of potential 'customers' and this will probably result in an expansion of private courses made available to older clients – a trend that would be in keeping with the Ministry's current emphasis on 'lifelong learning'.

Reform of the university entrance system

Traditional entrance exams in Japan have been under such sustained attack for so long that the government had to be seen to do something. In December 2000, the government's National Council for Educational Reform (NCER) issued a report that called for 'a shift in college entrance examinations from memory-centred tests to multiple routes with various screening methods' (Azuma 2002: 16). This change in emphasis was in keeping with recent education reforms that reduced the required course of study for junior and senior high schools, and reduced the school week from five and a half days to five days. Despite the centralised nature of Japan's education system, however, it has never been enough for the Ministry to simply issue directives in order to achieve change. It is questionable how much real reform would have been achieved without the help of demographic trends that are reducing the number of teenagers, and without the changes in the requirements of university graduates' future employers who no longer are content to look simply at the name of a job applicant's university.

In order to look more closely at the reforms that are taking place, this section will be divided into two parts: first, the new methods of entrance and how they differ from the old exam model and second, the opening up of the university entrance system to previously excluded groups in Japan. (Throughout this section the focus will be on, and most of the examples will be from, national and public universities rather than private universities; for more information on changes to admission procedures for private universities, please refer to Kinmonth's chapter in this volume.)

1 New Methods of Entrance

In the development of new methods of university entrance the emphasis has been put on finding methods that are better suited to the wishes of the individual candidates and to the needs of the particular faculties and departments to which they are applying. Various types of interviews, essays and practical tests have been introduced in an effort to match candidates to courses. In addition, 'admission on recommendation' by which high school students are directly admitted to university on the recommendation of their school principal, has become a very popular entrance method. In 2002, no fewer than 34 percent of new entrants (203,796 students in all) entered university via the recommendation method.[19] This proportion has been increasing year on year, although it should be noted that over 90 percent of recommendation entrants enter private universities. The Ministry is also encouraging universities to look at the extra-curricular activities of candidates, including their involvement in club and volunteer activities. One of the problems that university departments are now having to grapple with, however, is that students who are admitted without having to pass any paper exams may not have the basic scholarly requirements required to take existing courses. Thus, current curricular reforms taking place in many universities involve providing support for students lacking, for example, basic mathematical skills.

Some universities that have responded positively to Ministry suggestions have also set up new 'admission office' (AO) systems to provide the expertise and personnel required for the more lengthy procedures necessitated by more complex and varied kinds of admission policy. The first of these admissions offices was established by Keio University in 1990 and, by 2003, 278 private and eight public universities (five national, three prefectural) were using various forms of the AO system. In the 2004 academic year, the number of national and prefectural universities using AO admissions policies increased to 22 and 7 respectively. This means that by 2004 more than a quarter of public sector universities have followed the private university initiative of using flexible admissions policies. This can be seen as part of an increasing trend of organisational convergence as public sector universities adapt to their partial privatisation (*dokuritsu hōjinka*) that began on April 1, 2004. Up till now, one advantage that public sector universities have had over their private sector competitors has been the heavily subsidised student fees. Since the government is bound to use privatisation as an opportunity to cut these subsidies, national and prefectural universities have to plan for a future that will involve much more intense competition for students, especially good students. Another example of their preparation for this new era of tough competition is the increasing reliance by public universities on private companies for help in making entrance exams or checking exam questions. Kawaijuku, Yoyogi Seminar and Sundai, the three biggest *juku* chains in Japan have all been doing increasing business in this particular market (*Daily Yomiuri* 16 May 2003). Outsourcing the writing of entrance exams underlines the point made earlier in this chapter that one of the weaknesses of the traditional system was the fact that the vast majority of university entrance exams were being set by people with little or no relevant expertise in testing or assessment methodology.

The new, more varied university entrance methods are now being subjected to criticism of their own – the reverse of the criticism directed against the traditional system, i.e. for being too lax in their attitude to scholastic ability. Those alternative methods of entrance, such as the AO system or the recommendation system, that require no formal written exam, have been criticised for allowing too many unqualified young people to enter university.[20] Other methods of admission that require exams but only in a limited number of chosen subjects, have been criticised for encouraging over-specialisation at too young an age. As DeCoker points out: '[high school] students, realising that they may need to take exams in only two or three subject areas, begin to focus on these subjects at their *juku*. This narrowing of focus directly conflicts with the the Ministry's goal of broadening the high school curriculum' (DeCoker 2002: 149).

In other words there seems to be some nostalgia for the old exam-based practice whereby all academic-track students were supposed to study science, language and humanities up to the end of high school regardless of their later specialisation in university. The introduction of earlier specialisation can be seen as the continuation of the trend away from the kind of general, liberal education that was introduced during the American Occupation (1945–52). Up until the 1980s, the average student at a public university in Japan could expect to take a large number of compulsory courses right up to the end of their second year of university. The phasing-out of the 'liberal arts' education component (*kyōyōgaku*) that took up the first two years of a four-year university degree, has now been followed by a trend towards more choice and specialisation for all three years of senior high school as well. This means that whereas, under the traditional system, students in the same academic-track senior high school would generally study the same curriculum, they are now more likely to be broken up into different streams depending on the course they are aiming to apply for at university. For example, a senior high school may contain within it separate streams for humanities, sciences, foreign languages or information technology. Students will decide which stream they will follow either on entrance or after one year. The combination of new entrance methods with the choice that is now allowed by the Unified University Entrance Exam System means that present day Japanese senior high school students are more likely to make a choice about the broad direction of their university studies at an earlier age than was previously the case. Thus, as DeCoker pointed out above, one area of government education reform – university entrance reform – has had the effect of undermining another area of reform, namely efforts to enrich and diversify secondary education. Government reforms have also done nothing to stop the drift of school students to the private sector. As the curriculum for public sector secondary schools has been made less academically rigorous, parents have voted with their feet and taken their children to more *juku* classes or to private high schools.

2 Allowing graduates of Korean and other 'foreign' schools to enter university

If 'liberalisation' of the Japanese university system was ever going to be more than empty rhetoric it was going to have to include concrete measures to open up the system to those people living in Japan who had previously been excluded due to their ethnic origin. Korean nationals, who in 1994 numbered 688,144, form the largest ethnic minority group in contemporary Japan (Okano and Tsuchiya 1990: 111). Most came to Japan (or are descended from those who came to Japan) during the period of Japan's colonisation of the Korean peninsular from 1910 to 1945. The perception, inherited from the colonial era, that Koreans are second-class citizens remains widespread in Japanese society. This has lead to discrimination in employment, marriage and interpersonal relations as well as education. Surveys show that Korean children are less likely to enter university than Japanese students although the gap between them narrowed slightly in the 1990s (ibid: 113–4).

In the field of education, one of the main institutional barriers faced by Korean students was a Ministry regulation that stipulated that only graduates of Japanese high schools were eligible to take entrance exams for national universities. Although the majority of Korean children in Japan attend Japanese schools, there is a significant minority (about 20 percent of school-age Koreans) who attend Korean schools. Most members of this group attend North Korean-affiliated schools.[21] In July 1999, the Central Council of Education and the University Council (both advisory bodies to Ministry) approved a plan to allow the graduates of these Korean high schools and other foreign students to take the annual test known as *daiken* (*Daily Yomiuri* 10 July 1999). *Daiken* is a national test that was originally designed for people who had not completed a senior high school education but who wanted a chance to enter university. A candidate who passes the *daiken* qualifies to apply to universities and graduate schools in Japan.[22] Following on from the 1999 announcement, in March 2003, the Ministry announced that it was planning to allow students at Korean (and other Asian and international) schools in Japan to take university entrance exams directly without needing to go through the *daiken* stage (*Daily Yomiuri* 30 March 2003; *Daily Yomiuri* 3 August 2003). These reforms have been welcomed as steps that have removed an important barrier to equal participation by minority groups in the Japanese higher education system.

Conclusion

Critics of Japan's traditional university entrance exam system are many and they include people who have experienced the system at first hand. Even those who succeeded and were able to enter the nation's top universities, are prone to look back on the many years they had to spend cramming as an arduous and gruelling time. They are also well aware that those contemporaries who tried and failed could have been branded with that failure for the rest of their lives. During the time of Japan's 'economic miracle', such suffering and sacrifice was regarded by many as a price that had to be paid. 'Examination hell' was a rite of passage for Japan's youth, especially boys, who would then go on to become hard-working and obedient workers or dedicated and meritorious bosses. As Takeuchi comments, 'the mentality created by the examination system corresponds to the mentality desired by Japanese management' (1997: 195). According to this view, what is learned is not as important as the habits of work and diligence that are cultivated during that crucial, formative stage in a young person's life.

Those who criticised the exams on humanitarian grounds – that the suffering and the mind-numbing exhaustion inflicted on Japanese youth were evils in themselves – were banging their heads against a brick wall so long as the belief endured that the system was justified by its economic functionalism. This complacent position started to falter in the 1980s and was brought crashing down by the economic recession of the 1990s. This explains why the Japanese government and the universities are currently in the process of implementing far-reaching reforms in the way that school students are selected for places in universities. There are now many more avenues open to the aspiring student than the traditional entrance exam method. Problems with the way that exams are set and marked remain, but at least the days when the mindless cramming of vast numbers of facts was seen as a good in itself may soon be over.

The new methods of university entrance, however, have brought about different kinds of criticism. It still requires a lot of hard work to get into a top-level university in Japan but now applicants can specialise much more in their exam preparation. In this respect the entrance exam system has become more like the 'A' level system of England and Wales where candidates will specialise in three or four subjects at the age of sixteen. In this case criticisms point to the lack of a broad, rich curriculum for students at sixteen plus. Thus the changes in the entrance exam system in Japan have undermined government reforms in the area of improving secondary education.

For low-level universities in Japan the criticism often heard is that it is now too easy for students to get in. Because of demographic changes, universities often try to meet the criteria of new students rather than vice versa, as Kinmonth discusses in this volume. If a student cannot get into university through the traditional entrance exam, they can opt for entrance via recommendation or they can use the services of the admission office. The risk for the student that gets into a university too easily, however, may be that on graduation they find their degree lacks value in the employment market place. This is why changes in admissions systems are going hand-in-hand with curriculum changes. Japanese employers are becoming less interested in how hard a time a student had in getting into university and more interested in what they learned once they got there. Changes in the system of university entrance, therefore, should be understood within the broader context of the ongoing transformation of the whole Japanese university and high school system.

Notes

1 The *Guardian Weekly* ran the story under the following headline, 'Girl 2, strangled by school rival's mother' (2–8 Dec. 1999). The incident was also discussed on the BBC World Service programme 'Outlook' on 13 Jan. 2000.

2 In the days following the murder a more complex story emerged about the state of mind of the murderess when she committed the act of abduction and murder. However, the fact that so many in the press, and in the public,

jumped so quickly to the conclusion that the murder was related to school entrance competition is indicative of a national state of mind that is preoccupied with the whole process of getting into good schools, and the intense rivalry that surrounds it. (In December 2001, Yamada Mitsuko was sentenced to fourteen years in prison for the killing of Wakayama Haruna.)

3 For a detailed look at junior high schools in Japan, see LeTendre. He comments that '[m]any parents I interviewed in Japan thought that young adolescents in modern society had only narrow goals, such as passing the [high school] entrance examination' (2000: 94).

4 Even before elementary school, parents are considering the best strategy to get their offspring into a good university. The case of Wakayama Haruna, however, is unusual in that she was involved in an actual 'examination' for a prestigious kindergarten. (An 'examination' at such an early age usually takes the form of an interview with the parents and the child is not really tested.) Success in getting into such a kindergarten would lead to a fast track to university that would have spared Haruna the intense competition currently endured by other children in their teens. The vast majority of Japanese children do not have access to such a fast track and so they have to embark upon the 'marathon' that leads to university the conventional way.

5 From time to time, the Ministry criticises entrance exams for senior high schools (usually set by teachers in the schools themselves) for asking questions that are obscure or too difficult. For example, see 'Government warns schools to modify entrance exams' (*Daily Yomiuri* 25 Jan. 2000).

6 See Van Wolferen (1993: 115–17) for a critique of 'examination hell'.

7 DeCoker also makes the observation that the traditional Japanese approach to learning involves 'enduring hardship, both physical and psychological' (1998: 69).

8 Zeng has argued that western style IQ tests were never popular in Japan or other East Asian societies because they neglect the essential 'character-building' purpose of exams (1999: 81).

9 In Japan the academic year begins on April 1 and ends on March 31.

10 The sixth major subject area was created by dividing the old 'social studies' area into two: 'geography and history' and 'civics'.

11 Since it was introduced, the number of private universities making use of the NCUEE exams has increased from 21 in 1990 to 122 in 1996 (Ministry of Education 1996: 19).

12 See Roger Goodman's introduction to this volume for more on the demographic pressures to which Japanese universities are currently subject.

13 See Horio 1988: 12–13; Wray 1999: 138; Cutts 1997: 18 and McVeigh 2002: 87.

14 In this section, observations about the setting and marking of university entrance exams are derived from the author's own experience as a member of staff at two Japanese national universities as well as on conversations with faculty at other universities in Japan.

15 The TBS network made a documentary programme that was broadcast on May 30 1999. See review (*Daily Yomiuri* 10 June 1999).

16 For a typical account of these problems see 'Poor communication Japan's No. 1 enemy abroad' (AEN, 1 March 2000).
17 It would be wrong to say, however, that entrance exams were the only reason for the poor level of English language education at Japanese high schools, see Mulvey 2001.
18 Rohlen noted that 'when the public sector reforms, the private sector grows and prospers' (1983: 109). He was referring to private high schools as well as private cram schools.
19 See the Ministry web site, http://www.mext.go.jp/b_menu/houdou/index.htm.
20 See, for example, 'Soul-searching over the intellectual decline of Japan' (*Asahi Evening News*, 12 June 1999).
21 About 16,000 students study at 93 North Korean-affiliated schools in Japan. At times of tension in the international relations between Japan and North Korea (for example when North Korea fired a missile over Japan in 1998, or confessed to previous abductions of Japanese citizens in 2002), these students can become the targets of verbal or physical harassment from some Japanese people. When they leave school, some of these students enter the North Korean community's own university, which is located in Kodaira, Tokyo.
22 18,000 applicants took the daiken in 1999 and about half that number passed. 80 percent of successful candidates had previously dropped out of senior high school (Ministry of Education 2000: 151).

References

Arai, Katsuhiro (1999) 'Articulation toshite daigaku nyūshi' (Articulated university entrance exams), *IDE* June: 13–19.

Azuma, Hiroshi (2002) 'The development of the *Course of Study* and the structure of educational reform in Japan', in DeCoker, Gary (ed.), *National Standards and School Reform in Japan and the United States,* New York: Teachers College Press.

Blumenthal, Tuvia (1992) 'Japan's *Juken* industry', *Asian Survey* 32 (5).

Cutts, Robert L. (1997) *An Empire of Schools: Japan's Universities and the Molding of a National Power Elite,* Armonk, NY: M.E. Sharpe.

DeCoker, Gary (1998) 'Seven characteristics of a traditional Japanese approach to learning', in Singleton, John (ed.), *Learning in Likely Places: Varieties of apprenticeship in Japan,* Cambridge: Cambridge University Press.

DeCoker, Gary (2002) 'Deregulating Japan's high school curriculum: The unintended consequences of educational reform', in DeCoker, Gary (ed.), *National Standards and School Reform in Japan and the United States,* New York: Teachers College Press.

Dore, Ronald (1976) *The Diploma Disease: Education, Qualification and Development,* Berkeley: University of California Press.

Horio, Teruhisa (1988) *Educational Thought and Ideology in Modern Japan,* Tokyo: University of Tokyo Press.

LeTendre, Gerald K. (2000) *Learning to be Adolescent: Growing Up in U.S. and Japanese Middle Schools,* Yale University Press.

McVeigh, Brian (2002) *Japanese Higher Education as Myth,* Armonk, NY: M.E. Sharpe
Ministry of Education (1996) *Japanese Government Policies in Education, Science, Sports and Culture 1995,* Tokyo: Ministry of Education (Monbushō).
Ministry of Education (2000) *Japanese Government Policies in Education, Science, Sports and Culture 1999,* Tokyo: Ministry of Education (Monbushō).
Mulvey, Bern (2001) 'The role and influence of Japan's university entrance exams: A reassessment', *The Language Teacher* 25 (7).
Okano, Kaori and Tsuchiya Motonori (1999) *Education in Contemporary Japan: Inequality and Diversity,* Cambridge: Cambridge University Press.
Rohlen, Thomas (1983) *Japan's High Schools,* Berkeley: University of California Press.
Rohlen, Thomas and Gerald Le Tendre (1996) *Teaching and Learning in Japan,* Cambridge: Cambridge University Press.
Schoppa, Leonard J. (1991) *Education Reform in Japan: A Case of Immobilist Politics,* London and New York: Routledge
Takeuchi, Yo (1997) 'The self-activating entrance examination system – its hidden agenda and its correspondence with the Japanese "salary man"', *Higher Education* 34: 183–98.
Ukai Russell, Nancy (2002) 'The role of the private sector in determining national standards: How *juku* undermine Japanese educational authority', in DeCoker, Gary (ed.), *National Standards and School Reform in Japan and the United States*, New York: Teachers College Press.
Van Wolferen, Karel (1993) *The Enigma of Japanese Power*, Tokyo: Tuttle Press.
Wray, Harry (1999) *Japanese and American Education: Attitudes and Practices*, Westport, Connecticut: Bergin & Garvey.
Woronoff, Jon (1997) *The Japanese Social Crisis*, London: Macmillan Press.
Yoneyama, Shoko (1999) *The Japanese High School*, London: Routledge.
Zeng, Kangmin (1999) *Dragon Gate: Competitive Examinations and their Consequences*, London: Cassell.

11 Postgraduate and Professional Training in Japanese Higher Education: Causes and Directions of Change

Yumiko Hada

As Goodman notes in his introduction to this volume, the higher education sector has ben surprisingly neglected in the literature on Japanese education. It would also appear to be the case that postgraduate education is the least explored sector within higher education. Standard accounts of Japanese universities, whether in English or Japanese, have surprisingly little to say on the subject. In McVeigh's (2002) recent critique of the system, for instance, the terms 'postgraduate', 'graduate' and *daigakuin* do not appear in the index and 'research' only appears once – this, in an entry on research standards where McVeigh notes briefly that most research is done not at *daigaku* but in private companies, corporate laboratories or their affiliated research centers; that research standards in universities tend to be ignored by industry; and that university researchers often criticise their poor research facilities (McVeigh 2002: 139). Apart from this brief reference to science research, McVeigh concentrates almost entirely throughout his book on the problems of undergraduate education.

This is symptomatic of the wider neglect of the subject. With the exception of clinical medicine, searches of standard journal databases turn up very few sources on Japanese graduate training atall, apart from occasional press reports on the system in general and scattered references to programmes in law and business in particular. University graduate programmes in the mainstream social sciences and humanities are hardly ever mentioned, despite the very large number of students participating in them.

Despite this neglect, it can be argued that postgraduate programmes are of the utmost importance to the future of Japanese universities. They are not only the core elements in the production and dissemination of knowledge for the country as a whole, but they also provide the main source of training for the next generation of college and university teachers. The importance of these programmes is enshrined in the *Kyōiku kihonpō* (Basic Education Law) of 1944. Articles 2 to 4 state that the three-fold aim of master's degree courses is to provide students with extensive knowledge of a particular field, to foster their research ability and to provide professional training, while doctoral courses should promote basic research and train specialised researchers with the necessary skills. Article 65 proclaims that the postgraduate system is linked to culture through the development of theory and ways of applying it that will deepen society's understanding. Researchers are also expected to play a central role in the flow of information and in its practical applications, either through their publications or their contacts with business and industry. Government pronouncements over the years have mentioned other roles, such as professional training and the promotion of internationalisation (Daigaku shingikai 1991). The Ministry and the University Council have also been concerned about the shortage of resources available for education, research and internationalisation in Japan in comparison with Europe and America, and the shortage of

Table 11-1: Numbers of Universities in Japan, 1955–2003[1]

Year	National	Public	Private	Total
1955	228	72	34	122
1960	245	72	33	140
1965	317	73	35	209
1970	382	75	33	274
1975	420	81	34	305
1980	446	93	34	319
1985	460	95	34	331
1990	507	96	39	372
1995	565	98	52	415
1996	576	98	53	425
1997	586	98	57	431
1998	604	99	61	444
1999	622	99	66	457
2000	649	99	72	478
2003	702	100	76	526
Universities with Masters and PhD courses (2000)	346	80	31	235

researchers with PhDs in some areas. As a response, the government has sanctioned the establishment of more graduate courses over the years, in order to increase the numbers of post-doctoral researchers. As can be seen from Table 11-1, in 2000 there were 649 universities in Japan, of which 346 offered graduate courses up to doctoral level. By 2003 the number of institutions had risen to 702.

In this chapter, I will first analyse the development of postgraduate education in Japan in the post-war period, including the distribution of students between subjects, the roles of public and private universities, the changing sex ratio among graduate students and the jobs taken up on graduation. Secondly, I will consider the growing importance of professional training, particularly in law and management, in response to the changing government policies in these sectors. Finally, I will discuss briefly the links between postgraduate training, internationalisation and the development of Japan as a regional education hub.

Demography and Japanese higher education

The basic social trends affecting Japanese universities, as noted elsewhere in this book, are the declining birthrate coupled with greater rates of participation in higher education. Even though the number of 18-year olds in the population fell from 2,049,000 in 1993 to 1,500,000 in 2003, the total number of university students rose from 2,389,648 in 1993 to 2,803,901 in 2003 (Table 11-2). In two-year junior colleges (*tanki daigaku*), however, numbers fell sharply during the same period, from 530,294 in 1993 to 250,065 in 2003 (Table 11-3). Similar trends are reflected in the changing number of institutions. The number of universities rose from 534 in 1993 to 702 in 2003 (Table 11-1) while the number of two-year colleges decreased from 595 to 525 in the same period (Table 11-4).

What seems to be happening here, therefore, is a switch of students from two-year to four-year courses, accompanied either by the conversion of two-year college courses to four-year degree programmes or their closure. The population of 18-year olds is expected to decrease even further, thus increasingly affecting four-year degree programmes, although this may be temporarily offset by a continued rise in the proportion of the population attending university. The percentage of students continuing on to university from high school has now risen to 49.1 percent, a growth of 10.2 percent since 1992 (Ministry of Education 2003). But there is

Table 11-2: Numbers of students in Japanese universities, 1993–2003

Year	National	Public	Private	Total
1993	561,822	74,182	1,753,644	2,389,648
2003	622,403	120,463	2,061,035	2,803,901

Table 11-3: Numbers of students in two-year colleges, 1993–2003

Year	National	Public	Private	Total
1993	16,705	22,802	490,787	530,294
2003	4,515	17,999	227,551	250,065

Table 11-4: Numbers of two-year colleges, 1993–2003

Year	National	Public	Private	Total
1993	37	57	502	595
2003	13	49	463	425

probably a finite limit to this trend, given that the vast majority of children of middle-class parents with university education are already going to university. The combination of almost universal middle-class university education with a declining population of prospective students means that an increasing number of institutions will fail to meet their admissions targets and the result will be mergers and closures. As Kinmonth notes in his chapter, this state of affairs is already becoming a major problem for the smaller private universities and restructuring is taking place in the public sector as well, as shown in Table 11-5.

However, even though undergraduate enrolments may already be declining, graduate enrolments may not necessarily follow suit immediately. First, graduates faced with an increasingly competitive job market may decide to stay on at university for post-graduate training in the hope that this will improve their chances. Second, there is clearly a need for more trained professionals in professions such as law and management, and more law schools and MBA programmes are already being established to deal with this. Third, the level of qualifications of the university teachers themselves is rising. Until the 1990s, relatively few of the older teachers in Japanese

Table 11-5: Recent mergers between national universities

Mergers agreed
Tsukuba University + University of Library and Information Science
Yamanashi University + Yamanashi University of Medical Science
Kyushu University + Kyushu Institute of Design
Kobe University + Kobe Mercantile Marine University
Tokyo Mercantile Marine University + Tokyo University of Fisheries
Kagawa University + Kagawa University of Medical Science
Mergers in progress
Toyama University + Toyama Medical & Pharmaceutical University + Takaoka National College
Shiga University + Shiga University of Medical Science + Kyoto University of Education + Kyoto Institute of Technology
Kochi University + Kochi University of Medical Science
Oita University + Oita University of Medical Science
Miyazaki University + Miyazaki University of Medical Science
Saga University + Saga University of Medical Science

universities had doctorates. Now, many professors are acquiring them in mid-career and a completed PhD is becoming a requirement for the recruitment of new staff at the bottom of the scale. Finally, with increasing life expectancy, graduate programmes may find a growing market among older people looking for something new to do within the context of the 'lifelong learning society'.

The trend towards graduate education can be clearly seen from Ministry statistics. Table 11-6 shows the number of graduates advancing to higher-level courses in the Japanese system. In addition to the massive increase in absolute numbers over time, the percentage is also worth noting. This has fluctuated over the years, but generally it has risen from around 5 percent until the late 1980s to around 10 percent in the late 1990s. The figure is higher for men than for women, perhaps because of the massive popularity of engineering, and is also much higher for national than for private universities. Generally it is also higher for the science subjects than for the humanities and social sciences.

Table 11-6: New graduates moving to higher-level courses

Year	New graduates	Graduates advancing to higher-level courses	%
1955	94,735	6,520	6.6
1960	119,809	4,526	3.7
1965	162,349	8,024	4.9
1970	240,921	12,539	5.2
1975	313,072	15,365	4.9
1980	378,666	16,815	4.5
1985	373,302	22,056	5.9
1990	400,103	27,101	6.7
1995	493,277	46,329	9.4
1996	512,814	48,218	9.4
1997	524,512	47,906	9.1
1998	529,606	49,706	9.3
1999	532,436	54,023	10.1
2000	538,683	57,663	10.7
2000 figures by gender			
Male	333,753	43,690	13.1
Female	204,930	13,973	6.8
2000 figures by type of university			
National	103,740	31,457	30.3
Public	17,465	2,627	15.0
Private	417,478	23,579	5.6
2000 figures by discipline			
Humanities	91,824	4,464	4.9
Social sciences	216506	5,185	2.4
Sciences	18,241	6,923	38.0

Table 11-7 shows the numbers of graduates from master's degree courses proceeding to higher-level courses, presumably doctorates in many cases. Once again, there is a massive increase in absolute numbers, but the proportion of students moving has remained fairly stable, at around 20 percent. Even though the number of men in graduate education remains greater than the number of women, the percentages of male and female master's graduates continuing with their studies are more equal.

Table 11-8 shows the number of new entrants to master's courses. The discrepancy between the very high figure of 70,000 entering master's courses in 2000 as shown in Table 11-8 and the figure of

Table 11-7: Numbers of masters graduates advancing to higher-level courses, 1965–200, by gender, university, and subject

Year	New graduates	Graduates advancing to higher-level courses	%
1955	94,735	6,520	6.6
1965	4,790	1,818	37.9
1970	9,415	2,768	29.3
1975	13,505	2,991	21.5
1980	15,258	2,848	18.7
1985	19,315	3,207	16.6
1990	25,804	4,045	15.7
1995	41,681	7,022	16.8
1996	47,747	7,992	16.7
1997	50,430	8,091	16.0
1998	53,153	8,496	16.0
1999	52,850	8,462	16.0
2000	56,038	9,338	16.7
2000 figures by gender			
Male	41,963	6,726	16.0
Female	14,075	2,612	18.6
2000 figures by type of university			
National	33,651	6,430	19.1
Local	2,461	424	17.2
Private	19,926	2,484	12.5
2000 figures by subject			
Humanities	4,154	1,332	32.0
Social sciences	7,488	1,509	20.2
Science	5,351	1,567	29.2
Engineering	24,762	2,371	9.6
Agriculture	3,168	808	25.5
Health	2,544	525	20.6
Mercantile marine	18	4	22.2
Home economics	381	58	15.2
Education	4,465	394	8.8
Arts	1,207	113	9.4
Others	2,500	657	26.3

around 54,000 graduates moving into higher-level courses as shown in Table 11-6, is probably caused by the inclusion of around 5,000 students moving into clinical training, a substantial number of

Table 11-8: New entrants to master's courses, 1955–2000

Year	National	Public	Private	Total
1955	1,986	190	1,694	3,870
1960	1,691	149	1,620	3,460
1965	5,052	460	2,829	8,341
1970	7,243	599	4,515	12,357
1975	9,351	632	5,787	15,770
1980	10,995	596	5,253	16,844
1985	15,030	848	7,716	23,594
1990	19,894	1,190	9,649	30,733
1995	33,176	2,157	18,509	53,842
1996	34,834	2,262	19,471	56,567
1997	34,737	2,378	19,950	57,065
1998	36,258	2,633	21,350	60,241
1999	39,024	2,915	23,443	65,382
2000	41,278	3,307	25,751	70,336
2000 figures by gender				
Male	31,129	2,234	18,502	51,865
Female	10,149	1,073	7,249	18,471
2000 figures by subject				
Humanities	1,814	233	3,204	5,251
Social sciences	2,929	389	6,721	10,039
Science	4,464	391	1,430	6,285
Engineering	1,178	9,517	30,031	19,336
Agriculture	3,297	185	456	3,938
Health	1,661	326	1,437	3,424
Mercantile marine	15	-	-	15
Home economics	114	126	246	486
Education	4,564	17	631	5,212
Arts	366	246	825	1,437
Others	2,718	216	1,284	4,218

foreign students (discussed below) moving into graduate programmes and a number of mature students (*shakaijin*) or company employees entering graduate school (e.g. for MBA programmes) after an interval in employment. At any rate, the large increase in absolute numbers over the years and the massive importance of engineering compared with other branches of science are both very clear. What is also clear is the importance of the national universities in graduate training programmes, especially in the field of education. Private universities have a greater role in training in the humanities and social sciences.

Tables 11-9 and 11-10 show the numbers of students enrolled in master's and doctoral courses according to discipline. The most noteworthy feature here is the decrease in importance of engineering at the doctoral level. Presumably many engineers move directly into employment after completing their master's degrees.

Table 11-11 shows the number of foreign students in Japanese higher education. These figures are probably inflated somewhat by the inclusion of 'permanent residents in Japan', most of whom would be of Korean ancestry, but there has still been an impressive rise, especially from the late 1980s onwards. At the graduate level, foreign students make up a substantial proportion of the whole, probably in the order of 10 percent. About 20 percent of students from abroad are funded by the Japanese government and, as Table 11-12 shows, the great majority of them, nearly 90 percent, come from other countries in Asia. At the graduate level, foreign students can be seen to be concentrated in the national universities.

This mass of statistical information raises numerous issues, of which two will be explored in the remainder of this chapter: firstly, the relationship between graduate training and the labour market and secondly, the increasing involvement of universities in professional training, most notably in management and law.

Postgraduate education and manpower training

Tables 11-13a–d and 11-14a–d show the pattern of employment of master's and doctoral graduates respectively. Of the 35,000 master's graduates in 2000, the overwhelming majority (some 29,000) moved into professional and technical jobs of which the most popular sector by far was engineering; and 5,000 went into education or teaching. Of the nearly 7,000 graduates from doctoral courses in 2000, around a third went into medicine, another third into teaching and a quarter into engineering.

One of the major sources of employment for doctoral students, therefore, is the higher education sector itself. Tables 11-15a–b show the number of faculty in national, public and private universities divided by gender and position.

Tables 11-15 clearly illustrates a number of the important features of university faculty in Japan. First, they show the characteristic inverted pyramid struture, with professors making

Table 11-9: Number of students by field of study (master's courses)

Year	Humanities	Social sciences	Science	Engineering	Agriculture	Health	Education & Teaching	Other	Total
1960	2,870	2,370	987	1,223	372	140	291	52	8,305
1965	3,104	3,355	2,198	5,657	1,020	512	461	464	16,771
1970	5,157	4,607	2,983	10,251	2,063	909	946	798	27,714
1975	5,975	4,596	3,226	13,514	2,691	1,018	1,228	1,312	33,560
1980	5,469	4,050	3,741	14,864	2,546	1,497	1,863	1,751	35,781
1985	5,645	4,373	4,598	20,668	4,893	2,053	3,862	2,055	48,147
1990	6,009	6,366	6,484	28,399	4,046	2,710	5,328	2,542	61,884
1995	9,707	13,161	11,153	48,256	6,725	4,241	9,348	7,058	109,649
1996	10,366	14,277	11,973	50,272	6,958	4,576	10,012	7,468	115,902
1997	10,729	15,380	12,109	51,277	6,943	4,909	10,142	7,917	119,406
1998	11,023	17,090	12,117	51,951	6,941	5,204	10,107	8,822	123,255
1999	11,610	19,313	12,557	54,778	7,335	5,763	10,382	10,380	132,118
2000	12,234	21,457	12,785	59,076	7,810	6,492	10,842	12,134	142,830
2000 figures by gender									
Male	5,585	14,662	10,143	53,962	5,270	3,157	5,606	6,560	104,945
Female	6,649	6,795	2,642	5,114	2,540	3,335	5,236	5,574	37,885
2000 figures by type of university									
National	4,387	6,307	9,258	38,374	6,580	3,142	9,518	6,563	84,129
Local	547	784	748	2,272	370	624	48	1,100	6,493
Private	7,300	14,366	2,779	18,430	860	2,726	1,276	4,471	52,208

Table 11-10: Number of students by field of study (doctoral courses)

Year	Humanities	Social sciences	Science	Engineering	Agriculture	Health	Education & Teaching	Other	Total
1960	1,016	894	900	391	339	3,709	171	9	7,429
1965	1,281	1,086	1,245	1,282	424	6,101	247	17	11,683
1970	1,876	1,727	2,263	2,356	839	3,769	392	21	13,243
1980	2,860	2,430	2,589	2,358	1,095	6,191	548	140	18,211
1985	3,227	2,437	2,472	2,403	1,096	9,062	603	241	21,541
1990	3,594	2,654	3,067	4,315	1,742	11,794	668	520	28,354
1995	4,675	3,727	5,033	9,030	3,249	15,311	930	1,819	43,774
1996	5,145	4,234	5,533	10,155	3,439	16,395	1,068	2,479	48,448
1997	5,592	4,830	5,831	10,847	3,632	17,187	1,212	3,010	52,141
1998	6,019	5,217	6,123	11,170	3,823	18,091	1,388	3,815	55,646
1999	6,452	5,763	6,298	11,389	4,039	19,075	1,486	4,505	59,007
2000	6,871	6,195	6,410	11,818	4,204	20,051	1,537	5,395	62,481
2000 figures by gender									
Male	3,360	4,292	5,428	10,693	3,164	15,073	778	3,362	46,150
Female	3,511	1,903	982	1,125	1,040	4,978	75	2,717	16,331
2000 figures by type of university									
National	3,238	2,735	5,446	9,858	3,809	13,957	1,079	4,373	44,495
Local	310	398	432	465	135	1,288	29	169	3,226
Private	3,323	3,062	532	1,495	260	4,806	429	853	14,760

Table 11-11: Distribution of non-Japanese students by institution, and sources of funding

Year	University	Graduate school	Junior college	Total	Overseas students funding: Jap. Govt.	Overseas students funding: Private	Overseas students funding: Total
1960	3,874	557	272	4,703			
1965	6,250	1,459	557	8,266	482	2,985	3,467
1970	7,730	1,857	884	10,471	583	3,861	4,444
1975	10,697	2,255	1,362	14,314	1,050	4,523	5,573
1980	10,913	2,644	1,451	15,008	1,369	5,203	6,572
1985	14,264	5,477	1,601	21,342	2,427	10,062	12,489
1990	23,571	12,306	2,567	38,444	4,769	23,791	28,560
1995	32,567	18,712	3,044	54,323	6,932	36,679	43,611
1999	33,877	22,431	2,784	59,092	8,222	40,024	48,246
1999 figures by gender							
Male	18,443	13,690	554	32,687	5,488	21,243	26,731
Female	15,434	8,741	2,230	26,405	2,734	18,781	21,515
1999 figures by type of university							
National	7,463	15,855	17	23,335	7,185	14,984	22,169
Public	1,344	867	92	2,303	146	1,673	1,819
Private	25,070	5,709	2,675	33,454	891	23,367	24,258

Table 11-12: Distribution of non-Japanese students by subject and source of funding, 1999

	Japanese government				Private funds, etc.				
	University	Graduate school	Junior college	Total	University	Graduate school	Junior college	Total	Total Students
Arts									
Humanities	308	644	-	952	8,960	6,240	2,177	543	9,912
Social sciences	352	1,015	-	1,367	15,094	10,485	4,245	364	16,461
Education	102	350	-	452	1,920	792	1,095	33	2,372
Visual/ performing arts	10	70	-	80	935	522	303	110	1,015
Total	772	2,079	-	2,851	26,909	18,039	7,820	1,050	29,760
Science									
Physical sciences	27	447	-	474	572	121	414	37	1,046
Engineering	313	2,064	-	2,377	6,335	2,330	3,923	82	8,712
Agriculture	14	992	-	1,006	1,306	348	952	6	2,312
Health	34	874	-	908	1,744	229	1,502	13	2,652
Home economics	1	36	-	37	665	302	141	222	702
Total	389	4,413	-	4,802	10,622	3,330	6,932	360	15,424
Others	100	469	-	569	2,493	1,363	966	164	3,062
Total	**1,261**	**6,961**	**-**	**8,222**	**40,024**	**22,732**	**15,718**	**1,574**	**48,246**

Table 11-13a: Employment of master's graduates by field of industry

Year	Total	Constr.	Manuf.	Sales	Finance	Trans/ Com.	Services	Educat.	Pub.Serv.	Other
1965	2,282	77	924	34	7	38	952	782	121	129
1970	5,310	281	2,863	72	56	134	1,456	1,043	253	195
1975	8,160	425	4,394	128	54	252	2,014	1,375	506	387
1980	9,742	551	5,520	135	44	255	2,167	1,307	606	464
1985	13,419	668	7,644	138	96	249	3,232	1,780	871	521
1990	18,845	862	10,944	230	359	783	3,741	2,033	1,024	902
1995	28,051	1,695	14,619	445	288	1,151	6,458	2,936	1,864	1,531
1996	31,829	1,923	16,046	609	394	1,353	7,891	3,112	2,068	1,545
1997	34,223	1,955	17,117	679	394	1,522	8,847	3,268	2,150	1,559
1998	35,737	1,843	18,767	721	492	1,290	9,062	3,262	2,022	1,540
1999	34,296	1,572	17,685	657	471	1,272	9,177	3,160	1,966	1,496
2000	35,224	1,599	16,944	692	529	1,297	10,560	3,218	2,044	1,559

Note: In calculating totals, 'Services' includes 'Education'.

Table 11-13b: Employment of master's graduates by type of job

	Professional & technical							
	Engineering	Teaching	Medical	Other Prof./Tech	Total	Clerical	Sales	Other
1965	1,061	734	12	202	2,009	119	12	142
1970	3,340	1,011	60	279	4,690	336	33	251
1975	5,236	1,318	88	522	7,164	555	50	391
1980	1,027	525	119	389	8,709	6,331	1,238	113
1985	8,834	1,727	802	1,020	12,383	570	66	400
1990	12,688	1,993	315	1,768	16,764	1,230	107	744
1995	18,453	2,720	540	2,506	24,219	2,150	230	1,452
1996	20,908	2,899	712	2,417	26,936	2,878	297	1,718
1997	22,417	3,051	776	2,599	28,843	3,145	375	1,860
1998	23,182	2,994	918	2,965	30,059	3,465	465	1,748
1999	22,120	2,864	916	2,849	28,749	3,518	403	1,626
2000	22,215	2,900	1,040	3,166	29,321	3,628	391	1,884

up the largest single category, in direct contrast to European and American universities, where full professors are the smallest category. Second, it shows the small number of women in the system, although this has increased considerably since the early post-war period. Third, it illustrates the very small number of foreigners represented in university faculty. Fourth, the very large number of part-time teachers (concurrent faculty, *or hijōkinkōshi*) is clear and it is this group, which to a large extent keeps the system working. Rather characteristically also, the proportion of women amongst the part-time faculty is higher than among the full-time faculty and is highest among the non-Japanese faculty.

Table 11-13c: Employment of master's graduates by gender, degree subject, and field of industry, 2000

Year	Total	Constr.	Manuf.	Sales	Finance	Trans/ Com.	Services	Educat.	Pub.Serv.	Other
2000	35,224	1,599	16,944	692	529	1,297	10,560	3,218	2,044	1,559
2000 figures by gender										
Male	28,666	1,473	15,212	513	443	1,189	7,102	1,757	1,477	1,257
Female	6,558	126	1,732	179	86	108	3,458	1,461	567	302
2000 figures by degree subject										
Humanities	999	7	74	34	7	17	689	369	92	79
Social sciences	3,031	28	339	110	256	86	1,469	227	473	270
Science	3,028	28	1,399	71	87	127	1,077	221	142	97
Engineering	20,551	1,399	12,946	258	134	1,002	3,300	168	708	804
Agriculture	1,822	57	813	82	15	11	402	65	311	131
Health	1,714	-	707	63	-	2	863	177	55	24
Mercantile marine	8	1	2	-	-	-	3	1	-	2
Home economics	165	4	30	3	1	-	111	52	14	2
Education	2,292	1	68	30	7	12	1,965	1,657	148	61
Arts	328	9	46	8	-	1	229	142	6	29
Others	1,286	65	520	33	22	39	452	139	95	60

Note: In calculating totals, 'Services' includes 'Education'.

Table 11-13d: Employment of master's students by type of job, gender, and deegree subject, 2000

	Professional & technical							
	Engineering	Teaching	Medical	Other Prof./Tech	Total	Clerical	Sales	Other
2000	22,215	2,900	1,040	3,166	29,321	3,628	391	1,884
2000 figures by gender								
Male	20,196	1,618	441	2,258	24,513	2,401	293	1,459
Female	2,019	1,282	599	908	4,808	1,227	98	425
2000 figures by degree subject								
Humanities	40	296	27	191	554	302	20	123
Social sciences	120	169	25	315	629	1,813	87	502
Science	1,974	202	13	305	2,494	291	47	196
Engineering	17,927	136	7	1,263	19,333	435	98	685
Agriculture	978	56	10	351	1,395	194	77	156
Health	400	163	861	208	1,632	38	21	23
Mercantile marine	5	1	-	-	6	-	-	2
Home economics	28	41	17	35	121	40	1	3
Education	76	1,608	56	219	1,959	215	20	98
Arts	17	107	????	145	269	42	6	11
Others	650	121	24	134	929	258	14	85

Table 11-14a: Employment of doctoral graduates by field of industry

Year	Total	Constr.	Manuf.	Sales	Finance	Trans/ Com.	Services	Educat.	Pub.Serv.	Other
1965	1,268	4	45	-	-	1	1,157	924	23	38
1970	1,988	7	220	1	1	7	1,683	1,169	36	33
1975	1,859	7	216	4	4	11	1,487	1,180	32	98
1980	2,244	18	294	-	1	13	1,795	1,309	71	52
1985	2,798	4	324	3	2	12	2,259	1,296	106	88
1990	3,783	29	474	3	4	14	2,981	1,566	169	109
1995	5,019	75	759	13	6	24	3,658	1,975	291	193
1996	5,634	80	814	6	9	27	4,151	2,128	282	265
1997	6,201	101	922	13	8	25	4,516	2,188	334	282
1998	6,680	76	1,053	13	18	42	4,865	2,290	333	280
1999	7,120	91	962	19	36	49	5,186	2,452	436	341
2000	6,914	94	958	17	12	50	5,092	2,272	380	311

Note: In calculating totals, 'Services' includes 'Education'.

Table 11-14b: Employment of Master's graduates by type of job

	Professional & technical							
	Engineering	Teaching	Medical	Other Prof./Tech	Total	Clerical	Sales	Other
1965	58	776	296	88	1,218	5	-	45
1970	225	1,150	434	111	1,920	21	-	47
1975	224	1,143	200	170	1,737	39	3	80
1980	277	1,269	395	252	2,193	13	-	38
1985	296	1,228	880	294	2,698	21	1	78
1990	463	1,534	1,281	396	3,674	36	4	69
1995	823	1,853	1,473	654	4,803	68	8	140
1996	833	1,993	1,682	899	5,407	78	2	147
1997	1,008	2,009	1,880	970	5,867	85	7	242
1998	1,097	2,125	1,938	1,153	6,313	110	7	250
1999	1,036	2,187	2,049	1,437	6,709	117	8	286
2000	1,046	2,023	2,061	1,365	6,495	128	7	284

Professional training in law and management

In recent years, two other sectors of postgraduate education have been expanding in line with perceived demand in the labour market. In June 2002, the Judicial Reform Council decided to increase the number and quality of legal professionals in an attempt to speed up the glacial pace of court proceedings. Since the end of the Second World War, the bar examination had been extremely difficult to pass, with successful candidates restricted to 500 a year until 1995 (Nottage 2001: 116). The Council's plan envisaged that the number

Table 11-14c: Employment of doctoral graduates by gender, degree subject, and field of industry, 2000

Year	Total	Constr.	Manuf.	Sales	Finance	Trans/ Com.	Services	Educat.	Pub.Serv.	Other
2000	6,914	94	958	17	12	50	5,092	2,272	380	311
2000 figures by gender										
Male	5,761	90	892	12	11	47	4,123	1,787	325	261
Female	1,153	4	66	5	1	3	969	485	55	50
2000 figures by degree subject										
Humanities	299	-	1	3	-	-	267	232	10	18
Social sciences	459	1	9	3	1	2	406	366	6	31
Science	673	8	132	1	3	10	406	185	84	29
Engineering	1,725	71	609	6	3	33	698	489	161	144
Agriculture	466	7	76	3	1	1	278	153	57	43
Health	2,859	-	88	-	-	1	2,710	578	29	31
Home economics	18	-	4	-	-	-	14	12	-	-
Education	119	-	1	-	-	-	112	102	5	1
Arts	18	-	1	-	-	-	17	16	-	-
Others	278	7	37	1	4	3	184	139	28	14

Note: In calculating totals, 'Services' includes 'Education'.

Table 1-14d: Employment of doctoral students by type of job, gender, and degree subject, 2000

	Professional & technical							
	Engineering	Teaching	Medical	Other Prof./Tech	Total	Clerical	Sales	Other
Gender								
Male	976	1,580	1,697	1,154	5,407	102	6	246
Female	70	443	364	211	1,088	26	1	38
Degree subject								
Humanities	2	207	1	52	262	15	1	21
Social sciences	5	349	5	30	389	30	1	39
Science	136	147	2	273	558	34	-	81
Engineering	727	414	5	482	1,628	21	2	74
Agriculture	68	113	5	248	434	4	-	28
Health	54	555	2,040	184	2,833	7	-	19
Home economics	4	11	1	2	18	-	-	-
Education	2	100	-	12	114	3	-	2
Arts	-	14	-	1	15	3	-	-
Others	48	113	2	81	244	11	3	20

Table 11-15: Number of faculty in national, public and private universities, by gender and position

Year	National	Public	Private	Total	Women	%Women
1955	22,680	4,417	10,913	38,010	1,979	5.2%
1960	24,410	4,725	15,299	44,434	2,693	6.1%
1965	29,828	5,089	22,528	57,445	4,233	7.4%
1970	36,840	5,342	34,093	76,275	6,454	8.5%
1975	42,020	5,602	42,026	89,648	7,535	8.4%
1980	47,842	5,794	49,353	102,989	8,630	8.4%
1985	51,475	6,053	54,721	112,249	9,582	8.5%
1990	53,765	6,592	63,481	123,838	11,399	9.2%
1995	57,488	8,256	71,720	137,464	14,752	10.7%
1996	58,258	8,509	72,841	139,608	15,605	11.2%
1997	58,855	8,880	74,047	141,782	16,565	11.7%
1998	59,557	9,420	75,333	144,310	17,785	12.3%
1999	60,205	10,026	77,348	147,579	19,034	12.9%
2000	60,673	10,513	79,377	150,563	20,314	13.5%
2000 figures broken down by rank						
President	99	72	468	639	47	7.4%
Vice President	131	15	198	344	14	4.1%
Professor	20,463	3,463	34,211	58,137	4,595	7.9%
Assistant professor	16,717	2,587	15,568	34,872	4,575	13.1%
Instructor	5,466	1,585	12,061	19,112	3,594	18.8%
Assistant	17,797	2,791	16,871	37,459	7,489	20%
Graduate school faculty	47,302	5,681	27,910	80,893	6,098	7.5%
Non-Japanese faculty	1,632	352	3,054	5,038	1,095	21.7%
Concurrent faculty	38,189	8,712	90,667	137,568	27,877	20.3%
Non-Japanese concurrent faculty	1,484	436	6,860	8,780	3,106	35.4%

of successful candidates would increase from 1,000 after 1999 to 3,000 by 2010. In order to achieve this, major universities planned to establish law schools offering a graduate programme along American lines, lasting two years for students with a first degree in law and three years for students from other disciplines. Almost as soon as the Council's decision was announced, however, it became clear that vested interests in the legal profession had prevented the reforms from being as radical as they might have been, and insiders criticised the new measures as being surrounded by unnecessary regulations and controls. Furthermore, even with these new recruits, Japan will still have a smaller legal profession than the countries of Europe and North America, and the recruits will be from less varied backgrounds than was originally envisaged (*Nikkei Weekly* 1 July

2002). By the end of 2002, the universities planning to establish the new law schools were already experiencing difficulties in recruiting suitable staff and in drafting a curriculum (*Daily Yomiuri* 28 Nov 2002) and had found themselves in competition over recruiting judges to meet the requirement that 20 percent of the staff must be legal professionals (*Daily Yomiuri* 2 Dec. 2002). There were also worries that the high fees the schools would need to charge would scare off would-be lawyers (*Daily Yomiuri* 28 Nov 2002). Nottage argued that an opportunity for far-reaching reform was in danger of being missed and that the demand for legal skills in twenty year's time could be considerable as companies realise the utility of integrating these skills into their management and decision-making (Nottage 2001: 120–5).

The legal profession is not alone in Japan in having to face calls for reform. In the wake of an increasing number of malpractice suits, there have also been calls for the reform of medicine through the introduction of better postgraduate training (*Japan Times* 5 July 1999).

The other major area in which professional postgraduate training is expanding is that of business. With the economic recession, firms that used to provide their own on-the-job training for managers are recently beginning to rely increasingly on the universities to do it for them. According to Okazaki-Ward (2001), Japan lagged far behind the other major industrialised countries in business education until the late 1980s. Change began with the internationalisation of Japanese companies, and by the late 1980s around a third of Japanese companies listed on the Tokyo Stock Exchange and surveyed by Kobe University were sending employees to MBA courses abroad, mainly in the United States. But as Ishida notes (1997), many companies still held to the view that their own in-house management training systems were sufficient, and they only turned to the universities in order to train staff who had to deal with international business or who were being sent to their subsidiaries abroad. Ironically, the supply side of Japanese management training was in place before a strong demand for these qualifications emerged. To many companies, universities were places for training teachers and researchers, not businessmen. Another barrier was that according to Ministry regulations, master's courses required two years of full time attendance. It was only in 1988 that evening classes were also permitted, thus paving the way for the extension of training for in-post managers (Okazaki-Ward 2001).

As with law, it is the most prestigious universities, both public and private, which appear to be the most active in providing professional training, and their progress is being actively tracked in regular opinion surveys of corporate managers and companies. Keio University was for a long time the pioneer of business education in Japan (Ishida 1997) with a programme established in 1962. Until recently, it was still apparently at the head of the pack: the *Nikkei Weekly* (7 May 2002) reported that Keio had been ranked highest, in a survey of corporate managers, followed by Hitotsubashi and Waseda. Criteria for ranking included the quality of curriculum and faculty, the degree of 'globalmindedness' and the location. A majority of respondents, however, still felt that the Japanese business schools were not as good as those in America and thought that more MBA programmes were necessary in Japan. It also seems to be the case that Japanese companies still fail to reward their employees' new qualifications with promotion or extra compensation and this presumably dampens the demand for such courses. Another survey in which companies evaluated 114 universities, appeared six months later (*Nikkei Weekly* 7 Oct. 2002), and in this Keio was also ranked top, followed by Waseda, Tokyo and Kyoto. This survey was based on five criteria, including research (where Tohoku University was ranked highest), cooperation with the private sector, continuing and professional education, quality of alumni and international collaboration with overseas universities. Clearly international standing is an increasingly important issue in Japanese higher education, and this is reflected in government and private attempts to make Japanese universities more competitive and international, so that the best students no longer have to move overseas. These initiatives will be discussed in more detail in Eades' final chapter in this volume.

Problems with an emphasis on postgraduate education

In 1999, Kitamura noted that those in charge of more than 90 percent of postgraduate courses in national, public and private universities were either carrying out, or planning to carry out, reforms to take postgraduate training more seriously (Kitamura 1999: 191). It is, therefore, possible to see a general consensus that postgraduate schools should be given greater priority, and that an improvement in the quality of education and research is necessary in order to adapt to advanced technology and the requirements of globalisation. An increased stress on postgraduate education, however, raises a variety of issues:

1 The effects on undergraduate students

First, the policy of expanding and giving priority to postgraduate training may have a negative effect on undergraduate education by causing it to be taken less seriously. Many of the best research and teaching staff have become increasingly involved in the graduate school programmes, at the expense of undergraduate students for whom much of the teaching is being taken over by graduate student teaching-assistants. In addition, as universities compete for resources at the graduate level, the question of wider access to higher education institutions and equality of opportunity in education may also be given less importance. In reality, when the provision of postgraduate education expands, increases in expenditure and school fees are inevitable. Also, in the employment market, as the rate of postgraduate education increases, the bachelor's degree will begin to lose some of its status, resulting once more in increasing 'credentialism', or the stress on the importance of paper academic qualifications, and raising the level for entry to some sectors of the labour market.

2 Implications for postgraduate students

Secondly, there are the implications for postgraduate students of an increased emphasis on postgraduate education. Many universities are trying to increase their intake of graduate students, but some are not getting sufficient numbers for particular disciplines or programmes. In order to fill up their places, the less popular graduate schools are promoting the admission of mature students and overseas students. There are other considerations in relation to these students, such as language tuition both for Japanese students taking courses in English and foreign students taking courses in Japanese.

In relation to the national and public universities, there are also potential problems for graduate students. First, as the universities gain more autonomy, the economic burden of the university fees for postgraduate students is likely to increase. Second, due to the expanding number of postgraduate students in the market and the downsizing of many universities and research institutes, it will become increasingly difficult to find tenured jobs.

3 The implications for university teachers

The increased number of students may create a financial improvement, but it may not be accompanied by an increase either in the number of staff or institutional facilities, except in the departments securing Center of Excellence awards (see Eades' chapter) or other special funding. As a result, existing staff may find that they are facing an increased burden of classes and supervision. This would reduce the time available for the research and publication on which their careers, and the reputation of their universities, depend.

4 The stratification of higher education institutions

The gap between individual universities is also continuing to expand and competition is becoming more severe. The existence of a graduate school in Japan is becoming an indicator of the ranking of the university itself and the prestige of those who teach there. It is inevitable that the distribution of university resources and project funding will become more and more unequal as government sources of research funding are increasingly divided on the basis of research output. The difference between the universities based on whether or not they have graduate programmes will become more marked and entry exams will become more competitive. As the 'audit culture' spreads, number of refereed publications will be used as one of the major evaluation mechanisms, simply because it is both convenient and internationally accepted. As a result of the need to publish, academics will have to reduce the amount of time and energy they devote to teaching if they are to survive, and ultimately this will have a negative effect on both undergraduate and postgraduate students.

Conclusion: Looking to the future

As can be seen from the above tables, graduate education has enjoyed a steady expansion since the 1950s, along with the higher education sector as a whole. At the master's degree level, the main demand has been for engineers, many of whom move into employment after the completion of their master's degrees.

Medical postgraduate training is also clearly linked to the job market. The spread of disciplines at the doctoral level is more even and here one of the major sources of employment has been the expanding university sector itself. There are, however, three new elements complicating the picture at present.

The first is the increasing demand for other professional qualifications, not only from the engineering and medical sectors, but also in law and business. In the case of law, the demand for change is being stimulated by the government itself through its proposed legal reforms. In the case of business, the demand is coming from Japanese companies, which are increasingly globalised and which are realising the utility of both more highly trained manpower and of more effective training programmes than have traditionally operated in-house. Inevitably it will be the more prestigious universities with longer-established programmes, such as the Keio with its strong links to foreign schools, that will benefit from this market. But for many companies, the reason for training their senior staff is in order to send them abroad. Given that foreign language expertise is part of this package, there is a real question as to whether it makes sense to make use of the new Japanese programmes now coming on stream, or send their staff to longer-established and more prestigious programmes in North America or Europe. The logic must be in favour of the latter.

The second complicating factor is the increasing support from government for high-level research, both through established research funding channels and new programmes such as the Centers of Excellence (COE) initiative. The substantial government funds being invested in these programmes is to some extent distorting the market, so that the polarisation between the well-funded and more prestigious institutions and the rest will accelerate more rapidly than would otherwise have been the case. As an increasing number of academics now possess PhD degrees, the question of ranking between these degrees will also arise, with graduates from the most prestigious universities having an advantage over the rest in the job market. This will in turn mean that there will be more applicants for these universities, and the rest will find their graduate programmes failing to recruit sufficient good students to make them viable. The implication is that, for the lower-ranking institutions, a policy of launching graduate programmes in order to make up for the shortfall in undergraduates will at best only succeed in the short term, thanks to programmes like the COE which tend to benefit the best.

Third, there is the issue of the globalisation of higher education as a whole, as the countries with the most prestigious universities compete for the best students internationally. North America and the United Kingdom have long held an international advantage because they teach in English, and Australia is also well placed to penetrate the Asian market. Japan clearly has aspirations to become the major educational hub for Northeast Asia, and at the graduate level it is already recruiting a substantial number of foreign students. However, with the massive economic growth in the last thirty or forty years in countries such as Taiwan, South Korea and even mainland China, Japan is likely to face increasing competition, even within its own region. It is also probable that as English language teaching improves within Japan, and as English proficiency becomes increasingly important for Japanese company employees, a greater number of Japanese students will also choose to study overseas in order to enhance their own chances in the job market.

All these factors will increase the start-up costs for Japanese universities launching and expanding graduate programmes of a sufficient quality to attract the best students either from home or abroad. Many of them might well decide that, rather than reinvent the wheel, the most sensible way forward is to join forces with existing brand names and market leaders abroad, and form international partnerships in the form of exchange and double degree programmes. Meanwhile, we can expect that a large number of the graduate programmes currently available in institutions unable to become players in this global market will wither and disappear as the best staff and students go elsewhere. After the long period of steady expansion and consolidation in graduate education in the second half of the last century, the next few years promise to be much more volatile and uncertain as the forces of globalisation exert increasing pressure on Japan's undergraduate and graduate programmes alike.

Note

1 The statistics and tables referred to in this paper are taken from the Ministry site, http://www.mext.go.jp/english/statist/index11.htm, and are based on versions downloaded on 18 August 2003.

References

Ishida, H. (1997) 'MBA education in Japan: The experience of management education at the Graduate School of Business Administration, Keio University, Japan', *Journal of Management Development* 16(3): 185ff.

Kitamura, K. (1999) *Gendai no daigaku/kōtō kyōiku* (University and higher education today), Tokyo: Tamagawa University Press.

McVeigh, Brian (2002) *Japanese Higher Education as Myth*, Armonk, NY: Sharpe.

Nottage, L. (2001) 'Reform in Japanese legal education', *Ritsumeikan Journal of Asia Pacific Studies* 8: 112–42.

Okazaki-Ward, L.I. (2001) 'MBA education in Japan: Its current state and future direction', *Journal of Management Development* 20(3): 197ff.

12 Reform of the University English Language Teaching Curriculum in Japan: A Case Study

Gregory S. Poole

Introduction

In this chapter I will first review a few of the many theories proposed as to why Japanese have great difficulty in acquiring proficiency in English as a second language. The blame is usually laid on either the learners themselves or their learning environment. After all, the argument goes, motivation for learning English must be low in a country where more than 95 percent of the inhabitants speak Japanese as their first language.[1] There is little immediate necessity or perceived need for English, or any foreign language for that matter. When explaining these difficulties of English language teaching (ELT) and learning in the Japanese context, observers have rightly called for an examination of 'cultural and historical influences' (Koike 1978: 3). Unfortunately such an examination of the context of ELT in Japan is sometimes distorted into historically revisionist statements that attribute the failure either to the often heard 'island nation' (*tan-itsu minzoku)* explanation,*2* or culturalist arguments that emphasise how the unique traits of Japanese people present a major obstacle for ELT reform.[3] As Aspinall (2003) has pointed out, although such viewpoints have been recently couched in the progressive arguments of 'language ecology', they in fact become self-fulfilling in their prophecies and tend to say more about the politics of ELT in Japan than about the actual historical or sociocultural context.

Then, in keeping with the theme of this volume, I will examine changes in ELT at higher education institutions (HEIs) in Japan by exploring what exactly is being reformed. First I will focus on the context of language education in Japan, and specifically the sociocultural and historical constructs of ELT at the university level. What is the cultural history of English education in Japan, especially in terms of methodology, and how does this compare to the larger world of ELT around the globe? What reforms are being proposed? In terms of English education, what are the challenges facing universities in general? After addressing these questions of general context, I will then look at what reform means at one specific institution. How has an attempt at reform in the ELT curriculum at a private university in Tokyo been confounded by certain cultural and institutional 'roadblocks', while at the same time affecting the practice of the language teacher? Are these changes isolated attempts at reforms, or indicative of a university-wide implementation of 'accountability' and its concomitant 'audit culture'? I aim to include the teachers' voices in my discussion to better illustrate their views on these changes.

Failure of ELT in Japan

On the surface the lack of success with ELT in Japan appears discordant with the fact that Japanese education shows relatively good results in other areas. Japan is famous for 'borrowing' and 'copying' technology, and anthropologists have noted that such 'copying' is an important theme in Japanese education – '"imitation is the highest form of praise" in the Japanese cultural logic' (Rohlen & LeTendre 1996: 371). In fact, the Japanese language itself consists of fully 13 percent loanwords, mostly from English (Honna 1995: 45). Why then has there been such a widespread failure in, effectively, learning to 'imitate' the English language? For the past century lay persons and scholars alike have proposed various theories to explain this paradox.

Aspinall (2003) summarises the five major reasons put forward for ELT failure in Japan, arguments both as to why English education has 'failed' and why Japanese speakers of English as a second language (L2) are inept. Any English teacher in Japan would most likely offer one or more of these if asked why Japanese cannot speak English well:

1. there is a great linguistic disparity between Indo-European languages, such as English, and Japanese which is an Altaic language;
2. there is a lack of real need for English in a monoglottal society such as Japan;

3 the predominant ELT methodology has been grammar-translation, which is not an effective way to teach communicative skills;
4 the culture of the language classroom in Japan precludes effective language learning;
5 there is an exotic and fashionable image of English which emphasises entertainment value rather than the hard work necessary for effective language learning.

The most comprehensive explanation of language education failure I have come across is offered by the socio-linguist Loveday (1996: 95–99) who describes ELT in the context of language contact in Japan. Reiterating some of the reasons summarised above, he concludes that Japan is a case of a 'non-bilingual distant contact-setting' because of deficiencies that are related to 1) the system of education, 2) the teachers, 3) the institutions and 4) the socio-linguistic environment. He argues that the education system has failed because of the emphasis on grammar and translation, the wash-back of entrance exams and a history of reductionist concentration on receptive skills for decoding foreign texts. Teachers are at fault because of their often limited proficiency in English, lack of overseas experience and opportunities for practical training (faculty development, or 'FD' as it is often glossed at universities), and for perpetuating large, mixed ability classes with a strict syllabus and time limits using outdated, boring texts prescribed by the Ministry. There is an institutional conservatism that inhibits effective English language learning – the local classroom norm of teacher-centred lecturing, collective conformity, emphasis on rote-learning methods and absolute correctness, and students motivated only by the extrinsic demands of university entrance exams. Finally, socio-linguistic attitudes hamper proper second language learning due to 1) the linguistic distance between Japanese and English, 2) culturally specific styles of expression and interaction with an emphasis in Japan on self-control, modesty, reassurance and perfectionism (factors which when combined prioritise the written text over verbal communication and make for taciturn students in the language classroom), 3) a non-integrative attitude of ethnocentrism among Japanese speakers, 4) a lack of both perceived and actual need for foreign languages,[4] and 5) little support for maintenance of language skills after schooling leading to wide-scale attrition.

Although these hurdles for ELT in Japan parallel factors that hamper second language learning in other monolingual societies such as Britain or the United States (see Holliday, 1994 and Thornbury, 1998), there is a widespread belief in Japan, held by the person on the street and the education expert alike, that ELT has failed. Brian McVeigh sums up this belief nicely – 'If English teaching at the pre-tertiary level is a disaster..., it is at the tertiary level that English education becomes peculiar, with inverted, simulated ideas and practices that actually sabotage English learning' (McVeigh 2002: 157). This paper primarily addresses the tradition and attempted reform of these ELT practices by looking at changes in methodology and curriculum in higher education (HE) language programmes.

The changes in the university language programmes, and the HE curricula in general, reflect recent societal pressures in Japan. The effect of the post-war baby boom is now over and the phenomena of *shōshika* (declining birth rate) and *kōreika* (aging population) are appearing in the news on an almost daily basis. Educational institutions in general are now being challenged to adapt to these changes. For universities, the severe drop in the number of young adults in Japan has had serious consequences. Whereas up until only ten years ago the numbers of applicants produced a literal glut in the HE market as Roger Goodman mentioned in the introduction, experts predict that by 2009 at the latest the places available at HEIs will most likely equal the number of applicants.[5] Although the competition to enter elite universities will continue to be fierce, the lower-ranked institutions are already beginning to feel the crunch of *iki nokori* – survival of the fittest. In fact, the statistics for the year 2000 indicate that nearly a third of Japan's private four-year HEIs, and well over half of the private two-year colleges, failed to reach their enrolment targets. Since tuition fees account for over two-thirds of a private institution's income, their economic viability is clearly being threatened and they are being forced to find new markets for students. One of Japan's most vocal reformists and respected commentators, Amano Ikuo (1999, forthcoming), explains that although in the past HE has been predominantly a stagnant 'seller's market' in Japan, it is now being transformed by demographics and other pressures into a more diversified 'buyer's market'.

In the past, there was little pressure to reform the curriculum. The 'buyer's market', however, has forced universities to seriously reconsider the 'product'. Not only are admissions offices scrabbling to find new customers, but administrators and faculty are also beginning to recognise the equally crucial issue of retention. Efforts to keep students involved in the higher educational process has, for arguably the first time in 30 years, led to current theoretical debates about teaching and curriculum reform. This has led to a culture in some universities of faculty development (FD) and in others of parallel extension programmes. This paper will explain the approach taken by one private university in Tokyo that has decided to go the road of 'FD' in an attempt to improve its 'product'.

ELT at Japanese universities

The numerous descriptions and explanations of the poor state of English education in Japan usually emphasise how 'the poor English abilities of students are rooted in pre-tertiary-level training' (McVeigh 2002: 157). Many of these critical descriptions, though accurate, do not necessarily explain the changes that have taken place in ELT at Japanese universities over the past 50 years (Henrichsen 1989; Koike 1978; Seki 1988; Tanaka et al. 1987; Terauchi 1996 and 2001; Wadden 1993). Though admittedly inadequate in scope and only effecting incremental change,[6] nevertheless, there have been legitimate attempts to reform tertiary level English education in Japan. These changes to some degree parallel larger changes in applied linguistic and language teaching theory worldwide. As I have briefly noted above, much of the explanation of failure in English language training in Japan has often been based on arguments that are culturally-specific in nature. Certainly the socio-cultural context of ELT must be paramount in any analysis. However, as I have argued elsewhere (Poole 2001), the shortcomings of the reforms at the tertiary level may in fact reflect more upon the socio-cultural realities of the institutional milieu of ELT at HEIs worldwide – a 'smaller culture of the ELT classroom' – than on the 'larger culture of Japanese peculiarities'.

Context

As Goodman mentioned in the Chapter 1, Japan has one of the highest rates of post-secondary school attendance among all industrialised nations with 2.5 million undergraduates enrolled at over 600 national, public and private four-year universities (Hirowatari 2000). Over half of all Japanese teenagers, then, apply to take a college entrance exam for admission into a tertiary institution. As Aspinall describes in his chapter in this volume and I have described elsewhere (Poole, forthcoming), most such admissions exams include a compulsory English proficiency subtest although English as a Foreign Language (EFL) is not a state-required subject at primary, secondary or tertiary schools in Japan. Partly because of this, university entrance exams focus on English. While only a handful of students are exposed to language classes in primary school, over ten million twelve to eighteen year-olds, and another million or so university students, have no choice but to study English.

Not only is English a requirement to enter college, but most students also study the subject at some point during their four years of attendance. Nearly all tertiary institutions offer foreign language courses, and EFL is by far the most studied subject of these. In fact, although students sometimes have a choice of different English classes from which to choose, EFL in some form is a required subject at nearly every tertiary institution in Japan. In fact, the nature of the English language-teaching milieu at Japanese colleges corresponds closely to Holliday's description of a worldwide phenomenon he has defined as 'Tertiary English and Secondary English Programs' or TESEP (Holliday 1994). These TESEP attributes include:

1 EFL as a part of a wider curriculum and influenced by institutional imperatives[7]
2 ELT has a role alongside other subjects in socialising students as members of the work community
3 EFL is but one of many subjects taught and must work within the parameters and resources that are delimiting factors for all courses
4 ELT methodology choice is limited by institutional-wide approaches adopted across different subjects, as well as the expectations of the actors themselves (students, language teachers, teachers of other subjects, administrators and the Ministry.

In other words, though there are certain peculiarities that exist in Japanese ELT at HEIs (McVeigh 2002:157–158), many of the generalisations that describe the university context of language teaching and learning may in fact be attributes not necessarily unique to the Japanese experience but part of a wider phenomenon of tertiary English programmes worldwide. In fact, Kubota (1999) has argued, correctly in my opinion, that observers need to take more care in their evaluations of the Japanese context and that there exists an over-emphasis of essentialised 'features' of Japanese students in the research literature on ELT. Holliday points out a similar danger of assuming too much when he argues that '"learner" carries the implication that the only purpose for being in the classroom is to learn...[while "s]tudent", on the other hand, implies roles and identities outside the classroom' (Holliday 1994). Likewise, anthropologists have also noted that, for many students at HEIs in Japan, classroom learning is in fact not always the main priority and warn that the 'western' view of 'learner' may not fit with the Japanese model (McVeigh 1997; Poole 2003).

One example of the over-generalisations that are rather common in the ELT literature is the description of Asian students as 'often quiet, shy and reticent in ESL/EFL classrooms, indicating a reserve that is the hallmark of introverts. These ethnic groups have a traditional cultural focus on group membership, solidarity and face-saving, and they de-emphasise individualism' (Oxford, Hollaway and Horton-Murillo 1992: 445). While any EFL teacher who has spent time in a Japanese university language classroom would probably agree that many of their students are quiet, a language teacher in a North American college might just as easily label their class of eighteen year-olds as 'reticent' or 'face-saving' (see Sacks 1996). The dangers of generalisation aside, nevertheless, the fact remains that the perception of English language teaching at Japanese universities is that of failure, and this perception has challenged both university educators and Ministry officials for much of the twentieth century. Responses to this challenge have varied and for the most part real change has been superseded by mere rhetoric. What is interesting in the context of this volume, however, is what the tradition of ELT in Japan entails, what reforms have been discussed, and why they have failed in the end, or been doomed from the outset.

ELT methodology: The tradition of *yakudoku*

To address this question of ELT reform, it is necessary to first discuss the major trends in language teaching and learning in Japan, especially noting the change, or lack of change, in methodology over the years. In the university tradition of ELT, *yakudoku* (commonly defined as

Grammar-Translation or GT) methodology has often been the preferred teaching and learning style. *Yakudoku* has a long tradition in Japan, some (Henrichsen 1989: 104–107) trace its origin to the Nara and Heian periods (710–1185 A.D.) when Japanese Buddhist scholars were greatly influenced by the Chinese written language without regard for oral proficiency. Studying and reading Chinese in Japan evolved into an art of translation that attempted to compensate for the difference in grammatical structure between the two languages – with 'the target language…first translated word-by-word, and the resulting translation reordered to match Japanese word order' (Hino 1988; see also Hino 1993). Later in the Edo period, *rangaku* (the study of Western sciences through Dutch) began to complement this interest in Chinese and also necessitated the *yakudoku* approach to language learning (Wada and McCarty 1984: 28).

Though the GT method was predominant at the pre-war high schools and preparatory schools for university (*kōtōgakkō* and *yōka)*, once they had entered university, students were trained as specialists in subjects such as medicine, economics, law or engineering, and English lessons were not part of the curriculum. As a result of the Meiji programme to hire foreigners (*oyatoi gaikokujin*) to assist in modernisation efforts and to teach at tertiary institutions (McConnell 2000: 8–13), however, much of the university curriculum was delivered in foreign languages, similar to present day bilingual immersion programmes offered at some Canadian and European institutions. Since technical terms had not been translated into Japanese, even Japanese professors lectured in English, French, or German (Henrichsen 1989: 120). Mori Arinori, a Minister of Education during the Meiji period who was later assassinated for his modernising ideas, even proposed making English the official language of Japan (Amano 1990: 82). In late Meiji, however, the 1890 Imperial Rescript on Education, following the Education Ordinance of 1879, emphasised a growing nationalism. Soon all university courses were taught in Japanese and there was a resulting decline in English-speaking skills. While in much of the Meiji period university students studied '*in* English and *through* English, but never *about* English' by the twentieth century a change in the medium of instruction meant that students 'had reached the stage of learning *about* English *in* Japanese' (Henrichsen 1989: 122). *Yakudoku* methodology once again gained prominence as the preferred form of teaching English.

Reform – the oral approach

In pre-war Japan, then, while English taught through *yakudoku* was part of the liberal arts approach to preparing students for the imperial and private universities at *kōtōgakkō* and *yōka* respectively, the curriculum of the HEIs focused on specialised training. While the intention was not to develop proficiency in communicating in spoken English, nevertheless for those Japanese who traveled abroad, lack of communicative skills proved embarrassing.[8] Concern for Japanese students' lack of spoken-English ability prompted the intelligentsia to privately fund a special linguistic advisor to the Ministry in 1921. An international search landed the British linguist, Harold E. Palmer, from University College, London. An expert on language teaching methods, he was appointed director of the Institute for Research in English Teaching (IRET) and edited a professional journal published by IRET, *The Bulletin*, which dealt with language teaching methodology. Palmer's lecture tours and annual IRET conventions, aimed at spreading the gospel of 'Oral English' teaching methods, became popular sources of inspiration for many teachers around the country and his efforts were rewarded with an honorary doctorate from Tokyo Imperial University in 1935. His position, however, was peripheral to the Ministry and his recommendations, therefore, never became official policy. Nevertheless, the 'Palmer Oral English' approach was an important predecessor to a later reform innovation implemented in post-war Japan by the English Language Exploratory Committee (ELEC) and funded by the Rockefeller Foundation. This was known as the Fries Oral Approach to language learning (Henrichsen 1989).

Charles C. Fries established the first English Language Institute in the United States at the University of Michigan and is widely perceived to be 'the first applied linguist in the modern sense' (Howatt 1984: 313) and his 'Michigan Method' is known worldwide for its success in training American linguists during the Second World War. This effort by the ELEC at ELT innovation lasted for twelve years, from 1956 to 1968, with the unabashed goal of re-educating language teachers in Japan by 'the adoption of an almost revolutionised system of teaching English' (Henrichsen 1989: 34). The persistence of *yakudoku* methodology in spite of these efforts at reform suggests the pernicious strength and perceived efficacy of this tradition of teaching in Japan, and supports the argument that implementation of change in ELT must be predominantly an indigenous effort.[9]

Communicative Language Teaching (CLT)

Japanese ELT experts, themselves, have formed two factions, one supporting the *yakudoku* approach and one in favour of the 'communicative approach' – 'one saying that cultural enrichment through reading is important in the traditional manner, the other saying that English is needed for international communication' (Wada and McCarty 1984: 28). This latter group, though again employing theories from abroad, provided the impetus for a second wave of ELT reform at universities in Japan in the 1970s and '80s. During this period, language teaching worldwide underwent a change in perspective that has been called the Communicative Language Teaching (CLT) 'revolution'. A disenchantment with grammar-translation and a search for a more effective 'oral approach' to language learning was one impetus to the development of a communicative teaching theory and methodology, an approach that has indeed changed thinking about language teaching and learning in a 'revolutionary' way. Shifts in theory of language were also instrumental in the CLT 'paradigm shift' (Higgs 1985). The Chomskyan revolution in linguistics not only destroyed the behaviourism camp, but the resulting grammatical theory was not of much interest to teachers, as 'Chomsky himself loosened the bonds between linguistic theory and methodology' (Whitley 1993: 138). In Japan, tertiary level language teachers who had been proponents of Fries' Oral Approach saw CLT as the 'next step' in English teaching methodology and published a collection of reports on communicative methodology in the 1987 volume *Gengo shūtoko to eigo kyōiku* (Tanaka et al. 1987).[10]

Theory and practice – the gap

Tsuda, Suzuki and other Japanese ELT scholars have emphasised the need for nativist answers to questions of appropriate methodology. Aspinall (2003) argues convincingly that there is a strong political agenda in the case of Tsuda and Suzuki, but also points out that taken at face value there is relevancy to their claims. I agree with both Aspinall and Terauchi that, for the most part, 'attempts in the past to superimpose methods from overseas have generally been a failure not only because of the lack of appropriate training and shortage of materials, but also because of the existing approach to university education' (Terauchi 2001: 52). This failure to properly contextualise the method of learning with the learning environment has been the plague of ELT worldwide, not only in Japan. In North America and the British Commonwealth as well, there has arisen an unavoidable 'gap' between ELT theory in the literature and actual practice in the classroom. Through twenty years of observation of language classrooms and teacher training programmes in the United States, Europe, Australia and New Zealand, Thornbury (1998) concludes that the CLT method of ELT 'has never been anything but direct and that strong CLT – apart from its one moment of glory in Bangalore (Prabhu 1987) – has been and remains a chimera' (Thornbury 1998: 110). ELT teachers, whether in London, Cairo or Tokyo, are not convinced by research findings, rather they are concerned with whether or not the method is easily understood and can be adapted to their local situation (Whitley 1993: 147).

This 'gap' between CLT theory and classroom practice, while quite evident in North America, Britain and Australia, is especially pronounced in Japan and the rest of Asia. Bharghava (1986: 6) is quite resentful of 'the ignorance of the advocates of the communicative approach of the social, economic and educational conditions in...Asia and Africa'.[11] Other teachers in Asia dismiss the 'ethnocentrism' of the export of both the CLT approach (see Kuo 1995) as well as the education of international TESOL students in English-speaking countries (Liu 1998). Many ELT observers notice that though perhaps initially welcomed with great enthusiasm, 'the CLT approach has encountered a passive but enormous resistance from the majority of the EFL teachers and students' (Yang 1997: 187).

The reason for the general perceived 'failure' of CLT in Asia is often defined as the result of insensitivity to the cultural realities of the region. The influence of Confucianism in Asian education is often emphasised in these discussions (see Cortazzi and Jin 1996; Ellis 1994; Flowerdew 1998; Kelly and Adachi 1993; Oxford et al. 1992; Stapleton 1995). Partly because of these warnings and criticisms, teacher trainers in the Communicative Approach are certainly aware of the challenges and dangers of exporting western methodologies *in situ*, without considering the cultural and social milieu of the education environment (see Holliday 1994; Kramsch and Sullivan 1996).

However, as I mentioned above, though the so called 'cultural' explanations in the recent literature are at first convincing, some observers (Cheng 2000; Kubota 1999; Littlewood 2000) have warned that over-emphasising these factors when explaining challenges to CLT, risks a simplistic, cultural-deterministic argumentation that is not necessarily 'grounded' in reality. Holliday's (1999) proposal of a 'small culture' model is one pertinent approach to analysing social factors in language teaching in a more situationally-specific manner. As much as the CLT 'gap' in Asia can be attributed to 'large culture' differences, many of the practical challenges to the adoption in Asia of a 'strong' version of CLT (Howatt 1984) are not terribly different from the challenges that exist in 'the West' as Holliday (1994) has pointed out in his TESEP model mentioned above. Below I will provide a case study of ELT reform at one HEI in Japan to argue this point. In fact, if one looks at the specific CLT 'gap' in Japan, i.e. the challenge of reforming tradition at a Japanese university, the three reasons that Thornbury (1998: 110) suggests as the cause of this 'gap' in Britain, America, Australia and New Zealand , namely overcoming the hurdles of (1) the constraints imposed by grammatical syllabi, (2) the teachers' need for low-risk instruction strategies and (3) the students' expectations, appear to be equally applicable in the Japanese context.

University ELT reform: A case study

At my field site and place of employment, Edo University of Commerce (EUC),[12] there have been a number of curriculum changes over the past few years that, within the context of this private college, are serious attempts at reform. After first discussing 1) my fieldsite, 2) the faculty, 3) the changes in the *zemi* (seminar) and *gogaku* (foreign language) classes, and 4) the process by which these changes have been implemented, I will conclude with a discussion of how teachers feel these curriculum reforms may or may not affect actual ELT teaching practice.

The field site

Edo University of Commerce is part of Edo Gakuen, a private gakkō hōjin (educational corporation) which was founded a hundred years ago. Originally the Gakuen included a kindergarten and primary and secondary schools (later becoming a tertiary institution) but, because of the post-war educational restructuring and later Gakuen financial troubles, now only the kindergarten and the university remain. The urban campus is on a few acres of prime real estate in a rather affluent area of west Tokyo, 15–20 minutes from Shinjuku, the busiest station in Tokyo. EUC admits nearly 600 new students a year, and there are a total of about 2500 students enrolled in the four-year undergraduate program. There are more men than women (80/20) – probably due to the fact that the school was originally for men only.[13] There are two schools, the Faculty of Commerce and the Faculty of Management, and students choose from a number of different programmes of study. In curricular matters, the third division (Liberal Arts – of which I am a member), plays a strictly supportive role to the other two faculties and while there are numerous classes on offer in the humanities and sciences, students can only major in one of the business courses. There is also a small graduate programme, which offers an MBA and PhD degree in business management, mostly through evening and weekend classes.

The faculty

As at many Japanese universities, there is a very striking and important distinction between 'core' and 'periphery' faculty at EUC. The university employs about 55 full-time[14] and over 100 part-time faculty. Full-time staff teach between three and eight 90-minute classes (*koma*) per week in addition to various committee and departmental responsibilities. A few teachers with responsibilities in the graduate programme teach more *koma* than this. The *gogaku keiretsu* (Foreign Language Group or FLG), of which I am a member, comprises six full-time and about 25 part-time adjunct teachers. The six tenured members of the FLG have between four and twenty years experience at the University. In addition to teaching between five and seven *koma* per week, all six teachers are responsible for committee work; three of the FLG faculty are presently chairing university committees.

Given the preconception that centralisation is a hallmark of Japanese institutions, it might be surprising to discover that at private universities, at least at EUC, hiring is handled almost entirely at the *keiretsu* (departmental) level. The subject teachers decide the necessary qualifications, and this information is passed to the administration and then announced at the *kyōjukai* (General Faculty Meeting) and publicised through the relevant inter-university and public channels in the case of full-time positions. More often than not, however, there is little time to properly advertise for part-time positions, and full-time teachers use their networks to fill the vacancies. Every member of the *keiretsu* comments on the qualifications of the applicants and then, for the full-time positions, the prospective employees are interviewed by a hiring committee. The result of this screening process is then brought to the *kyōjukai* for approval. This approval process is at first consensus-seeking but, in the case of full-time staff, a vote is called and the majority of the Faculty Senate must approve the appointment. Although no public lecture or teaching presentation is required of applicants, careful scrutiny at the *kyōjukai* level tends to ensure employment of a capable, if not the most capable, candidate.

Teaching schedules are also decided by consensus amongst the teachers in a given *keiretsu*. Since there are six full-time and 25 part-time adjunct teachers in the FLG and between them they teach on average more than 4 *koma* a week (Monday to Saturday) making up a total of 130 *koma* of language instruction per week, deciding who teaches what on which day is not an easy task. This is complicated by a number of factors: half of the entire undergraduate student body (all first and second year students or about 1,200 in total) are enrolled in mandatory English Communication (EC) classes; the students in these classes are streamed into three levels by means of a proficiency test in the first week of April and an achievement exam given in the last week of December; over half of the 130 language *koma* are electives; there are five different foreign languages on offer, and students can choose from a selection of more than ten different types of language class. Although there is some attempt made to match teacher interests and abilities with the type of class to be taught, scheduling concerns do tend to dictate teacher assignments.

The adjunct part-time ELT faculty at EUC can be divided into two groups: those with full-time positions at other schools (the minority) and those who have a full schedule of entirely adjunct work (the majority). Part-time colleagues are not always formally and systematically included in university curriculum planning or implementation and professional exchange is, therefore, not an overt priority. The primary responsibility of part-time faculty is classroom teaching. The part-time faculty are not expected, or even allowed, to attend the many 'confidential' staff meetings held by full-time faculty throughout the year nor would most want to attend even if it were possible. As most full-time teachers have experience as part-time faculty at other institutions, they have no illusions as to the role of adjunct professors in providing input into the language programme. Conversely, a few of the (foreign) adjunct faculty feel that the tenured teachers 'work too hard [at administration]' and need to 'get a life [outside the college] during school vacations'. There is the perception that the full-time faculty choose to live and breathe the university even though the assumption is that they have a choice not to be so 'busy' outside the regular 9-5 workday. This interpretation, however, misses the symbolic significance[15] of the core/periphery distinction at EUC. Although the tenured teachers actually have a lighter teaching load than the adjunct teachers, they acquire status from their involvement in the powerful 'core' activities of the university, not least of which involves being a member of the *kyōjukai*.

Another dichotomy is that between the Japanese and non-Japanese faculty. Of the approximately 25 language teachers at EUC, over half are 'foreigners'. There is very little interaction between the Japanese and 'western' teachers of English, for example. There is a strongly-perceived gap in teacher methodology. The foreigners tend to believe that all Japanese teaching pedagogy is basically grammar-translation (GT), while the communicative classes taught by foreign teachers are often considered *rakushō* (easy or 'gut'[16] classes) by the Japanese teachers.[17] Probably both due to different ideas of teaching methodology and contrasting work ethics, the *gaijin* (foreigner) staff are sometimes accused of not being 'serious' by the Japanese staff, though in the past few years this may have changed.

The teachers lounge is also divided, if not physically then socially, into two groups: 'westerners' and Japanese. Although discussions are predominantly not about work-related issues, peer support is evident and teaching methodology and classroom management is shared openly among 'western' colleagues. One of the major perceived differences involves different ideas of college education. Although most foreign language teachers are lenient in their assigning of year-end grades, 10 percent of all students still fail to pass the first-year English classes required for graduation. Both informal interviews and year-end questionnaires reveal that the majority of these students fail classes taught by non-Japanese teachers because of lack of attendance. Special classes are set-aside for second year students to 'repeat' the coursework they failed to complete in their first year. When I questioned the pedagogical appropriateness of this segregation, a Japanese full-time faculty member commented that the practice, though not educationally sound and certainly not 'western', was in line with the 'Japanese philosophy of college education'. However, a more pragmatic interpretation is that by 'giving' unmotivated students credits merely as a convenience there is less conflict. This burden of a growing number of students, who do not have enough credits to graduate, falls on the full-time Japanese staff and this reality necessitates a different 'philosophy'.

Curriculum reforms

Over the past two years, the foreign language and first-year seminar (*zemi-ichi)* curricula at EUC have undergone substantial changes. Still in their early stages, these reforms have initially focused on 1) providing a better-integrated overall curriculum and 2) streaming the students according to level, in the case of the language programme, and interest, in the case of the *zemi-ichi* or first-year seminar group. These reforms are not insignificant if one takes into consideration that 1) traditionally, professors, at the majority of the private and public colleges and universities throughout Japan, have each had nearly total autonomy in teaching matters[18] and 2) that, historically, streaming took place only during the entrance examination process – once at a particular university all students have been effectively regarded as the same irregardless of ability or interest.[19]

The impetus behind the above reforms was multi-faceted. The introduction of a new school of management at EUC necessitated a university-wide reform of the curriculum. The process was decentralised by the Committee for Academic Affairs (*kyōmuiinkai*), which asked all the departments including the *gogaku keiretsu* (FLG) to rethink and adjust their individual curricula. A further impetus was the dissatisfaction with the university curriculum in general and, in particular, with the foreign language programme which was exposed as failing in its mission. This was partly because of the sheer size and visibility of ELT at EUC where the *gogaku keiretsu* was by far the largest in terms of number of classes on offer and number of teachers employed. This visibility was boosted by the presence of foreign, 'native English' teachers on campus. In terms of the *gogaku keiretsu* also, the third facet of this drive for change to the curriculum was the willingness amongst the full-time teachers to both engage in *hansei* and to look for creative solutions, though this willingness also involved self-serving reasons as noted below. In the past, before the 2001 school year, neither the ELT nor the *zemi-ichi* curricula and class syllabi had been decided institutionally; individual teachers, not academic affairs committees or subject departments, were given total responsibility for both the planning and content of these classes. However, such a *laissez-faire* approach changed last year, as the department (in the case of the EFL classes) and the academic affairs committee (in the case of the *zemi-ichi*) decided to take control and revamp the curriculum for these two freshman courses.

The first 'dumbing down' of the curriculum[20] to cater to the perceived decline in student ability was in the area of languages. In the English *gogaku* curriculum the two required EFL classes had been taught by non-Japanese instructors (natives speakers), who were primarily adjunct faculty, while the small number of elective classes were taught by Japanese teachers. Although under the new curriculum most classes are still taught by part-timers, the ratio has changed. The FLG decided that incoming first year students could not handle the required English Communication classes taught exclusively by native speakers. Since 2001, therefore, the curriculum was changed so that Japanese teachers of English would be responsible for all first year students, and the foreign staff would teach only second year or above. Significantly, therefore, in terms of their symbolic importance, full-time Japanese English teachers are now teaching core classes that are compulsory and not merely peripheral (electives) to the ELT and EUC curriculum.

Full-time Japanese teachers are also more involved in the curriculum by streaming the incoming first year students into different levels and the syllabi by designing the wide range of elective classes now on offer. To adjust to the increasing need for EUC students to possess more and more 'qualifications' and 'certificates' (*shikaku*) to list when job-hunting, the first-year ELT syllabus was adjusted to help students attain a better score on the TOEIC exam. Furthermore, using a standardised testing instrument, incoming students are now streamed according to ability. These reforms have resulted in substantially more work for the full-time EFL teachers, most of whom are now teaching seven *koma* as well as spending many hours in curriculum planning and programme development. As a result, a few dedicated part-timers have been enlisted to help ease the workload of the full-time professors.

The *zemi-ichi*, since it is a 'home-room class', has always been taught exclusively by full-time faculty members. In the past, however, there has never been a common syllabus, or even a common objective, for this course. Teachers have had total freedom in doing as much, or as little, in the way of teaching, counseling, lecturing and leading student research projects, as they felt inclined. There has been no direction for new teachers. Even as a new foreign teacher, I was given no guidance. An entirely new *zemi-ichi* programme, however, was implemented at the beginning of the 2002 school year and not only is there now a common syllabus and a clear objective, but all students have been assigned the same textbook as well (*Daigaku de nani o manabu ka*). Both the *zemi-ichi* programme and the individual teachers have been given the full support of the academic affairs committee and administrative staff. In addition, as part of the new *zemi-ichi* curriculum the university decided (at the considerable expense of several hundred thousand dollars) that all first-year students and *zemi-ichi* faculty would participate in a two-day orientation in Izu Peninsula, a famous resort area in Shizuoka Prefecture, west of Tokyo. This was well planned in advance, of course, and executed smoothly in a regimented fashion typical of such institutional outings in Japan. The resulting feeling was that incoming students needed more practice in basic study and research skills and so, to help them adjust to the academic demands and freedoms of a university, the *zemi-ichi* was redesigned as this sort of remedial class. Practice in reading, writing, summarising, discussion, presentation and even etiquette were all to be part of the syllabus whereas before teachers were allowed to teach anything they wanted (or not teach at all, as a very few were accused).

Process of change

Shōshika, the declining birth rate in post-baby-boom Japan, is perceived by some teachers as being the impetus behind these curriculum reforms but there does not seem to be as direct a relationship as I had originally thought. As two teaching staff members told me, 'curriculum and teaching reform will not necessarily impact on the number of applicants as this is usually determined by the name of the school and its location. Rather by giving more support to first-year students these changes might help to retain students that are already enrolled'. In other words, the implicit understanding amongst some faculty is that this may be a strategy to gain control over the educational process at EUC in hopes that 'better' schooling may reduce the attrition rate. This was a topic that the *gakucho* spent considerable time addressing at both the entrance ceremony and the first year students' orientation. In recent years the dropout rate at EUC has reached an alarming rate of over 10 percent.[21]

Through my observations, and conversations with teachers, it has become clear that the *gogaku* and *zemi-ichi* changes were implemented partly as an attempt to reform practice amongst instructors (and thus to more effectively teach students). This increased control over practice is multi-faceted and for the *gogaku* courses it involved the following considerations, as I have witnessed them:

1. The L2 teaching-style of the foreign instructors was considered by Japanese teachers to be too much of a 'culture shock' for *ichi nensei* (first-year students).
2. The firing of teachers in Japan is generally difficult but the curriculum changes (coinciding with the new *gakubu*) gave a ready excuse for terminating the contracts of a few part-time teachers. Likewise, professors explained the curriculum changes as being necessitated by the Ministry. This approach to change has been described as 'higher education as risk management' (Bradley 2002).
3. Curriculum change was a less radical option than a proposal strongly advocated by one full-time language teacher – that of outsourcing the entire ELT programme to a private educational corporation.[22]
4. Previously, Japanese teachers of English were not directly involved in the compulsory classes of the core curriculum and they felt concerned that their role in the university may become marginalised.

Due to the considerable open opposition from faculty towards the changes in the *zemi-ichi* curriculum, it was necessary to accomplish the process in two steps: first, in 2002, the selection process by which the new first years chose their *zemi-ichi* classes was changed; then, in 2003, the entire syllabus was reformed. Many of the *senmon* (business) teachers explained to me directly in conversation, and argued indirectly in the *kyōjukai*, their view that more control was needed over the *zemi-ichi* classes because: (1) of the need for a better 'advisory' system to help students adjust to college life, and (2) the importance of helping students with writing and self-presentation skills so they may have a head start in job-hunting.[23]

The administrative staff echoed these rationalisations for change. The head of the *gakuseika* (Student Affairs Office) gave me a detailed explanation as to how the first-year orientation had emphasised the need 1) for students to learn 'college study skills' (*manabikata*) and 2) to provide an 'EUC orientation' to new students.

An interesting tangential development to the curriculum reforms has been an increased interest in faculty development (FD) workshops amongst the FLG teachers. In 2002, two seminars were conducted – the first on computer-assisted language learning and the second on project-based language learning. Though arranged and organised by the full-time staff, both workshops were conducted by part-time teachers who volunteered to share their expertise and their time. Regardless of the ensuing effect on the actual quality of teaching practice, these events certainly added an air of professionalism to the department, helped to bridge the divide between part-time and full-time teachers and raised the status of the FLG within the EUC as a whole.

Conclusions

For the professoriate, the most controversial of the reforms appeared to be that related to changing their practice from focusing on research to teaching. Interesting for me, as an anthropologist, is how this controversy appears to highlight the tip of a larger cultural iceberg centred on the concept and role of 'the professor' (*kyōju*) – is the professor ultimately a researcher (*kenkyūsha*) or a teacher (*kyōikusha*)? The success of curriculum reform and FD hinges on this issue debates about which go on just below the surface. The discussions on this deeper issue reflect the differences among teachers and the level to which they accept or are committed to the current reforms.

From listening to the voices of the actors themselves, I have discerned three important issues within the larger debate surrounding practice. These are 1) the importance of identifying with, and feeling, a stronger sense of responsibility toward the institution of EUC rather than one's academic field of research;

related to this is 2) the importance of teaching and *gakusei shidō* (student guidance); and 3) the importance of devoting time and energy in a volunteer effort on committees and working groups (*gyōsei*) to actually implement these reforms. Not all the teachers are equally committed to these reforms and their voices seem to be qualified along lines of both generation and gender.

Identifying with the university

The new President of EUC, himself a graduate of the college, often sums up the curriculum reforms on the importance in professors having a commitment and responsibility to the university itself. His vision is one of 'the body corporate [EUC] shining brilliantly... (*hōjin ni haeru*)'. In interview, therefore, I decided to ask some of the teachers how they felt about their professorial role.

I asked for example, 'Do you see yourself as a professor at EUC, or do you see yourself as a professor of international marketing?' I elaborated, 'By definition, as *kyōin* (a professor) we have a foot in both camps, in our field and our workplace. Which foot are you leaning on more heavily?'

One male professor in his mid-thirties said, 'It is more natural for me to say, "I am a professor at EUC" than for me to say, "I am a researcher or professor of accounting science"'. The youngest member of staff, also male, explained that, 'At this point I identify more strongly with my workplace than with my field of research. Frankly, if the university goes under I will not be able to conduct research anyway...so at this point in time my priority is on [improving] my workplace rather than my field of research'.

Women, however, tended to disagree. One recently hired staff member explained herself, 'Honestly, I don't see myself as a member of the EUC faculty for that long, so I don't feel I can make a commitment [to volunteering time to work toward reform]...I have the confidence that, based on the quality of my research, I will be able to sell myself to another university. I don't think [I will be able to change jobs] based on my administrative skills or volunteer work on committees'.

There seemed to be a generational difference as well. Indeed, such expressions are probably behind the President's strongly-held opinion that teachers over fifty years-old are hopeless in terms of group spirit or responsibility to the body corporate. On the other hand, he told me that 'teachers in their 30s and 40s are flexible (*sunao*) and understand the importance of the organisation (*soshiki*)'.

Role as teacher

After school hours, the President explained to me his view as to the importance of teaching over research. 'Anybody, no matter how busy, can be a successful researcher – in fact, the busier the scholar the better the research. Service to the university should be paramount for all teachers. I have no respect for teachers that try to escape their teaching duties by complaining of the workload in terms of number of classes, or by saying irresponsible things like recruiting visits to high schools (*kōkō hōmon*) is "a waste of time and we should be given more time for research"'.

When I interviewed the faculty and asked them whether they thought that the reforms at EUC would change the teachers' identity by focusing on teaching rather than research, one professor in his forties replied, 'Yes, I do. It is already happening. But we must be better at evaluating teaching, not just research'.

I also asked, 'What is the most important role of the university professor?' 'A university professor's main role is to teach one's academic subject and approach to this subject or method of research to students', replied one associate professor in his thirties. Older professors and women, however, tended to disagree. A woman in her mid-thirties responded, 'Research is the most important role of a university professor'. Another woman of similar age was more specific – 'Half of a university professor's job is as a researcher, and half is as a teacher. And because we are judged more on our research, in actuality it is more like 60/40'.

Despite the fact that some staff still hold to this view, however, there is less and less room for prioritising research over teaching at EUC. Internal assessment of teachers was implemented in 2001 in the form of student evaluations. The curriculum changes, and the subsequent focus on teaching, are also parts of the market-driven reforms and the new view of students as 'customers'. As the President said in so many words, teaching is, of course, an essential ingredient in this new formulation.

Some teachers are feeling the pressure and opting for early retirement or moving into other positions at different universities. One professor of labour economics, well-respected in his field in Japan as a prolific scholar, decided to quit his position before the mandatory retirement age and move into a think-tank. He was not popular with the students because of his condescending attitude in the classroom. 'We can't stand the guy!' two students told me when I asked them about his teaching. I would argue that this debate of *kyōiku* versus *kyōikusha* at EUC was a factor in 'helping' this professor to 'decide' to retire.

Gyōsei – administrative and committee work

Contrary to the preponderance of age-based hierarchies in Japanese society, in order to effectively implement the reforms at EUC, most of the committee chairs appointed since 2001 have been in their thirties or forties, while the older professors have been given less of a voice in administrative matters.

Interestingly, some younger male teachers did not necessarily resent this added workload. The youngest member of the faculty told me that, 'I feel that my most important role at this university is to help make changes. Though this may come across as somewhat conceited, I honestly feel that if I do not help to make and implement changes [in the curriculum], nobody will'.

In contrast, women have not been given roles of responsibility within the administrative and committee structures at EUC. Nor do they necessarily want such positions, knowing full well the time commitment involved. For example, one woman told me, 'as a woman I am not asked to participate in a lot of meetings and committees. This can be seen as either a positive [more time to focus on research and teaching] or as a negative [being excluded]'. This situation is cause for concern, however, among certain people at EUC and some wonder aloud whether it is healthy. At a secret 'inner circle' meeting, with only young male members of the professoriate in attendance, a younger faculty member complained directly to the University President: 'What about the women teachers? President, none of your choices for committee chairs involves women. I feel you are wasting a valuable resource as many of the women teachers are capable leaders and interested in taking on committee responsibility…'

This awareness of gender issues is atypical, however, as one female professor noted in an interview: 'Not only at EUC, but at many universities there are [male] professors who express openly their opinion that women should not be given positions of responsibility [within the university]'. She continued, on the other hand, that 'there exists this over-sensitivity that is openly asserted that "we must include more women on committees [and in the reform process]" which I think is missing the point [that individuals should be judged on their ability and not their gender]'.

Changing practice

A few of the full-time teachers were puzzled as to why they had to change their practice and seemed indignant at being asked to follow a new *zemi-ichi* syllabus. They questioned the ability of the professors to teach to a common syllabus. Others welcomed the reforms but had little faith in the teachers' ability or willingness to change their practice and assumed that most would merely pay lip service to the changes. One of the younger full-time economics teachers told that she did not feel that 'there ha(d) been any recognisable change in practice (*ninshiki saretenai*)' amongst the profesors. She went on to say that, 'although I agree that the *zemi-ichi* seminar was a success, I feel that in teaching freshmen it is not right to assume that they are not adults. I think it is wrong to take a condescending attitude'. A physics professor told me that although he felt the curriculum change was a step in the right direction, he did not believe this reform would be enough necessarily to impact on the deeply-entrenched concept of the *sensei* – 'We won't really be able to change our attitude until there is better evaluation of teaching and not merely research'. Another professor agreed that though the curriculum had changed substantially, he felt only the younger teachers would be able to 'keep up with' these changes. In the end, he said, there was no strong feeling of collective 'identity' among the teachers who were, after all, 'just a collection of individualities with very little real will or intent for cooperation'.

Certainly for many professors, it was business as usual regardless of change at the university. Though few professors would question the 'common sense' (*jōshiki*) of the reform per se, in actual practice most teachers I spoke to indicated that there had been little if any change in actual teaching and research practice. That said, however, over the months following the introduction of the reforms, I heard and participated in many more discussions of 'the educational process' than in past years. I contend, therefore, that at EUC the changes in both the curriculum and in the make-up of the professoriate (ten new full-time faculty were appointed in 2001–3), although arguably 'makeshift reforms', were responsible for creating an environment that allowed for new discourses not only on faculty micro-politics or research agendas but also on the central issues of practice. These new discourses resonate with the terms of the 'audit culture', discussed by Roger Goodman in the introduction to this volume, as they are student (or customer), *chōsa* (survey) and *hyōka* (assessment) driven.

Ancillary to these debates was a pervasive feeling of somewhat increased pressure on the students to learn than in recent years – a pressure that began with an increased commitment from the teachers. Amongst faculty there was a general feeling that the 'quality' of the student body was dropping every year. As the pool of high school applicants grew smaller and smaller, the admissions committee, in order to meet quotas felt they must admit students they would not have taken ten, or even five, years previously. Of course, since the quality of the entrance exams and admissions process was suspect anyway (Poole 2003, forthcoming) it was hard to assess objectively whether or not the actual academic level was actually dropping. More importantly though was the perception among teachers that the students were not of the same calibre as in years past. This led to the afore-mentioned curriculum changes, which are significant in the eyes of those implementing these reforms.

Arguably the move to reform the professoriate has had some affect on practice. Between 2001–3, I noticed a change at EUC in the seriousness of intent amongst teachers. This attitudinal shift was initiated by a general change in mood at the university in terms of the individual accountability (to borrow another term from the 'audit culture') of teachers. This started with simple notices in the teacher's room stating, for example, 'Please conduct a full 90 minute class' and with verbal warnings by the *gakuchō*. By mid 2003, however, it had culminated in the news that the *gakuchō* and administration would be tying one of the (twice yearly) bonuses to performance. Henceforth, teachers were told that they would be graded in the areas of research, teaching and administration and that the 'hardest working' teachers would be given a greater proportion of the performance bonus. At the time of writing, it remained to be seen how exactly this rule would be applied and whether the assessment would be a 'true' measurement of teacher performance. For example, it was understood that assessments of teaching practice would not, initially at least, be done through student or peer evaluations of actual performance but simply by counting teacher absenteeism. Interestingly, this reflected the general grading policy for students in many of the smaller liberal arts and seminar classes – ie. if a student has excellent attendance they normally receive an excellent grade irregardless of actual performance or participation.

I believe this approach to teacher evaluation may be seen as an example of what anthropologists refer to as 'a multi-vocal symbol'. While most teachers at EUC appeared to agree that we were being challenged to better educate each incoming student cohort, there was also a diversity of interpretations as to what is a 'good' learner, a 'good' teacher or a 'good' education. The measurement of absenteeism as a means to assess teaching performance is considered 'crude' and 'meaningless' by some but is apparently deemed to be an effective starting point on the road to accountability by the *gakuchō* and other managers at the university. Though the difference in salary, as a result of earning the small performance-related bonus, would be at most 200,000 yen over the entire school year, this policy is symbolically very significant.[24] In this form, I wonder if such an assessment of 'good practice' is not a rather progressive implementation of an institutional audit practice since I sense the effect may be more of a carrot than a stick for those seen as struggling. In addition, the calls for assessment and evaluation were not initiated only by the university administration as many of the already hardest-working faculty members supported the President in implementing these changes.

Finally, descriptive studies of reform at individual universities may show that there is in fact what could be called 'reformational' change occurring in departments across Japan, whether language departments or otherwise. I suspect that while comparative work on universities around the country might show some positive aspects of the 'audit culture', ethnographic studies might at the same time add to our knowledge of the 'cultural impediments' (see Poole 2000) to change and the issues of 'immobilist politics' (see Schoppa 1991) that exist in the various individual 'university cultures'.

Acknowledgement

The efforts of many individuals have helped to make this a better paper. William Bradley of Ryukoku University kindly offered a detailed critique of an initial draft. Likewise, James Friedman of the Science University of Tokyo and Ann Butler of Keio University contributed tips that have helped to make the paper more readable. Discussions with Robert Aspinall of Shiga University and members of the Anthropology of Japan in Japan helped formulate my ideas for this paper. I am indebted to the entire faculty at my field site, the 'Edo University of Commerce'. Finally, I must thank the editors, Roger Goodman and Jerry Eades. Roger Goodman, especially, provided the initial impetus as well as invaluable support and advice during the writing process. Needless to say, any shortcomings are entirely the author's responsibility alone.

Notes

1 Granted, there is a language diversity within the Japanese community in Japan that is seldom acknowledged in the popular literature and local mindset (see Denoon et al. 1996; Lie 2001; Loveday 1996; Maher and Yashiro 1995; Maher, 1996; Miller 1982; Sugimoto 1997) which usually assumes a 'uniqueness' of Japanese, a distinctiveness that in reality 'relates not only to Japanese linguistic experience but actually to all human language' (Miller 1982: 26).

2 'Our lack of proficiency in English may be ascribed to certain national traits developed over a long period of historical and geographical isolation' (Suzuki 1973: 114).

3 One author has summarised the challenge for English language education as the need to 'modify a nation's 2,000-year-old mental habit or psychological complex' (Harasawa 1974: 77), while recently, religious differences, in particular Confucianism, has been invoked as a major obstacle (Stapleton 1995).

4 I have heard that more foreign texts are translated into Japanese than any other language worldwide. This claim is not difficult to accept by those with extended experience in Japan.

5 One possible consequence may be the transformation of some universities into non-competitive 'community colleges' serving the local working populace for retraining and continuing education.

6 Unless the university entrance exam system is drastically changed, most critics of Japanese ELT feel there can be no real reform (see Aspinall in this volume and Poole, forthcoming).

7 National imperatives are also a part of the equation since the state of confusion in the liberal arts (LA,) and ELT curricula specifically, can be traced back to 1947 when the U.S. converted the state-run high schools (*kōtōgakkō*) along with the independent, post-secondary prep schools (*yōka*) into the first and second years of LA curricula at public and private undergraduate institutions nationwide. These *kōtōgakkō* and *yōka* were literally transferred in their entirety into the universities – materials, methods, and faculty – with little effort at integration into the more

specialised subjects of the university faculties. In fact, the yōka curriculum of the 1920s is nearly identical to the LA curricula at many universities today, 80 years later (Terauchi 2001: 19). ELT, obviously, was one of the subjects transferred from the yōka into the 'university' and thus relegated to this 'under-class' of faculties (Matsuyama 1993: 51). No attempt was made to incorporate a system of majors and minors that might have better harmonised the disparity. Instead, a dichotomy between LA teachers and specialist faculty has evolved. In fact, many in Japan could not accept the lack of differentiation or specialist training that was imposed by the American Occupation. These were clearly inferior institutions labeled 'universities' (Schoppa 1991: 36). English language teaching has been caught in the middle of this dichotomy for the past 50 years.

8 After attending a meeting in Washington D.C. in 1921, one of the Japanese participants lamented that '(w)e make a poor showing at international conferences when compared with the Chinese' quoted in Henrichsen 1989: 122.

9 One author recommends that the story of the defeated efforts of the Oral Approach reform 'be required reading for any foreigners new to Japan who imagine they are going to reform language teaching' (Tripp 1985: 30).

10 In the same year the Japan Exchange and Teaching (JET) programme was inaugurated by three different ministries of the Japanese government. At an expense of half a billion dollars a year, Japan decided to 'import' thousands of foreign nationals yearly to work in public schools partly to bring more CLT methodology to the English teaching process (McConnell 2000).

11 Bharghava's description of 'eurocentrism' is vivid: 'A situation where an average class is sixty to eighty strong, where an overwhelming majority of learners are from the economically and culturally weaker or disadvantaged sections of society, where there is little or no motivation to learn a foreign language, where the linguistic and communicative competence of the average teacher is extremely poor, where library facilities are hopelessly inadequate and where a moribund examination system controls and governs all teaching and learning – a situation of the above description is simply inconceivable for these high-brow theorists. For many native speakers of English, Asia and Africa still continue to be academic colonies to be civilized by self-professed "experts" peddling their expensive wares in the third world countries' (Bhargava 1986: 7).

12 A pseudonym

13 This reflects the fact that the subject matter, commerce, does not fit with the typical 'finishing school' mindset of a traditional Japanese college education for women (see McVeigh 1997).

14 At most HEIs in Japan there is no system of tenure. Normally, however, full-time faculty members have job security equivalent to tenured faculty at institutions in the west. The exception to this rule is the practice at certain private and public universities of only giving short-term contracts to some full-time faculty members, often foreigners.

15 This difference is not only symbolic, of course, if one considers the income of the full-time staff.

16 American slang for a university elective class that is passable with minimal effort.

17 Perhaps this is partly explained by a cultural difference – foreign teachers generally favour evaluating students based on in-class participation and performance rather than the year-end testing that is common in many classes taught by Japanese staff.
18 In most cases individual faculty members decide what and how they will teach, set their own syllabus, teach the course, design their own exam and then mark this exam and assign grades. There has until very recently been absolutely no external assessment, let alone formal discussion amongst teachers within a department, of the teaching on offer. This is usually very surprising to colleagues involved in HE institutions in North America, Britain, Australia or New Zealand.
19 In Japan egalitarianism is a strong social more in educational circles.
20 Palfreyman (2001) discusses this phenomenon in the context of higher education in Britain.
21 Though North American higher education institiutions often have considerable rates of attrition, at Japanese universities the norm is different. Usually every effort is made to 'help' the student to graduate (see McVeigh 2002).
22 Recently more than one university in Japan has purchased the services of an outside company to both hire part-time teachers and deliver the ELT curriculum.
23 Kelly (1993) argues that the societal role of the university in Japan differs vastly from that of American higher education institutions. One of the needs a Japanese university fulfills is to provide an opportunity for students to find employment. This activity is called *shūshoku katsudo*, (job-hunting) and for many students this consumes much of their energies during their third and fourth year of university.
24 Transposed to the U.K. higher education environment, where starting salaries are in the range of 17,000 GBP, this amount (roughly 1000 GBP) would probably take on more than symbolic importance (Goodman, personal communication).

References

Amano, I. (1990) *Education and Examination in Modern Japan* (trans. W. K. Cummings & F. Cummings), Tokyo: University of Tokyo Press.

Amano, I. (1999) *Daigaku: Chōsen no jidai* (Universities: Challenging times), Tokyo: University of Tokyo Press.

Amano, I., and G. S. Poole (forthcoming), 'The Japanese university in crisis', *Higher Education*.

Aspinall, R. W. (2003) 'Japanese nationalism and the reform of English language teaching', in Goodman, Roger and David Phillips (eds.), *Can the Japanese Change Their Education System?,* Oxford: Symposium Books.

Bhargava, R. (1986) 'Communicative language teaching: A case of much ado about nothing', paper presented at the Annual Meeting of the International Association of Teachers of English as a Foreign Language, Brighton, England.

Bradley, W. (2002) 'Higher education reform as risk management: The case of Japan', paper presented at Japan Anthropology Workshop 2002 Conference, Yale University, New Haven, CT.

Cheng, X. (2000) 'Asian students' reticence revisited', *System* 28: 435–46.

Cortazzi, M., and L. Jin, (1996) 'Cultures of learning: language classrooms in China', in Coleman, H. (ed.), *Society and the Language Classroom*, Cambridge: Cambridge University Press.

Denoon, D., Mark Hudson, Gavan McCormack and Tessa Morris-Suzuki (eds) (1996) *Multicultural Japan: Palaeolithic to Postmodern*, Cambridge: Cambridge University Press.

Ellis, G. (1994) *The Appropriateness of the Communicative Approach in Vietnam: an interview study in intercultural communication,* Melbourne: La Trobe University, Australia.

Flowerdew, L. (1998) 'A cultural perspective on group work', *English Language Teaching Journal* 52: 323–29.

Harasawa, M. (1974) 'A critical survey of English language teaching in Japan: A personal view', *English Language Teaching Journal* 29(1): 71–79.

Henrichsen, L. E. (1989) *Diffusion of Innovations in English Language Teaching: The ELEC Effort in Japan*, New York: Greenwood Press.

Higgs, T. (1985) 'The input hypothesis: an inside look', *Foreign Language Annals* 18: 197–203.

Hino, N. (1988) '*Yakudoku*: Japan's dominant tradition in foreign language learning', *JALT Journal* 10 (1 and 2): 45–55.

Hino, N. (1993) 'Nihon no gengo bunka to yakudoku', *IRICE Plaza* 4: 36–52.

Hirowatari, S. (2000) 'Japan's national universities and *dokuritsu gyōsei hōjin-ka*', *Social Sciences Japan* 19: 3–7.

Holliday, A. (1994) *Appropriate Methodology and Social Context*, Cambridge: Cambridge University Press.

Holliday, A. (1999) 'Small cultures', *Applied Linguistics* 20 (2): 237–64.

Honna, N. (1995) 'English in Japanese society: Language within language', in Maher, John and K. Yashiro (eds) *Multilingual Japan,* Clevedon, England: Multilingual Matters, pp. 45–62.

Howatt, A. P. R. (1984) *A History of English Language Teaching*, Oxford: Oxford University Press.

Kelly, C. (1993) 'The hidden role of the university', in Wadden, P. (ed.), *A Handbook for Teaching English at Japanese Colleges and Universities,* Oxford: Oxford University Press, pp. 172–91.

Kelly, C. and N. Adachi (1993) 'The chrysanthemum maze: Your Japanese colleagues', in Wadden, P. (ed.), *A Handbook for Teaching English at Japanese Colleges and Universities,* Oxford: Oxford University Press, pp. 156–71.

Koike, I. (1978) 'English language teaching policies in Japan: Past, present and future', in Koike, I., M. Matsuyama, Y. Igarashi and K. Suzuki (eds.), *The Teaching of English in Japan*, Tokyo: Eishosha.

Kramsch, C. and P. Sullivan (1996) 'Appropriate pedagogy', *ELT Journal* 50: 199–212.

Kubota, R. (1999) 'Japanese culture constructed by discourses: Implications for applied linguistics research and ELT', *TESOL Quarterly* 33 (1): 9–35.

Kuo, H. S. (1995) 'The (in)appropriateness and (in)effectiveness of importing communicative language teaching to Taiwan', *University of Hawai'i Working Papers in ESL* 13: 21–47.
Lie, J. (2001) *Multiethnic Japan*, Cambridge, Mass.; London: Harvard University Press.
Littlewood, W. (2000) 'Do Asian students really want to listen and obey?', *ELT Journal* 54: 31–36.
Liu, D. (1998) 'Ethnocentrism in TESOL: Teacher education and the neglected needs of international TESOL students', *ELT Journal* 52: 3–10.
Loveday, L. (1996) *Language Contact in Japan: A Socio-Linguistic History*, Oxford: Clarendon Press.
Maher, J. and K. Yashiro (eds) (1995) *Multilingual Japan*, Clevedon, England: Multilingual Matters.
Maher, J. C. (1996) 'North Kyushu creole: A language contact model for the origins of Japanese', in Denoon, D., M. Hudson, G. McCormack and T. Morris-Suzuki (eds) *Multicultural Japan: Palaeolithic to Postmodern*, Cambridge: Cambridge University Press, pp. 31–45.
Matsuyama, T. (1993) 'Daigaku ni okeru eigo kyōiku no juyōsei', in JACET (ed.), *21 seiki ni mukete no eigo kyōiku*, Tokyo: Taishukan Shoten, pp. 50–55.
McConnell, D. L. (2000) *Importing Diversity: Inside Japan's JET Program*, Berkeley: University of California Press.
McVeigh, B. J. (1997) *Life in a Japanese Women's College: Learning to be Ladylike*, London: Routledge.
McVeigh, B. J. (2002) *Japanese Higher Education as Myth*, Armonk, N.Y.: M.E. Sharpe.
Miller, R. A. (1982) *Japan's Modern Myth: The Language and Beyond* (First edn), New York: Weatherhill.
Oxford, R., M. E. Hollaway and D. Horton-Murillo (1992) 'Language learning styles: Research and practical considerations for teaching in the multi-cultural tertiary ESL/EFL classroom', *System* 20: 339–546.
Palfreyman, D. (2001) 'Higher education in the United Kingdom: A viable elite-mass "Third Way"?', *Ritsumeikan Journal of Asia Pacific Studies* 8: 30–41.
Poole, G. S. (2000) 'English language eat a Japanese college: Kabe no sekai', paper presented at the Anthropology of Japan in Japan, Minnesota State University-Akita, Japan.
Poole, G. S. (2001) 'The theory of the "communicative revolution" and the practice of CLT in Japanese tertiary education', in Barbereau, R. R. D. (ed.), *Proceedings of the International ELICIT Conference*, Paisley UK: Paisley University Language Press, pp. 95–103.
Poole, G. S. (2003) 'Foreign language classes at Japanese universities: a rationale for a learning-centered, computer-enhanced syllabus', *Takachiho Ronso* 37 (3 and 4): 225–246.
Poole, G. S. (forthcoming) 'Assessing university entrance exams in Japan', *Studies in Educational Evaluation*.
Prabhu, N. S. (1987) *Second Language Pedagogy*, Oxford: Oxford University Press.

Rohlen, T. P. and G. K. LeTendre (1996) 'Themes in the Japanese culture of learning' in Rohlen, T.P. and G. K. LeTendre (eds) *Teaching and Learning in Japan,* Cambridge: Cambridge University Press, pp. 369–376.

Sacks, P. (1996) *Generation X goes to College: An Eye-Opening Account of Teaching in Postmodern America,* Chicago: Open Court Publishing.

Schoppa, L. J. (1991) *Education Reform in Japan: A Case of Immobilist Politics*, London: Routledge.

Seki, M. (1988) *Nihon no daigaku kyōiku kaikaku: Rekishi, genjō, tenbō*, Tokyo: Tamagawa Daigaku Shuppankai.

Stapleton, P. (1995) 'The role of Confucianism in Japanese education', *The Language Teacher* 19(4): 13–16.

Sugimoto, Y. (1997) *An Introduction to Japanese Society*, New York: Cambridge University Press.

Suzuki, K. (1973) 'Some recommendations for improving English education in Japan', *Workpapers in Teaching English as a Second Language* (University of California at Los Angeles) 7: 107–115.

Tanaka, H. et al. (eds.) (1987) *Gengo shūtoko to eigo kyōiku*, Tokyo: English Language Education Council.

Terauchi, H. (1996) *English for Academic Purposes in Japan: An Investigation of Language Attitudes and Language Needs in a Department of Law,* Coventry: University of Warwick.

Terauchi, H. (2001) *English for Academic Legal Purposes in Japan,* Tokyo: Liber Press.

Thornbury, S. (1998) 'Comments on Marianne Celce-Murcia, Zoltan Dornyei and Sarah Thurrell's "Direct approaches in L2 instruction: a turning point in Communicative Language Teaching?": A reader reacts', *TESOL Quarterly* 32: 109–119.

Tripp, S. D. (1985) 'Review of *A History of English Language Teaching* by A.P.R. Howatt', *The Language Teacher* 9 (2): 28–32.

Wada, A. and S. McCarty (1984) 'The history of foreign language education in Japan', *The Language Teacher* 8 (5): 28–29.

Wadden, P. (ed.) (1993) *A Handbook for Teaching English at Japanese Colleges and Universities*, Oxford: Oxford University Press.

Whitley, M. (1993) 'Communicative language teaching: an incomplete revolution', *Foreign Language Annals* 26: 137–54.

Yang, P. (1997) 'Communicative language teaching in China: An analysis from a cultural perspective', paper presented at the Educating in Global Times, Canada.

13 The Paradox of the 'IT Revolution' and Japanese Higher Education Reform

Jane M. Bachnik

Japanese education is well known for its success in achieving widespread literacy and high levels of general education. The *World Competitiveness Yearbook* (World Economic Forum 2001) gives Japan top ranking among forty-nine countries in secondary school enrolment, and runner-up ranking in higher education enrolment. Yet the same survey ranks Japan last among the forty-nine countries surveyed in terms of an education system that meets the needs of a competitive economy.[1]

In response to these problems, the Ministry has developed a comprehensive package of educational reforms. It has also markedly increased its budget for educational technology in the past three years and is promoting information technology as a crucial component in its educational reforms. The Ministry is also in the process of turning the national universities and research centres into 'independent administrative institutions' (*dokuritsu gyōsei hōjinka*) which reputedly will give them autonomy to manage their own campuses and to compete successfully in providing education to prepare students for the workplaces of today's fast-changing global economy.

However, a gap has appeared between plans and implementation of the information technology (hereafter referred to as IT) revolution in education. The difficulty is that implementing IT is not as simple as connecting schools to the Internet and teaching computer literacy. In fact, the IT revolution brings a series of broad challenges to education, which is already under pressure to carry out the range of reforms that have been proposed. Moreover, the challenges raised extend beyond the classroom to the political and social environment of education and its broader links to Japanese society. The 'gap', discussed above, between plans and implementation of IT has its origins in the politico-social structure of the education system and especially in its close linkage to the state.

In this chapter I will argue that IT has played the role of a weathervane in signalling the need for education to respond more adequately to the challenges it faces. Three sets of challenges, in particular, have become apparent during the process of implementing information technology in Japanese education. I will argue that responding to these three challenges and the issues of change they raise for the broader socio-political environment of education are crucial for affecting any serious educational reforms. In discussing these issues I will focus on two specific reforms: (1) the development of IT support centres in Japanese national universities and, (2) the Ministry's latest reform initiative relating to the creation of 'independent administrative institutions'.

Challenges to education raised by information technology

Let us now look more closely at the challenges to education raised by IT. The first challenge is the considerable increase in skills that are needed for employment as a consequence of the IT revolution. One feature of permanent employment in Japanese firms has been the 'de-specialisation' of workers who, as 'generalists', were trained largely by the firm and rotated to different jobs throughout their careers. However, the increasing specialisation requirements brought by technology have challenged the organisation of this system. A majority of occupations in all the developed countries now require education or training beyond high school.[2] Along with this trend, the most substantial change in Japan's occupational structure is 'an increase in the share of professional and technical occupations, which is predicted to grow from 10.5 percent in 1985 to a staggering 17 percent in 2005' (Castells 2000: 242).

The educational system is thus challenged to provide advanced training and specialisation for a number of career paths. But this is not in line with the university entrance examination system through which students are selected for admission to a hierarchically-ranked order of universities, with the University of Tokyo at its apex. Upon entry the student receives the equivalent of an institutional 'brand name'[3] and ultimately becomes a 'University of Tokyo graduate' or a 'Waseda graduate'. The point is that 'brand name' is far more important than a chosen course of study (Dore 1998)[4] and, in fact, the status ranking of one's university (rather than one's grade point average, skills or other personal qualifications) is the primary criterion for getting a job in Japan's lifetime employment system. The selection process for employment operates by the institutional status ranking system. Education takes a back seat in this system, and skills training has little place after the primary school level.[5]

In effect, the hiring criteria discussed above put the university largely in the role of a parking lot where students wait for four years before taking up employment. Gregory Clark, the former president of a Japanese university, put this succinctly: 'students have little incentive to study properly – their future having already been decided by the name of their university the moment they enter that university – [moreover] why should teachers have much incentive to teach properly?' (*Japan Times* 8 August 1998). Moreover, because entrance to the university becomes the defining criteria for employment, rather than educational achievement at the university, the status of one's university comes to be equated with one's academic ability as well. As Samuel Coleman (1999) has noted: '(n)o matter how bright or promising a young scientist may be, if the degree was earned at a second- or third-tier university, much less a technical school, the perception in industry and government is of inferior ability' (see also *Daily Yomiuri* 23 April 2000).

The parking lot approach to higher education is already creating serious dislocations in the employment process for graduating students. As Ōtoshi Takuma, President of IBM Japan states, companies increasingly need trained personnel, and training requirements (especially for IT) have become far too specialised for 'generalists' to pick up on the job or for company training systems to provide. The dislocation is evident: 'a survey of corporations by the Japan Institute of Labor revealed that fewer than half the companies surveyed – 44.6 percent – were able to hire the people they needed' (Ōtoshi 2001: 7). Over fifty percent of these firms stated that they were unable to hire because of a lack of applicants who had the skills that they need (emphasis mine). Japan unemployment rates are now the highest in the post-war period and rates for graduating students are higher than those for any other age group.[6] This means that in a very tight labour market, more than half the companies surveyed had vacant positions, largely because they couldn't find employees with the skills they needed!

The second challenge IT has brought to education is the rise of the Internet which has ushered in a new era. How well a country is networked is a measure of its ICT competitiveness and, in the 2003 *World Competitiveness Yearbook*, Japan ranked only 20th in the world in this index, far behind its GNP ranking of second in the world.[7] It is curious that Japan, while avidly promoting technology, has lagged well behind other developed countries in adopting the Internet. Japan has also consistently fallen behind its Asian neighbors, including Singapore, Taiwan, and especially Korea (*Nikkei Weekly* 2001, Hopfner 2000) in broadband infrastructure, use of Internet and e-commerce. In fact, Korea was ranked 14th on the same Networked Readiness Index where Japan ranked 20th (Dutta and Jain 2003).

The university has played a crucial role in the development of Internet. In contrast to the 'grandiose plans for encouraging the spread of computerisation – such as the Technopolis Scheme, initiated by MITI... the use of the Internet has been a bottom-up process, initiated by a small group of academics with virtually no government support and spreading in a largely unplanned and spontaneous way' (Morris-Suzuki and Rimmer 2003: 158–9). Yet at the same time, universities, which would be expected to use the Internet most for educational purposes, have made the least progress among all the educational levels in utilising it (Narita 2003).

But here, the flexibility, openness and bottom-up organisation of the Internet comes into conflict with the hierarchical nature and opaque tendencies of universities in Japan. The state's general 'guidance' of higher education and its focus on education as an administrative, rather than an academic, enterprise have made university administrations both slow and resistant in their responses to the Internet (Kumar et al. 2003). More specifically, the attempt to 'manage' the Internet through bureaucratic process has subjected it to a lengthy, committee-based decision-making process, which prioritises administrative regulations over effective use. The regulative focus also promotes a static perspective on the Internet (which is reflected in university websites) rather than promoting its interactive possibilities for education (Bachnik 2002).

In fact, the Internet poses a challenge to the education system precisely because it requires an organisational shift from a bureaucratic, regulatory perspective to a networked perspective grounded in performance, which is based on the individual. As Ōtoshi notes '(t)hrough Internet the individual has become the key player in economic life' (Ōtoshi 2001: 3).

This individually-based initiative is closely linked to the third challenge which Garelli has described as 'the priority of a competitive nation to develop the people who will operate the new technological infrastructure and strive to be on the leading edge of future developments' (Garelli 2001). Since knowledge is the most critical factor in a modern workforce, this requires a young and qualified labour force with good IT skills and entrepreneurial spirit. Obviously, this is linked to the first challenge as well, but the focus also involves a shift from IT viewed as 'products' and infrastructure, to a focus on people as the core of the IT revolution. 'New information technologies are not simply tools to be applied, but processes to be developed' (Castells 2000: 31) and processes must be developed by people who have the skills and creativity to innovate.

All of the three challenges discussed above require an educational shift, from training diligent workers who dedicate themselves to nationalist goals, to developing people who possess originality, individuality, creativity, initiative and leadership abilities. The individual who has become 'the key player in economic life' (Ōtoshi 2001: 3) and has acquired the skills to create his own career path, differs considerably from the worker who dedicates himself to his company and is rotated through jobs that the company demands. In effect the information revolution requires a new kind of individual, with a new relation to the economy – and to the nation. Noyori Ryoji, a Nobel Prize co-recipient in 2001, was quick to emphasise this kind of individual in critiquing the nationalist focus on science in his first press conference after receiving the prize: 'Science is not something we learn for the sake of the nation. It's something we learn for us...It is a wrong-headed policy to have students study science harder in order to make Japan a scientific and innovative nation' (*Daily Yomiuri* 18 Oct. 2001).

Responding to these challenges is not a simple matter of creating plans and slogans. The new economy requires a shift from central control and hierarchy to flexible organizations, and from individuals who are 'beaten down like nails' if they 'stick out' (deru ku(g)i wa utareru) – as the saying goes – to individuals who are not afraid to challenge decisions. 'To develop a new airliner, for example, engineers need to challenge design decisions continually, no matter how high in the hierarchy they may have been made. Without such an approach, design improvement is impossible' (Porter et al. 2000: 173). Rather than assuming that such people don't exist in Japan, it is more accurate to understand that the socio-cultural, political, economic and educational environment does not support them adequately.[8]

The stakes of the educational shift

For the education system to respond to the three challenges outlined above, it is not enough to create plans and buzzwords: substantial organisational shifts are required. All of the following are urgently needed:

1 A new type of organisation – that focuses on the educational process taking place within the institutions instead of the institution as a status-oriented 'brand-name'.
2 A new type of relationship between the educational organisation and the administrative ministry – that focuses on the learning process taking place for individual students instead of on education as a bureaucratic and administrative system.
3 A new type of individual student (and educator) – who supports the qualities of creativity, leadership and entrepreneurial spirit required for the new era rather than that of teacher-centred, fact-based learning.

In fact, substantial overlap exists in the requirements of meeting all three challenges discussed above. All of these require a shift from a focus on education that is administrative, bureaucratic and teacher-centred; to one that is student-centered and focuses on the education process of the students.

The educational reforms outlined above also raise questions about the relationship of the state – and the Ministry – to the organisational transformations outlined above. Can the Ministry manage to instil creativity, originality, innovation and individuality that centres on the students themselves while directing, guiding and monitoring the movement from above? Can it create students capable of 'flexibility and responsiveness to change' in institutional contexts whose responses to change (including implementing IT) are based on maintaining the status quo? Can it manage to reinvigorate teaching and learning in a system of higher education where little incentive exists for either due to the prioritisation of institutional status ranking? The contradictions involved in this 'balancing act' also highlight a clash between two different – and incompatible – perspectives on the information revolution.

As Manuel Castells points out, 'An information society is more than a society that uses information technology' (1998: 239). The technological revolution is not only reshaping the material basis of societies, but also transforming societies themselves. As a means for bringing about the IT revolution, technology can be viewed either (1) as a means for economic development carried out within the existing social environment (status quo), or (2) as a means to assist meeting the social challenges of the information revolution. The first perspective regards technology as yet another vehicle for economic growth, but viewed in a social vacuum; the second views technology as a vehicle for transforming the relationships between economy, state and society.

Viewed in the same light, the educational reforms can be seen either (1) as a means of improving students' knowledge (assessed by test scores) within the existing socio-economic environment (status quo), or (2) as a means of transforming that environment in order to achieve the kind of education that will prepare Japanese students for the new economy. Just as with the IT revolution, this would require transforming the relationships between economy, state, and society.

As Brian J. McVeigh notes, discussions on educational reform are filled with terms that convey the development of the individually-oriented focus noted above, including 'initiative', 'individuality', 'diversity', 'creativity', 'choice' and liberalisation' (2002: 8). But he adds that, in Japan, this discourse doesn't have the meaning that it implies. 'Talk about "diversity", "creativity" and "choice", as if the problem were a lack of art classes or not enough optional classes' (McVeigh 2002: 9) misses the point that the entire focus of the system needs to be changed in order to realise such reforms. To the extent that the necessity for deeper change is either not realised or ignored, a gap is created between plan and practice, such that reforms are increasingly difficult to implement.

IT as weathervane: Development of IT support systems in Japanese national universities

I will now examine the way in which IT has played the role of a weathervane in signalling the need for education to respond to the challenges above. Providing support for teachers and students is crucial in the successful introduction of IT in education systems in every country (Anderson 2003) and the development of IT support centres in the Japanese national universities relates to each of the challenges outlined above.

An investigation into the development of IT support centres in the national universities (Bachnik 2003b) resulted in the following discoveries: IT support centres in the national universities are organised in a pyramid which has three tiers (see Figure 13-1). What is noteworthy about this method of organisation is that every support centre in the pyramid manifests the same organisational structure. The organisations vary only in size – meaning the number of personnel and the size of the mainframe computers (and scope of the constituency they serve) which are the focus of the centres. In fact, the organisational structure of the pyramid and its size continuum, replicates the status-ranking order of the national universities. The higher status universities had the largest IT support centres, while the converse was true as well. At the apex of the pyramid was the support centre of the university with the highest status – Tokyo.

To be more specific, the apex of the pyramid consists of seven institutions, which trace their histories back to the old imperial universities. The University of Tokyo centre, at the top of this apex, is differentiated by having the largest mainframe computer; the largest number of personnel and a different name (*Jōhō kiban* centre instead of *Jōhō kyōiku* centre). Following Tokyo are the six other former imperial universities: Kyoto, Kyushu, Nagoya, Tohoku, Osaka, and Hokkaido; all of which have large mainframe computers and larger personnel organisations although smaller than those possessed by Tokyo. The middle tier of the pyramid consists of 29 institutions, each of which has a university-wide information-processing centre (IPC). However, these centres are small with only a handful of personnel each. The bottom (and largest) tier consists of 73 universities which only have small computer 'rooms' or IPCs within engineering departments with few personnel (see Figure 13-1).

The organisational development of this pyramid also gives us valuable information about how the education system responds to new needs. Establishing the new IT support centres was managed largely by the Ministry which authorised the creation of the centres and the faculty positions and approved the personnel. Moreover, since these were new organisations, the approval of the Ministry of Public Management[9] was required for the organisational structure, and funding was routed from the Finance Ministry. Thus the organisation of the centres was clearly defined by the ministries and from outside the institutions. The question then arises as to how well these organisations responded to local needs. Is it necessarily

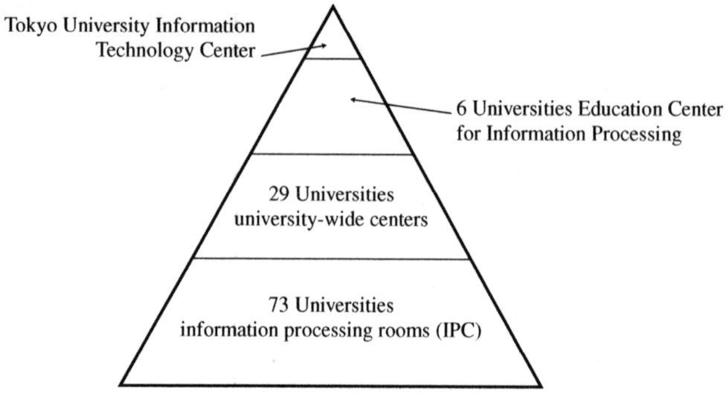

Figure 13-1: IT support systems in Japanese national universities

the case that smaller centres fit the needs of every lower-ranked university – or that the former imperial universities had the greatest needs for larger centres? In other words, did the status-ranking pyramid actually fit the needs of the universities in the pyramid?

To respond to this question we need to look at the role of individuals, who also played crucial roles in the development of the IT support centres. It was individual faculty who largely developed the infrastructures and lobbied for IT and support services to be introduced into their universities (Ando 2003; Kumar et al. 2003). For example, one small national university introduced IT, in1982, through the efforts of a visionary professor in the engineering division. This professor started the first information processing 'room' within the engineering department (the bottom tier of the pyramid) and became its first 'volunteer' director (Bachnik 2003b: 95). A group of 'volunteer' faculty members was also formed to support the centre and they developed an infrastructure that was quite sophisticated for the size of this university. The development and maintenance of this infrastructure was done entirely by enthusiastic faculty who volunteered their time and expertise and who also promoted IT throughout the university on their own. Eventually, however, the growing sophistication of the technology, and the time demands this made on the volunteer faculty, caused them to reach burn-out (Ando 2003). In 1997, the Ministry eventually established a university-wide support centre at the mid-level tier of this university (even though its size would have put it in the lower tier).

The fact that Japanese IT support organisations had to be provided externally by the ministries affected their development in numerous ways. To summarise briefly:

1 The universities were unable to set up their own organisations, which could respond to their own local support needs. One result was a serious inadequacy in the support staffing. For example, in the pyramid in Figure13-1, the computer 'rooms' were largely supported by volunteers. The middle-tier centres also had few full-time staff members.
2 The IT centres had virtually no ability to respond dynamically to the rapidly changing needs of the technology with organisational change. Instead, change was limited to an external process whereby the Ministry chose two universities each year to be 'moved' from the lowest to the second tier of the pyramid. The pyramid itself remained intact.
3 No professional support staff has been created in Japanese universities. Either faculty 'volunteers' or full-time faculty hired as support personnel are expected to carry out support activities.
4 Support personnel are also 'generalists' and specialists have not been created to respond to specific needs such as servicing the infrastructure and supporting faculty IT needs. For example, the individual faculty member, who worked in the IT support centre in the case above, had to single-handedly service all the infrastructure and faculty support needs at his university.
5 Consequently, the IT support that does exist focuses on infrastructure, while faculty support is neglected both in national and private universities (Slater 2003; Yoshida and Bachnik 2003: 35–36). In nationwide surveys of all Japanese universities conducted in 1999 and 2000, 95 percent of faculty identified lack of support staff as a major barrier to IT utilisation (Yoshida and Bachnik 2003: 34; Yoshida 2001; Yoshida and Taguchi 2002).
6 The result is a severe limitation of all IT services in Japanese universities. Services for faculty such as help hotlines, walk-in services, faculty skill development or pedagogy workshops; or consultation services for creating teaching materials are scarce or non-existent. Infrastructure services are also inadequate. Network management staffing is insufficient and equipment is inadequately maintained and repaired.[10]

To a considerable extent, the pyramid figure symbolises what is wrong with the university approaches to IT support. All the support organisations are set up from outside the universities by the Ministry and they are all organised in a uniform manner. The rigidity of the resulting organisations makes them totally incapable of responding to the rapidly changing demands of information technology and their divorce from the local environment makes them unable to adequately fulfil the local level support needs at any of the universities. A major reason for this failure is that the establishment of support organisations has been focused on meshing with *the status-ranking of the universities rather than their individual needs*. To the extent that this focus remains, responding to the individual institutional needs is impossible. But for Japanese universities to create appropriate responses to the needs generated by IT, they must be able to manage their own organisational responses to these needs. For this they need a much greater degree of autonomy.

The independent administrative institution (IAI) reforms

The most important large-scale educational reform movement at present is the IAI reforms (*dokuritsu gyōsei hōjinka*), which began in 2001 and are still underway. These were originally linked to the reorganisation of the central government's ministries and agencies; as part of which 89 institutions, including state-run museums and research institutes, were scheduled to become IAIs. Later, the 99 national universities were added and slated to become IAIs after April 2004, as discussed by Goodman and others in this volume.

The IAI reforms appear to respond to the need for more institutional autonomy for national universities – which was made clear in the discussion of the IT support centres. Indeed, the Ministry presented the IAI reforms as a means for the national universities to gain autonomy, since they would be granted independent juridical status (which they do not previously have), thus allowing them to gain more flexibility and control in spending their budgets, as well as governing their personnel who would no longer be subject to the laws for civil servants (Hirowatari 2000: 4). The benefits of the reform have also been couched in terms of relating universities to market forces. The institutions would be made responsible for their own management, enabling them to become more competitive and able to establish their own distinctive identities in order to attract a sharply declining student pool. The changes in legal status giving more autonomy to the universities were largely welcomed. In terms of how the reforms would work in practice, however, a number of serious problems have been raised.

In approaching these problems it is crucially important that the origins of this reform are understood as not educational but administrative. The IAI system 'was originally conceived as a measure to reduce the size of the national administrative apparatus, as part of the central government policy for administrative reform'(Hirowatari 2000: 4). The Ministry went along with the IAI reforms only when the administrative pressure – to reduce the number of civil servants by 25 percent in ten years – became intense under the Obuchi administration. The Ministry saw the IAI reforms as a way to accomplish this, since the national university system includes 125,000 national employees and it would avoid large personnel cuts by converting the universities to IAIs (Hayakawa 1999). Consequently, the 'independence' of the universities was a way to dress up the real cost-saving motive of removing the university personnel from the civil service. As Dando notes, 'these discussions do not arise from an awareness of the need to find solutions to the already abundant issues that plague universities. It is, rather, a move that is being made from the front lines of administrative reform'(1999: 1).

Consequently, many faculty have objected that, in the actual working of the reforms in practice, institutional independence would be severely restricted because the universities would not be able to set their own goals. The functions of the institutions are to be split into two divisions: planning and implementation. The planning functions are to be carried out by the central government – the Ministry in the case of universities – and only the implementation functions would be retained by the universities themselves. Consequently, the chief executive of the institution will be appointed by the cabinet minister with jurisdiction over the agency. 'Intermediate objectives' – or plans drafted by the planning division – would be set by the Ministry for the universities who would then submit three- to five-year plans on how they will achieve the 'intermediate objectives'. The institutions will then be evaluated, both yearly and at the end of the planning period, by 'independent committees' appointed by the Ministry on how well they are carrying out the plans. This evaluation will provide the basis for the institution's budget, the course of its future operations and its very survival – since its programmes, units or even the entire institution can be eliminated by the decisions of the evaluation committees (Hirowatari 2000).

Many university faculty members have responded to the proposed reforms with sharp criticisms.[11] Most are concerned that the IAI reforms would greatly increase Ministry control and that the controls which until now had been indirect, in the form of 'guidance', would become direct (Toyoshima 2002). According to the faculty objections, far from becoming 'independent', the universities would be even more sharply restricted within the confines of Ministry 'plans' which it is supposed to carry out. The administrative basis of the reform is also seen as antithetical to education: 'the unsuitability of the title "administrative agency" for a university is almost universally accepted by those involved in the issue' (Hirowatari 2000: 7). The reforms are also widely viewed as impinging on academic freedom and freedom of academic teaching and study. However, very little public debate has occurred on these issues (Hayakawa 1999). Moreover, it is hard to evaluate the reform when so much remains ambiguous about how it would actually work.

Assessment of the IAI reforms

The crucial question is whether the IAI reforms will address any of the organisational shifts outlined above. Will they transform the focus from the status-ranked 'pyramid' of universities discussed above to universities that are competitively oriented, diversified and focused on providing education (rather than status 'brand names') to their students? Will the reforms produce a shift in the state's role in education?

In his introduction to this volume, Goodman sees the state as 'relinquish[ing] some of its hold on universities and allow[ing] them to set their own agenda although it won't withdraw from the higher education sector altogether. Instead the state's role will be changed from one of control to one of supervision. It is here that the universities in Japan are having to learn yet another new language, one which Strathern (2000) calls that of the "audit culture"... audit practices in education are associated with a whole cluster of new terms including "performance", "transparency" and "accountability"'. Perhaps the term that most encapsulates the IAI reforms is that of 'evaluation'(*hyōka*).

But for the 'audit culture' to actually come into being, the organisational shifts outlined above in response to the three challenges would already have to be accomplished. This is because the 'audit culture' can't operate effectively in a status-ranking system. I will briefly elaborate why this is so. The discussion of the IT support centres above indicates that each university in the status-ranking pyramid (see Figure 13-1) was highly dependent on the Ministry to provide for its needs; and that the degree of funding, personnel and other assistance each university received reflected its status-ranking. Looked at another way, Ministry approval was necessary to preserve each university's status-ranking, which was in turn the basis of its funding. The universities, therefore, had to curry favour with the Ministry in order to smooth out the process which meant that the gaze of each institution was constantly 'turned upward'. A by-product of currying favour involved careful adherence to the bureaucratic regulations and Ministry 'guidance'.

But institutions that are currying favour by 'turning upward' are not very good at developing competitive market strategies, for the same reasons that the national universities were not very good at developing IT support centres. Responding to local needs requires autonomy, leadership and initiative, and strategy-making at the university level. If the universities develop these kinds of initiatives, they cannot also be focused on currying favour with the Ministry because *two different goal orientations are involved, and these are mutually incompatible.* This is why implementing the educational buzzwords such as 'initiative', 'individuality', 'diversity', 'creativity', 'choice' and so on, requires a shift to a different kind of organisation, a different kind of relationship with the Ministry and a different kind of student (and teacher).

If the terminology of the 'audit culture' is to be implemented, the same kinds of organisational shifts are required in order to implement them. While everyone acknowledges that evaluation (*hyōka*) is necessary, and it is already getting considerable attention throughout the system, it is not clear that agreement exists either on what *hyōka* means or on how to carry it out.

The difficulties in carrying out the 'audit culture' are encapsulated in the ambiguities that remain fundamental to the process of evaluation in Japanese universities. If movement toward a competitive market is crucial, then it is necessary to develop standards of evaluating individual initiative in the education system. But such a standard has been lacking in Japanese education because it does not fit well with the Ministry reward system (as described above). While this lack of evaluation is frequently termed 'egalitarian' or as 'institutional equality', McVeigh points out that it is really an institutional 'standardization' (2002: 4). Such standardisation masks individual differences in performative abilities, and makes it unnecessary to evaluate and reward these individual differences. Thus individuals are not commonly singled out, either for outstanding contributions or for incompetencies, either in the classroom or on the job. (Dore 1987; McVeigh 2002). In higher education, salary levels are commonly defined by years of service to the institution, rather than by evaluating individual abilities or the degree of one's contribution to the organisation.

It is necessary to keep in mind McVeigh's insights on the usage of terms in Japanese discourse on reform. He warns that terms that convey the development of an individually-oriented focus (such as 'initiative','individuality','diversity', 'creativity', 'choice' and 'liberalisation') often have different meanings in the Japanese discourse on reform (McVeigh 2002: 8). I think we can be more precise as to what these 'different meanings' involve, if we focus on the term 'evaluation'. The process of evaluation has specific connotations in English where it means the supervision or assessment of some aspect of one person's performance or output by another.

In my experience as a faculty member of a research institute, evaluation in Japanese institutions is commonly carried out by the self, in the form of *jiko tenken* (literally, self-examination). This takes the form of a detailed listing of one's work in a unified manner on specified forms. Following this, the individual *jiko tenken* listings can then be combined by adding together the listings for each category for all the individuals in the institution. This net 'score' is then utilised as a mechanism for *institutional status-ranking*. I became aware of this when several faculty were talking with the institute director one day and he was bemoaning the fact that our 'evaluation' lists had produced an institutional ranking that was too low. (Whether the solution was to produce better lists, or more research and publications to go on the lists, I am not sure).

The point is that 'evaluation' criteria that are commonly used to focus on *individual* output (for example in America), are commonly reinterpreted in Japan to become indices of *institutional* status-rankings. This means that all of the terms in the 'audit culture' could be reinterpreted so that they become institutional/ status-ranking indexes instead of individually focused indexes.

Ironically, the very initiation of the IAI reforms has put considerable pressure on institutions to court the Ministry in order to ensure a favourable 'timing' (or sometimes inclusion in a favourable 'grouping') for putting the process of *hōjinka* into action. Just as my institute was preparing for *hōjinka,* the Ministry then introduced *ninki seido* in which the existing tenure system was changed to one of five-year contracts. Although this contract system had considerable implications for the faculty, my institute accepted it without objection in order to remain on good terms with the Ministry and thus ease the process of *hōjinka*. In this case the institute opted to use a contract employment system – which supposedly hinged on individual evaluation – as a status-ranking index for their own *hōjinka* process.

The paradox, of course, is obvious. The definition of 'independence' here seems to be just as problematic as that of 'evaluation'. Contrary to the rhetoric of *hōjinka,* the very relationship that was supposed to be weakened – that between the Ministry and the institution – is instead being given more weight as a result of the IAI reforms. By the same token, this can also explain why institutions that were initially critical of *hōjinka* have now conceded and why an individual in the higher education system can only criticize *the system itself* from a very strong position. It is no accident that Noyuri Ryoji, the recent Nobel Prize winner, made precisely this criticism at his first press conference.

On this same point, Toyoshima argued that the *hōjinka* system will *increase* each university's dependence on making a good impression on the Ministry, since much more is at stake now that the Ministry (or its appointed committee) has the power to manipulate funding; direct changes to the institution's performance or even close down the institution itself. These are all very powerful incentives to curry favour. 'If this system is implemented, the universities will, more than ever before, worry about winning bureaucrats', not peoples' favor'(Toyoshima 2002: 2).

Since the 'independence' of the institution is so restricted that it can be exercised only in carrying out Ministry directives – it appears that the term is a misnomer, and that it is 'dependence' that is being promoted in the IAI reforms. The idea that an institution has some latitude as to the manner in which it carries out Ministry directives can actually be termed 'independence'. Rather 'independence' would mean that the Ministry had given up its power to impose such a directive in the first place. Once more, we are back to square one. None of the organisational shifts appear to be taking place in the educational reforms. Therefore, although a language of reforms has been adopted, it does not mean what it appears. Therefore, the gap between plans and implementation that characterised the IT revolution can also be said to characterise educational reforms more generally, including the IAI reforms.

At stake is something larger than contradictions between both the IT and the IAI reforms and the organisational frameworks which prevent them from being implemented. Rather, these contradictions both encapsulate what Castells calls 'the fundamental contradiction emerging in Heisei Japan: the incompatibility between the developmental state – the actor of Japanese development and guarantor of Japanese identity – and the information society that it decisively helped to bring to life' (1998: 236). In effect, the reforms are being carried out against an unspoken (and largely unseen) backdrop which assumes that the status quo of Ministry/state relationships to education will remain unchanged. But, in a nutshell, the three challenges outlined at the beginning of this chapter, make it clear that educational reform must address these relationships. To the extent that it preserves, rather than challenges, the status quo, the IAI reforms appear to be thwarting the very reform process it is intended to initiate.

Notes

1 Some of the issues raised in this paper summarise more extensive discussions in Bachnik 2003. However, the particular focus on these issues, especially that relating to the 'independent administrative institutions' is developed for this paper. I thank David Groth for his insightful comments on this paper and Ando Hidetoshi, Narita Masahiro and Sugimoto Taku for their assistance during interviews regarding the I.T. support centres in their respective universities.

2 'In fact, more than two out of three of the thirty fastest-growing occupations and nearly half of the thirty with the largest number of jobs, had a majority of workers with education or training beyond high school in 1990' (Silvestri and Lukasiewicz 1991: 82, Castells 2000: 240).

3 I am grateful to David Groth for this phrase (personal correspondence, February 2002).

4 "Every university... slots into the hierarchy at its appropriate place, and every high school into its local prefectural hierarchy" (Dore 1998: 3).

5 A tradition of skill development does exist as a parallel learning system outside of formal education. This parallel learning system includes cram schools which teach test-taking skills, and technical schools which teach IT skills, along with schools for public speaking, traditional arts, and piano playing, to name a few (Stephen Nussbaum, personal correspondence 2001). The status ranking of technical schools is often low.

6 The percentage of this spring's college graduates who found employment was 60 percent, down five percent from last year (Dando 1999: 1).

7 The Networked Readiness Index includes a comprehensive assessment of a country's network environment (including development of knowledge-based economy, political and regulatory support and development of infrastructure, along with the network readiness of individuals, business and government and the usage of these three stakeholders (Dutta and Jain 2003).

8 To support this assertion, Porter et al. present a set of 'new emerging' Japanese companies that are fostering different dynamics (including results, action and enthusiasm over age, seniority and academic background) (2000: 175–79).

9 The Ministry of Public Management, Home Affairs, Posts and Telecommunications (Sōmushō) was formerly the Bureau of Public Management (Sōmushō) before the changes of January 2000.

10 In fact, the initial development of IT in this university strongly parallels that in US universities I researched, where engineers set up the initial network infrastructure at the university and then established small 'rooms' within their departments. The difference was in the ways in which the IT support organisations were institutionalised following this initial development. In the case cited above, the Ministry response was slow (taking fifteen years to set up the support centre). While the impetus in introducing IT came from the bottom-up – the faculty – in both cases, the Japanese university leadership failed to respond to the impetus by taking the initiative to develop organisations that would support IT implementation (Narita 2003). Yet in another sense, they were unable to provide this leadership because they lacked the autonomy to develop their own organisations in response to the requirements of the new technologies. Consequently, all the IT support organisations in the Japanese national universities had to be established externally and thus their organisational structure, staff and focus was both authorised and funded by the Ministry. While this chapter does not allow me the space to provide a detailed comparison (see Bachnik 2003b), it is telling that the IT support in United States state universities, which did have the autonomy to develop their own organisations, diverged quite markedly from that of the Japanese universities from this point onwards. To summarise briefly: 1. Not only were American universities able to set up their own support organisations – they were able to do so at different levels within the university, including university-wide, division, and department levels. This meant that if one level (for example, university-wide) was slow to respond, a dean of a division could manage to set up support organisations, and staff them, within that division. 2. This institutional flexibility produced an array of new organisations that varied greatly, not only between universities, but between division and department

units within the universities. 3. These organisations evolved very quickly, changing their focus, merging and being reorganised, as they responded to rapidly evolving technologies. 4. A professional staff of IT specialists was created for establishing and maintaining extensive IT support. Support was offered for both infrastructure and faculty needs (for example, servicing their technical needs and assisting them in utilising IT in teaching and research). 5. An extensive array of services was provided, usually at all three organisational levels within the universities. These include extensive telephone and walk-in services, as well as workshops and consultation services for an array of instructional uses of IT, such as web page design, construction of multimedia instructional materials, and statistical and mainframe services. There was also extensive development of infrastructure, including a professional maintenance staff, and a research programme for further development. Nor is this list exhaustive.

11 Several organisations were formed opposing the IAI reforms, including 'The Peoples' Network against the Plan to Destroy Japan's National Universities' (with a website at the University of Saga in Kyushu); 'The Kanto Area Network against IAI' and a website posting English language articles on the reforms (at Hokkaido University) to name a few. There was a clear international focus to the protest: adverts were taken out in the New York Times by the faculty/staff union, and letters were written to the Chronicle of Higher Education and to the Secretary General of UNESCO. A partial list of websites focusing on the reforms includes: (in English): http://fcs.math.sci.hokudai.ac.jp/dgh/e-index.html (in Japanese): People's Network against the Plan to Destroy Japan's National Universities http:/ //pegasus.phys.saga-u.ac.jpznete.html and the government's explanation of the IAI reforms: http://ww.kantei.go.jp/foreign/central_government/ 03_more.html

References

Anderson, Ronald E. (2003) 'Teaching, learning, and computing in Japan and the United States', in Bachnik, Jane M. (ed.), *Roadblocks on the Information Highway: The IT Revolution in Japanese Education,* Lanham Maryland: Lexington Press, pp. 231–47

Ando, Hidetoshi (2003) 'The unbearable lightness of being an IT service provider: A case study', in Bachnik, Jane M. (ed.), *Roadblocks on the Information Highway: The IT Revolution in Japanese Education,* Lanham Maryland: Lexington Press, pp. pp. 61–68.

Bachnik, Jane M. (2002) 'The social challenges of Internet to Japanese society', paper presented at the International Symposium of the Association of Internet Researchers, University of Maastricht, Maastricht, The Netherlands, October 13 –16.

Bachnik, Jane M. (2003a) 'Introduction: Social challenges to the IT revolution in Japanese education', in Bachnik, Jane M. (ed.), *Roadblocks on the Information Highway: The IT Revolution in Japanese Education,* Lanham Maryland: Lexington Press, pp.1–22.

Bachnik, Jane M. (2003b). 'Do IT yourself: Short circuits in technical support services', in Bachnik, Jane M. (ed.), *Roadblocks on the Information Highway: The IT Revolution in Japanese Education,* Lanham Maryland: Lexington Press, pp. 77–125.

Castells, Manuel (1998) *End of Millennium*: *Economy, Society and Culture,* Oxford: Blackwell.

Castells, Manuel (2000) *The Rise of the Network Society, (*2nd edition.), Oxford: Blackwell.

Coleman, Samuel (1999) *Japanese Science: From the Inside,* London: Routledge.

Dando, Yasuharu (1999) 'Confusion deepens in universities', in *Japan Research and Analysis through Internet Information*, August 26. http://dandoweb.com/e/univ.html.

Dore, Ronald (1987) *Taking Japan Seriously*, Stanford: Stanford University Press

Dore, Ronald and M. Sako (1998) *How the Japanese Learn to Work* (2nd. edition), London: Routledge.

Dutta, S. and A. Jain (2002) 'The networked readiness of Nations', in *Global Technology Report 2002–2003, Readiness for the Networked World,* Oxford: Oxford University Press, pp. 1–25.

Garelli, Stephane (2001) 'Executive Summary', in *World Competitiveness Yearbook,* World Economic Forum. http://www.imd.ch/wcy/esummary/.

Hayakawa, Nobuo (1999) 'Giving national universities the status of independent administrative institutions', on NHK Radio, 28 October. http://fcs.math.sci.hokudai.ac.jp/dgh/99a28-radio-japan.html.

Hirowatari, Seigo (2000) 'Japan's national universities and *dokuritsu gyōsei hōjinka*', *Social Science Japan* (19 September): 3–7.

Hopfner, Jonathan (2000) 'Fast country', in *Japan Inc.*, December. http://www.japaninc.net/mag/comp/2000/12/dec00_fast.html.

Japan Institute of Labor (2001) 'Shokuin saiyō tassei jōkyō' (Percentage of hiring plans accomplished) in *IT katsuyō kigyō ni tsuite no jittai chōsen* (Survey of conditions of IT usage in industry), June. http://www.jil.go.jp/statis/doko/itkatsuyo/itkatsuyo.htm, http://www.jil.go.jp/statis/doko/itkatsuyo/2-5.htm.

Kumar, R., Karen A. Shire and Jane M. Bachnik (2003) 'Developing a university website: A webmaster's perspective', in Bachnik, Jane M. (ed.), *Roadblocks on the Information Highway: The IT Revolution in Japanese Education*, Lanham Maryland: Lexington Press, pp. 197–213.

McVeigh, Brian (2002) *Japanese Higher Education as Myth*, Armonk, New York: M.E. Sharpe.

Morris-Suzuki, Tessa and Peter J. Rimmer (2003) 'Cyberstructure, society, and education in Japan', in Bachnik, Jane M. (ed.), *Roadblocks on the Information Highway: The IT Revolution in Japanese Education*, Lanham Maryland: Lexington Press, pp. 157–70.

Narita, Masahiro (2003) 'Barriers to educational use of the Internet in a Japanese university', in Bachnik, Jane M. (ed.), *Roadblocks on the Information Highway: The IT Revolution in Japanese Education*, Lanham Maryland: Lexington Press, pp. 171–79.

Nikkei Weekly (2001) 'Net services in Japan lag behind', 15 August.
Ō toshi, Takuma (2001) 'Expectations for higher education in Japan', International Symposium: 'How Can IT Help Universities to Globalize?' Chiba, Japan: National Institute of Multimedia Education, 31 October.
Porter, Michael E., Hirotaka Takeuchi and Mariko Sakakibara (2000) *Can Japan Compete?*, Cambridge Mass.: Perseus Publishing.
Silvestri, George T. and J. Lukasiewicz. (1991) 'Outlook 1990–2005: Occupational employment, wide variations in growth', *Monthly Labor Review* (November): 58–86.
Slater, David H. (2003) 'No faculty service stations on the information highway: A case study', in Bachnik, Jane M. (ed.), *Roadblocks on the Information Highway: The IT Revolution in Japanese Education*, Lanham Maryland: Lexington Press, pp. 69–76
Strathern, Marilyn (ed.) (2000) *Audit Cultures: Anthropological Studies in Accountability, Ethics and the Academy*, London: Routledge.
Toyoshima, Koichi (2002) 'The alleged "independence" may deprive universities of their freedom', translated from *Shūkan Kinyobi,* 19 April, pp. 45–47. Downloaded from http://fcs.math.sci. hokudai.ac.jp/dgh/e-index.html.
World Economic Forum (2001 and 2003) *World Competitiveness Yearbook*, Oxford: Oxford University Press.
Yoshida, Aya (2001) 'Kōtō-kyōiku kikan ni okeru multimedia riyō jittai chōsa: 1999' (A national survey of multimedia utilization in higher education in Japan:1999), Chiba, Japan: National Institute of Multimedia Education (Research Report No. 19).
Yoshida, Aya and Mana Taguchi (2002) 'Kōtō-kyōiku kikan ni okeru multimedia riyō jittai chōsa : 2000' (A national survey of multimedia utilization in higher education in Japan:1999), Chiba, Japan: National Institute of Multimedia Education (Research Report No. 31).
Yoshida, Aya and Jane M. Bachnik (2003) 'A nationwide assessment of IT implementation in higher education', in Bachnik, Jane M. (ed.) *Roadblocks on the Information Highway: The IT Revolution in Japanese Education,* Lanham Maryland: Lexington Press pp. 25–60.

14 The Japanese 21st Century Center of Excellence Program: Internationalization in Action?

J.S. Eades

Introduction

The image of Japan in relation to its higher education system often appears to be schizophrenic. On the one hand there are the well-known published critiques of the system, from the polemics by Cutts (1997) and Hall (1998) against Tokyo and Tsukuba Universities, to Brian McVeigh's dismissal of the Japanese higher education as 'myth' (McVeigh 2002). On the other hand, there are the international ratings of universities, in some of which Japan scores quite well, and the technological strength of the Japanese economy, which suggests that someone must be getting something right. Where is the reality? Does it lie somewhere in between? Or are both sets of images actually correct, because they are images of different parts of what is a very large and diverse higher education sector?

In this chapter, I argue that the last of these positions is probably most plausible, and that this can be seen in relation to the 21st Century Center of Excellence Program, an initiative by the Japanese Ministry of Education to raise standards of research in universities across the board by rewarding innovation and excellence with large sums of extra money. In doing this, Japan is following what seems to be an international trend: embracing the 'audit culture' (Shore and Wright, 1999; Strathern 2000; Goodman 2001), moving from regulation to monitoring and evaluation, and using the results of evaluation as the basis for the distribution of rewards. This is a model which has been used in Britain since the Margaret Thatcher premiership of the 1980s, a period which began with a massive reallocation of university funding, and which continued with the institution of the Research

Assessment Exercise (RAE) which has been carried out at regular intervals ever since.[1] In this exercise, the research output of departments throughout the country is evaluated on a seven-point scale, from 1 to 5*, i.e. from poor to internationally excellent. A portion of the grant for universities, around a billion pounds a year, the equivalent of 200 billion yen, is distributed in line with the RAE findings, so that there is a financial advantage in having highly rated researchers, in addition to the research grants and contracts that they bring in.[2] The results have been an increasing polarization between the 'research universities' (e.g. the self-styled 'Russell Group'),[3] and the rest. The situation was complicated by the upgrading of the former polytechnics to the status of universities in 1991, doubling the size of the university sector. As these 'new universities' had never been able to compete for research grants before 1991, they remain primarily teaching institutions, though most of them have one or more departments that are highly rated for their research. Meanwhile, Oxford, Cambridge and the major London colleges have a great majority of departments which are rated 5 or 5*. These institutions also tend to get the pick of the graduate students, not least because they also have the best library facilities. As the most famous institutions internationally, they also tend to get the pick of the overseas students as well. However, even the lower-ranking institutions have some clusters of productive and highly ranked scholars that they regard as the jewels in their crowns for marketing purposes, and they keep them there by offering them sufficiently attractive salaries and working conditions to make sure that they stay.

The Japanese 21st Century COE Program originated from similar audit culture thinking, the identification of subsets of universities and departments in which to concentrate national research funding. The phrase 'Center of Excellence' has been in circulation since at least 1993, in a funding scheme operated by the Japanese Science and Technology Agency with an original budget of 3 billion yen a year. Later, from 2002 to 2004, it was appropriated for the 21st Century COE Program proper, which is the subject of this paper, resulting in substantial awards for some 274 projects from over 90 universities, totaling over 13 billion yen a year. A parallel scheme, offering even larger amounts of money to a very small number of universities has been in operation since 2001, though with nothing like the publicity accorded the 21st Century COE program. Known in Japanese as *seiryakuteki kenkyū ikusei*, or 'strategic research training,' it is also known popularly as the 'super COE' program, but so far involves only a handful of the leading universities. Here I concentrate on its larger and better-known sibling.

In terms of total budget and number of institutions involved, the 21st Century COE Program is by far the largest of these center of excellence schemes. As described below, it was originally intended to be focused on the country's thirty leading universities. However, during implementation, it evolved into a more flexible system, in which individual departments and research units in any university, whether national, public (i.e. run by a city or prefecture), or private, could compete for funds. Even though the majority of the money did go to a small number of leading institutions, a substantial number of lower ranking institutions have also enjoyed a small share of the action, as detailed in the Appendix to this paper.

But the COE Program also sheds other light on the internal workings of the Japanese higher education system, most recently through the first interim evaluation of COE projects carried out during the course of 2004. After the first two years of operation, the first batch of COE programs were required to present reports and samples of their research output for review, and the membership of the review committees were largely the same as that of the committees that had allocated the money two years previously. The outcome of the evaluation was published at the end of November 2004, and one of the most interesting results was that the evaluations of the Human Sciences committee appeared substantially out of line with those of the other committees.

This paper examines this difference, and argues that it is symptomatic of a fault-line between the sciences and humanities in Japanese academe, in terms of both their modes of operation and their international standings. This in turn has important implications both for the extent to which Japanese universities can internationalize in future, and the ways in which initiatives like the COE program can hasten the process.

Two images, two realities?

In what is perhaps the most sustained and devastating critique of Japanese universities published in the West to date, Brian McVeigh (2002) has argued that Japanese higher education is a 'myth.' Japanese children get a comparatively good grounding in maths, science and Japanese language in schools, but teaching of other languages and critical thinking is much weaker. 'It is the state and capitalist forces that sanction certain forms of knowledge that appear on examinations' (2002: 39), and it is the examinations which determine the learning and studying style. English is one of the most important subjects in the examination system, and yet what is learned is a form of 'fantasy' English, which is of little use as a communications tool (ibid: 41; see also Poole in this volume). Finally, McVeigh argues, reforms fail because they, too, are exercises in simulation. The only times Japanese education has undergone substantive change were during the Meiji period and the American post-war Occupation. But generally, he suggests, 'reform practices...often target not repairing education in a fundamental sense but rather increasing the efficiency of the education-examination machinery. Consequently 'reform' efforts end up maintaining the status quo' (ibid: 43).

How valid is this critique? If we look at the international league tables of universities, Japanese universities do not seem to perform all that badly. In the much-cited ranking by the Jiao Tong University in Shanghai, four out of the top five Asia Pacific universities are Japanese, namely Tokyo (1), Kyoto (2), Osaka (4) and Tohoku (5). (the Australian National University was ranked 3).[4] Another five, namely Nagoya, Hokkaido, Kyushu, Tokyo Institute of Technology and Tsukuba, make it into the top 17, over half of which are therefore Japanese. If we look at the Jiao Tong world rankings, the Japanese still do not do all that badly. Tokyo is ranked 14, the highest of any university outside the US and UK. There are five Japanese universities in the top 100, comparable to the numbers for France (4) or Germany (7).[5] The Times ranking of the world's 50 best universities is not dissimilar, with Tokyo ranked 12 and Kyoto ranked 29. Only two French universities and only one from Germany make it into the same list.[6] What both lists have in common, of course, is the dominance of the Anglophone countries. In comparison with other non-Anglophone countries, Japan appears to be relatively successful. How can we account for this apparent discrepancy between the McVeigh account and the international league tables?

Two answers to this question immediately spring to mind. The first is that McVeigh is talking about the run-of-the-mill universities in Japan, not the elite institutions. 'My focus is not on students from a short list of famed state-run schools or the well-known private universities...Rather, I am more interested in the hundreds of unknown universities and colleges attended buy most students' (ibid: 22). McVeigh also admits that Japan's educational system is probably no better or worse than that of any other G-7 industrialized nation in reproducing the kind of manpower required by the economy. (ibid: 12). The international rankings by definition tend to focus on the research output of elite institutions. But a second possibility is that there actually coexist in Japan two academic cultures, one which is capable of being internationally recognized, mainly in the natural sciences and technology, and one which produces work which has little impact or recognition outside Japan, mainly in the humanities. The social sciences straddle the gap, with the more quantitative and/ or experimental disciplines such as economics or psychology behaving more like the natural sciences, while the more qualitative social sciences tend to behave more like the humanities. This is a suggestion that I want to explore in this paper, because it may help explain some of the more interesting features of the outcome of the Center of Excellence program itself, including the discrepancy between the evaluations in the human sciences and the other disciplinary committees.

The Center of Excellence Program

Up to 1998, the Ministry of Education's view of the tripartite division between national, public (i.e. city or prefectural) and private universities was that national universities should meet the needs of the nation, public universities should meet the needs of the local communities that established them and private universities should be mainly responsive to the market (Eades 2001: 95). However, soon after this, the pace of reform of the university system began to accelerate, including deliberate erosion of the differences between the three sectors.

The first major initiative came in 1999 when then-education minister, Arima Akito, conditionally approved a plan to turn national universities into independent administrative institutions (*dokuritsu gyōsei hōjinka*) in order to give them more autonomy. The politics behind this move towards 'incorporation' are discussed in detail by Hatakenaka in her chapter in this volume, but at the time this seemed to represent a U-turn on the part of the Ministry of Education, which had, up to that time, resisted criticisms of higher education and calls for greater autonomy. Despite considerable controversy, both over the intent of the plan and the likely results, legislation was passed in July 2003, and the measure was implemented in April 2004.

There is still little consensus as to the main rationale for this change or what its effects on universities in the three sectors will be in the longer term.[7] However, there are several important implications. First, it seems clear that the tripartite model of the higher education sector has been abandoned, and all universities are expected to compete on a level playing field from now on, rather as they have in the UK since the upgrading of the polytechnics to universities. Second, at the management level, the proposal has been accompanied by a new discourse in which university presidents, vice presidents and deans are presumed to take a more active managerial role, at the expense of the *kyōjukai* (faculty meetings) which traditionally had the veto on decisions relating to academic matters. This again is reminiscent of the move to managerial leadership in the UK from the 1980s onwards. Third, the Ministry's direct administrative role seems to be turning into an indirect supervisory role, with many decisions being made by increasingly independent organizations based on peer review, as indeed they are in the United Kingdom. Already, many kinds of routine decisions and processes have been devolved from the ministry to individual institutions such as the Gakujutsu Shinkōkai (Japan Society for the Promotion of Science or JSPS) which is responsible for administering the COE program and Japanese government research funds. On October 1, 2003, the JSPS was given administrative autonomy, and officially ceased to be a quasi-governmental organization.[8]

Fourth, as Kinmonth reminds us in his chapter, all of this is taking place within the context of Japan as a rapidly aging society, with a dwindling supply of students. As Hada's chapter notes, mergers are already taking place in the middle ranks of national universities, and in the much larger private sector it seems likely that many institutions unable to compete for bodies will eventually disappear. The implication of incorporation is that in future, when any universities – including the former national universities – run into budgetary problems, they will have to sort themselves out. Building maintenance costs tend to be fixed, irrespective of staff and student numbers, so if schools want to save money, the only way to do it is by reducing the number of teaching staff. This may in turn require replacing tenured staff with staff on short-term contracts and increasing the number of part-time teachers, a trend also visible in UK universities. By allowing the national universities autonomy, the government can also delegate to them responsibility for the harsh decisions which will have to be taken in the medium-term future: i.e. slashing budgets and staff, and closing programs or entire schools, thus shielding the government from any fallout or unpopularity generated by these decisions.

The second initiative dates from discussions in 2001 between Prime Minister Koizumi and his education minister, Toyama Atsuko, concerning ways in which education could help make the Japanese economy more competitive. The 'Toyama Plan' had three main proposals. Two of them built on the Arima Plan: the reorganisation and consolidation of national universities (rather ominously described as 'scrap and build'); and the introduction of private sector management methods, e.g. in the enhanced role for university executives. The third proposal envisaged the employment of an external evaluation system to select the top thirty universities in the country for special treatment, and it is this part which evolved into the 21st Century COE program described below.

This third proposal was naturally the most controversial: there was predictable protest from institutions with little chance of being selected. It was felt that, in particular, the seven former imperial universities (Tokyo, Kyoto, Osaka, Nagoya, Tohoku, Hokkaido and Kyushu) would have an unfair advantage.[9] In January 2002, the Ministry proposed an alternative plan, which held out the promise of spreading the resources more evenly. The idea was to establish 'Centers of Excellence' (COEs) at those institutions which seemed most likely to produce work of international quality. Evaluation committees were to be established in 2002, 2003 and 2004 to consider bids from individual universities wishing to establish these centers. The requirements were stringent: universities wishing to apply had to have a critical mass of scholars with good track-records in research to have a fighting chance. This meant that either they had to come from disciplines already strongly represented in these institutions (e.g. some of the core science or social science departments), or they had to recombine existing staff around a new, innovative interdisciplinary concept. The whole program was headed by one of the country's most distinguished scientists, the 1973 Nobel laureate in Physics Professor Leo Esaki, who expressed his hopes that the program would help reinvigorate research and development in Japan.[10]

The committees set up for 2002 covered environment and life sciences; chemistry and materials science; information technology and electronics; and 'human literature'. Those set up for 2003 dealt with medicine; mathematics; physics and earth sciences; mechanical, civil and construction engineering; and social science. An additional committee, covering interdisciplinary and new areas of research, met in both years. 'Human literature' was eventually redefined as 'human sciences' including psychology, philosophy, education, anthropology and the fine arts. The budget for the programme was substantial with 18.2 billion yen allocated for 2002. A smaller final round of awards in 2004 concentrated solely on new fields of enquiry. In real terms, each programme would receive an average of around 100 million yen per year for five years (the annual budgets ranged from 26 to 330 million yen), and the budget for the final three years would be dependent on an interim progress review after two years. The money could be used in a number of ways: to fund international exchanges; for PhD research and post-doctoral fellowships; for research support and training; for symposia and workshops; and for the provision of new equipment and space for research.

The government's underlying agenda can be clearly seen in the criteria for evaluation for the status of COE. These are worth quoting at length:

1. **Fact Sheet for research and education activities**
   - Whether the research and education activities are excellent *by the world's standard* in the designated field
   - Whether the research and education activities have the potential required to perform the plan for becoming COE
   - Whether the institution will be able to reach *the world's standard* in the future, whereas the current research and education activities are not sufficient enough.
2. **Future Plan and Plan to become COE**
   - Whether the institution plans to become a COE *by the world's standard* under the management by the President of the institution
   - Whether the content of the Plan to become a COE is intended to have the institution *to be of the world's standard*
   - Whether the Plan to become a COE is trustworthy and realistic, and is intended to be active as a COE
   - Whether the Plan describes how to become COE where young researchers can independently show their ability
   - Whether the Plan includes a system where students will be able to be active as important resources in the future
   - Whether creative and epoch-making research results can be expected

- Whether the Plan to become a COE is understood as the strategy of the whole institution

3. Rationale of the Proposed Budget

- Whether the content of the proposed budget is reasonable and indispensable to pursue the plan. (Shinohara 2002, English as original, emphasis added).

There appeared to be three ideas underlying this proposal: (1) the establishment of research institutes of 'world standard' (however defined – the phrase recurs throughout the COE documentation, including the questions on the application forms and the evaluation forms sent to reviewers), (2) the fostering of creativity and young researchers, and (3) the strengthening of the role of the university president and management in leading these initiatives. As an exercise in the extension of the audit culture by central government, it can be compared with some of the UK initiatives implemented from the 1980s onwards.[11] Indeed conversations with both Japanese and UK officials in the late 1990s suggested that Japanese ministry officials were well aware of the UK experience.[12] However, the COE initiative was not simply a copy of a British model, but shared features with a number of British initiatives: the annual competition to establish Research Centres run by the research funding councils; the periodic New Blood programmes to open up new fields of study in the UK through the establishments of new teaching posts; and the Research Assessment Exercise (RAE) carried out at regular intervals in the United Kingdom since 1985. Like the RAE, the COE programme has produced a clear list of winners and losers in terms of the distribution of rewards among the major universities, providing a ranking which universities now regularly use in their own publicity and marketing campaigns.

Once the main outlines of the COE programme were decided, it was carried out with considerable speed and efficiency. For the 2002 round of evaluations, institutions were given just a few weeks to draw up their applications. The evaluation committees were also assembled very quickly, drawing on companies, foundations and research institutes, in addition to national and private universities (see Table 14-1).

The committee members from universities were established professors rather than university managers: presidents, vice-presidents and deans of faculties were excluded. The most prestigious national universities were well represented, as might

Table 14-1: Composition of COE review committees, 2002

Affiliation of Members	Number
National Universities	26
Research Institutes	26
Private Universities	23
Companies	12
Foundations	6
Foreign Universities	2
Public Universities	1
Other	3
Total	99

Source, based on JSPS lists, http://www.mext.go.jp/.

have been expected. Fifteen out of 26 members from national universities came from the former imperial universities: Hokkaido (2), Tohoku (3), Tokyo (3), Nagoya (1), Kyoto (4), Osaka (1), and Kyushu (1). The list of members from private universities was perhaps more surprising, with only two from Waseda and none from Keio. In addition, JSPS tried to bring in outside evaluation, through its recruitment of panelists from the foundations, companies and research institutes.

The applications were circulated at the beginning of August and evaluated by the committee members who then met for two days in early September to draw up a shortlist of successful institutions. The final stage was a series of hearings in late September when representatives from the short-listed institutions (usually the university president and the project leader) gave presentations on their proposals.[13] The older national universities got their acts together very quickly and put in a large number of applications. In the 2002 round, there were 464 applications, of which 113 or 24 percent from 48 universities were finally approved. Tokyo and Kyoto were the most successful universities in the first round, with eleven awards each. The other former imperial universities also did well: Nagoya (8), Osaka (7), Tohoku (5), Hokkaido (4), and Kyushu (4). Three of the private universities, Keio (5), Waseda (4) and Ritsumeikan (3) were also relatively successful. The only other universities to gain more than one award were Tsukuba, Tokyo University of Agriculture, Tokyo University of Foreign Languages, Yokohama National, Toyohashi, Nara Institute of Science and Technology, and Hiroshima, all national universities with two awards each. Only four awards were made to public (i.e. prefectural and city) universities. A full listing is given in the Appendix.

However, the speed of the operation meant that the ways in which the committees reached their decisions were rather different from that of the RAE in the United Kingdom. In the case of the RAE, the evaluation committees are more numerous and relatively small and their deliberations extend over several months, including reading the mass of publications submitted by departments. The short timescale of the COE exercise made this kind of exercise impossible. The human sciences committee, for instance, consisted of around twenty individuals spread over a wide range of disciplines, including anthropology, archeology, philosophy, psychology, linguistics and the fine arts. The materials made available to the committee members were the application forms (which included the CV's of the main researchers), and reports by two or three outside assessors on each project. The mode of proceeding with the applications was left to the committee members, rather than dictated by the JSPS officials. There was some discussion by sub-groups dealing with different disciplines, but given the time constraints, the most important function of the committee was to rank the applications in order of merit. This actually worked quite well as there was considerable agreement both on the best applications and the total non-starters, and there were also very few contentious cases where external assessors and committee members disagreed. Once the applications had been ranked, the number that actually received funding was determined by the budget available: funds were allocated starting from the top of the list until the money ran out.

Many of the new programs began to generate a substantial body of newsletters, journals, conference materials and other publications very quickly. Much of the money was spent on bigger and better forms of *kokusai kōryū* (international exchange) involving visits and conferences with foreign scholars, both in Japan and abroad. A second category of expenditure was on research fellowship programs, to promote the work of younger scholars. A third category of expenditure was on establishing new journals and other publications series, with some institutions devoting considerable sums to high-quality printing. The fourth main category of expenditure was on infrastructure – particularly IT support.

With the research review established, the Japanese government once more followed older British precedents by starting to take an interest in the quality of teaching provided by the universities: it announced 'Center of Learning' awards in September 2003. There were fewer COL than COE awards and only seven percent of Japan's four-year institutions were recognized. Those awarded include institutions where much of the teaching is in English, such as Ritsumeikan Asia-Pacific University and Sophia University. The funds available under this award scheme were rather smaller than those for the COE, so it is likely that the latter will have the greater impact on Japanese universities in the future.

The 2003 and 2004 COE rounds

Two further rounds of COE bids were processed in 2003 and 2004. In 2003, there were 611 bids of which 133 or 22 percent were accepted, slightly less than 2002. The majority of the awards once more went to the national universities, 97 out of 133 (73 percent), with 31 going to the private universities (23 percent) and only 5 to the public universities (4.6 percent). Once more, the former imperial universities did very well: Hokkaido (6 awards), Tohoku (7 awards), Tokyo (15 awards), Nagoya (6 awards), Kyoto (11 awards), Osaka (7 awards) and Kyushu (4 awards). Kobe (6 awards) and Hitotsubashi (3 awards) were also comparatively successful. Of the private universities, Keio did best with seven awards, compared with four for Waseda and one for Ritsumeikan. One other leading private university in Kansai, Doshisha, also appeared in the rankings for the first time, with two awards.

There was a final much smaller round of awards in 2004. Only one committee met, dealing once more with new areas of research. By this time the good news of a fairly high acceptance rate had spread, and universities put in a large number of final bids. As a result, 320 applications were received, though only 28 were accepted, less than 9 percent. Once more the bulk of the awards (23 out of 28 or 82 percent) went to the former national universities. Only one award went to a public university (Osaka City), while four went to the private sector, including one to Waseda.

Thus in the three rounds of COE bids over three years, 274 awards were made, and of these around half (134) went to the 'usual suspects', i.e. the seven former imperial universities, plus Keio and Waseda. As might have been expected at the outset of the exercise, Tokyo University gained the most awards, with 28, followed by Kyoto with 23. Nagoya and Osaka gained 15 each, followed by

Tohoku (12 awards), Hokkaido (12 awards) and Kyushu (8 awards). Other winners from the former national universities were Kobe (6 awards), Hiroshima (5 awards), and a cluster of specialized Tokyo schools, including Tokyo Institute of Technology (8 awards) and Hitotsubashi (3 awards). The major winners among the private universities were Keio (12 awards), Waseda (9 awards), and Ritsumeikan (4 awards). The only city or prefectural universities with more than one award were Osaka City University with three, and Tokyo Metropolitan University with two (for further details, see Appendix). Clearly, the result of the exercise was the concentration of resources in about twenty universities, most of them in the Tokyo, Kansai and Nagoya regions. To anyone familiar with the Japanese university system, this would have come as no surprise.[14] The fears of those that worried about the former imperial universities dominating the program turned out to have been well-founded.

The Interim Review

In 2003–04, the Interim Review process of the COE projects was carried out, aimed initially at the Centers of Excellence projects chosen in 2002. (The projects started in 2003 and 2004 are scheduled to be evaluated in 2005 and 2006 respectively.) The results of the first batch of reviews were announced at the end of November 2004: the JSPS was clearly concerned with transparency, and large amounts of documentation were made public on the Internet, on which this section draws.[15] This review not only made possible the first comprehensive overview of the progress of these projects, but also suggested some possible differences in research cultures between disciplines, especially between the sciences on the one hand and the humanities on the other, with the social sciences split down the middle.

The review process comprised several stages. First, each COE had to complete review forms giving details of expenditure, activities, research output and publications in the first two years. Second, each COE had to provide a sample of its research output for evaluation by the committee members, usually in the form of journal articles. Third, members of each center had to present a presentation to the review committee and answer questions from the committee members. The process was also designed to include further hearings, site visits and interviews with university presidents where necessary, though in the event these were reserved only for the most problematic cases. The first meetings were held in February 2004, and the hearings were carried out over the summer.

The details of these hearings in relation to specific institutions must remain confidential, but two points quickly became clear on the human sciences committee on which I was sitting. First, the purpose was not simply to rubber-stamp the continuation of the projects. The questions put to the directors of the projects were both searching and, in some cases, highly critical. Whether it was the same in the other committees is impossible to say, though it is clear that the published evaluations of the human sciences review were more critical than those of the other committees.

Second, the materials presented to the committees by different academic disciplines within the human sciences committee were very varied. While researchers in quantitative social sciences such as psychology were apparently carrying out much of their research and publishing in English, much of it in mainstream peer-reviewed journals, the situation in other disciplines was radically different. Some COE's were carrying out joint research with foreign institutions, but were leaving the foreign-language publication to their partners, concentrating themselves on publishing in Japanese. At the other end of the spectrum, some programs were publishing their output only in Japanese, mostly journals, conference proceedings and research reports produced by the COE's themselves. This is the traditional pattern for the humanities and some of the qualitative social sciences in Japan (Eades 2000). For these scholars, the production of research of 'international standard' clearly did not imply that research results would be disseminated internationally, through internationally recognized outlets.

When the results from the different committees were issued at the end of November, 2004, it was clear that the human sciences committee was somewhat out of line with the others. This can be seen not only from the statistics (Table 14-2), but also from the reports on each project that were released at the same time.[16]

A number of features of this table stand out. First, in the natural and applied sciences, together with new fields of research, the evaluations were more favorable than they were in the human sciences. Only two out of the 20 human science projects were graded A, a rate of 10 percent compared with a rate of 36 percent

Table 14-2: 2002 COE Projects, Interim Evaluation, by subject area

Evaluation	Life sciences	Materials sciences	IT and electronics	Human sciences	New Fields	All fields
A	12	13	6	2	8	41
B	16	8	13	10	13	60
C	0	0	1	6	3	10
D	0	0	0	2	0	2
E	0	0	0	0	0	0
Totals	28	21	20	20	24	113

Key: A = Should continue as it is, B = Should continue, taking into account committee's comments, C = Problems, project needs to be rethought; D = Problems, project should be scaled down; E = Problems, project should be scrapped. Source: "21 Seiki COE Puroguramu, Chūkan Hyōka ni tsuite," available at http://web.jsps.go.jp/j-21coe/05_chukan/index.html.

overall. Second, a majority of the C grades and both the D grades came from the human sciences committee: In other words, 40 percent of the projects were judged to have serious problems, compared with 11 percent for the program as a whole.

Press reports of the announcement of the results concentrated not on the satisfactory grades given to most of the projects, but to the two projects awarded D grades and the fact that they were being downsized, rather than scrapped completely. The Japanese edition of the *Yomiuri Shimbun* of November 30th gave devoted some space to this, and speculated why the original decision to scrap the projects had been changed. The article explained it as follows:

> **Taking pity? Interim university evaluation: JSPS surveys funding.** On the 29 November, the JSPS announced the results of the interim evaluation of the 21st Century Center of Excellence Program, its first survey of its progress. The COE program is a major funding initiative for universities to create a world-class research and education system.
>
> Among 113 research programs from 50 universities, one each from Kyushu University and Hosei University was given a D grade, meaning that support should be withdrawn. In response to this, the four grades of evaluation were changed to five one month before the public announcement. There are complaints about the lack of transparency in the details of how the two universities escaped from the lowest rank, after the initial decision that their funding would be stopped.

> The interim evaluation covered the 113 programs selected in 2002, and was carried out by a committee of experts drawn from the program committee, chaired by Professor Leo Esaki. As a result of the survey, 41 programs received an A grade, 60 received a B grade, 10 received a C grade, 2 received a D grade, and none received an E grade.
>
> The two D grade programs were both in the human sciences. The Kyushu University program on 'East Asia and Japan: Interaction and Change,' led by Professor Yoichiro Imanishi, was described as 'notably reliant on past achievements: the object of the program appears unclear to those in charge of it.' The Hosei University program on 'Declaration of international Japanese studies' [sic], led by Professor Eifu Nakano, was also criticized: 'The reason for starting the project was to go beyond [conventional] Japanese studies, but there is no evidence that this is happening, while important perspectives are being ignored.' As a result, it was proposed that the projects of both universities should be drastically reduced, and that their future progress should be monitored. Kyushu University said that it would 'take the evaluation seriously.' Hosei University commented that it 'accepted the severe judgment, and was waiting for the outcome.'
>
> In considering these two programs, the committee in charge of the evaluation had originally decided on a D grade, meaning that the program would be stopped. However, because the Universities had no opportunity to appeal, a higher-level committee reconsidered the evaluation process. As a result, a new right of appeal was instituted, and an additional grade was added to the scale, for which project funding would be reduced.
>
> There is criticism both from universities which failed to be selected for the COE program and from private tutoring institutions that trust in the evaluation process has been eroded. However, Professor Esaki explained the situation at a press conference. 'As a result of looking into a proposal from the universities, we decided that it was possible to continue the projects. The truth was that the evaluation categories were insufficiently worked out. The rationale was never to bail out the two universities.'
>
> The COE program provides support for five years. The projects selected in 2002 are costing 45 billion yen over 3 years, These two projects have already received more than 200 million yen. (*Yomiuri Shinbun*, 2004.11.30, my translation)

The politics behind this report must remain a matter for speculation, but Professor Esaki's comments do touch on a relevant point. The members of the review committees were invited to comment on each project in the form of a questionnaire. The last of these questions was to suggest an overall grade for the project on a four point scale. The gist of the ranking was as follows: A = Should continue as it is, B = Should continue, taking into account the committee's comments, C = Problems, the project needs to be rethought; D = Problems, the project should be scaled down or terminated. Thus decisions to cut the budget or terminate the project were conflated in the lowest point on the scale. This four-point scale was used as the basis for the numerical rankings on which the committee as a whole based many of its decisions. The five-point scale which emerged during discussions in effect formalized the division implicit in the original ranking scheme, between projects to be downsized, and projects to be scrapped.

The comments made on individual projects and made public on the Internet also suggest a broad difference between the human sciences committee and the others.[17] For a start, the individual comments were on average nearly twice as long as those for the other projects, reflecting their more critical nature. The longest comments were reserved for the projects perceived to have failed, but they encapsulate many of the problems the committee felt with many of the other projects under review. Those in the public domain can be summarized as follows.

In relation to the Kyushu project on Japan and East Asia, the committee noted that at the outset it had had great expectations, but that there was a large gap between these and the results achieved after two years. In spite of the original plan, it was clear from the hearing that the results of the project were heavily dependent on previous research, and the researchers had ignored the fact that this was supposed to be world-class research. The research was uncoordinated, with each participant going off in separate and unrelated directions. A final comment was that there was no clear relationship between the research and the research infrastructure which had been set up. The response of the university, which the committee eventually accepted, was to reorganize it under the leadership of the university president around two issues: the process of state formation in the countries of the region, and the relationship between the coastal and inland areas.

In the case of the Hosei Unversity Japanese studies project, the committee conclusions were similar. There was a gap between the original proposal and the results achieved, and the various parts of the project lacked coordination. In addition the project had not sufficiently taken account of the importance of Japanese studies outside Japan in languages other than English. Thus the project posed problems from the point of view of theory, structure, and implementation, and after two years seemed unable to meet its original objectives. As with Kyushu University, Hosei had proposed downsizing the project under the leadership of the university president, reducing the number of issues being researched, and providing better coordination. As with Kyushu, the project was allowed to continue on a scaled-down basis, subject to later review. It is not yet clear how drastic the downsizing will actually be.

Two academic modes of production?

It was probably important for the future credibility of the COE program that the review process should be seen to have teeth and that substandard performance should be sanctioned in some way, even though there was clearly high-level uncertainty as to how far these sanctions should be taken. However, in the light of problems such as these, achieving the original object of world-class research seems to be a very tall order for many of the programs, particularly those in the humanities.

In an earlier essay where I discussed problems of research and publication, I argued that the academic modes of production of Japan and the West are in many ways different, particularly in relation to publishing (Eades 2000). On the evidence of the COE experience, this thesis may well need revising. I would argue now that there are two ideal-typical academic modes of production in Japan, one found mainly in the sciences, which is mainstream and international, and which explains the high ranking of Japanese academic in the surveys mentioned earlier. The other is more domestic and parochial, and is found mainly in the humanities. The social sciences straddle the divide: some, like psychology or physical anthropology, have long traditions of publishing in English in mainstream international peer-reviewed journals. Others, such as cultural anthropology, cultural studies or history, publish more locally, through Japanese publishers, in Japanese language peer-reviewed journals, and – perhaps most important of all – in in-house journals published by the universities themselves. As I have discussed in previous papers (Eades 2000, 2004), publishing in Japanese, either through commercial publishers or in in-house journals, is astonishingly quick by Western standards, with a turn-round time measured in weeks or months rather than years as is common in the West.[18] It is therefore much easier for scholars to publish their results locally than internationally, particularly as the latter requires a very high level of writing and editing in English. While many of the COE projects and their members are already in the international mainstream, others are clearly not, and these divisions were most apparent in the human sciences committee.

Mainstream international research and publishing are probably much easier for scholars in the sciences who are already used to publishing in English in refereed journals, collaborating with foreign researchers, and working as a team. For the scholars in the humanities, it is much more difficult. First, as was clear from the CV's of the scholars supplied in the original applications, many had very limited experience of writing in English or of collaborative research, either with foreign scholars or with each other. The actuality of much 'team' research in Japan is that it allows individual scholars to pursue their own paths, without much coordination being required. Japanese research has traditionally placed more emphasis on assembling data rather than creating theory (anthropology is a good example), so creating new theory in the humanities or soft social sciences as an umbrella for disparate research agendas was by definition a tall order. Creating world-class theory which would have an international impact was always likely to be more difficult still.

The lack of a coherent theoretical starting point was shown in many of the experimental titles of the human sciences projects, which looked equally strange in Japanese or English. 'A construction of bio-thanatology concerning culture and value of life' (Tokyo University), 'Studies of the integrated text science' (Nagoya University), 'Interface humanities' (Osaka University), 'Declaration of international Japanese studies,' (Hosei University), 'Research institute of enhancement of peripheral cultures in Asia,' (Waseda University) and 'Kyoto art entertainment innovation research' (Ritsumeikan) are typical examples.[19] Even odder from the point of view of an outside scholar were some of the official English language descriptions of the projects which ended up being posted on the official Ministry of Education site. For instance, the Hiroshima University COE on 'The Construction of the 21st Century Higher

Education System and Quality Assurance' advertised its wares in the following way. In addition to the rather vague terms of reference of the program itself, the quality of the grammar and spelling are clearly unfortunate in a program dedicated to educational reform (the English is reproduced as in the original):

> This program intends to congribute to higher education policy as well as higher education research by resolving the problem of the construction of higher education system and quality assurance to meet with the changing social structure.
>
> *Objectives:* This project is expected to contribute to both Japanese and international society through making contribution to international scientific community. It is also expected to form a ceter of learning as COE for international scientific exchange by constructing the powerful institution possesing international competitiveness.
>
> *Needs:* For this objectives, middle and long lendge framework related to 'construction of the 21st Century higher education system and quality assurance', which is internationally thought to be important, is indispensable. Concretely, it focusses on the realization of three interelated objectives: 1 promotion of higher education research; 2 coducting international academic seminars every year; 3 dispatching scientific informations and also construction of data base.[20]

With examples such as this, one might well ask to what extent many of the COE projects could have been expected to achieve their original objectives of world-class research however defined, or whether the discourse of international standards and internationalization was more for domestic than external consumption.

This is related to a final issue: how significant are the sums of money involved in the COE, compared with similar programs in Japan or the flows of money in the Japanese higher education system as a whole. At first sight, the program appears substantial, with a budget of around 15 billion yen a year, roughly $US 145 million or 75 million in sterling at the current (early 2005) rates of exchange.[21] For individual departments, the additional research funds are extremely tempting, despite the problems of actually managing and executing the research alluded to above. But in relation to an economy and higher education sector the size of Japan's, the sums are relatively modest. The COE funding was only a tenth as large as the regular JSPS Grant-in-Aid scheme of the which stood at 141.9 billion yen in 2000.[22]

To put this in international perspective, in the UK, an economy less than half the size of Japan's, the Economic and Social Research Council alone has an annual research budget equivalent to 12–13 billion yen, i.e. of the same order of magnitude as the COE program.[23] The Engineering and Physical Sciences Research Council has a budget nearly ten times as large, around 100 billion yen a year.[24] Finally, the amount of money allocated for research under the RAE evaluation scheme runs to about two hundred billion yen a year ten times as much as the COE. This kind of money has achieved real change in the British university system. While some may deplore the result – an emphasis on regularity of publication rather than creativity, a preference for shallow short monographs rather than long path-breaking work which takes too long to write and publish – its supporters would argue that RAE is at least partly responsible for the currently relatively high profile of the British universities in the world rankings. In the sciences, Japan already has a high profile. But to achieve one in the humanities will take a lot more money, much more internationalization, an emphasis on mainstream publication abroad as well as publication for local audiences,[25] and an early retirement scheme to shake the dead wood out of the system. So it is probably safe to conclude in relation to the COE that it is a useful first step, but only a small one in relation to what has to be done if the original goals of the scheme are to be fully achieved – in the humanities as well as the natural sciences.

The money to make things happen is probably there of course. By the late 1990s, the annual budget of the Ministry of Education amounted to 5.8 trillion yen, of which 2.7 trillion was spent on national educational institutions. Around 370 billion, or 6.4 percent was going in subsidies to private universities.[26] Other big ticket items involving universities were the 112 billion yen in Grants-in-Aid for research, 101 billion for cooperative research between universities and industry, and 55 billion yen spent on foreign students, as part of the program to raise the numbers to 100,000 by the end of the century. It is clear that there are very substantial amounts going to universities in one form or another. It is interesting to speculate what would happen if the government were to follow the British or Australian strategy, reserving a sizable percentage of the higher education budget (of the order of 10 or 15 percent) for redistribution following the results of peer review. There is a possibility, of course, that a very high percentage is already going to the top institutions, and that their success in the

COE program is just the tip of the iceberg. In that case a redistribution would have little effect. But it is also possible that out there, in the vast Japanese university system, there are small groups of scholars in many universities with the potential for research of international standard, and the question is how to recognize them and give them the resources they need to upgrade and disseminate their output. The COE program is pointing in the right direction by focusing at the level of university departments rather than whole institutions as was envisaged in the original version of the Toyama Plan. If this peer review built into the COE process could be made more general and money channeled accordingly throughout the system – and to the best scholars – the effects could be electrifying.

Conclusion

One of the most interesting features of the COE was the hybrid nature of the program. It became in effect an exercise to promote both established departments claiming to be centers of excellence already, and new research groups aspiring to become them. The two kinds of unit are difficult to evaluate together and could have been the objects of different exercises. Some of the units evaluated were already cohesive departments, producing substantial flows of research and publications; the COE has effectively given them more money to do more of the same. The new research groups have had a harder time, and some have foundered, as we have seen above. However, the evidence from the UK is that new research programs do take substantial time to settle down, particularly given the length of time needed to publish in the West, and eighteen months or two years is, by international standards, a very short period on which to base an evaluation.

It could be argued that in Japan, the establishment of new research units is better done through the long-established regular JSPS Grant-in-Aid programs. This would leave the COE or its successor as a separate exercise to evaluate the research excellence in established departments, rather like the RAE in the UK. The framework of evaluation could then become internationally recognized disciplines, making expert external peer-review easier to organize. There is a clearly a need for genuinely innovative interdisciplinary research groups, but establishing these is a quite different exercise from evaluating the mainstream university departments where most of the research and teaching is based, and rewarding those which are performing most effectively.

The scope of the relatively small number of committees in the COE was very wide, and perhaps this could also be considered in the next time around. In the case of the RAE, the committees were smaller, and were composed entirely of specialists. In the case of the human sciences committee of the COE, nobody could have been an expert in all the disciplines represented, which ranged from psychology, cultural anthropology and philosophy to education, area studies and religion. It is clearly difficult for specialists in one field to evaluate work in another expertly and objectively, particularly where there are such clear differences in academic cultures, as for instance between psychology on the one hand and Japanese-style comparative religion on the other. It might be better to establish a larger number of smaller committees to provide more expert evaluation of closely related disciplines.[27]

The evaluation of some disciplines can also be left to the market. One of the most interesting trends in Japanese graduate education in recent years has been the development of professional programs in law (Nottage 2001, Milhaupt and West, 2003), and business administration (Kagono 1996, Okazaki-Ward, 2001). Intriguingly, one of the first effects of the incorporation of the national universities in 2004 was the move to secure better publicity, both through opening offices in other major Japanese cities, and hiring former advertising executives to direct public relations (Nakanishi 2004). Another straw in the wind is the decision of the Japanese government to recognize foreign universities operating in Japan, theoretically opening up the Japanese sector to further internationalization and foreign competition (Brender 2004, but see also John Mock's chapter in this volume).

Overall, however, the outcome of the COE reinforces the idea that there are two distinct academic cultures co-existing in Japan. On the one hand, many scientists are already experienced in writing and publishing in international journals in English. They may also write in Japanese for domestic audiences, but these writings often serve a quite different purpose. At the other pole are humanities projects where research output is only published locally, in Japanese alone. Clearly, if 'international standard' is taken seriously as an objective, Japanese academe will have to adopt objective internationally accepted measures such as citation indices as part of the evaluation. The corollary is that publications unlikely to be read outside Japan, such as in-house journals or conference proceedings, are not very useful for the international dissemination of research findings. But in any case, the hybrid nature of the first round of COE awards meant that it was difficult to use a single measure of quality, given that some of the units were established departments, whereas others were new research units which were founded specifically to capitalize on the COE program.

Finally, a comparison with the British experience suggests that if the COE program or its successors are to achieve the original goals, they will have to be carried out on a much larger scale, putting much more significant sums of money on the table. Some of this could be well spent making it possible and financially worthwhile for universities to pension off less productive faculty in the process. The universities will also have to move away from the present system of almost automatic full professorships for permanent teaching staff over 45, to one in which promotion and salaries are based more clearly on performance. Promotion of exceptional younger scholars to full professorships at a much younger age, allowing them more extensive participation in faculty management and graduate programs, would be an obvious step forward. Despite a surge in the number of university teachers with PhD's in the 1990s, most promotions from associate to full professor still take place around the age of 45–50, irrespective of quality of teaching or research output. The *dokuritsu hōjinka* has given the national universities greater ability to hire and fire, while an expanded COE would give them the incentive to seek out the best scholars and pay them the going market rate for excellence. Japanese salaries are already generous by international standards: it would take little adjustment to provide world-class salaries for world-class scholars. As for those already in the system, evaluation schemes tied to substantial resources could both help identify who they are, and give them the incentive to increase their productivity and international profiles.

The speed at which such a program can create change in a university system is clear from the British experience. The RAE was introduced on a regular basis in 1985. By the early 1990s, it had become clear that the potential rewards of research were sufficient to encourage extensive staff changes. By the late 1990s, much of the dead wood in the university system, particularly in the higher ranking research universities, had been retired and replaced by younger, more active researchers able to compete internationally.

Because very few PhD's had been produced in the 1980s due to an earlier cut in government scholarships, many of the new professors were either very young (i.e. in their early 30s, with extensive publications and research funding) or were recruited from abroad, helping the internationalization of the system. If the JSPS, the Ministry of Education and the Japanese government were willing to make similar changes in tandem with an extended COE- or RAE-type evaluation program, the changes in Japan could be just as swift and dramatic, and could help lead to the genuine internationalization of the Japanese system, in the humanities and social sciences, as well as the sciences.

Notes

1 For details see http://www.hefce.ac.uk/research/assessment/. The latest proposals are that the exercise should be carried out every six years (Roberts Report 2003: 7).
2 Based on the 2005 figure of GBP 1.06bn, given at http://www.hefce.ac.uk/research/funding/resfund/.
3 An association of 19 leading UK Universities. For membership of the group, see www.planning.ed.ac.uk/Russell_group.htm.
4 http://ed.sjtu.edu.cn/rank/2004/Top%20100%20Asia%20Pacific%20Universities.htm, downloaded December 25 2004.
5 http://ed.sjtu.edu.cn/rank/2004/top500(1-100).htm downloaded December 25 2004.
6 http://www.timesonline.co.uk/article/0,,2-1343281,00.html, downloaded December 25 2004.
7 For a short but useful account of the reform agenda plus a list of internet sources, see Nishibayashi (2003).
8 JSPS Report, 2004–5, http://web.jsps.go.jp/english/about_us/data/2004_e.pdf.
9 *Daily Yomiuri*, Friday, October 4, 2002, page 2.
10 'Centers of Excellence program to reinvigorate R&D in Japan' Leo Esaki, Daily Yomiuri , Monday, September 1, 2003, page 8.
11 On the concept of the audit culture, see Shore and Wright (199), Strathern (2000). The model has spread widely. For its effects in East Asia, see Goodman (2001), and for Hong Kong, see Faure 2001. One of the most comprehensive set of audit institutions are those in place in Australia, on which see Higher Education Division (1999).
12 Comparative research on university reform in Japan and the UK was carried out together with Yumiko Hada in the Summer of 1999. We are grateful to vice chancellors and other senior academics in the UK and ministry officials in both countries for invaluable off-the-record briefings on the state of reforms.
13 On the human sciences committee, the number of institutions invited to the hearings, determined by the number of time slots available over two days,

was only slightly more than the number of projects which could be funded, so that most of those invited to these hearings eventually received money.

14 Indeed, the final list of winners from the program and their ranking has a close correspondence to the list of universities supplying large numbers of public officials thirty years ago. See Johnson (1982: 58, Table 3.).

15 The reports are available in Japanese at the JSPS COE site, http://web.jsps.go.jp/j-21coe.

16 For the PDF files of reports on individual universities, see http://web.jsps.go.jp/j-21coe/05_chukan/index.html.

17 This summary is based on the documents '21 Seiki COE Puroguramu Chūkan Kekkahyō' (21st Century COE Program Interim Evaluation Results), available in PDF format at the JSPS site http://web.jsps.go.jp/j-21coe/05_chukan/index.html. This site contains summaries of each project, including the Kyushu and Hosei University summaries which are paraphrased below.

18 Some western journals publish for each article details of when it was submitted, revised, and finally accepted. As an example from anthropology, the average time between submission and publication in the *American Ethnologist* in the mid-1990s was running at just under two years.

19 http://www.mext.go.jp/english/news/2002/11/021101/d.pdf,

20 From the English text available at http://www.mext.go.jp/english/news/2002/11/021101/d.pdf.

21 At the time of going to press US$1= approx. 105 yen.

22 http://www.jsps.go.jp/english/e-grants/grants02.html.

23 http://www.esrc.ac.uk/esrccontent/researchfunding/index.asp. At the time of going to press, the pound sterling was equal to about 200 yen.

24 http://www.oxtrust.org.uk/pooled/profiles/BF_COMP/view.asp?Q=BF_COMP_27028.

25 The problem of audiences and language in anthropology is discussed in Yamashita, Bosco and Eades (2004).

26 Figures taken from http://www.mext.go.jp/english/news/1997/04/970401.htm, which gives a detailed breakdown of the 1997 budget.

27 Interestingly, the Roberts Report on the RAE has recommended that the number of 'units of assessement' (i.e. subject areas) in the 2007–8 RAE be reduced to around 20–25, with up to 60 sub-panels working under them (Roberts Report 2003: 12), more comparable to the number of COE committees used in Japan.

References

Brender, A. (2004) 'Japan recognizes U.S. and other foreign universities on its soil', *Chronicle of Higher Education*, October 15, 2004.

Cutts, Robert L. (1997) *An Empire of Schools: Japan's Universities and the Molding of a National Power Elite*, New York: M.E. Sharpe.

Eades, J.S. (2000) 'Why don't they write in English? Academic modes of production and academic discourses in Japan and the West', *Ritsumeikan Journal of Asia Pacific Studies* 6: 58–77.

Eades, J.S. (2001) 'Reforming Japanese higher education: Bureaucrats, the birthrate, and visions of the 21st century', *Ritsumeikan Journal of Asia Pacific Studies* 8: 86–101.

Eades, J.S. (2004) 'Local research, global audiences: Linguistic hegemony and transnational publishing in the information age,' in Matthews, Peter J. and Jun Akamine (eds.), *Research Writing in Japan: Cultural, Personal and Practical Perspectives*, Osaka: National Museum of Ethnology, pp. 3–16.

Esaki, Leo (2003) 'Centers of Excellence program to reinvigorate R&D in Japan,' *Daily Yomiur*i, Monday, September 1 2003, p. 8.

Faure, David (2001) 'Higher education reforms and intellectual schizophrenia in Hong Kong', *Ritsumeikan Journal of Asia Pacific Studies* 8: 80–85.

Goodman, Roger (2001) 'The state of higher education in East Asia: Higher education in East Asia and the State', *Ritsumeikan Journal of Asia Pacific Studies* 8: 1–29.

Hall, Ivan. P. (1998) *Cartels of the Mind.* New York: Norton.

Higher Education Division (1999) 'The Quality of Higher Education', Canberra: Higher Education Division, Department of Education, Training and Youth Affiars, available at http://www.dest. gov.au/archive/highered/pubs/quality/contents.htm#contents, downloaded 5 Feb, 2005.

Holden, Constance (1998) 'Crackdown by Japan's universities?' *Science* (Washington) (Nov 6, 1998): 1035.

Johnson, Chalmers (1982) *MITI and the Japanese Miracle*. Stanford: Stanford University Press.

Kagono, Tadao (1996) 'Part-time MBA education in Japan,' *The Journal of Management Development* (Bradford) 15 (8): 53–64.

McVeigh, Brian. J. (1998) *The Nature of the Japanese State*, London: Routledge.

McVeigh, Brian J. (2000) 'Educational reform in Japan: Fixing education or fostering economic nation-statism?', in Eades, J.S., Tom Gill and Harumi Befu (eds.), *Globalization and Social Change in Contemporary Japan*, Melbourne: Trans Pacific Press, pp. 76–92.

McVeigh Brian J. (2002) *Japanese Higher Education as Myth*, Armonk New York: M.E. Sharpe.

Milhaupt, Curtis J. and Mark D. West (2003) 'Law's dominion and the market for legal elites in Japan', *Law and Policy in International Business* (Washington) 34 (2): 451–98.

Nakanishi, S. (2004) 'Universities seeking to boost PR', *Daily Yomiuri*, Friday, April 2 2004, p. 8.

Nishibayashi, Yosuke (2003) 'A summary of the situation in Summer 2003: Japanese universities in the midst of drastic reform', Cambridge, Mass.: Harvard University, Reischauer Institute of Japanese Studies, available at http://www.fas.harvard.edu/~rijs/unibib_summer2003_summary.html.

Nottage, Luke (2001) 'Reformist conservatism and failures of imagination in Japanese Legal Education', *Ritsumeikan Journal of Asia Pacific Studies*, 8: 115–43.

Okazaki-Ward, L.I. (2001) 'MBA education in Japan: Its current state and future direction', *Journal of Management Development* (Bradford) 20 (3): 197–234.

Roberts Report (2003) 'Review of Research Assessment: Report of Sir Gareth Roberts to the UK Funding Bodies Issued for Consultation May 2003', London: HEFCE, available at http://www.ra-review.ac.uk/reports/roberts/roberts_summary.doc.

Shinohara, Kazuko (2002) 'Toyama Plan: Center of Excellence Program for the 21st Century', *National Science Foundation Report* (Memorandum No.02-05,) Tokyo: Tokyo Regional Office, http://www.nsftokyo.org/index.htm.

Shore, C. and Susan Wright (1999) 'Audit culture and anthropology: Neo-liberalism in British higher education', *Journal of the Royal Anthropological Institute* (N.S.) 5: 557–75.

Strathern, Marilyn (ed.) (2000) *Audit Cultures: Anthropological Studies in Accountability, Ethics and the Academy*, London: Routledge.

Yamashita, Shinji, Joseph Bosco and J.S. Eades, 2004. 'Asian anthropologies: Foreign, native and indigenous', in Yamashita, Shinji, J. Bosco and J.S. Eades (eds.), *The Making of Anthropology in East and Southeast Asia*, New York: Berghahn, pp. 1–34.

Appendix: Distribution of COE awards 2002–04, by University

Rank	University	Status	2002	2003	2004	Total
1	Tokyo U	national	11	15	2	28
2	Kyoto U	national	11	11	1	23
3–4	Nagoya U	national	8	6	1	15
3–4	Osaka U	national	7	7	1	15
5	Tohoku U	national	5	7	1	13
6–8	Hokkaido	national	4	6	2	12
6–8	Keio U	private	5	7		12
6–8	Tokyo Institue of Technology	national	4	5	3	12
9	Waseda U	private	5	4		9
10	Kyushu U	national	4	4		8
11	Kobe U	national	1	6		7
12	Hiroshima U	national	2	2	1	5
13–17	Chiba U	national		3	1	4
13–17	Hitotsubashi U	national		3	1	4
13–17	Osaka City U	public	2	1	1	4
13–17	Ritsumeikan U	private	3	1		4
13–17	Tsukuba U	national	3	1		4
18–38	Doshisha U	private		2		2
18–38	Gifu U	national	1		1	2
18–38	Gunma U	national	1		1	2
18–38	Japan Institute of Advanced Technology, Hokuriku	national		1	1	2
18–38	Kanazawa U	national	1		1	2
18–38	Kinki U	private	1	1		2
18–38	Kumamoto U	national	1	1		2
18–38	Nagaoka U. Tech.	national	1	1		2
18–38	Nagasaki U	national	1	1		2
18–38	Nara Institute of Advanced Tecnology	national	2			2
18–38	Nihon U	private	1	1		2
18–38	Ochanomizu U	national	1	1		2
18–38	Okayama U	national		2		2
18–38	Tokushima U	national		2		2

Rank	University	Status	2002	2003	2004	Total
18–38	Tokyo Agricultural U	national	2			2
18–38	Tokyo Foreign Languages University	national	2			2
18–38	Tokyo Medical and Dental University	national		2		2
18–38	Tokyo Metropolitan U	public		2		2
18–38	Tottori U	national	1		1	2
18–38	Toyohashi Inst. Tech.	national	2			2
18–38	Yokohama National U	national	2			2
39–91	Aichi U	private	1			1
39–91	Akita U	national	1			1
39–91	Aoyama Gakuin U	private	1			1
39–91	Chuo U	private	1			1
39–91	Ehime U	national	1			1
39–91	Fujita Health U	private		1		1
39–91	Fukui U	national		1		1
39–91	Hamamatsu Medical U	national		1		1
39–91	Himeji Inst. Tech.	public	1			1
39–91	Hosei U	private	1			1
39–91	Hyogo Prefectural U	public		1		1
39–91	International Christian U	private		1		1
39–91	Iwate U	national			1	1
39–91	Jichi Medical School	private		1		1
39–91	Jochi/Sophia U	private	1			1
39–91	Jutendo U	private		1		1
39–91	Kanagawa U	private		1		1
39–91	Kansai Medical U	private		1		1
39–91	Kitasato U	private	1			1
39–91	Kochi Technology U	private			1	1
39–91	Kokugakuin U	private	1			1
39–91	Kurume U	private		1		1
39–91	Kwansei Gakuin U	private		1		1
39–91	Kyoto Pharmaceutical U	private			1	1
39–91	Kyushu Inst. Design	national		1		1
39–91	Kyushu Inst.. Technology	national		1		1
39–91	Kyushu Sangyo U	private			1	1
39–91	Meijo U	private	1			1
39–91	Miyazaki Medical U	national	1			1
39–91	Nara Women's U	national			1	1
39–91	Nat. Grad. Inst. for Policy Stud.	national		1		1
39–91	Nihon Fukushi U	private		1		1
39–91	Niigata U	national		1		1
39–91	Nisho-Gakusha U	private			1	1
39–91	Obihiro U. of Agriculture and Veterinary Medicine	national	1			1
39–91	Saga U	national	1			1
39–91	Science U of Tokyo	private		1		1
39–91	Shinshu U	national	1			1
39–91	Shizuoka Prefectural U	public	1			1
39–91	Shizuoka U	national			1	1
39–91	St Luke's Coll. Nursing	private		1		1
39–91	Tamagawa U	private	1			1
39–91	Tokai U	private	1			1
39–91	Tokyo Denki U	private		1		1
39–91	Tokyo Institute of Polytechnics	private		1		1
39–91	Tokyo Women's Med. U	private		1		1
39–91	Toyama U	national		1		1
39–91	Toyo U	private		1		1
39–91	University of Elect.ro-Communications	national		1		1
39–91	U of the Ryukyus	national			1	1
39–91	Yamagata U	national		1		1
39–91	Yamanashi U	national		1		1
39–91	Yokohama City U	public		1		1

Index